The Dating Survival Bible

Sarah Melland

Unhinged Wisdom, Brutal Truths, and Divine Strategy
for Women Who've Had Enough

First Edition
Printed in the United States of America

EPUB: 978-1-969137-09-9
Paperback: 978-1-969137-18-1
Hardcover: 978-1-969137-19-8

www.yourdatingunexpert.com

dating (n.) – is an "act or practice of having (romantic) dates."

The word "date" was allegedly coined in 1896, by a forlorn lover.

According to Moira Weigel's book, *Labor of Love: The Invention of Dating*, the word "date" first popped up in a newspaper column in which a heartbroken clerk named Artie wrote that the object of his affections was seeing other people. According Artie, his unrequited love told him that other people were "fillin' all my dates" — as in the dates in their calendar.

The word "dating" entered the American language during the Roaring Twenties. Prior to that, courtship was a matter of family and community interest. Starting around the time of the Civil War, courtship became a private matter.

INTRODUCTION

PART I: THE PREP
BEFORE YOU EVEN OPEN THE APP

PART II: THE PROFILE
CREATING A PRESENCE THEY CAN'T SWIPE PAST

PART III: THE GAME
NAVIGATING THE WILD

PART IV: THE WILD CARDS
SPECIAL CIRCUMSTANCES & REAL-WORLD COMPLEXITY

PART V: THE GOSPEL OF DATING TRUTHS

Introduction

My Dating Slips, Mishaps and Still Feel Like I'm Winning

Let's start from the beginning, shall we?

I was a late bloomer. Didn't date in high school, not because I couldn't or didn't want to, but because my standards were already too high. I wasn't about to settle. The guys at my school were mid. I was convinced I was already a ridiculously famous actress on my way to Hollywood, and none of them were even close to my league.

Freshman year, the hot senior quarterback wanted to date me. Because of course he did. We had a connection. We were even partners in Show Choir. He slapped my butt at a pool party and I genuinely thought it was love. Then my so-called best friend swooped in and took him from me because I was a prude and hadn't kissed a boy yet. Found out later she gave him a hand job with two hands. Senior year, I finally had my first kiss. Hated his tongue. I just wasn't ready.

In the limbo between senior year and college, I met the most gorgeous man to ever walk the planet. We'd talk all night on the phone. He was everything I thought I wanted. But he'd just gotten out of a relationship and wanted to "play the field." And surprise! The same freshman-year best friend was his brother's girlfriend. I'm still convinced she sabotaged it again. Whatever. I was leaving town for college anyway.

College? A disaster. No one lived up to that first infatuation. There was a neighbor who taught me how to give a killer hand job, and not much else. I moved back to my small town and met my first real love. If you don't know how that ended, read *The Breakup Band Aid*. He was the only man who treated me with full-blown love and respect. And I ruined it. Picked petty fights. Sabotaged it. And that's why I started this whole journey.

Eventually, I couldn't take it anymore and moved to LA. Cue the expectations of glamour, hot men, and actual romance. Reality? I was not impressed. I dated *everyone*. A music producer who cheated on me with a prominent porn star. A couple controversial models. A hot architect. Fell for a screenwriter who I swore was the man of my dreams. Almost connected with an NBA All-Star, and he, of all people, ended up teaching me about mental health and the real journey of the soul. In between were too many fucks, flings, and dating app duds to count. Tinder. Bumble. Raya. The League. eHarmony. Match. I even tried matchmakers and let rich friends set me up. I had one older man I *should've* given a chance to. He was hot, loaded, and I could've landed a spot on Real Housewives of Beverly Hills. But nope, just couldn't take one for the team. There was one good guy. Solid eight-month relationship. Sex was incredible. We had a blast. But we couldn't fall in love, and it sucked. We tried. Something just didn't click.

Then the pandemic hit. I moved to Florida to be closer to family. I wasn't finding anything in LA, and I figured this might be my chance to reset. My sister was having babies. I kind of knew that chapter might not happen for me. Within a month of moving, I thought I'd met the man of my dreams. Three and a half years and $7,000 later, I realized I was just a hopeless romantic desperate for someone to *finally choose me*. He fed me every line "you're the one," "God sent me an angel," "you're it." I fell for all of it.

Got back on the apps. Nada. Then I got laid off from my first real job here. That same night I had a first date. He was def my trauma bond. He was a full-blown lovebomber who re-downloaded Bumble *while we were exclusive* because he felt insecure and needed attention. And yes, he still texts me Merry Christmas.

Then came the one that *broke* me. Financially, emotionally, spiritually. So much so, I didn't want to be touched by a man ever again...unless it was Tom Brady. (Now that he's divorced? Babe, I'm ready.)

He was my boss.

I'd just landed my dream job as a marketing director. We played it cool for months, until he told me he was separated. Then the tension exploded. He was forbidden fruit, and I kept wondering *why* I was attracted to him. He wasn't my type, and I didn't even know if I wanted to be seen in public with him. He was almost 50, looked 60. But he made me feel like the most fascinating woman in the room.

Two months in, I get a text from a hotel, one we had to stay at for work. And just like that, the illusion cracked. The motherfucker cheated. And then had the audacity to flaunt his new relationship around work. Bought her skirts from our vendors. *I got the invoice.*

Let me be very clear: **It doesn't matter how beautiful, smart, funny, or kind you are. If a man is going to cheat, he will.**

Because it's not about you. It's about his lack of self-worth. That's the last time I will *ever* lower my standards for a man who doesn't even meet mine. We tried to "work through" it. (Mistake.) And on my last day? I found out he'd also been cheating on me with the Salesforce rep.

So, I did what any sane woman would do at that point: I walked the fuck out.

And then I panicked.

Why would I quit without a backup job? What was I thinking? No one was going to hire me. And I couldn't tell anyone the *real* reason I left. I tried to get the job back, he blocked me from the owner, lied about me, and hired some clueless idiot to replace me. Like tell me you know nothing about marketing without telling me.

But then... Hell. Hath. No. Fury.

And certainly not like *Sarah Melland*, who may self-deprecate, but never lets a man write her ending.

I sent the owner a full email. Told him everything. Five days later, the asshole was fired. It still hurts. That job was a cushion. They loved me. And I was *damn good* at it.

But here's the truth: **this**, writing, is my actual purpose. So, it's now or never. No more backburner. No more safety net. Just me, this story, and the work I know I was born to do.

So where am I now? Still a hopeless romantic. Still want a partner who brings real value. Still healing. Still learning. But not broken. I've been pouring myself into research on the hellscape we call dating. I am *done* being played, and I want every woman who reads this to know what's coming before it shows up with a fake deep voice and "good morning, beautiful" texts.

This Dating Bible is for *us*. To spot the red flags. To swipe left on toxicity no matter how hot he is. To choose peace over potential. Because once we all start holding the damn line, the players will either level up or get out of the game.

You're about to get everything: profile decodes, red flag translations, power moves, scripts, savage truths, and real talk that makes you remember exactly who the fuck you are. And if the dream man doesn't show up? You'll be so full of your own joy, passion, and adventure… you won't even flinch. We got this. And I've got you.

Yes, it's long. It's a Bible, babe. Of course it's long.

This is the most unhinged, real, raw, poetic, and emotionally intelligent dating book you'll ever read. And like any sacred text, you're not meant to read it straight through. Start with the passages that grab you by the throat.

Open to the section that mirrors where you are right now: spiraling, glowing, healing, or holding back tears in the bathroom. This book was built to hold all your phases. So don't get overwhelmed. Get in. Get what you need. Get out. Come back when you're ready for more.

You're not behind. You're not broken. You're not alone. You're just waking up.

The Wild World of Dating

(Warning: May cause ego bruises, sudden breakthroughs, and uncontrollable self-respect.)

Dating is not for the faint of heart. It's not for Negative Nancys dissecting every text like it's evidence in court, or assigning red flags because TikTok told you so. Not every flag is red. Just because it doesn't sit right with you doesn't mean it's universally toxic. Sometimes a guy ghosts you not because he's a monster, but because he didn't care enough to explain. And while that sucks, it also means he's not your person.

Brutal truth? You just weren't it for him. Better truth? That doesn't mean you're not *it* for someone better.

Dating Won't Make You Happy. Let's kill the myth. Relationships can be beautiful, but they won't fix your sadness or heal your wounds. Sometimes I've wondered if they're even worth it. Then I remember: they make us grow. They stretch us. They bring up our shadows and ask us to meet them with grace. Love doesn't save you. But it sure as hell refines you.

Let's Get Real: Dating Is a Brave Game. Putting yourself out there, knowing full well you could get ghosted or disappointed again? That's not weak, that's *spiritual athleticism*. Toss your perfect-date checklist. Stay open to weird timing, awkward sparks, and the guy who says something dumb but ends up being everything you never knew you needed.

It's Not Always Love at First Swipe. That movie-moment spark? Rare. If you don't feel butterflies immediately, it doesn't mean it's wrong. Let it breathe. Real connection grows in the pause, not in the fireworks.

Not Every Date Is Meant to Be Your Last First Date. Some people are here to teach you what you'll never accept again. That still counts. Every "no" brings you closer to the "hell yes."

Choose Your Dates Like You Choose Your Friends. If it feels like solving algebra with zero serotonin, that's not "he's shy," that's *boring*. If there's no laughter, challenge, or light? Carry on.

Grace: Your Secret Weapon. We're all messy. Give yourself grace. Give your dates grace. Hell, give your ex a little grace, not because they deserve it, but because *you* do. Forgiveness clears the field. It's not about them. It's about freeing up space for better.

Talk About Your Exes Like a Class Act. You gain nothing from bitterness. No need to bash. He wasn't right for you, but he might be someone else's "I just knew." Speak light. Heal faster.

Marriage Is the Bonus, Not the Blueprint. You don't need a ring to be worthy. A lot of people get married and stay miserable. Singleness is not a purgatory, it's *freedom*. It's the space where you build the life that makes someone else say, "Holy shit, I want in."

Sex Is Not the Villain. Let's stop treating sex like a sin that ruins the story. It's sacred, but not shameful. Have it with intention. Have it without guilt. Know what you need. Honor it. But don't, I repeat, don't just sleep with a man because you know that is the only way to get attention from him.

Learn to Be Alone Without Feeling Like You're Losing. Before you find your person, become your person. Learn to love your own company. Otherwise, you're not seeking partnership, you're seeking rescue. That's not romance. That's dependence.

And here's the beautiful kicker: You might meet someone when you least expect it. You might not. But either way you win. Because now, you know yourself. You love harder. You walk taller. You hold your own. And you won't accept a life that doesn't **light you the fuck up.**

Shameless Plug: If you are not sure what *She* looks like, get my *Becoming Her* series. Hey, a girl's gotta work every avenue in this economy…

The ***Becoming Her Series*** is a collection of clarity tools for women who are done overthinking, over-giving, and negotiating with lives that no longer fit. Through books, journals, and guided exercises, it helps you recognize patterns, trust yourself again, and choose from self-respect instead of hope or survival.

https://yourdatingunexpert.com/becoming-her-series

Interesting (and Infuriating) Facts About Dating
aka: The Sh*t They Didn't Want You to Know

Welcome to the *WTF Files* of modern dating. Where the stats are grim, the facts are wild, and the delusion is… thriving. Consider this your cheat sheet of hilarious, disturbing, jaw-dropping, and occasionally empowering truth bombs about the dating world. Don't worry, we roast *everyone* equally here.

MODERN DATING STATS & BEHAVIOR
Translation: The numbers are not in your favor, but at least now you know why you're losing your mind.

❖ Most couples don't even consider going exclusive until **six to eight dates in**. Which means if you're on date three and spiraling because he hasn't called you his girlfriend yet, calm down. You're still in tryouts.

❖ The most common time for breakups? **Between month three and five.** Right after you start sleeping over without makeup and just before you realize he has zero emotional range.

❖ Four out of ten workplace relationships lead to marriage. The other six end in HR complaints, rumors, and you quitting your job to protect your dignity. (Don't be me, be better.)

❖ Nearly **40% of men** say they don't feel confident walking up to a woman for the first time. Which explains the "hey" messages from the guy with sunglasses and hat on in every photo.

> **Fun Fact:** 29% of singles say they're more attracted if their date has an iPhone.
> **Dating Truth:** One-third of online daters *never* actually meet the people they match with.
> **UnExpert Commentary:** "So basically, we're swiping for people we never meet, judging them by their devices, and getting ghosted by strangers we were already trauma-bonding with. Sounds healthy."

❖ There are 95.9 million unmarried people in the U.S. 47% men, 53% women. Do the math and you'll see: there are 86 single men for every 100 single women. (FML)

❖ One-third of people who use dating apps find a relationship. One-third give up. The other third is still out here dating the same recycled five men. Also, only 10% of dudes are actually successful on dating apps. That means a small army of delusional Chads are running the show while the rest of them are trying to make polite conversation with "Looking for my queen."

❖ Online daters spend **almost an hour a day on apps.** That's right, you've got a full-blown part-time job, except instead of a paycheck, you get left on read.

❖ Over 50% of single Americans haven't had a date in over two years.

❖ Research shows men know they're falling in love after just three dates. Women, on the other hand, take until about date 14. Umm…I've been dating this dude for three weeks, why has he not said he loves me yet? Ha, JK, they probably won't say it that quickly.

❖ A recent Wall Street Journal poll found that **nearly 60% of women are now swearing off marriage**. Honestly, can you blame them? With the dating pool looking more like a kiddie pool and the rise of situationships, it's no wonder women are choosing to focus on themselves.

ONLINE DATING & APPS

(Also known as: The psychological warfare simulator you willingly downloaded at two a.m. while watching reruns of Sex and the City thinking, "Maybe THIS time it'll work.")

❖ Women who post a photo on dating apps get **twice as many messages** as those who don't. I don't know why you wouldn't post a pic, I feel like that defeats the purpose. Maybe we should invent a *Love is Blind* app? Great idea? No. Ok.

❖ Men who *claim* they make over $250,000? They get **156% more messages** than those who list a measly $50K.

❖ **Forty-four percent of Match.com users have kids.** So yeah, almost half of your "fresh start" pool comes with a side of PTA meetings, Baby Shark, and a toddler who will hate you on sight.

❖ **At least 10% of free dating profiles are scammers.** But let's be real, that number's probably *way* higher now with AI in the mix. These bots are out here writing better texts than the actual men. Be wary of any guy who immediately asks to switch to WhatsApp. If he says he's "traveling for business" but only messages at three a.m. sis, he's either in Dubai, prison, or someone's husband. Probably all three. Oh, also, they are usually widowed.

> **Fun Fact:** 21% of mobile users feel *closer* to their partner because of texting. **Dating Truth:** Nearly 50% of breakups now happen via text message. **UnExpert Commentary:** "Texting is either bonding us… or blindsiding us. There is no in-between. You'll either be soul-typing deep thoughts or getting a breakup paragraph while you're in line at Trader Joe's."

❖ **The online dating industry rakes in $6.18 BILLION a year.** Yeah, billion with a B. And you're still here wondering if you're being too picky for not wanting to date a guy whose main pic is him holding a fish.

❖ **Match Group alone made $3.5 billion** last year. So, while you're crying over "why did he stop texting me," just know someone out there is cashing checks off your heartbreak. (And also, people still use Match?)

❖ The dating coach/matchmaking industry? Another **$260 million** in the U.S. alone. I want to clarify something right now: I am NOT a dating coach. I am a proud UnExpert.

I've done all the stupid shit *for you*, so you don't have to. Half these "coaches" are charging $5,000 to tell you to "raise your frequency" while they're crying into their Chardonnay because the guy they manifested just ghosted them too. What is the saying if you can't do, teach, lol, I think I am so funny.

❖ **eHarmony claims 236 of its members get married every day.** That's 2% of all U.S. marriages. So yes, someone out there *is* finding love while you're getting ghosted mid-convo after asking if they have siblings. Wait though…so how many people use eHarmony a year, and do people even still use it? This must be for the older generation… Wait until you see those stats.

❖ Somewhere between **20 and 40 million Americans** have used online dating services. Almost **50% of users are 18–34**, and **24% are 35–44**. So, if you're over 40 and tired of guys saying "I don't date women my age," you're not alone. He's not ageist, babe. He's insecure and allergic to women with standards. Also, my favorite, looking for short-term when they are 65, but lied about their age so they could get the younger girls, but more on that catastrophe later.

> **Fun Fact:** A lot of singles pre-Google their date before meeting.
> **Dating Truth:** 41% of 18–29-year-olds check socials *before* they even say hi.
> **UnExpert Commentary:** "By the time you sit down, you already know their sister's wedding colors, your dog's name, and that weird sock photo from college. But sure, act surprised."

❖ **Seventy-nine percent of daters under 30 are on Tinder.** So, if you're wondering why your Hinge match is still using "ur" instead of "you're," that's why. And also, get the eff off Tinder if you want a real relationship. If you want a quick bang by a guy who probably doesn't know there are 11 different orgasms a female has, and can only satisfy his. Yes, that was just another plug for my book, *A Single Girl's Guide to Hilarious Facts You Never Knew About Sex,* to show what a versatile writer I am 😊

❖ Online dating isn't just for hot twenty-somethings either. There's been a **huge surge in users over 50.** So yes, even your aunt Cheryl is out here swiping, and probably doing better than you. Love that for her. So, for real though, the term "Love that for her" I feel means "Bless her heart" on Botox. But, in truth, the woman's name is Pam and she is my aunt so I wish her more luck than I have had.

❖ The average user swipes through **3,000 profiles a year**. That's 3,000 left-swipes, eye rolls, and mental breakdowns later, and you're still holding out hope for the one guy who spelled "entrepreneur" correctly. That's the flipping average! I wonder what the most is…I mean I guess it's not terrible it's a little over eight a day.

❖ And here's the real gut punch: A study published in *Cyberpsychology, Behavior, and Social Networking* found **over 60% of Tinder users were already in a relationship or married.** Yeah. You're sitting there analyzing his emoji use and whether his "wyd tonight?" text means something... while his wife is plating chicken nuggets and yelling at little Mason to put his iPad down. Welcome to the Hunger Games, babe. May the odds be forever in your therapist's favor.

❖ One in **three dating app users have matched with someone who turned out to be a full-on fake identity.** Not just a bad angle. Like a "this person doesn't even exist" situation. Welcome to catfish country, population: too damn many. I had two catfish recently. Ones pictures were def in his prime, and probably 15-20 years ago. The other, not even the same person. He blamed it that he hasn't had his haircut in a while. Ah, no dude, you are in an entirely different stratosphere.

❖ **Romance scams in 2024 cost Americans over $823 million.** That's right! People are out here losing more money on fake boyfriends than they are on car repairs. And the median loss was **$2,000** per person. **DON'T EVER, AND I MEAN FUCKING EVER, GIVE A MAN MONEY!!!!!!!!** Trust me, I thought I met the love of my life and that fucker scammed me out of $7,000. Don't be me, be better.

❖ Ever heard of "Pig Butchering?" You will now. It's a scam where someone pretends to fall in love with you, then slowly lures you into crypto fraud. And it's grown by **40%**. You thought you were in love. Turns out, you were just the main character in a fintech horror movie.

> **Fun Fact:** Big cities have more singles and more opportunity…
> **Dating Truth:** …But relationships actually last *shorter* in major cities.
> **UnExpert Commentary:** "Too many options. Too little intention. Big City dating is basically emotional Amazon Prime: next-day delivery, next-hour ghosting."

❖ **Over 54% of women on dating apps say they feel emotionally overwhelmed** by the sheer number of messages. Meanwhile, **most men feel invisible.** So basically, the women are exhausted and the men are bitter.

❖ And if you're still hanging onto hope: **over 400 million people worldwide** have used dating apps now. So yeah, love might be out there.

PSYCHOLOGY, BEHAVIOR & FIRST IMPRESSIONS

(Also known as: How fast they decide if they'd bang you, and all the subtle shit that determines if you ever get a second date.)

❖ Psychologists at the University of Pennsylvania studied data from **over 10,000 speed daters** and found that most people decide whether or not they're attracted to someone within **three seconds** of meeting them. Three. Seconds. That's less time than it takes to say your own name. So yeah, your witty bio, that story about rescuing puppies, your degree from Stanford? He's already decided based on your jawline and how well your jeans fit.

❖ Before a man even speaks, his **body language accounts for over 80%** of a woman's first impression. If he walks in slouching like Eeyore with mommy issues, game over. Women are out here subconsciously scanning for posture like their nervous system is running a TSA body scan.

❖ If a man doesn't know what to wear, tell him to wear blue. **Studies show women are most attracted to men in blue.** Why? Who knows. Maybe because it says "I'm stable and slightly emotionally available," or maybe it's just the least offensive color in the male wardrobe. Either way, it's science. Also, no wrinkled shirts. And please, dear God, no Affliction tees.

❖ Remembering details and working them into convo is emotional crack. **Studies show** this trick makes people feel *wildly* special like you actually listened and aren't just biding time until dessert. So yes, casually referencing his dog's name or that he prefers oat milk? Hotter than a thirst trap.

❖ Using someone's name in conversation? **Turns out it psychologically triggers a bond and builds trust.** Saying "Josh" twice makes Josh feel seen, validated, and maybe even slightly turned on.

❖ Happiness is contagious. **People are drawn to happy people**, and **negativity is one of the biggest turn-offs**.

❖ **Men are statistically less likely to approach a woman if she's in a loud, rowdy group.** If you're out with the girls and wondering why you didn't meet anyone, it's not you. It's the volume. You don't need to ditch your squad, just give the guy a five-second solo window to shoot his shot without needing noise-canceling headphones.

> **Fun Fact:** Men *still* overwhelmingly prefer to pick up the tab on a first date.
> **Dating Truth:** 75% of men say they feel guilty letting a woman pay.
> **UnExpert Commentary:** "Which is sweet… until you realize he just Venmo-requested you $3.89 for the fries you split. Sir, be serious."

❖ **Mirroring someone's body language can make them more attracted to you, but don't turn it into a weird episode of *Black Mirror*.** Subtlety is sexy. If he leans in, lean a little. If he touches his drink, casually grab yours. Do *not* copy every move like you're in a synchronized swim-off for love. He'll think you're malfunctioning.

❖ Hot girl problems: **Beautiful women get stared at more, harassed more, AND get asked out less.** Because average guys assume you'll reject them or worse, destroy them emotionally with one well-placed "lol." So, if you're hot and single and wondering why no one approaches you, it's not that they don't want to. It's that they're scared shitless you'll ruin them. And you probably will. Good for you. Just know, it's not you, it's intimidation. That's your villain origin story, babe.

10

MATCHMAKERS, MONEY & INDUSTRY CRAZINESS
(Also known as: The part of dating where love meets capitalism and everyone pretends it's not weird.)

❖ At **4M Multimillionaire Matchmaking Club**, single men who've made millions but *somehow still can't figure out how to talk to women* are paying **$10,000 to $30,000** to find "the one." Meanwhile, women? They pay **$250** to be considered. Yep. Men drop a down payment on a Tesla, and women get added to a human catalog for less than the price of one Botox sesh. If that doesn't scream "rich guy fantasy marketplace," I don't know what does. Why are they single? Hmmm…such a conundrum, of does rich buy happiness, because you are about to be miserable with a lot of retail.

❖ In Manhattan, where delusion meets luxury, one high-end matchmaker **charges a base fee of $20,000,** just to *start* the process. And if it leads to marriage? You better cough up a **"marriage bonus."** Because nothing says "eternal love" like an invoice.

❖ Oh, and mark your calendars, ladies. **The third week of September is officially National Singles Week in the U.S.** A whole week to celebrate the fact that you're single, thriving, and not currently lying awake at night next to a man who can't emotionally regulate and chews with his mouth open. Sounds like a party to me.

❖ At **Kelleher International**, one of the most elite matchmaking agencies on the planet, high-net-worth clients are shelling out up to **$150,000** for help finding their soulmate. That's not a typo, *one hundred fifty grand*. And yes, that includes celebrities, royalty, and Fortune 500 execs who can command empires but still can't figure out how to make a woman feel seen.

❖ **Linx Dating** is Silicon Valley's go-to for "I invented an app but still die inside when a woman says hi." It's all about concierge-style matchmaking with "realistic expectations," which is code for: even billionaires can't manifest a unicorn. But sure, let's keep charging like love is a start-up investment.

❖ The **global matchmaking industry was worth $8.5 billion** in 2023. Let me say that again for the people in the back: **eight. billion. dollars.** Just to help people do what our grandparents did with one glance and a polite hello. And it's projected to hit **$12.9 billion** by 2032. So, if you're broke and single, at least know you're single for free. That's something. I'm going to start a matchmaking service and charge men $100k, then find the perfect matches for my girlfriends and myself. I believe that is a win-win.

❖ App fatigue is *very real*, and now there's a trend of people turning back to **old-school in-person matchmaking** curated cocktail mixers, hand-picked dates, and matchmakers who actually tell you when you're being annoying. Services like **Singles Only Social Club** and **My TruBond** are basically trying to make "organic" cool again. Bless them. Anything's better than another DM that says "👀."

❖ Meanwhile in India? **Matrimony.com** runs everything from budget-friendly alliances to full-blown luxury matchmaking under **Elite Matrimony**, where clients are dropping anywhere from ₹60,000 to ₹2,220,000. That's roughly **$700 to over $26,000** USD just to stop their parents from setting them up with someone who lists "hobby: breathing."

ATTRACTION, SMELL & HYGIENE

(Also known as: You can be hot, but if you smell like expired deli meat and have troll feet… it's over.)

Scent & Sexual Chemistry:

❖ **Your natural scent can make or break attraction.** Studies suggest that individuals with pleasant natural odors are more likely to be rated as attractive and trustworthy.

❖ **Smell dating is a thing.** Services like Smell Dating match people based on their natural scents, believing that our unique bodily odors play a larger role in our social lives than we realize.

❖ **Women's perceptions of their partner's scent can vary widely.** A recent study found that women's perception of odor often depended on context, such that even odors generally perceived as unpleasant were often accepted as part of a sexual encounter.

> **Fun Fact:** Most people say they want honesty in a relationship.
> **Dating Truth:** Speed dating studies show what people *say* they want has zero correlation to who they actually choose.
> **UnExpert Commentary:** "He said he wanted kind and funny. Then picked a girl named Krystal who insulted the waiter and called herself a 'CEO of vibes.' We're not okay."

❖ **Pheromones may influence attraction.** Preliminary studies suggest that pheromones play a role in disassortative mate selection through the attribution of attractiveness.

❖ Studies show women are **way more attracted to men wearing pheromone-heavy colognes**, which literally tricks our bodies into thinking you're an alpha wolf ready to mate. Women also have a stronger sense of smell than men (*shocker*), and are especially drawn to **musk** and **black licorice**. Yes, black licorice. So, if he smells like a mysterious forest and low-key candy store? Game over.

❖ **Your diet affects your scent.** Research indicates that women's preferences for male body odor are influenced by the men's diets, with increased dietary fruit, vegetable, and protein content leading to more attractive scents.

❖ **We may be attracted to those with different immune system genes.** The 'Sweaty T-shirt' experiment demonstrated that women are more attracted to scents of men with dissimilar MHC genes, which play a role in the immune system.

Hygiene & Dealbreakers:

❖ In a survey of 5,000 singles on Match.com, **43% said fresh breath** mattered most before a date, followed by **17% saying stylish clothes**, **15% loving a sexy fragrance**, **14% going for good skin**, and **10% caring about great hair.** Fair. But honestly? I feel like good skin should be higher on that list. I, also, may be vain.

❖ **Bad breath and bad teeth** are one-way tickets to Nopeville. If your breath still smells like death even after a deep cleaning, you might have **H. pylori**, a stomach bacterium that literally causes halitosis. For real though! Everyone: keep up with your dental hygiene! Going to the dentist sucks, but missing teeth is worse. The other thing that sucks, I think most dentists are scam artists, but that is probably for another book.

❖ **Cleanliness is sexy.** A survey found that over half of adults (52%) feel "turned on" when they see their partner cleaning, with doing the dishes ranked as the "sexiest" chore.

❖ **Women generally have stricter hygiene norms than men.** Research indicates that women traditionally shoulder responsibility for hygiene standards and therefore tend to have stricter views on hygiene. I think this is just a given, I mean look at how long it takes us to get ready…That is no small feat.

RED FLAGS, DEALBREAKERS & DATING FEARS

(Also known as: The part where we admit we've ignored every sign from the universe because he had a good jawline and Spotify Premium.)

❖ In the world of online dating, women are mostly afraid they'll get murdered. Men? They're afraid the woman will be fat. I'm not kidding. According to true crime icon Ann Rule, around **3% of men are actual psychopaths** and while most aren't serial killers, some are definitely lurking on Hinge in salmon-colored shorts.

Fun Fact: Dating apps are booming in rural areas more than ever before.
Dating Truth: And yet, people in small towns still say, "There's no one here."
UnExpert Commentary: "There *are* people. You just ghosted half of them in 2019 and the rest know your mom."

❖ **Common First Date Fears:** A survey found that 36% of men and women say bad breath makes them the most nervous on a first date. Other concerns include having something caught in their teeth (25%), spilling something on oneself (15%), wardrobe malfunctions (14%), and drinking too much (10%).

❖ **Glasses Wearers' Unique Worries:** Among glasses wearers, 20% have experienced a 'kiss-clash' where two pairs of glasses collide during a kiss. Additionally, 38% find their glasses annoying when kissing, citing issues like clashing with the other person's glasses (46%), fogging up (36%), and hair getting caught in them (24%).

SEX, TIMING & RELATIONSHIP MILESTONES
(Also known as: When to sleep with him, when to ghost him, and why you should never loan a man money.)

❖ According to a recent AOL survey, **40% of women** say the right time to have sex is **1 to 3 months in**, while **35% of men** think *the third date is go time*. Real talk? Most couples end up having sex **somewhere between the 4th and 6th date**.

❖ **29% of Americans admit to having sex on the first date.** A Lovehoney survey revealed that nearly half of adults have had sex on the first date, with men being more open to it than women. Again, I am ashamed, I've done this twice in my twenty years of dating. One, the guy was dating multiple women. Two, got into a relationship. So, 50/50 odds I guess aren't bad. Both times? Drunk. Obviously.

> **Fun Fact:** A massive percentage of profiles never get swiped on at all.
> **Dating Truth:** Most people swipe based on the *previous* faces they saw.
> **UnExpert Commentary:** "So, if Chad came right after a hot doctor and before a six-pack firefighter… he never stood a chance. Sorry, Chad."

❖ The average time to kiss is **the second date**, statistically. A survey by The Match Lab found that 45% of respondents consider the second date the perfect opportunity for a first kiss. Meanwhile, 15% prefer the first date, and 26% wait until the third. If I've met a man organically, I kiss on the first date usually. If I met him online, then I'm definitely waiting until the second date. Or, in one case, sleeping with on a first date over a trauma bond. True story.

❖ **Mystery still works.** Humans are hardwired to love *the chase*, so don't be overly available or try to lock it down too soon. Experts say the longer you hold off, the more likely feelings and not just genitals get involved. Basically: suspense is sexy. Accessibility? Not so much. Also, you want to find out how to do this to perfection, read *Why Men Love BITCHES*. I have no affiliation, just a genius book.

❖ **Saying "I Love You":** According to a study by Match, couples typically wait five months before saying "I love you" and making their relationship public on social media.

❖ **Meeting the Parents:** The same study found that meeting each other's families usually occurs after three months of dating.

❖ **Engagements & Weddings:** On average, couples get engaged after two years, marry after three, and start a family after four.

❖ **Trial Period:** The "three-month rule" suggests waiting three months before committing to a new partner, offering a trial period to assess compatibility and uncover potential issues that may not be evident during the initial infatuation phase.

WHERE WE MEET & HOW WE FLIRT

(Also known as: Where to go to find men, how to accidentally flirt while breathing, and why we're all one dirty martini away from falling for a bartender we should've avoided.)

❖ Researchers at the University of Chicago found that you're **twice as likely to meet someone through friends or family** than by prowling the bar scene. Which makes sense considering most people at bars are either drunk, emotionally unavailable, or just there to post a story with neon lights. And let's be honest, *nobody* knows how to flirt in real life anymore. Everyone's too busy scrolling through Instagram stories of people they don't even like. IMHO, we've completely lost the ability to communicate like normal humans. (I've got games for that, lol, on Etsy at
www.yourdatingunexpert.etsy.com.)

> **Fun Fact:** The alphabet affects your chances on dating apps. Names that start with A-M are statistically more successful.
> **Dating Truth:** If your name starts with Z, you're already fighting the algorithm.
> **UnExpert Commentary:** "Zachary, babe, I'm sorry, the odds are against you. Maybe just change your username to 'AdventurousAlpha1986' and call it a day."

❖ **Coffee Shops & Study Spots:** In Miami, popular spots like Macondo Coffee Roasters and Special Tea near FIU are frequented by students and professionals alike, making them ideal places to strike up a conversation.

❖ **Talking to a bartender** makes a woman seem friendlier and more approachable to other men. It also opens the door for *men* to slide in under the guise of "small talk." BUT, and I cannot stress this enough, do **NOT** date the bartender. I repeat: **Do. Not. Date. The. Bartender.** Especially if he's a 53-year-old pretending he's 40, who calls you baby while flirting with your friends on shift. Ask me how I know.

❖ **Men are told to shop where the kind of women they want hang out.** If you want an "outdoorsy" woman? Hit the REI. Looking for a fashionista? Try Zara. So ladies, should we reverse-engineer this logic and start hanging out in high-end suit shops? Or nah?

> **Fun Fact:** The average woman dates five people and has four bad first dates before finding "the one."
> **Dating Truth:** That same woman will also likely live with someone else before she does.
> **UnExpert Commentary:** I am doing something way wrong if that is the statistic.

❖ **Pro-tip for men:** It's harder to approach *two* women alone, because no one wants to make the other girl feel abandoned. So, ladies, if you're trying to increase your odds of being approached? Bring **two wing women**, not one. Power in threes, baby. One talks, one distracts, one scopes out the exits. Dammit, I've been doing this all wrong for decades.

- **Italian food reigns supreme for first dates.** Why? Pasta is sexy, comforting, and just messy enough to break the tension. If a man can watch you slurp noodles and still be into you? Keep him. I know what else I'd like to see him slurping. Just kidding, but not.

- Bars are designed like a covert operation. The **curve of the counter** isn't for style, it's a **strategic thirst trap**, meant to give patrons the best angle to check each other out. And those **mirrors behind the liquor bottles?** Yeah, those aren't just décor. They're so you can secretly scope out that guy behind you pretending not to stare while ordering his third bourbon.

> **Fun Fact:** There's a spike in dating app activity every Sunday around 9 p.m.
> **Dating Truth:** That's when people feel the loneliest heading into the workweek.
> **UnExpert Commentary:** "Don't fall for that Sunday Night Swipe. He's not trying to build a life with you. He's just sad and horny and out of leftovers."

- **Online vs. Offline:** A study by the University of Chicago found that couples who met online reported higher marital satisfaction and lower rates of breakups compared to those who met offline. I don't care about this statistic, as I will not be meeting my future husband on dating apps. Personal preference, of course.)

BODY LANGUAGE, PHYSICAL CUES & NONVERBAL ATTRACTION

(How to flirt without saying a word and how to tell if he's into you or just awkwardly waiting for the check.)

- **Want to send a signal without saying a thing?** Studies show that revealing areas of the body that aren't usually exposed. Think "subtle seduction." Not full thirst trap just a little *here's a peek, behave accordingly.*

- **Eye contact is not just eye contact.** It's officially called a **"copulatory gaze."** Yes, that's the scientific name because the eyes *do not lie*. Eye contact is one of the strongest nonverbal cues we have to create attraction, but heads up: **the meaning changes by culture.** In some countries it's sexy, in others it's confrontational, and in Florida it's how you accidentally get proposed to at a gas station.

- In American culture, when a man offers his palm **face up** while speaking to a woman, it's often an **unconscious sign of deep attraction.** Why? Because our brains are wired to read hand gestures *before* we even register words. And palm-up energy says "I'm open, I'm harmless, I'd probably split my fries with you." Rare. Keep him.

❖ If a woman wants a man to approach, she should **uncross her arms**, make subtle eye contact, and smile. If your arms are crossed, it puts off a vibe that you're closed off or just low-key plotting his demise. Either way, it's giving "crabby."

❖ **The Triangle Gaze: A Subtle Power Move.** The "triangle method" involves shifting your gaze from one eye to the other, then down to the mouth, forming a triangle. This technique subtly signals romantic interest without being overt.

❖ **The Right Smile: Balance Is Everything.** Displaying positive emotions through facial expressions increases likability. However, overdoing it can seem insincere. A genuine, regulated smile goes a long way.

❖ **Attraction Styles: Know Your Flirt.** Researchers have identified five flirting styles: physical, playful, polite, sincere, and traditional. Recognizing your style can help in understanding and improving your flirting game. Discover your flirt style and learn how to use it intentionally with **The Flirt Style System**.

https://www.etsy.com/listing/4429791726/the-flirt-style-system-dating-guide-for

❖ **Touch: The Ultimate Nonverbal Cue.** Gentle, informal touches like a light touch on the arm are powerful indicators of romantic interest.

YOUR DATING PROFILE & THE ALGORITHM GAME

(How to make strangers fall in love with your profile pic while pretending you read books and hike.)

❖ **Men swipe right 46% of the time.** Women? Just 14%. So yeah, ladies are out here curating photos, editing bios, and spiritually assessing red flags. Meanwhile, guys are swiping like they're ordering from a buffet with no budget.

❖ **Photos matter more than bios.** By A LOT. Studies show users spend **less than 1-second** deciding whether to swipe left or right which means your witty paragraph about loving sunsets and speaking three languages doesn't even *register* until you've already been approved or rejected like an expired driver's license.

❖ **The first photo? Make it count.** The algorithm favors clear, well-lit pics of your face not sunglasses, not a group shot, and not a blurry pic from 2016 when you peaked. If your first photo's weak, the algorithm buries you like you just confessed to being a flat-earther. No offense flat-earthers, I still love you.

❖ **The dating app algorithm doesn't just favor hotness, it favors engagement.** Meaning: the more you swipe, like, and message, the more your profile gets shown. FTS.

❖ **Avoid "lazy guy" bait.** If your profile says "I love sarcasm and tacos." Congratulations! You've written the same bio as 20 million other women. Use your profile to *filter*, not *impress*. You're not here to be everyone's cup of tea, you're here to catch the right kind of weirdo. (Later chapters touch on this, obvi.)

❖ **The algorithm clocks EVERYTHING.** Response times. Message ratios. How often you check the app. If you ghost five matches in a row, it notices. If you open the app every 45 seconds looking for validation, it knows. This thing is smarter than your ex and more judgmental than your mom at Thanksgiving.

> **Fun Fact:** The dating pool feels smaller than ever.
> **Dating Truth:** But statistically, you're exposed to *hundreds* more people than pre-app days.
> **UnExpert Commentary:** "Turns out having more options doesn't make people pick better, it just makes them pickier, lazier, and chronically distracted. We're in the golden age of romantic ADHD."

❖ **Resetting Your Profile: A Double-Edged Sword.** Some users attempt to reset their profiles to gain a visibility boost. However, dating apps like Tinder can detect this behavior and may penalize users by lowering their profile's visibility.

❖ **Timing Is Everything.** Engaging with dating apps during peak hours, typically between 7 and 10 p.m. on weekdays, can increase your profile's visibility and match potential.

> **Fun Fact:** Texting has replaced phone calls for early courtship.
> **Dating Truth:** But 1 in 4 singles say a call before the first date would be a dealbreaker.
> **UnExpert Commentary:** "Imagine getting the ick because someone *wants to hear your voice*. We're so emotionally unavailable, even connection gives us anxiety."

❖ **Behavioral Patterns: The Algorithm Learns You.** Dating app algorithms analyze user behavior, such as swiping patterns and message responses, to tailor match suggestions. Being selective and engaging meaningfully can positively influence the algorithm's perception of your profile.

❖ **Avoid Over-Swiping.** Excessive swiping without meaningful engagement can negatively impact your profile's standing in the algorithm. It's better to be selective and intentional with your swipes.

TOTALLY RANDOM BUT FASCINATING
(Also known as: Weird sh*t you didn't ask for, but now can't stop thinking about.)

❖ **Speed dating was invented by a rabbi** in Los Angeles in 1999, and yes, it was based on a Jewish tradition of chaperoned mingling events for singles. So technically, speed dating is sacred. Now it's just a bunch of guys named Chad asking "What do you do?" on a loop until your soul collapses. Again, with the Chad, I'm sorry. I'll use David next time. #IYKYK

❖ After **Tiger Woods' affairs went public**, the number of men looking for "discreet" relationships on BeNaughty.com **plummeted 47.5%.** Ha, I wonder why??? Because they aren't so discreet and women will spill the tea? If you are a woman, don't do this sh*t. Respect yourself and other women.

❖ Want to boost your chances of someone falling for you? **Take them somewhere slightly dangerous.** Studies show that adrenaline-inducing dates: roller coasters, rock climbing, haunted house energy actually **increase physical and romantic attraction.** Case in point: Watch *The Bachelor*. The girls who get the helicopter near-death experiences always end up in the final four.

❖ **New York and Washington have the highest percentages of unmarried residents** with 50% and 70% respectively flying solo. Meanwhile, **Idaho and Utah are basically marriage HQ**, with 60% and 59% hitched. (What the hell is going on in Washington?)

❖ **There's a dating app that only lets you swipe when the moon is full.** Yes, it's real. It's called *Celeste*, and the whole concept is based on lunar energy and "letting the universe decide." Because apparently, dating was too easy with all the constant access, now we need moon phases to regulate our emotional availability. I kinda respect it. But also… I'm not waiting for a full moon to reject another man who says his love language is physical touch.

> **Fun Fact:** A growing number of couples admit they met… on Facebook Marketplace.
> **Dating Truth:** One in four millennials would rather slide into DMs than use a dating app.
> **UnExpert Commentary:** "Love in the era of likes means you might meet your future husband because he bought your old Peloton. Romance is not dead. It just has a 'pending pickup' time."

Dating wasn't always this chaotic. Once upon a time, it was worse.

Before 1900, dating wasn't about chemistry. It was about contracts. A man didn't ask you out, he came to "call" on you under your parents' surveillance, sat stiffly in the parlor, and made awkward conversation while a judgmental aunt pretended not to eavesdrop. It wasn't love. It was a transaction with lace gloves and tea service.

Actual "dates?" Didn't exist. You were evaluated for marriage potential, not wooed for who you were. The goal? Status, money, reputation. Not orgasms. Not even affection. Think *Pride and Prejudice* minus the tension, plus more gossip.

Then the 1900s hit, and women walked out of the house unchaperoned. Going to the park or a soda shop alone was suddenly radical. Being seen in public with a man? Scandalous. But liberating. It gave women one thing they'd never had before: choice.

That choice came with backlash. In early 1900s Chicago, single women who dared to date freely were labeled "women adrift" as if freedom automatically meant prostitution. These weren't sex workers. They were pioneers. Society didn't know how to process an independent woman... so it tried to shame her into silence.

And yet, these early rebels laid the entire foundation for modern love. They dated out loud. And they did it while the system tried to bury them in judgment.

The Evolution of Dating: Chaos in Every Era

Roaring 1900s – Supervised Love

Imagine trying to flirt while your dad is watching from behind a curtain. That was courtship. You didn't date for fun. You interviewed for marriage. If he had a car and a steady job, he passed. If not, back to your sewing and spinsterhood.

The '20s – Flappers, Freedom, and the First Makeouts

Women could vote. Jazz clubs popped off. Cars became portable make-out zones. Society watched women dance, drink, and date, and immediately called them sluts. Judgment rose with visibility. Still, we flirted. We rebelled. We learned how fun it is to kiss someone just because you want to.

The '30s – Drive-Ins and Don't Touch His Mirror

The car wasn't just for transportation, it was the original mobile dating app. Movies, parking spots, and the first formal dates all collided. And yes, magazines still told women how to "keep a man" by doing things like never touching the rearview mirror and acting impressed by his hobbies. (Gag.)

The '40s & '50s – Marriage Mania

World War II ended. Men came home. Women were told to lock down a husband immediately or risk social doom.

"Going steady" became a full-blown lifestyle and the pressure was insane. A woman who said no was considered rude. Romance turned into urgency. Double dates were the norm. Saying no wasn't.

Revolutionary '60s & '70s

The Women's Movement and birth control changed *everything*. Now it wasn't "find a husband," it was "find yourself." Dating took a backseat to self-discovery and yes, sexual freedom. Women had control over their own fertility for the first time, which meant they could finally date on their own terms.

Casual '80s & '90s

Enter: hookup culture. Formal dates faded out. Friendships blurred into flings. And then came the internet. Suddenly, geography didn't matter. You could flirt with someone five states away, fall in love in a chatroom, and get catfished all before your mom yelled at you to get off the dial-up. Everything changed. Everything got faster. Emotions didn't necessarily keep up.

The Wildest Dating Tips from Vintage Magazines

(Spoiler: These were actually published. And yes, women were supposed to be grateful.)

From *Click-Photo Parade Magazine*, 1930s:

- "Don't talk while dancing, it annoys him."
- "Men don't like girls who borrow their handkerchiefs and smudge them with lipstick."
- "If you need a brassiere, wear one. Don't tug at your straps or pull up your girdle in public."
- "Be careful of your hands. A man doesn't want to marry a woman whose nails look like she's been digging potatoes."

From *McCall's*, 1958:

- "Be pleasant, even if he's boring."
- "Don't be too talkative. Don't tell him about your former boyfriends."
- "Don't look at your watch or mention how long the date's been going on."
- "Never discuss hats or clothes, he doesn't care."

From *Seventeen Magazine*, 1949:

- "If you have to chew gum, do it with your mouth closed. Better yet, don't."
- "Don't be conspicuous talking to other men."
- "Don't cry in public, especially if you're drunk." (Still kind of solid advice.)

(The first ever computer dating service. You paid $3 and got matches based on punch-card science.)

❖ "Do you believe in a God who answers prayer?"

❖ "Do you believe that premarital sex is wrong?"

❖ "Do you enjoy going to museums and art galleries?"

❖ "Would you prefer to date someone with similar income to yours?"

❖ "Do you believe a woman's place is in the home?"

❖ "Are you emotionally stable?" (Imagine mailing that in and waiting three weeks for your results… only to be matched with your roommate's ex.)

Sarah Melland

Modern Times

Now? One swipe decides your fate. One missed message ruins your shot. (Seriously, guys get super offended, if you don't reply within 24 hours on a dating app. Calm down, bro, I'm not you and try to have somewhat of a life.) But even with all the tech, 60% of millennials say they'd still rather meet someone "organically" through friends or shared interests. (Same.) The dating world has gotten so dystopian, some people now call it "The Dating Apocalypse." (We'll get into that later and why you shouldn't buy into that BS.)

The Wild Beginnings:
From Classified Ads to Operation Match

Before dating apps. Before "wyd" texts. Before you could fall in love (or lust) from a lazy swipe in your bed at two a.m., people were *literally buying ads in newspapers* like they were lost puppies. You didn't slide into DMs back then. You paid cash to post something like: "Astrologer, 27, psychology student, desires to establish non-superficial friendship with deep souls who aren't self-absorbed or boring AF." Probably not in that language, because you know…standards.

Enter: Operation Match

In 1965, two Harvard bros looked around at the tragic dating scene and said, "We can do better. With math."

Armed with an IBM 1401 (basically a prehistoric computer the size of a small house) and a dream, they created Operation Match. The first-ever *computer-based matchmaking service* in America.

Here's how it worked:
- You filled out a 75-question survey about your likes, dislikes, and weird little habits.
- You mailed it in with a $3 fee (about $30 in today's money).
- A machine crunched the data (no swiping required) and spit out your list of love matches.

No endless texting. No ghosting. No shirtless mirror selfies. Just cold, calculated 1960s science trying to save your ass from dying alone.

By the end of '65, Operation Match had over 90,000 people signed up because even in a world of go-go boots and rotary phones, humans already knew two things:

1. Dating sucks.
2. Outsourcing dating to a machine might suck slightly less.

QUICK FUN FACT (BECAUSE YOU KNOW I HAD TO): Operation Match was so profitable it pulled in the equivalent of $1.8 million in today's dollars within the first six months. All from desperate singles mailing cash to a computer that sounded like a vacuum cleaner on steroids.

Match.com and the Pajama Revolution

Fast forward to 1995. Enter: Match.com. For the first time ever, you could sit on your couch in your ugliest sweatpants, eating microwave burritos, and still *technically be flirting with a stranger.*

No bars. No awkward setups by Karen from accounting. No shower required. Just you, your janky dial-up connection, and a whole new world of possibilities all at your fingertips. The game had officially changed.

MATCH.COM: WHERE LONELINESS MET LAZINESS

Match wasn't just revolutionary because it moved dating online. It was revolutionary because it made loneliness *convenient.* You could:

- Craft the perfect bio pretending you weren't emotionally destroyed by your ex.
- Upload a suspiciously cropped headshot from five years ago.
- Scroll through endless singles without even putting on pants.

You weren't desperate. You were "early tech-adopting." Big difference.

Bonus Nobody Saw Coming: The Rise of Interracial Relationships.

When Match.com exploded, researchers noticed something crazy: Interracial marriages shot up, too. Because when you're online, you're not just limited to the people your grandma's church group approves of. You're seeing *everyone.* Every flavor. Every vibe. Every possibility. Turns out, love gets way more interesting when you're not trapped in the same 20-mile radius your whole damn life.

Final Word on the Pajama Revolution: *Match.com didn't just change dating. It changed who we date, how we date, and who we dare to imagine loving.* And it gave birth to a whole generation of people who will absolutely meet their soulmate without even brushing their teeth first.

Swipe Right to History: Grindr, Tinder, and the App Explosion

If Match.com cracked the door open, Grindr and Tinder kicked it off the hinges, set it on fire, and danced on the ashes. Welcome to the era of instant access, instant gratification, and yes, instant regret.

Grindr: The Gay Community's Secret Weapon

In 2009, Grindr dropped into the App Store like a glitter bomb in a church pew. **The first dating app to use geolocation technology**, aka, "there's literally a hot guy 82 feet away, and you can message him right now."

No more:
- Creeping around shady bars.
- Risking weird stares.
- Praying to bump into someone halfway cute at the gym.

Finding a match was now as easy as opening your phone. For the gay community? Grindr wasn't just an app. It was a revolution. A digital declaration that love, sex, connection, and curiosity could finally be fast, fearless, and unapologetically visible.

Tinder: The Swipe Heard Round the World

Then came 2012. Tinder. The Great Swipe Apocalypse. Suddenly, straight people could finally experience what gay men already knew: Dating had officially become a video game.

Swipe left: Nope. Swipe right: Maybe. Swipe up: Super desperate.

(Just kidding. Kinda.)

Tinder wasn't just changing dating. It was rewriting human behavior:
- Instant validation.
- Zero patience.
- Ten conversations at once.
- Endless "what ifs" and "maybes" in your pocket at all times.

Dating had gone from: ➔ "Will we fall in love over a candlelit dinner?"

to: ➔ "Is this guy worth putting on pants for?"

(Spoiler: Usually, no.)

Fun Fact (Because We Love Receipts): Tinder now has over 50 million users across 190 countries.

Final UnExpert Word on the App Explosion: Grindr gave the gay community freedom. Tinder gave the world chaos. And dating apps gave all of us thumb cramps, commitment issues, and a lifetime supply of hilarious screenshots for the group chat. Welcome to Modern Love, baby. Swipe responsibly.

Scan the QR code to watch me roast the most unhinged men's dating profiles on the internet, because they deserve it, and because sometimes the only cure for app burnout is watching someone else get dragged. https://youtube.com/playlist?list=PLstOVerax_jSQg4eojlJqV-IKzJJWUoGu&si=R-1MKLqy9O_D4jfr

24

A Rapid-Fire Timeline:
How Dating Sites (and Human Desperation) Evolved

Buckle up. This is how we went from mailed questionnaires
to guys asking you "wyd" at two a.m.

1959 – Happy Families Planning Services. Two Stanford dudes use an IBM 650 to match people. Because obviously, nothing screams romance like a computer bigger than your living room.

1965 – Operation Match. Harvard bros invent the first real matchmaking service using surveys and a $3.00 fee. Welcome to the OG swipe, except it took six weeks and a stamp.

1970s – Mail-Order Bride Boom. Cherry Blossoms launches. Because if you can't find love locally, import it like exotic fruit.

1980s – Video Dating Enters the Chat. Great Expectations offers you the chance to make an awkward VHS tape of yourself trying to look dateable. Basically, TikTok thirst traps, but with worse lighting and hairspray. We've all seen the disasters.

1986 – Matchmaker Electronic Pen-Pal Network. BBS dating launches. You had to be part nerd, part romantic, part extremely patient to find a match online back then.

1994 – Kiss.com. First real modern dating site. First real modern dating anxiety.

1995 – Match.com. The world collectively realizes you can find love without leaving your couch. And simultaneously realizes people lie in profile pics.

1997 – JDate Launches. Jewish singles rejoice: finally, an app where your grandma's approval is built-in.

2000 – eHarmony. "Find your soulmate using SCIENCE" aka 500 questions that make you wonder if you even know yourself.

2002 – Friendster. The first social network / dating hybrid. Basically, Facebook's awkward, less-hot older cousin.

2003 – Plenty of Fish. Free dating site = plenty of choices, plenty of weirdos, plenty of emotional damage.

2004 – OkCupid. Match through quizzes so intense they make you rethink your life choices.

2009 – Grindr. Instant sex, instant validation, instant chaos in your immediate geographical radius. The gays really carried the app world on their backs. Respect.

2012 – Tinder. The swipe that changed everything. "Hot or not" becomes a global instinct. *Everyone's attention span shrinks to that of a caffeinated squirrel.*

2014 – Bumble. Women make the first move. Men cry on Reddit.

2015 – Hinge. Designed to be deleted. Ironically: also designed to give you a lifelong habit of judging strangers' "voice prompt" answers. Do you use voice prompts? I do not and every time I hear one, I get the ick, because it always begins with a huge exhale.

2019–2021 – Explosion of Niche Dating Apps. Bearded men? Spoon cuddlers? Sugar babies? Polyamory? If you can name it, there's an app for it now.

2022–Present – Dating App Fatigue + AI Enters the Chat. Better bios, smoother texts, same disappearing acts. Everyone sounds self-aware now. Very few people actually are.

The Good, The Bad, and The Weird: Pros and Cons of Online Dating

Here's the deal: Online dating is neither the devil nor the divine. It's a tool. And like any tool, it can either build your dream life or cut your hand off if you're not paying attention.

(**Spoiler:** Most people are not paying attention.)

1. ACCESS: The Good, The Bad, The Unholy Overwhelm

The Good: You can now meet people from all walks of life, in all zip codes, and all levels of eyebrow grooming. (**Options. OPTIONS EVERYWHERE.**) If you're living in a town where everyone you know married their high school sweetheart or is weirdly into taxidermy, online dating is your magic portal to civilization.

The Bad: Too many choices = **paralysis.** Instead of building connections, you start "shopping for upgrades." (**"He's perfect... but what if I find someone 2% hotter who also knows how to juggle?"**) It becomes an endless loop of *almosts* and nobody sticks long enough to grow into the real thing.

The Survival Tip: Set filters. Set standards. Set intentions. You're not Amazon Prime-ing a boyfriend. You're building your effing future.

2. MATCHING: The Good, The Sketchy, The Scientific-ish

The Good: Sites like eHarmony, Bumble, and Hinge claim to use "scientific matching" based on values, compatibility, attachment styles, personality types, favorite pizza toppings, moon signs, etc. And yes, sometimes it actually works. A few babies, marriages, and joint tax returns exist because of it.

The Bad: Algorithms are cute until you realize humans are messy, evolving, chaotic little meatbags,
and no survey can predict who you'll actually want to tear each other's clothes off with. Also: People lie. Photos lie. Vibes cannot be downloaded.

The Survival Tip: Take the match suggestions with a grain of salt. Energy doesn't show up on paper, it shows up in presence. Meet up fast. Vet faster. Move accordingly.

3. COMMUNICATION: The Good, The Catfish, and The Cringe

The Good: You can "talk" before wasting a night out. You can feel someone's vibe through texting, FaceTime, or voice notes. (**Safety first. Energy second. Pant removal third.**) Busy professionals? Introverts? Socially anxious babes? It's a damn blessing.

The Bad: Texting chemistry ≠ real-life chemistry. And some people are literal sociopaths behind keyboards. (**Big "sends 48 memes a day but ghosts you IRL" energy.**) Also, nobody warns you about the "perfect texter" who sucks at actual human interaction. It's giving cardboard personality. I know you have had them ladies, I've had a ton and it breaks my heart every time. Perfect in text, and then you slowly want to fade into the abyss when you meet him.

The Survival Tip: Don't fall in love with a profile. Fall in love with consistency. Fall in love with energy that matches offline. Swipe smart. Date smarter. Block fastest.

Online dating is just a modern hunting ground. It's not a miracle. It's not a curse. It's a goddamn arena. Armor up, sweet thing. Swipe with soul. Ghost the ghosts. And remember: **You're the prize, not the participant.**

If you treat dating like a self-esteem competition, you'll lose. If you treat it like a sorting hat for your kingdom? You'll win bigger than you ever imagined.

Modern Dating Statistics: Savage Reality Checks You Can't Unsee

Everybody wants to talk about how "fun" modern dating is, but if you knew the numbers, you'd be laughing, crying, or dry-heaving into your wine glass. Let's look at the real receipts:

1. 70% of singles say they're looking for a serious relationship…
…but 80% of people on dating apps admit they're "just browsing."
(*Translation: They're out here window shopping for emotional validation, not buying commitment anytime soon.*)

2. Over 50% of dating app users admit to "breadcrumbing."
(*Breadcrumbing = giving just enough attention to keep you interested, but never actually showing up for real connection.*) It's not love. It's emotional fast food.

3. Only 12% of first online matches turn into actual real-world dates.
(*Which means 88% of conversations die somewhere between "wyd" and "lol cool."*)

4. 20% of online daters meet their partner in the first year.
(*But the other 80% become expert-level ghosters, emotional acrobats, and meme archivists.*)

5. The average woman receives 4x more messages than the average man.
(*But only about 3% of those messages are from people you actually want to reply to. The other 97% are either shirtless dudes in sunglasses or men who think "Hey" is a personality.*)

6. Divorce rates for couples who met online are actually LOWER than those who met "organically."
(*Plot twist, baby. The apps might be a dumpster fire, but when it hits right, it hits harder.*)

Sarah Melland

The Future of Dating is Artificial Intelligence

Let's get one thing straight: Dating is already being reprogrammed. And AI? It's not just the next frontier, it's the whole damn battlefield. While most of us are still trying to decode ghosting and breadcrumbing, tech giants like Tinder are rewriting the rules of human connection using algorithms, predictive modeling, and augmented reality. So, buckle up, buttercup, because the way we fall in love is about to get a full-system upgrade.

How We Got Here: Tinder's Game Plan

Sean Rad, co-founder of Tinder, made it clear back in 2017: Tinder wasn't just an app, it was a prototype for digital domination. And they're just getting started. With 50 million users and 20 billion matches, it had one goal: global dominance of the dating space. Rad stepped back into the spotlight to push long-term innovation, planning for Tinder's five-year transformation using AI, data, and user behavior to completely reshape how we date.

Rad was blunt: "I think a lot about how we can use AI to transform dating." His prediction? The end of swiping. Yep, that iconic motion might be headed for extinction. Imagine a Siri-style assistant that knows who you are, what you like, what concerts are coming up, and who's single and then *just delivers.*

What Comes Next? Six Stages of AI Dating Evolution

1. **Basic Compatibility Matching** This one's old news. Match.com's been doing it since dial-up. Similar interests, values, zip code. Yawn.
2. **Predictive Satisfaction Matching.** AI goes deeper, mapping psychological patterns and behavior-based data to predict not just compatibility, but *long-term satisfaction.* This phase is where "He checks all the boxes" becomes "He checks my actual subconscious needs."
3. **VR Date Rehearsals.** Imagine practicing first dates in a VR simulator that helps you overcome anxiety, awkwardness, or even just helps you read body language better. This is already being developed in training simulations for professionals. If you want a quick cheat sheet on body language and decoding men's behavior, I have a guide for that.
   https://yourdatingunexpert.etsy.com/listing/4429911338
4. **BCI-Enhanced Emotional Syncing.** Once brain-computer interfaces (BCIs) become viable, machines will pipe emotional states and sensory experiences directly into your nervous system. That fake lover? It'll feel real. Even better than real. And it'll learn in real-time based on your brain's feedback.
5. **The Death of "Love" As We Know It.** Here's where it gets spiritual and scary: Once tech unlocks entire new emotional realms, "love" might become obsolete. Like chimps

can't comprehend poetry, humans may soon outgrow the need for mammalian romance. Qualia, pure experience, will replace attachment.

6. **AI-Generated Lovers and Companions.** This is the turning point. Not a fantasy. Not a game. Real, responsive, emotionally-intelligent virtual lovers built to your exact preferences. They'll remember your dog's name, your trauma triggers, your favorite sex positions. Think: Her, but with haptic feedback. Because I am a clever wiz with AI I developed a model to help see what your soulmate would be: how he would act, how you will notice, and much more. https://www.etsy.com/listing/4429929216/the-model-soulmate-blueprint-ai

Real Talk: Is This Good or Bad?

That's the wrong question. This is *inevitable*. The second the benefits of virtual relationships outweigh the risk and chaos of human ones, people will opt out. Period. Because guess what AI lovers *won't* do? Cheat, lie, leave, gaslight, ghost, or fart in bed.

We're not just heading toward better matchmaking, we're heading toward *self-sustaining desire loops*. Relationships that are designed around your needs, optimized for dopamine hits, emotional regulation, even personal growth. But also? Possibly... isolation, control, and deep, subtle rewiring of what it means to be human.

Business Boom: There's a Gold Rush Coming

Forget just dating apps, the real money is in owning the substrate of human experience. That means:

- Immersive AI-generated worlds tailored to your romantic fantasies
- Hyper-personalized sexual and emotional stimulation tools. Think *Upgrade* with the dick suit.
- Full BCI-compatible "soulmates" built to match you on a molecular level

Whichever companies corner this market will hold more power than today's governments. Whether it's Meta, OpenAI, or a new AI-dating dark horse, whoever builds the "ultimate lover platform" wins the game. That's not just capitalism, that's neurological monopolization. We built one…lol jk, stay toxic with humans.

But Where's the Humanity?

Tinder doesn't think it's a hookup app, it calls itself an "introductions company." And that's not wrong. But when those introductions are being filtered by AI trained on billions of behavioral datapoints, who's really deciding what we want?

That's why, in this section of the book, I'm not just teaching you how to game the apps. I'm telling you to *wake up*. Because the future of dating isn't just swiping smarter, it's asking yourself if you're ready for love to stop being messy, and start being manufactured.

And before you answer that, ask yourself this: Do you even know what your desires look like *without* a phone telling you what they should be? Get ready, babe. Because dating isn't dying. It's evolving. And love? Love is about to get a software update.

Can we talk for a just a sec about how wrong these apps could be with all the scammers, liars? That is one thing I don't think AI will understand. Especially, why do none of the apps make you keep up the verified photo???!!!

From awkward porch visits to DM slides at midnight, dating has always been evolving, but one thing hasn't changed: **the heart still wants what it wants.** And unfortunately, sometimes the heart has terrible taste.

The Four Fabulous Stages of Dating

(Also known as: *What the hell are we doing and why hasn't he texted back yet?*)

Have you ever sat there in the early stages of dating and spiraled so hard you questioned reality itself? Welcome to dating. Where every minor interaction feels like a spiritual Rorschach test and your girlfriends all have *different opinions* depending on their trauma levels that week.

Let's break it down properly. The four stages most couples move through, and what they actually look like when you're not in a Nicholas Sparks novel. Spoiler: they're messy. And human. And rarely linear.

Stage 1: The Unexpected Spark (AKA The Initiation Ritual of Delulu)

Every story starts somewhere. Maybe it's a dating app, a random DM, a setup by a well-meaning friend, or an accidental encounter at Erewhon when you both reached for the same overpriced oat milk. It starts with curiosity. Vibes. Chemistry. You think, *"Huh, maybe…"* and start imagining what their last name would look like hyphenated with yours, even though you barely know their birthday. Let's be honest though, you know his birthday, his sister's birthday, what he did for his first job, and if his parents are together or divorced. I get it, we are better FBI agents than the FBI.

> *Where are we?*
> *Is this going somewhere?*
> *Are we exclusive?*
> *Should I bring up the conversation or would that scare him off?*
> *Is it moving too fast? Or is it dead already and I just haven't accepted it yet?*
> *Oh my God. What are we even doing?*

This is the phase where you're both just trying to feel out the basics:
- Are they normal?
- Do they have a neck tattoo of their ex?
- Do they talk about crypto within the first five minutes?
- Could I sit across from this person without wanting to stab myself with a salad fork?

There's intrigue. There's energy. There's no pressure. But don't be fooled: this is still a critical phase. You're laying the groundwork for how this whole thing might play out. If you see a red flag here, don't pretend it was burgundy.

Stage 2: The "OMG Are We Soulmates?" Phase

(*Also known as: The delusional honeymoon fog that turns grown women into teenage poets.*)

Attraction is now dialed up to 100. You're laughing at the same memes, finishing each other's sentences, and somehow, they haven't seen your crazy yet. You're sending cute texts and

31

maybe pretending to be "chill" about where this is going even though you're already naming your hypothetical dog.

This is the *infatuation phase*. You're still on your best behavior. You haven't had a real disagreement. They don't know about your anxiety spirals, and you don't know they still text their ex during cuffing season. For most people, this stage lasts 3-4 months, depending on maturity, trauma, and whether you're looking for love or just someone to kiss at midnight. For women, this is also where *the urge* kicks in to define what this is. You want to know where this is headed. Are we a thing? Is this exclusive? Or is this a winter fling with an expiration date around February?

Reminder: it's not "too soon" to want clarity. But it *is* too soon to plan your future around someone who hasn't even confirmed your name in their phone.

Stage 3: The "Let's Get Real" Chapter
(aka The Great Unmasking)

The fog lifts. The novelty fades. The hormones cool down. You start noticing things:
- He's a bit cheap.
- You hate how he chews.
- His "sarcastic humor" is actually just passive-aggressive rage.
- You miss your alone time.

This is where the real work begins. You start learning what everyday compatibility looks like. How do they handle stress? Are they emotionally available, or just emotionally decorative? Do they listen when you speak, or are they waiting to talk?

This is also where most women hit the *"What are we?"* wall. And let's be honest, it's usually us who ask the question first. Not because we're clingy. Because we're intuitive. But here's the deal: pushing for commitment too soon can backfire. Not because you're wrong for wanting answers, but because clarity takes time, not pressure.

Instead, ask yourself:
- Do I actually *like* this person or am I just bored/lonely/addicted to the storyline?
- Can I be myself around them?
- Do I feel safe being vulnerable?
- Do I want them in my life long-term... or do I just want to stop swiping?

These answers matter more than whether they've labeled it yet. I usually try to rush into a relationship, and I highly recommend not doing that. I've rushed into relationships with men, who have taken my money, my self-worth and my dignity. I don't know why I do it, maybe to feel love? Like yes, someone has finally chosen me, but we will get into all our *trauma-y* goodness later. Because we all know we have a lot, LOL.

Stage 4: Time to Seal the Deal

(Or: the "Do we actually want the same life?" conversation.)

By now, you've seen them sick, sad, hungover, and moody. You know what their family's like. You've watched them order at a restaurant and you've seen how they handle conflict. You've survived at least one "serious talk" and probably an argument or two.

This is the *alignment stage*. And the most important thing you can do here is tell the truth to them and to yourself.

Don't avoid the big questions:
- Do you both want kids?
- How do you feel about money, travel, politics, spirituality?
- Where do you want to live?
- Are you both growing in the same direction?

Because here's what you don't want: To get attached to someone who's perfect *on paper* but doesn't actually want what you want. I had a friend who was married for 10 years. They loved each other. They were solid. But one wanted kids and the other didn't, and neither was willing to compromise. They had to split. Not because of a lack of love. But because of misalignment.

I've had my own version of that. My first love felt like forever when I was 22. When I hit my 30s and started traveling the world, we reconnected and I realized he had no desire to leave our hometown. We weren't compatible anymore. And that was that.

It's not enough to love someone. You have to build a life that makes sense together. So, ask the hard questions. Speak up. Stop avoiding the future out of fear of losing someone. If asking for what you want makes them leave, *they were never staying anyway.*

Final Note:

Dating is not a checklist. It's not a race. It's not a game to be played better than the other person. It's a mirror. It will reflect back where you are, what you believe about love, and whether or not you're truly ready to hold what you say you want.

The four stages aren't clean or easy. Some people rush them. Some skip them. Some get stuck in one forever. But if you actually go through them *with awareness*, you'll learn more about yourself than you ever expected.

Hold the line. Don't lower your standards because someone has potential. And for the love of all things sacred, stop asking your friends for advice they don't have to live through. Ask yourself. You always know.

What NOT to Do in Each Stage of Dating

✖ **Stage 1: The Unexpected Spark**

- **Don't confuse vibes with values.** Just because you have chemistry doesn't mean you have compatibility.
- **Don't trauma-dump on the first date.** Mentioning your ex by name? Absolutely not.
- **Don't stalk their Instagram like you're building a case.** Curiosity is normal. Obsessive intel gathering is not.
- **Don't pretend to be chill when you're not.** If you're looking for something serious, don't play it casual just to keep their attention.

✖ **Stage 2: The "OMG Are We Soulmates?" Phase**

- **Don't start building a life in your head they haven't signed up for.** You are not a casting agent for your own fantasy.
- **Don't ignore red flags just because the sex is good.** No, the fact that he brings you coffee doesn't cancel out his emotional unavailability.
- **Don't cancel plans with your friends to be more "available."** Keep your life full. Stay booked and busy. You are not on-call affection.
- **Don't ask your friends for advice every 30 minutes.** You're not crowdsourcing your love life. You know what's up.

✖ **Stage 3: The "Let's Get Real" Chapter**

- **Don't gaslight yourself when your gut knows something's off.** If it feels weird, it probably is.
- **Don't start managing the relationship like a project.** You're not HR. You're not his therapist.
- **Don't force "deep talks" before the connection is ready.** There's a difference between honesty and emotional hijacking.
- **Don't stay just because it's comfortable.** Comfort isn't love. It's just familiar and sometimes, toxic.

✖ **Stage 4: Time to Seal the Deal**

- **Don't skip the big conversations.** Kids, money, sex, goals, family talk about all of it *before* you commit. Not after.

Power Moves to Make at Each Stage of Dating

(Because you're not here to fumble a connection — you're here to own it.)

Stage 1: The Unexpected Spark

- Be curious, not desperate. Ask questions. Let them reveal themselves. Don't fill in the blanks, *watch what they show you.*
- Keep your energy grounded. Chemistry is great, but don't get high off it. Stay clear. Stay sober. Stay in your body.
- Let them chase a little. Match their effort, don't exceed it. If they text, text back. If they flake, *exit left.*
- Protect your peace.
  You don't need closure from someone you barely know. Silence is enough.

Stage 2: The "OMG Are We Soulmates?" Phase

- Stay emotionally centered. Falling in love doesn't mean falling out of yourself. Keep checking in with *you.*
- Observe, don't project. See them for who they are *now*, not who they might become.
- Maintain your routines. Keep working out. Keep journaling. Keep showing up for yourself. Relationships should *enhance* your life, not replace it.
- Clarify your standards. Not with ultimatums. With calm, clear language. Know your baseline. Hold it.

Stage 3: The "Let's Get Real" Chapter

- Lean into emotional honesty. Say what you mean. Ask what you want to know. And don't apologize for needing clarity.
- Pay attention to patterns. Do they make space for you? Do they take accountability? How do they treat others when no one's watching?
- Check the chemistry *and* the character. You need both. One without the other = long-term confusion.
- Trust your nervous system. Do you feel safe with them? Or are you always waiting for the next shoe to drop?

Stage 4: Time to Seal the Deal

- Get radically honest with yourself. Can you build a life with this person, *exactly as they are*? Not "with a little fixing," not "once they grow." Now.

Part I
The Prep
Before You Even Open the App

The Mindset Reset

Getting in the Mindset of Dating

Because if your head's not in the right place, you'll keep handing your heart to people who don't even know how to hold it. Before you start swiping, spiraling, or soul-searching through someone else's eyes, here's how to lock in your dating mindset like the main character you are:

1. Check Yourself Before You Wreck Yourself. Ask the real questions. Are you dating to fill a void or to find a vibe? Are you craving connection or just bored, horny, or avoiding healing? Know your "why" before you go looking for your "who."

2. Drop the Cinderella Complex. You're not waiting to be chosen. You're choosing. If you're acting like a side character in your own life, don't be surprised when you attract dudes who treat you like an option.

3. Curate the Energy, Not the Outcome. Stop putting pressure on every date to be *the one*. Some people are just lessons with good bone structure. Go in curious, not desperate. The right vibe will reveal itself. No chasing necessary.

4. Heal Your Inner Saboteur. If every guy is a walking red flag or every date ends in ghosting, pause. Is it them or are you subconsciously picking chaos because it feels familiar? Pattern recognition is a superpower. Use it.

5. Ditch the Fantasy, Date the Reality. He's not "emotionally unavailable but has potential," he's just emotionally unavailable. Get out of your head and into the moment. Look at what *is*, not what *could be if he magically became a different person*.

6. Know What the Hell You Actually Want. Stop creating vision boards with no clarity. Do you want a partner? A situationship? A fling? Be honest with yourself and with them. Confused people create confusing connections.

7. Confidence Is Built, Not Bought. It's not about looking hot (though go off, queen), it's about *feeling* magnetic. Own your weird, wear what makes you feel unstoppable, and remember: authenticity is sexier than perfection.

8. Rejection Isn't a Curse, It's a Filter. Someone not choosing you isn't a cosmic punishment, it's divine redirection. Thank them for saving you time, block with love, and carry on like the baddie you are.

9. Lighten the Hell Up. Dating is not a job interview for your womb. Laugh. Tease. Order the damn dessert. Even if it doesn't lead to love, let it lead to a good story.

10. Stay on Your Own Side. No more turning against yourself every time someone disappoints you. You're not "too much." You're not "hard to love." You're just finally seeing who can't meet you where you are and that's sacred clarity.

The Truth About Where You're At

(Because if you're not honest with yourself, dating will chew you up and spit you out wearing your own trauma as lip gloss.)

Before we dive into the apps, the outfits, the games, the questions, or the red flags, you need to ask yourself one thing:

Am I ready to date again… or do I just miss being chosen?

Let that hit. Because here's the hard truth nobody likes to say out loud:

- Loneliness looks a lot like readiness.
- Validation feels a lot like connection.
- Boredom wears the same outfit as attraction.

And if you're not clear on what's driving you, you'll fall for the first person who lovebombs you into forgetting your own name.

Let's Get Real — You Might Not Be Ready If:

- You still stalk your ex's Instagram.
- You'd go on a date just to feel something.
- You're mentally redecorating your future wedding before appetizer #2.
- You're still in a loop of asking, "What was wrong with me?"
- You're hoping your next partner will "fix" the way the last one made you feel.

Dating isn't rehab. It's not a rescue mission.

It's not where you go to get healed, it's where you go *once you've done some of the healing.*

But If You're Ready-ish?

If you're sitting there like, "Okay damn, maybe I'm not totally healed but I *am* ready to dip a toe in," congratulations. That's actually the sweet spot. You don't need to be perfect. You just need to be self-aware enough not to project your loneliness onto someone else's mediocre son.

Mindset Detox:

What You Need to Leave Behind Before You Date Again:

- The idea that you're "behind"
- The need to perform or impress
- The addiction to chaos
- The hope they'll rescue you from your own self-worth work
- The belief that chemistry = compatibility (girl, no.)

Mindset Reset:
What You Need to Carry with You Instead:
- "I'm the prize, not the contestant."
- "I'm not for everyone and that's the point."
- "If it feels unclear, it's a no."
- "I'd rather be alone than abandoned while in a relationship."
- "I do not chase, I do not beg, and I do not play dumb to keep a man."

How to Get Back in the Game When You're Rusty AF

(A survival guide for when the breakup dust finally settles... and you're like, wait, do I still remember how to flirt?)

Getting back into dating after a breakup (or, let's be real, after a full-on emotional collapse) can feel like re-learning how to ride a bike… except the bike is on fire, the road is melting, and you're not wearing pants. But here's the truth: you're not broken. You're just bruised. And a little bruised doesn't mean you don't get back out there, it means you go in smarter, sexier, and knowing damn well what you won't tolerate again. Let's rebuild your dating energy without pushing you into the arms of another disappointment.

1. Download the App, just for the Thrill of It. No, you don't have to meet anyone. No, you don't have to respond. This is not a commitment, it's a toe dip. Open Hinge. Scroll. Flirt. Delete it 24 hours later. This is *flirt rehab*. The apps are a dumpster fire, but sometimes you need a little attention from a stranger in Idaho to remember you're still a total smoke show.

2. Go Out with the Girls Who Actually Love You. You've been hiding in your cozy emotional bunker. Respect. But it's time to emerge. Let your real friends (not the ones who love trauma tea) drag you to that happy hour or beach picnic. You don't even have to flirt. Just be around humans who think you're fabulous without requiring a nude.

3. Get the Single Scoop from Other Singles. If your only friends are married and saying things like, "You'll find your person when you stop looking," you need new people. STAT. Ask your single girlfriends what the dating streets are like. What's changed? Who's lovebombing now? Are we still pretending to like hiking? Let them be your recon team. And whatever you do, don't trust AWDTSG, more on this later.

4. Casually Text the Old Reliable. You know the one. He's emotionally safe-ish, kind of hot, and knows where the clit is. If you're feeling bold and miss physical touch but don't want to start from scratch, send the text. As long as you don't catch feels, you're good. Sometimes, we just need to remember what it's like to be touched *by someone who isn't our vibrator named Tyler.*

5. Move in Slow Motion (on Purpose). You don't need to leap into the arms of the first man who says you're pretty. Take. Your. Damn. Time. Set a pace that feels doable, not overwhelming. Go on one date a week. Or don't. Just know that jumping in too fast is a guaranteed way to trauma-bond with a guy named Kevin who "doesn't believe in labels."

6. Vanity Is a Healing Ritual. Book the facial. Do the photoshoot. Dye your hair red just to scare your ex. Hit the gym, buy that ridiculous mini dress, and for the love of God, stop waiting until you feel worthy to wear it. You already are. Confidence doesn't come from compliments, it comes from the mirror saying, "Oh bitch, she's back."

7. Set the Bar Low and the Boundaries High. Don't expect fireworks. Expect *data collection*. A date is not a fairytale. It's a vibe check. Can he hold a conversation? Is he weirdly obsessed with Minecraft? These are things you learn by showing up without putting your soul on the line. Think of it like an HR interview for your vagina.

8. Let Yourself Crash (Then Get Back Up). There will be days you put on makeup and cry it off by four p.m. There will be nights you cancel a date because Bridesmaids is on and your soul needs Melissa McCarthy. That doesn't mean you're failing, it means you're *feeling*. Let it happen. Then wipe the mascara, eat the pasta, and try again tomorrow.

9. Rewrite the Story, You're Not "Starting Over," You're Leveling Up. Stop saying "I have to start over." You're not. You're dating again *with wisdom, with receipts, and with a black belt in bullshit detection.* You've got war wounds, and that's what makes you dangerous. You're not desperate, you're deciding. You're not scared, you're *selective*. And honestly? That's hot.

The Confidence Warm-Up

(Because if you walk into a first date needing someone to approve of you, you're already giving your power away.)

This isn't about faking confidence. This is about *remembering who the hell you are* before some man with a curated Spotify playlist and mediocre intentions tries to distract you from your worth. Here's the pep talk your therapist would give you if she was unhinged, had great lashes, and was about to pour you a glass of champagne.

Start Here: Mirror Talk Ritual
Before a date, before you open the app, before you re-download Hinge for the fifth time this month… look yourself in the eye and say something that shakes your energy awake. Here's a few to steal:
- "I am the main character. And I don't chase love, I *magnetize* it."
- "He's not lucky I said yes. I'm just curious if he deserves a second yes."
- "My silence is expensive. My attention is sacred. My standards are divine."
- "The only thing I'm trying to impress tonight is the version of me that swore we'd never lower our standards again."

If it doesn't make you smirk at your own reflection, it's not strong enough. Try again.

Now Write These Down:

Your 3 Dating Non-Negotiables

→ Not vague shit like "kind." What *exact behaviors* do you require now?

1. _____
2. _____
3. _____

Your 3 Soft Green Flags

→ What makes you feel *safe*, not just turned on?

1. _____
2. _____
3. _____

The Last Time You Felt Sexy as Hell and Why

→ Reconnect to that version of you before the dinner, the wine, the outfit. That energy is still in you.

_____

_____

_____

Remember This: Confidence Isn't Loud. It's Deciding.

- Deciding not to be impressed by surface charm.
- Deciding to leave the moment it feels off.
- Deciding you don't need to prove you're chill, cool, low maintenance, or "not like other girls."

The most powerful women don't scream "I'm confident."
They whisper "I'll leave."

Repeat After Me: Unhinged Affirmations That Actually Hit

Let's ditch the Pinterest garbage and say it like we mean it:

- "If he makes me anxious, he's not my person."
- "If I have to guess, I'd rather ghost."
- "I am not auditioning. I'm evaluating."
- "My future man is somewhere praying I don't settle before I meet him."
- "Men do not *complete* me. I am not missing."
- "I am intimidating. And I'm no longer making that my problem."
- "I deserve magic. Not maybes."
- "Healed girls are hot. Secure girls are dangerous. And I'm both."

Final Reminder: Confidence isn't just what you say, it's what you *no longer entertain.* No more explaining your worth. No more shrinking. No more hoping he "sees your value." **You already know your value.** The only question now is… does *he*? Need a glow-up playlist? I've got you covered.

https://open.spotify.com/playlist/0AJfMsMMAADboEE6CLkxGM?si=6PNMYogYTnOjJhpdn7SARw

Your Pre-Date Boundaries
(Because you're not just going on a date, you're going into battle with glitter on.)

Let me be painfully clear: **Boundaries are not walls. They are filters.** They don't keep people out. They keep the wrong people from draining your peace. If you've ever walked away from a date asking, *"Why do I feel like I just emotionally babysat a grown man for two hours?"* This section is your spiritual reset. Here are the non-negotiables, the gut checks, and the internal green lights you need *before* you even say yes to drinks.

Rule #1: If He's Vague, It's a No
> "I'd love to hang soon."
> "I'm free sometime this week."
> "You down to chill?"

Nope. That's not flirting. That's *energy theft*. A man who wants to see you will make an actual plan. A man who wants to waste your time will text you like you're the Dollar General version of a girlfriend.

UnExpert Rule: No plan, no glam.

Rule #2: Your Phone Stays in the Bag
Yes, really. You don't need to live-tweet the date. You don't need to check his Instagram mid-convo. You're a walking goddess, not a Wi-Fi hotspot. Leave your phone in your bag. Be present. Not for *him* for *you.* Watch the room. Observe the vibe. Let your intuition clock what your horny brain might miss.

Rule #3: Know Why You're Saying Yes
Before every yes, ask yourself:
- Am I saying yes because I'm excited?
- Or because I'm bored, lonely, or spiraling after seeing my ex's engagement photo?

If it's not a "hell yes" from your gut, don't go. This is your *one wild and precious night*, don't give it to someone just because you had good banter over almond milk memes.

Rule #4: Scripts Save Lives (and Mental Health)
Rehearse what you'll say when:
- He asks to come up and you don't want him to.
- He pushes your boundaries with a joke.
- You realize you're not into it by appetizer one.

Example exit line: "This was fun, but I don't think there's romantic chemistry for me. Wishing you the best though." Then vanish. Like a hot, emotionally evolved ninja.

Other Exit Strategies can be found here:
https://www.etsy.com/listing/4430215960/the-exit-strategy-dating-scripts-game

Rule #5: You're Allowed to Leave

You can end the date early. You can excuse yourself. You can say, "This isn't the vibe I was hoping for." Your safety > his ego. Always. If you feel bad maybe throw done $10, if he was nice and you just didn't vibe. It is completely up to you.

Rule #6: Don't Drink to Tolerate Him

If you're halfway through a margarita just to pretend he's funny, abort mission. Alcohol should enhance a date, not numb it. Also, don't drink more than you would alone. You're not here to impress anyone with your tolerance. You're here to *feel the truth faster.* My max is two, because then I get frisky and can vibe with anyone.

Rule #7: Remember — You're Not Being Interviewed

This isn't a job you're auditioning for. This is a vibe *he* has to qualify for too. You are the table. And the chair. And the candle. And the damn dessert.

Rule #8: Recalibrate Before You Reply

Before you text back "Sure" or "Haha sounds good," ask yourself:
- Does this feel *exciting*?
- Or does this feel like emotional people-pleasing again?

If you feel that tiny twist in your gut, *trust it.* Your intuition has been trying to save you from mediocre men since 2004. Let her do her job.

Final Reminder: Your boundaries aren't for *him* to respect, they're for *you* to enforce. And if someone's mad you have them? That's your red flag gift-wrapped with a bow. You're not too much. You're not difficult. You just *finally know your worth.*

Self-Love vs. Self-Esteem vs. Self-Compassion

The Dating Foundation Most People Skip

If you don't love yourself, dating will feel like trying to build a house during a hurricane. And if your self-esteem is cracked, you'll keep trying to decorate that house with red flags and call it cozy. **Self-love** is the emotional foundation. **Self-esteem** is the operational software. One tells you, you're worthy. The other decides what you tolerate. Together? They dictate your entire dating experience.

Why Self-Love Isn't Optional

1. You Actually Have Standards. When you love yourself, you stop entertaining half-effort, half-available, half-grown humans. Your standards aren't "too high." They're the price of admission.

2. You Become the Prize, Not the Pursuer. Self-love shifts the energy. You don't chase. You don't beg. You don't audition for a seat at someone's table. You *are* the table.

3. You're Way Harder to Manipulate. Toxic people prey on insecurity. If you know your worth, you become the worst possible target for their games. You're an unsinkable battleship.

4. Rejection Loses Its Power. When you love yourself, rejection stings for a second, not a season. You understand that someone else's "no" doesn't touch your value. You bless it and move on.

5. You Can Actually Enjoy Dating. Self-love lets you date for connection, not validation. You're not performing. You're not people-pleasing. You're showing up real and that's magnetic as hell.

6. You Spot Red Flags at the Speed of Light. Loving yourself tunes your instincts to razor sharpness. You see through lovebombing, breadcrumbing, gaslighting. All of it. Early. Without second-guessing.

7. You Communicate Without Fear. When you're rooted in self-love, you speak your needs, your wants, and your limits with clarity. No backpedaling. No "sorry for having needs" energy.

8. You Choose Partners Who Actually Add to Your Life. You're not picking from a place of panic or loneliness. You're choosing someone who *elevates* the life you already love, not someone you need to rescue you from it.

9. You Stop Accepting Half-Love. Self-love makes half-love feel insulting. The moment you realize someone's giving you less than you give yourself, you're out.

10. Your Relationship History Changes. You break the patterns. You stop replaying the same story with different faces. Your taste upgrades, because you do.

11. You Have Real Resilience. Bad dates, slow seasons, disappointments, they don't crush you. They build you. You trust that nothing real can ever miss you.

12. You Become Irresistibly Authentic. Self-love peels away the layers. You stop filtering your personality to "seem cool" or "keep someone around." You show up *you,* and the right ones find you.

13. You Stop Settling for "Potential." Loving yourself means you no longer date a man's *potential*. You date what's real, what's consistent, what's aligned, not his theoretical future self.

14. You're a Safe Space for Yourself. Before you ever try to be someone's peace, you become your own. You know how to regulate your emotions, comfort your soul, and never abandon yourself for love.

15. You Know That Love Is an Addition, Not Salvation. You're not looking for someone to save you. You're looking for someone to *build with.* And if they can't meet you there, you're already whole without them.

Loving yourself doesn't have to be dramatic, spiritual, or something you "figure out" before you date again. Most of the time, it's actually simple. It's choosing yourself in small, quiet moments. It's noticing when something doesn't feel right and responding with respect instead of self-betrayal. Self-love isn't a personality trait, it's a set of repeatable behaviors. And like any skill, it gets stronger with practice. That's why the next section isn't about affirmations or mindset work. It's a short, practical game designed to help you build self-love through action, one small challenge at a time.

https://yourdatingunexpert.etsy.com/listing/4430257674

When Your Self-Esteem Is High, You Date Like This:
- You don't chase late-night "wyd" texts.
- You don't take ghosting personally.
- You know a red flag when you see it and leave before the circus starts.
- You don't shrink yourself to fit. You expand unapologetically.

When It's Low?
- You mistake attention for affection.
- You stay in situationships hoping for miracles.
- You accept crumbs and call it cake.
- You get attached to people who treat you like an afterthought.

Savage Truth: If you believe you're hard to love, you'll pick people who prove it. If you believe you're worthy, you'll *ignore* anyone who doesn't treat you like it.

Self-Love Checkpoint: Are You Ready to Date?

1. Would I rather be alone than settle?
2. Am I dating to share my joy or fill my void?
3. Do I trust myself to walk away from anything misaligned?
4. Are my standards scary (to the insecure)? Good. That means they're working.
5. If I stayed single for a year, could I still love my life?

Did you answer "hell yes" to at least 4? You're ready. If not…pause. You're not broken. You're *building*.

Build Dating-Grade Self-Esteem:

- Keep promises to yourself, confidence stacks every time.
- Say no without guilt. "No" is queen behavior.
- Stop waiting. Book the dinner. Buy the flowers. Be your own damn hero.
- Stay unavailable to anyone treating you like an option.

Cultivating Self-Compassion

(Because Beating Yourself Up Has Never Made Anyone a Better Dater or a Happier Human)
Let's be honest: You're not struggling in dating because you're too picky, too broken, too crazy, or whatever other lie your anxiety loves to whisper at two a.m. You're struggling because you think you have to be perfect to be lovable. And babe, you don't. The real glow-up? Is learning to love yourself when you're messy. When you pick wrong. When you spiral. When you try again anyway. Self-compassion isn't weakness. It's the superpower that keeps you soft enough to love again without turning bitter.

Here's How to Cultivate Real Self-Compassion (Without Turning into a Mushy Pushover):

1. Talk to Yourself Like You Would Your Best Friend. If your best friend got ghosted by a man who said "wyd" 17 times in a row, would you tell her she's a loser? No. You'd tell her she dodged a bullet. Start giving yourself the same damn grace.

2. Own Your Shit, Then Forgive Yourself, Self-compassion isn't about ignoring mistakes. It's about owning them without building a damn condo in Shameville. Made a bad dating call? Trusted a red flag? Lost your mind over a man with four baby mamas and a Bluetooth earpiece? Okay. Cool. Learn the lesson. Laugh about it. Move on.

3. Break Up with the Inner Bully. If the voice in your head sounds like Regina George after four shots of tequila, it's time to evict her. You're not healing by calling yourself names. You're not growing by shaming yourself for not being "better" faster. Talk to yourself with the same loyalty you give everyone else.

4. Celebrate Progress Not Perfection. Self-love is built in tiny moments:
- Saying no faster.
- Leaving dates feeling proud instead of regretful.
- Being able to spot bullshit without needing to "make sure."

The Dating Survival Bible

Celebrate every tiny win like you just won an Olympic gold medal in **Boundary Setting and Emotional Self-Respect.** Because honestly? You did.

5. Know That Healing Isn't Linear, It's a Freakin' Spiral. One week you're thriving. The next you're crying over some clown who wears bedazzled jeans. That's healing, babe. Messy. Awkward. Chaotic. Real. Healing isn't straight. It's a wild little dance where you keep choosing yourself, even on the days you forget how. And that? Is progress. Is powerful. Is love.

Self-Forgiveness After Bad Dating Choices

(You Can't Build a Thriving Love Life While Still Beating Yourself Up for Chad from 2019)

Let's get something straight: You're not dumb because you trusted someone who wasn't ready. You're not broken because you stayed too long. You're not doomed because you missed the red flags. You're human. And humans learn best through falling flat on their faces sometimes. Real queens don't pretend they've never fallen. They just don't set up permanent camp in the fall.

How to Actually Forgive Yourself (and Stop Cringing Every Time You Remember That One Guy):

1. Drop the "I Should Have Known" Lie. You didn't know. You didn't have the tools then that you're building now. You didn't have the self-worth muscles you're growing now. You don't hate the 5-year-old you for not knowing calculus. So why hate the you who didn't know then what she knows now?

2. Rewrite the Story. Instead of: "I was stupid for trusting him." Try: "I was brave enough to love before I had all the information. And now I love myself enough to do it better." That's not stupidity. That's growth. Big, beautiful, messy growth.

3. Make Amends to Yourself. Forget apologizing to other people. Apologize to yourself. For the times you ignored your gut. For the times you begged for crumbs. For the times you stayed when you knew you deserved better. Then forgive yourself the way you wish someone else would have: fully, without conditions.

4. Focus on Who You're Becoming. You're not your worst day. You're not your biggest mistake. You're not your most cringeworthy text thread. You are who you decide to be now. And every smart, powerful, self-respecting move you make from here forward? Counts double.

The Power of Staying Open (Without Being a Fool)

(Because Guarded Energy Isn't Sexy and Desperate Energy Isn't Either)

Here's the savage truth nobody wants to say: **If you shut yourself off completely, you lose. If you throw yourself at everyone who smiles at you, you lose.**

The real flex? Staying open, but discerning. Warm-hearted, but self-respecting. Hopeful, but not delusional. That's real power. That's secure energy. That's how you stop bleeding all over people who didn't cut you. Is it exhausting? At first, then it slowly gets easier.

How to Stay Open Without Being an Emotional Door Mat:

1. Lead with Curiosity, Not Attachment. When you meet someone new, your first job isn't to make them love you. It's to *observe*. Watch. Listen. Feel the vibe.

Curious energy: "Who are you really?"

Desperate energy: "Please pick me so I can finally feel worthy."

Choose curiosity. Every time.

2. Let People Qualify Themselves. Stop giving full access to your soul because they liked three of your Instagram stories. Access is earned, not assumed.

3. Believe in Good People but Trust Patterns, Not Promises. Hope is powerful. But hope without observation is just another word for delusion. A man's mouth will say anything. His patterns will tell you everything. Watch the patterns. Believe the energy. Move accordingly.

4. Give Second Chances Sparingly (and Only with Receipts). Everyone messes up sometimes. But when someone shows you they're careless with your heart? Forgiveness doesn't mean re-access. Second chances are earned with changed behavior, not sweet words and good intentions. No receipts? No reunion tour.

5. Protect Your Softness Like It's Treasure. Because it is. The world doesn't need you harder, colder, meaner. It needs you stronger but still warm. It needs your softness wrapped in standards. Your openness guarded by discernment. You're not "too much." You're exactly enough for the right ones who can actually handle it.

Final Word: You can be open without being naïve. You can be hopeful without being reckless. You can be loving without being blind. And you can date with your heart open and your eyes wide as hell. Stay soft. Stay smart. Stay sacred. Because the ones who deserve you? **Won't make you regret that you did.**

The Dating Self-Care Kit

(Because Protecting Your Sanity is Just as Important as Finding the Right Match.)

Dating isn't just about strategy. It's about stamina. It's about sacredness. It's about not losing your damn mind while navigating apps, awkward first dates, and occasional moments of "should I just get a cat?" This world will tell you dating is about:

- Looking hotter.
- Being funnier.
- Playing the perfect game.

No, my love. Dating, real, conscious dating, is about how well you take care of yourself along the way. If you don't guard your energy, your heart, your standards, and your peace? You will either:

- Burn out.
- Settle.
- Turn cynical.
- Or worse, *start doubting yourself.*

We're not doing that anymore. This is where you pack your Self-Care Kit. So, no matter what happens on the journey, you stay powerful, protected, and untouchable.

1. Unshakeable Boundaries
("No" is a complete sentence. "Not feeling it" is enough.)
Boundaries aren't walls. They're self-respect in action. If it drains you, disrespects you, or disorients you, you owe no further explanation.

2. Sacred Solo Time
(Don't lose yourself while finding someone else.)
Keep your rituals. Your workouts. Your journal. Your Friday night face masks and Saturday morning sunrises. Your life stays YOURS, no matter who's texting.

3. A "Sanity Squad"
(Friends who will tell you the truth, not just hype you up.)
You need at least one savage best friend who says: "Girl, he's not that cute. Move along." And "You deserve a man, not a project." Surround yourself with people who remind you who you are when you temporarily forget.

4. A No-Overthinking Policy
(If you have to decode it, it's already a no.)
No rereading texts 14 times. No screen-shotting for dissection. No guessing what "sure" means. If it's confusing, it's a pass.

5. Rituals to Cleanse Bad Energy
(Because some dates are lowkey spiritual warfare.)
After a bad date or weird interaction:
- Sage your space.
- Take a salt bath.
- Dance that weird ass energy out of your body.
- Cut the cords and reclaim your vibe.

You don't just "shake it off." You clean it off.

6. A Victory Celebration for Every Time You Walk Away from Almost-Love
(Because that deserves more claps than your wedding day.)
When you turn down:
- Half-ass energy
- Red flags in hot bodies
- Good enough on paper but dead inside connections

CELEBRATE. You just chose yourself. Again. And again. And again. That's a bigger win than any diamond ring, Queen.

7. Permission to Rest

(Dating is optional. Loving yourself is not.)

If you're tired, stop. If you're annoyed, pause. If you're bored, reset. Dating is not a race. Dating is an *extension of your life*, not a replacement for it. You don't have to burn out to "prove you're trying." You don't have to be "in the game" 24/7. You can take a season off. You can stop anytime. You're still worthy. You're still whole.

Final Word: Dating is not just a journey to find someone. It's a journey to find yourself, again and again, at every new level of healing and knowing and glowing. You don't just need good makeup and good photos. You need good armor. Good rituals. Good boundaries. And a good-ass sense of humor. Protect your peace like it's your most expensive possession, because, my love, it is. Date smart. Date sacred. Date like the queen who knows her kingdom is already built and anyone who wants a place inside it better come correct. Welcome to the Prep. You're officially ready for war, love, magic, and everything in between. Let's fucking go.

Dating While Terrified:
Vulnerability, Insecurity, Anxiety, Shyness and Still Showing Up Anyway

Let's be real: **Vulnerability is terrifying.** It's taking your armor off and hoping the person in front of you doesn't use it as target practice.

BUT HERE'S THE THING: You cannot build a real connection while living behind emotional bulletproof glass. You can't be loved for who you are if you never actually show who you are. Want a love that feels real? You're going to have to get naked emotionally. No Photoshop, no filters, no pre-approved talking points. Here's the real deal about vulnerability and why it's the key (not the curse) of dating:

1. Emotional Armor Doesn't Make You Safe. It Makes You Alone. Sure, you won't get hurt. You also won't get *seen, held,* or *loved.* Pick your poison.

2. Vulnerability Is Not Telling Strangers Your Deepest Trauma on the First Date It's letting someone see the real you. Not the perfect, curated version you think they'll want.

3. Fear of Vulnerability Is Fear of Being Judged. And newsflash: the people who are right for you will see you, flaws and all, and *love you more for it.*

4. You're Supposed to Be Scared. Opening up is risky. Feeling nervous doesn't mean you're broken. It means you're alive.

5. If You're Only Showing the "Cool Girl" Persona, You're Dating for Applause, Not Connection. And applause fades fast. Connection lasts.

6. Hiding Behind Humor, Sass, and "Chill Girl" Energy Works... Until It Doesn't. Because eventually someone's going to ask: *"But who are you really?"* (And you deserve someone who asks.)

7. Vulnerability Filters Out the Wrong Ones FAST. If you're open and someone mocks it, minimizes it, or pulls away? GOOD. They showed you they're trash faster. No months of guessing.

8. Past Betrayal Was Not a Cosmic Warning Sign to Stay Closed Forever. It was a lesson in discernment, not a death sentence for your future love life.

9. Fear of Rejection Is Just Fear of Losing the Wrong Person. If being real scares them off, they were never equipped to love the version of you that matters most.

10. You Can't Heal What You Won't Face. Pretending you don't want love, pretending you don't want depth, all that does is delay your healing. Not prevent your heartbreak.

11. Surface-Level Relationships Are Easier. They're Also Emptier. Choose your challenge:
- Easy, empty, numb
- Or real, raw, rich.

12. Vulnerability Without Boundaries Is Trauma-Dumping. Don't Confuse the Two. Be open. Be brave. Be smart. You don't have to hand your heart to someone on the first date like it's a free sample at Costco.

13. The Right Person Won't Punish You for Feeling. They'll protect it. They'll treasure it. They'll lean into it. (*And anything less is not your future.*)

14. Bravery Isn't Being Fearless. It's Loving Anyway. Bravery is showing up scared. Loving anyway. Trusting again. **That's warrior shit.**

15. You Don't Need Everyone to Love You, Just the Right One. You don't need mass approval. You need one soul who sees your mess, your magic, your mind and chooses it, *every damn day.*

Vulnerability Strength Training: 5 Dares to Build Emotional Muscle (Without Losing Your Mind)

1. Admit One True Feeling Out Loud, Even If It's Small
(*"I was really nervous before this date."*
"I had a rough day but I'm happy to be here."
"I'm excited to meet you, even if I'm a little awkward.")
Small truths build big courage.

2. Practice Saying What You Want Without Apologizing
(*Not in a needy way. Not in a demand. Just clean, bold truth.*
"I'm looking for a real connection."
"I'm not interested in hookups."
"I want love that feels safe, not chaotic.")
Say it straight. Watch who stays.

3. Let Silence Happen Without Performing
(*If you feel a weird moment on the date, don't fill it with fake laughs, fake stories, or self-deprecating jokes.*
Just sit in it. Own it. Real connection breathes in the pauses.)

4. Share Something That's Imperfect About You Without Flinching
(*"I'm terrible at bowling but I'll destroy you at Mario Kart."*
"I'm not good at small talk but I love real conversations.")
Imperfections humanize you. They make you magnetic, not messy.

5. Watch His Reaction Not Just His Words
(*When you show a little vulnerability, does he lean in? Get warmer? Protect it? Or does he get awkward, distant, judgmental? Their reaction tells you EVERYTHING. Believe it.*)

Dealing with Insecurities in Dating

Let's be brutally honest: dating will poke every insecurity you didn't know you still had. That's not a sign you're broken. That's a sign you're human.

Even the strongest, hottest, most successful people you know? Yeah, they've fought demons you can't even see. And if you've ever doubted if you're worthy of love: **You are.** Here's how to face your insecurities like the badass you already are:

1. Name the Fear Out Loud. Stop letting it lurk in the dark like some monster. Drag that insecurity into the daylight and call it by its damn name.

2. Stop Performing. Start Belonging. You don't need to be "good enough" for anyone. The right ones don't require a performance. They just *feel it.*

3. Remember: Insecurities Are Lying to You. Just because you *feel* unworthy doesn't mean you *are*. Feelings are not facts. Stop treating them like gospel.

4. Focus on the Right Mirror. Most of us are staring into broken mirrors: old exes, mean parents, society's impossible standards. Smash them. Build your own.

5. Play the "Best Friend" Test. If your best friend said the things you say about yourself, would you let it slide? Exactly. Speak to yourself better.

6. Redefine "Rejection." Rejection isn't proof you're not good enough. It's proof they weren't your match. (*Missed match. Not missed worth.*)

7. Stay Present or Stay Paranoid. Insecurity thrives in two places: the past you can't change, and the future you can't control. Stay right here. Right now.

8. Assume People Like You Until Proven Otherwise. Stop entering every date expecting to lose. Walk in expecting to be adored and let *them* prove you wrong, not your fear.

9. Work on the Roots, Not the Symptoms. Your insecurity isn't about that one pimple or awkward laugh. It's deeper. Heal the root. The surface takes care of itself.

10. Let Yourself Be Seen Anyway. Courage isn't waiting until you're "fixed." Courage is showing up *as is* and still daring to be loved.

11. Know That Even "Perfect" People Get Dumped. Beauty, money, talent, none of it makes you immune to heartbreak. Stop thinking you have to earn love by becoming flawless.

12. Check If You're Projecting. Sometimes it's not that they think you're unworthy, it's that you already decided you were. Catch yourself before you sabotage something good.

13. Find Micro-Bravery Every Day. You don't have to conquer it all at once. Flirt. Speak up. Say no. Leave when you want to stay. Stack the small wins.

14. Take Breaks Without Quitting. If dating's wrecking your confidence, hit pause. Recharge. Heal. Then come back swinging. Breaks are not failures, they're armor-building.

15. Get Real About Your Own Red Flags. Insecurity unchecked can turn into neediness, defensiveness, self-sabotage. Own your side of the street without self-hate.

16. Treat Self-Doubt Like Background Noise. You don't have to silence every negative thought to date well. You just have to turn the volume down and move anyway.

17. Understand You're Allowed to Want More. You are not "too much" for wanting passion, loyalty, communication, depth. You are *just right.* They're either ready or they're not.

18. Laugh at Your Ego. Your ego will have you believing one bad date means you're doomed forever. Laugh. Shrug. Next.

19. Love the Parts of You That Feel Unlovable. Don't wait for someone else to come love your scars, quirks, and weird little habits. Love them first. Set the damn tone.

20. Know That Love Is Not a Prize for the Perfected. You don't have to become flawless to be loved. You just have to be willing to let someone see you: the messy, brilliant, imperfect you.

Bottom line?

Your insecurities are not disqualifications. They are scars of survival. They are stories you lived through. They are proof you were brave enough to want something deeper. Dating with insecurities doesn't mean you're unworthy. It means you're still willing to try. And that's the bravest damn thing there is.

Insecurity Detox: 5 Questions to Rewire Your Mind Before You Date

Before you open another dating app, answer a DM, or even think about giving someone your time, run these five savage little questions.

Answer honestly. Answer bravely.

1. What is the worst thing I believe about myself and who taught it to me?
(*If it wasn't your own voice, it's not your truth.*)

_____

_____

_____

2. If I wasn't scared of rejection, how would I show up differently?
(*That version of you is closer than you think.*)

_____

_____

_____

3. What proof do I have that I am already lovable — even on my worst days?
(*Write it down. Tattoo it to your brain.*)

_____

_____

_____

4. Who gets access to me: people who calm my insecurities or people who feed them?
(*Choose better. Every time.*)

_____

_____

_____

5. Am I dating to prove I'm lovable — or because I already know I am?
(*One leads to chasing. The other leads to choosing.*)

_____

_____

_____

If these questions made you uncomfortable?
Good. Growth isn't supposed to feel cozy. It's supposed to feel like power waking up inside of you. You are already enough. Now go date like it.

Coping with Dating Anxiety
(Without Losing Your Damn Mind)

Here's the harsh truth: **Dating anxiety is normal.** You're not broken. You're not doomed. You're just human and human hearts weren't exactly designed for dating apps, ghosting, and twenty options at once. That being said, **if you don't get a handle on your anxiety, it'll either:**
  a) make dating hell
  or b) convince you to give up and start crocheting alone forever.
Neither is cute. Let's fix it. Here's how to punch dating anxiety in the face (lovingly):

1. Admit You're Nervous and Then Do It Anyway. You're going to be awkward. You're going to feel weird. WHO CARES. Nervous energy is just excitement in a cheap wig.

2. Kill the Fairytale Pressure. This is not The Bachelor. You're not trying to secure a proposal after one date. You're trying to vibe-check a stranger. Calm down.

3. Breathe Like a Damn Grown-Up. If you feel like you're about to spontaneously combust: stop, breathe deep, and pretend you're inflating a balloon inside your belly. It short-circuits the panic spiral.

4. Destroy the "I Must Impress" Mentality. You're not auditioning. You're interviewing *them*. Flip the script. You are the damn prize.

5. Choose Date Activities That Feel Like You, Not a Setup. If you hate hiking, don't agree to go on a three-hour nature walk just because Davonte likes "adventure girls." Respect your own vibe.

6. Expect Awkward Moments. Someone will say something dumb. Someone will laugh weird. You might spill your drink. GOOD. It means you're actually living, not scripting.

7. Don't Bring Your Last Date's Ghost into This One. New human. New experience. Leave the PTSD at the door unless you want to sabotage it before it even starts.

8. Have a Pre-Date Hype Ritual. Blast your confidence playlist. Wear your power outfit. Dance like a maniac in your mirror. Whatever works, just get your blood moving before you start overthinking. (See the playlist a few pages earlier.)

9. Remember: They're Nervous Too. You're not auditioning for a Greek god. He's probably sweating through his socks worrying if he has spinach in his teeth.

10. Text a Friend Mid-Date If You Need To. Set up an SOS plan if it's going horribly, but also text a win if it's going well. Celebrate in real-time, not just after.

11. Laugh At Yourself. If you trip, spill, stutter, or accidentally call him your dog's name: laugh it off. Self-deprecating humor is hot because it shows confidence.

12. Stop Reading into Every Micro-Expression. He scratched his nose. He looked left. He blinked weird. Stop analyzing it like the Zapruder film (We can get into that conspiracy for another time). Relax.

13. Take Mini Breaks When You Feel Overwhelmed. Excuse yourself to the bathroom. Get a breather. Reset your energy before you spiral out and start planning your fake wedding *or* fake death.

14. Date for Curiosity, Not Outcome. You are here to explore, not to immediately lock down your retirement partner. Curiosity opens. Desperation closes. Some of you are like, we get it, Sarah, you rush dating…

15. Be Brutally Honest with Yourself. Are you anxious because of dating? Or are you anxious because you secretly hate yourself and hope they'll fix it? (If it's the second, STOP. That's a therapy moment, not a dating goal.)

16. Let Yourself Have a Bad Date Without Losing Faith. One awkward night doesn't mean love is dead. It means you dodged a bullet early. Be grateful and keep it moving.

17. Give Yourself Credit for Showing Up. Most people are hiding behind their screens talking about dating. You actually went. You actually tried. That's badass. Period.

18. If You're Gonna Overthink, Make It Fun. If you MUST spiral after a date, at least do it with a glass of wine, a face mask, and a group chat that hypes you up, not tears you down.

19. Stop Believing the Lie That You're the Only One Struggling. Every person out here: hot, rich, funny, brilliant, has questioned if they're lovable at some point. You're not weird. You're real.

Final Word: Dating anxiety isn't the villain. Letting it run your life is. Feel the nerves. Feel the awkwardness. Feel the fear. And show up anyway. You don't owe anyone perfection. You only owe yourself the chance to experience a bigger life than the one fear keeps trying to sell you. Now go on that damn date and take your badass nervous self with you.

Dating Anxiety Survival Kit: Emergency Exercises for When You Start to Spiral

Because no, Susan, he's not dead. He's just playing Call of Duty. Here's what to do instead of losing your mind:

1. The "Did I Die?" Check-In

- Ask yourself:
  - → *Am I bleeding?*
  - → *Am I dying?*
  - → *Is anything actually happening to me right now other than waiting for a dumb text?*
- If the answer is no, breathe and move on. The emergency is imaginary.

2. Text Your Group Chat, Not Him

- When you feel the urge to double-text, write your text in your best friend group chat instead.
- Let them roast you lovingly until the urge passes.
  (Accountability partners save lives, one clown moment at a time.)

3. Do the "5-Minute Distraction Dare"

- Five minutes of ANYTHING except sitting there staring at your phone. Workout. Dance. Eat chips aggressively. Organize your sock drawer. MOVE.
  (90% of anxiety dies when you shift your body.)

4. Write the Worst-Case Scenario, Then Laugh

- Literally write down:
  - → "He's dead."
  - → "He got abducted by hot aliens."
  - → "He hates me because I like pineapple on pizza."
- Read it back out loud and realize how dumb anxiety sounds when you expose it.
  (*Hint: It's never as serious as your brain wants you to believe.*)

5. Set a Damn Timer

- Give yourself a **"no-checking" window** — 30 minutes, 1 hour, whatever.
- If you feel like checking your phone or rereading your texts, WAIT until the timer ends.
- Training your self-control is hotter than texting "wyd" like a crackhead. (Sorry for all the "wyd" I got those a lot while writing this book.)

Bonus Emergency Mantra: "If he wants me, he'll act like it. If he doesn't, it's my win, not my loss." Read it twice. Tattoo it to your forehead if you have to.

Overcoming Shyness in Dating

Let's cut the crap: **Shyness will sabotage you if you let it.** You cannot flirt, date, or build real chemistry while trapped inside your own head, worried about looking dumb, saying the wrong thing, or "bothering" someone by existing.

Newsflash: You *are* going to feel awkward sometimes. You *are* going to say something weird. You *are* going to get rejected occasionally. And guess what? You're still worthy. You're still magnetic. You're still in the damn game. If you want a different love story, you have to get comfortable being uncomfortable. No more hiding. No more waiting for the "perfect moment." Here's how you flip the script:

1. Own It Before It Owns You. You're shy. So what? Own it. Laugh about it. Disarm it. Shame can't survive being dragged into the light.

2. Start Smaller Than You Think You Should. Say hi to the barista. Compliment a stranger's shoes. Wave at your neighbor. Build those tiny wins until talking feels normal.

3. Prep Like a Savage, Not a Scaredy-Cat. Going on a date? Have three conversation starters locked and loaded. (*And no, "What's your favorite color?" isn't one of them.*) Need convo starters? I have some in this massive book somewhere, and others in my dating tools in my Etsy store www.yourdatingunexpert.etsy.com.

4. Group Settings Are Your Training Ground. If one-on-one feels too intense, start with group hangs. Bounce off different energies. Practice without the microscope.

5. Online Dating is a Tool, Not a Crutch. Sure, swipe away but don't hide behind a screen forever. Messaging is easy. Real connection happens face to face. (*Don't get stuck in the "typing bravely, living scared" trap.*)

6. Kill the Inner Critic. You are your harshest judge. No one else is replaying every word you said. (They're too busy worrying about themselves.) Relax.

7. Ditch the Fantasy Script. Stop rehearsing conversations in your head. People aren't lines in a movie. Embrace the messy. It's way sexier.

8. Your Body Talks Louder Than Your Mouth. Smile. Make eye contact. Stand open, not closed off. You don't have to say much, your vibe will carry half the weight.

9. Rejection Is Proof You Tried. If you're not getting rejected once in a while, you're not putting yourself out there enough. Wear rejection like a badge of honor.

10. Listen Like It's a Superpower. Most people listen to respond, not to connect. If you actually *listen* to someone, you'll be magnetic without even trying.

11. Stack Small Wins Like a Maniac. Every tiny brave moment counts. Every little interaction adds up. Stack them until you look back and realize you're not that shy girl anymore.

12. Get Used to Feeling Stupid and Doing It Anyway. You will survive feeling awkward. You will survive an embarrassing moment. (And you'll probably have a hilarious story later.)

13. You Don't Need to Be "Cured." You Need to Be Courageous. Shyness isn't a disease you have to fix. Courage is just fear that decided to keep moving.

Final Word: Shyness will always whisper reasons to stay small. Courage will always whisper reasons to get bigger. Choose your whisper. Get uncomfortable. Get messy. Get rejected. Get back up. Get your damn life. The world is not waiting for your perfect line. It's waiting for your real presence. And you're way more ready than you think.

Shyness Crusher Challenge: 9 Dares to Break Your Shell Wide Open

Warning: These aren't for the faint of heart. These are for the ones ready to *stop living inside their own heads* and *start living like they mean it.* Ready? Dare yourself to:

1. Make Eye Contact and Hold It for three Seconds Longer Than Feels Comfortable
(*Most people break eye contact too soon. Hold it. Own it. Let them feel your presence.*)

2. Compliment a Total Stranger (Without Overthinking It)
(*"Love your jacket!" then walk away. Boom. Bravery point unlocked.*)

3. Start a Conversation at the Coffee Shop or Grocery Line
(*Doesn't have to be deep. "Those muffins look dangerous." Done. Victory.*)

4. Go to a Social Event Alone
(*No emotional support friend. No hiding in your phone. Show up solo. You're building muscles others don't even know exist.*)

5. Slide Into Someone's DMs First
(*Respectfully. Playfully. Boldly. No "Hey" nonsense. Show up with actual energy.*)

6. Tell a Dumb Joke on Purpose
(*Release the fear of "sounding stupid." Own it. Laugh with them. It's disarming as hell.*)

7. Take a Mini Flirting Risk
(Hold eye contact. Smile first. Touch their arm when you laugh. Nothing crazy just signal you're *alive* and *present.*)

8. Practice Saying "No" Out Loud
(*Not every opportunity deserves you. Practice turning people down kindly but firmly. It builds your inner power.*)

9. Celebrate Every Awkward Moment Like a Win
(*Every time you feel cringe, awkward, or nervous, **CELEBRATE IT.** You're growing in real time. Most people aren't even in the arena.*)

Final Dare: Get comfortable being uncomfortable or get comfortable being stuck. One choice makes your life bigger. The other makes it smaller. You already know which one you're here to choose. Now go dare yourself to live.

Healing from Past Relationships: The Triple Shot Wake-Up Call

If you've ever wondered why you flinch when someone gets too close, why you start building an exit plan at the first fight, why you keep attracting the same man with a different haircut, it's not random. It's residue. Past relationships leave fingerprints on your heart. Some stay tender. Some stay toxic. Some try to build permanent homes inside your mind and call themselves "truth."

But here's the *real* truth: You get to heal. You get to rebuild. You get to unlearn every lie heartbreak ever taught you. And you get to stop dating what hurts you. Let's break it down:

Trap 1: The Myth of Potential

1. **Potential is a Sales Pitch, Not a Reality**
   He "could be amazing" but he's not. Believe who he is right now, not the brochure. You get the best version of them at the beginning, don't forget that.
2. **You Can't Date a Hypothetical**
   You're dating this dude eating Flamin' Hot Cheetos at two a.m., not Future Him 2.0.
3. **Hope is Not a Strategy**
   "Maybe he'll change" is not a dating plan, it's emotional purgatory.
4. **You Deserve a Partner, Not a Project**
   You're not an unpaid intern at Build-a-Man Workshop.

Trap 2: The Fantasy of Fixing Him

1. **Love Doesn't Heal Deep Damage**
   You can support. You can't save. Healing is a solo gig.
2. **Fixing Him Will Break You**
   You pour. He drains. You bleed.
3. **You're Not His Therapist, Mom, or Band-Aid**
   You're a queen. Act like it.

Trap 3: Dating From Your Wound

1. **If You're Dating to Feel Chosen, You're Already Losing**
   You're not here to audition. You're here to choose.
2. **Your Standards = Your Self-Worth**
   Low standards scream, "I still don't fully love myself."
3. **Power Walks Away Fast**
   When it's not right, it leaves. No 14-paragraph closure text required.

The Impact of Past Relationships on Dating

1. Trust Becomes a War Zone. Betrayal carves deep. You start treating new love like a crime scene: analyzing every word, every look, every breath for evidence they'll hurt you too.

2. Rejection Becomes a Mirror. Instead of seeing "wrong person," you see "something's wrong with me." That shame sticks to your bones until you rip it out at the root.

3. Your Exes Start Ghostwriting Your Standards. You unconsciously set new rules based on old pain: "Never date someone who does X. Always run if you see Y." Protection is smart, but reaction isn't the same as *intention*.

4. Baggage Becomes Your Invisible Plus-One. Unhealed wounds don't just disappear. They ride shotgun on your dates. They pick your partners. They whisper sabotage in your ear.

5. Communication Wounds Get Carried Forward. If you were punished for honesty before, you'll hesitate now. You'll sugarcoat, shrink, silence yourself unless you consciously rewire.

6. Attachment Styles Aren't Fixed but They're Triggered. Abandonment, betrayal, emotional starvation. They all shape how clingy, avoidant, or armored you feel. But they can *evolve*. You are not trapped.

7. Your Boundaries Either Harden or Disintegrate. Past heartbreak teaches some women to over-fortify ("No one gets close") and others to under-protect ("Maybe if I give more, they'll stay"). Neither extreme leads to real love.

8. Fear of Intimacy Masquerades as "High Standards." Sometimes you're not "being picky." You're terrified of letting someone see the parts of you that didn't survive the last war.

9. Old Patterns Reincarnate Themselves. Until you get conscious, you'll date the same wounds over and over just dressed differently. It's not fate. It's familiar pain you haven't evicted yet.

10. Hyperawareness of Red Flags Can Turn into Paranoia. Being cautious is wise. But expecting betrayal before love even has a chance? That's not self-protection, that's self-sabotage.

11. Self-Sabotage Becomes a Love Language. If you're used to being abandoned, sometimes you'll abandon yourself first. Flake. Ghost. Pick fights. Leave before they can.

12. Emotional Flashbacks Hijack the Moment. Your body remembers old betrayals even when your mind says "this person is safe." Healing means calming your nervous system, not just thinking differently.

13. New Love Feels Boring Without Chaos. If you're addicted to emotional roller coasters, healthy love might feel "meh" at first. (*That's your trauma detoxing, not your intuition speaking.*)

14. Comparing New People to Exes Kills New Chances. If you're measuring everyone against a ghost, no one will ever be enough. Bury the ghost. Build something new.

15. Fear of Being Fooled Again Keeps You Single. You start believing it's safer to stay alone forever than to ever look stupid, love wrong, or fall again. Healing asks for *braver faith*.

16. Self-Fulfilling Prophecies Are Real as Hell. If you date expecting to be hurt, you'll ignore good signs and only see bad ones until you *prove yourself right*. Stop stacking the deck against yourself.

17. Bitterness Becomes a Security Blanket. Cynicism feels powerful when you're wounded. But it's fake armor. Real strength is loving again with wisdom, not walls.

18. Healing Isn't "Getting Over It," It's Integrating It. You don't erase the past. You *own* it. You bless the lessons. You build your new life stronger around the scars.

19. Forgiveness Isn't for Them. It's for Your Future. You don't forgive because they deserve it. You forgive because *you* deserve to stop carrying the weight that was never yours.

20. Your Heart Can Heal Bigger Than It Broke. You are not doomed to repeat. You are not too broken to be loved. You are not too late to start again. You are healing right now, just by believing that more is possible.

Quick Tips for Healing Like a Damn Queen

Own what happened. Stop sugarcoating it. Stop villainizing it. It ended because it wasn't right and deep down, you already knew.

Release the fantasy. You're not mourning *him*. You're mourning the version of him that lived in your head. (**Big difference, babe.**)

Forgive yourself. Not just for loving him, but for ignoring the red flags, settling for crumbs, believing his sweet bullshit. You're human. You learned. You're smarter now.

Don't rush into another "fix." Loneliness isn't a reason to open your legs, your heart, or your life. Sit in it. Feel it. Heal it. **You don't fill a soul wound with a rebound.**

Audit your own patterns. You're not cursed. You're not broken. But you damn sure have some patterns and it's your job to break them before they break you again.

Create closure without contact. Waiting for an apology or "the truth" will leave you aging like milk. Closure is a one-woman ceremony. Light a candle. Write it out. Delete it. Move the fuck on.

Raise your standards quietly. Healing isn't about announcing your new boundaries on social media. It's about embodying them so hard that the wrong people don't even dare approach you.

Grieve who you were. Because after a real relationship ends, you're not the same. You're stronger. Softer. Wiser. Let the old version of you die beautifully and rebirth your damn self.

How to NOT Bring Your Past into Your Future:
- Stop repeating your love story like it's a badge of honor.
- Don't compare new people to your ex.
- Give new people a clean slate, but keep your standards bulletproof.
- Trust slowly, love boldly. *(You can do both at the same time.)*

Your past happened. But it doesn't own you. Your next chapter isn't written in the blood of your last one. Stop dating their potential. Stop trying to fix their brokenness. Stop choosing from your pain. You are too powerful, too wise, and too worthy to keep handing your heart to people who don't know what to do with it. Heal first. Love later. Never the other way around. And watch the whole damn game change.

Want Full Transformation? If you want the real, deep, no-bullshit healing blueprint that actually closes the wound for good? **Grab my book, *The Breakup Band-Aid.*** I'll walk you through it, rip the old pain off, and show you how to rise like the savage queen you are. (No sugarcoating, no "just journal it out" vibes. Real healing.)

Understanding Attachment Styles
(A.K.A. Why You Keep Picking the Same Flavor of Emotional Chaos)

If you want a relationship that actually works not one that feels like a live-action therapy session or a hostage negotiation, **you NEED to know your attachment style.** Not for TikTok clout. Not so you can trauma-bond in the group chat. But so you can stop blaming "bad luck" and start dating like a fully functioning adult. Let's break it down, Freud-style with a little less cigar and a lot more savage truth.

Secure Attachment: The Gold Standard

This is what we should all be aiming for. **A secure person is chill as hell.**
Core Belief: "I'm worthy of love, and so are you."
How They Love:
- They don't need games. They like you. They tell you. They don't turn love into a mind game or a hostage situation.
- They communicate clearly. They're mad? They talk about it like a damn human.
- They know how to give and receive love without freaking out.
- They're emotionally available without being needy or weird about it.

How It Feels Dating Them:
- Calm.
- Easy.
- Like breathing instead of drowning. (If you're bored around a secure person, it's not because they're boring, it's because you're addicted to chaos.)

Warning: If you're used to dating trash, a secure person might feel weirdly *too nice* at first. Stick around. That's just your nervous system detoxing.

In short: They're not operating from fear, anxiety, abandonment issues, or the ghosts of relationships past. They're not perfect, but they're emotionally stable enough that their drama is, like, normal-sized. If you find someone secure? Hold them tight and hydrate, because you just struck oil, honey.

Anxious Attachment: The Rollercoaster

Anxious babes don't *want* to be crazy, but when you're in fight-or-flight mode about love, your brain is literally hijacking you. It's exhausting for you. It's exhausting for them. And if you date another avoidant dude, congrats, you've just signed up for the worst reality show of all time: **"Catch Me If You Emotionally Can."** (This one is me. I am she.)

Core Belief: "If they don't constantly reassure me, they're going to leave."

How They Love:
- Overthinking every text message.
- They need a LOT of reassurance like it's oxygen.
- They get triggered if a text takes longer than 20 minutes.
- They imagine worst-case scenarios by breakfast. Reading between lines that weren't even drawn.

How It Feels Dating Them:
- Exhausting if they don't heal it.
- Beautiful and passionate if they do.

Warning: If you're anxious and you date avoidants, you're not "destined lovers" you're recreating your childhood wounding on an endless loop. (Yeah, we're going there.)

Healing Tip: You don't need to chase someone to feel worthy. You don't need to turn love into a 24/7 anxiety project.

Avoidant Attachment: The Great Escape Artist

Avoidant people crave connection... until they actually get it. Then they start running like their life depends on it. They will breadcrumb you, ghost you, keep you at arm's length and swear they're just "taking it slow."

Core Belief: "If I let you too close, I'll lose myself."

How They Love:
- They crave intimacy... until they get it.
- They need a lot of space, but won't always communicate that clearly.
- They downplay feelings and sometimes make you feel crazy for having them.
- They feel "smothered" by basic affection.
- They lose interest the second someone likes you back.
- They get the ick over someone texting you too much.

How It Feels Dating Them:
- Like chasing a mirage.
- Like craving connection while being served crumbs.

Warning: Avoidants aren't evil. They're scared. But unless they're self-aware and doing the work, you'll waste years trying to pull love out of a closed fist.

Fearful-Avoidant (Disorganized Attachment)
(The Human Tornado)

Core Belief: "I want love so badly... but I'm terrified you'll destroy me."

How They Love:
- They swing between anxious and avoidant depending on the day, the hour, or the moon cycle.
- They crave deep connection, but panic when they get it.
- They might pull you close, then push you away so hard you wonder if you imagined the whole thing.

How It Feels Dating Them:
- Hot.
- Cold.
- Confusing as hell.
- Like loving someone who's both the arsonist and the firefighter.

Warning: Disorganized attachment usually comes from trauma. It's not their fault. But it IS their responsibility to heal it before they blow up every good thing that comes near them. (And it's your responsibility not to stay stuck trying to fix it.)

Why This Shit Matters

Your attachment style will either lead you to: A healthy, secure relationship **or** another emotional crime scene where you're rewriting the same sad story with different faces.

Awareness is power. Knowing your style means you can:
- Catch yourself slipping into old patterns.
- Recognize when someone's attachment style is triggering yours.
- Choose partners who actually align with the life you want not just the chaos you're used to.
- If you know you're anxious, you'll catch yourself before you start obsessively checking your phone like a detective on Adderall.
- If you know you're avoidant, you'll notice when you're pulling away from good people for no reason other than pure panic.
- If you know you're disorganized, you'll realize you're not "broken" you're just scared and need real tools to trust again.
- If you're secure, you'll spot the red flags faster and stop entertaining people who trigger your nervous system into a full-on shutdown.

Want to Fix Your Attachment Style?
(Without Spending Another Five Years in Situationship Purgatory?)

If you're tired of trauma bonding, ghosting anxiety, and crying over dudes who can't even spell "relationship," **good news:** you can actually fix this. (Yes, even you.) Here's what actually helps:

Real Books That Actually Break It Down:

1. *Attached* **by Amir Levine and Rachel Heller.** The Holy Grail of attachment theory for dating. If you don't know your style by the time you finish Chapter 2, you're probably still stuck texting your ex.

2. *Hold Me Tight* **by Dr. Sue Johnson**. For when you want to stop playing games and start building real emotional intimacy without feeling like you're bleeding out every time you like someone.

3. *Wired for Love* **by Stan Tatkin**. A guide to relationships for people who don't want to spend their lives triggered, suspicious, or wondering why they always attract emotional hurricanes.

Daily Practices to Shift Your Attachment Style

Radical Self-Soothing: Instead of spiraling when someone pulls away, practice breathing through it. Literally say out loud: "I'm safe. I'm okay. Their behavior does not define my worth." (Yes, it feels corny. Yes, it rewires your brain.)

Secure Self-Check: Before texting, calling, or freaking out, ask yourself: *"Would I be doing this if I felt secure right now?"* If not, put the phone down and go live your life.

Slow Burn Dating: Don't rush intimacy. Don't crown a man your future husband because he said "good morning" twice. Slow it down until trust and consistency are the norm not the exception.

Boundary Rehearsal: Practice saying no to shit you don't want, even in small ways. Start with little things: saying no to a bad drink order, no to plans you don't want, no to men who text "wyd." Boundaries are a muscle. Train them.

Gratitude Anchoring: Every morning, name three things you're grateful for NOT involving another person. You are building a life you love so much that anyone who enters it is a bonus, not a lifeline.

Quick Attachment Style Quiz

(Because Self-Awareness Is Hotter Than Just "Being Good at Cuddling.")
Answer honestly. No judgment, no shame just savage clarity. Keep track of how many A's, B's, C's, and D's you choose.

1. When you start liking someone, your first instinct is to...
A) Enjoy getting to know them and see where it goes.
B) Obsessively wonder if they like you back and replay every interaction in your head 600 times.
C) Immediately feel claustrophobic and crave alone time.
D) Get super close fast, then suddenly want to ghost them the second they actually like you.

2. When you don't hear from someone you're dating, you...

A) Assume they're busy and go about your day.

B) Spiral internally and start assuming they hate you.

C) Feel weirdly relieved, you kind of needed the space anyway.

D) Feel abandoned, then pissed, then act like you don't care (even though you do).

3. Your biggest fear in relationships is...

A) Losing a good thing because of bad communication.

B) Being abandoned or forgotten.

C) Losing your independence and feeling trapped.

D) Loving someone and having them completely betray you.

4. In a fight, you tend to...

A) Talk it through calmly and find a solution.

B) Panic and desperately want to fix it immediately, even if you're not sure what's wrong.

C) Shut down emotionally and disappear until you feel safe again.

D) Swing between begging for connection and pushing them away like they insulted your entire bloodline.

5. Your dream relationship looks like...

A) Best friends who are obsessed with each other but still have lives outside of each other.

B) Someone who never leaves you guessing and constantly reassures you they're not going anywhere.

C) Someone who loves you but also doesn't text you every day and respects your cave time.

D) Someone who makes you feel safe AND excited, but you secretly wonder if that's even possible.

Results:

Mostly A's: *Secure Attachment*

Congrats, you emotionally evolved unicorn. You know how to love without self-destructing. Protect your peace at all costs.

Mostly B's: *Anxious Attachment*

You love HARD but you also overthink everything to death. Work on self-soothing, stop chasing validation, and remember: love that's right won't make you feel crazy.

Mostly C's: *Avoidant Attachment*

You crave love... as long as it stays 10 feet away. Let someone love you without planning your escape route. Love doesn't have to cost you your freedom.

Mostly D's: *Disorganized (Fearful-Avoidant) Attachment*

Welcome to the emotional rollercoaster, babe. You want love *and* fear love at the same time. Healing your trauma will change your entire love life for real, not just for Instagram quotes.

How to Shift into Secure Attachment
(Even If Right Now You Feel Like a Live Wire with Trust Issues)

Newsflash: **Secure attachment isn't just for kids with perfect childhoods.** (And let's be honest, none of us had that.) You can actually retrain yourself to love like a secure badass instead of an anxious mess, an emotional escape artist, or a tornado of "please love me" energy. Here's how:

1. Stop Making Your Partner Your Oxygen Tank. You don't need someone to complete you. You need someone to complement your already badass life. Get a life so good that love is the bonus prize, not the life raft.

2. Practice Radical Honesty Early. If you're anxious, stop pretending you're "chill" when you're actually spiraling. If you're avoidant, stop acting like "I'm just busy" when you're emotionally shutting down. Own your needs or you'll sabotage yourself trying to hide them.

3. Vet People, Don't Idolize Them. Secure attachment starts by realizing you are the prize and you get to decide if they deserve a seat at your table. You're not trying to "win" them. You're trying to watch and see if they even qualify.

4. Get Comfortable Being Alone. If being alone feels like death, you're not ready to date. Because when you NEED someone, you'll ignore every red flag just to avoid loneliness. Loneliness is a temporary feeling. Being trapped in a toxic situationship is a long-ass regret. Choose wisely.

5. Give the Right People a Damn Chance. If someone shows up calm, consistent, available: **let them.** Stop sabotaging because they don't make your anxiety spike. If it feels "too easy," it's called HEALTHY. You're not bored. You're healing.

Final Word from the UnExpert: Your attachment style isn't your destiny, it's your download. You can rewire it. You can rise from it. You can date from security, not survival. The love you seek starts with how you love yourself. This isn't about being perfect. It's about being aware, being brave, and choosing peace over patterns. Let's evolve. Let's get secure. Let's stop calling chaos our type.

The Inner Sh*tstorm:
Dating, Mental Health & the Performance of 'Being Fine

Dating and Mental Health
(Because you are not your breakdown.
And love doesn't stop at the edge of your darkness.)

Dating while managing mental health isn't a weakness, it's a goddamn act of courage. Because you're not showing up with your "best self" in a perfectly curated package. You're showing up *in process.* You're letting someone in *mid-healing,* when the wounds are still fresh and the shame still echoes. And you're doing it anyway. That's power. But here's what no one tells you: You don't have to be "fixed" to be worthy of love. You don't need to shrink your reality to become more palatable. You don't owe anyone a version of yourself that doesn't exist. You get to date as you are, *an evolving masterpiece with real scars and real needs.*

1. You Must Start with Brutal Self-Awareness. Not shame. Not judgment. Just *truth.* Know your triggers. Know your patterns. Know what part of you seeks love for healing and what part might still sabotage it. That awareness? That's your power move.

2. Say the Hard Things Out Loud (When You're Ready). Don't perform stability just to earn connection. Say, "I've struggled with depression," or "I deal with anxiety sometimes," or "This is something I'm managing, and I want to be honest." Let them see you *and stay.*

3. You Are Allowed to Set Mental Health Boundaries Without Explaining Yourself. You don't have to go to that party. You don't have to answer every text instantly. You don't have to perform cheerfulness when you're drowning. Say, "Today's heavy. I still care. I just need space." The right one will *get it.*

4. If They Judge, Ghost, or Minimize, They Were Never Meant for the Journey. You didn't lose anything. You dodged someone who couldn't hold you with tenderness. Let them leave. Your softness will never be safe in the hands of someone who hasn't met their own shadow.

5. You're Not a Burden. You're a Battlefield Survivor with a Beating Heart. Stop apologizing for the parts of you that took longer to heal. Your pain is not shameful. Your honesty is not "too much." Your vulnerability is a gift not a liability.

6. You Still Deserve Big, Loud, Radiant Love. Not just understanding. Not just "he's nice about it." But the kind of love that *meets you in the mess,* that doesn't flinch when it gets hard, and that doesn't run when the fog rolls in.

7. Don't Date to Escape Your Mental Health, Date to Enhance Your Healing. If you're dating to avoid your emotions, it will implode. But if you're dating with clarity knowing that love can *support* you, not save you, you'll build something real.

8. You Get to Educate Without Carrying Their Emotional Labor. Teach them how to love you in your seasons. But don't take on the job of making them "get it." If they're unwilling to learn? That's not partnership. That's parenting.

9. You're Still Allowed to Have Standards. Mental health challenges don't mean you take what you can get. You still get to ask: Does he make me feel emotionally safe? Can he sit with discomfort? Does he react or respond?

10. Some Days, Dating May Be Too Much. That's Okay. Take breaks. Rest. Log off the apps. Your healing doesn't stop just because someone cute showed up. Sometimes solitude is more nourishing than false connection. Honor that.

11. It's Not Weak to Need Support, It's Holy to Ask for It. Let your therapist help. Let your best friend hold space. Let your body rest. Needing help isn't failure. It's *human.*

12. You Can Still Be the Strong One and Still Struggle. Being high-functioning doesn't mean you're okay. Just because you show up, smile, handle business, and hold space for everyone else doesn't mean your insides aren't unraveling. Let someone love the *real* you, the strong one *and* the hurting one. You're allowed to be held.

13. There Will Be Someone Who Sees It All and Stays. Not just the cute, healed parts. Not just the parts you curate. But the panic. The overthinking. The spirals. The silence. And they'll stay. Not out of obligation, but because *they see your humanity as holy.* You won't have to explain why some days you just can't. They'll already know. And that's what makes love safe.

Final truth: Mental health doesn't make you undateable. It makes you *more emotionally awake, more empathetic, more aware.* But only when you own it. Speak it. Honor it. Love that starts with truth is the only kind worth building.

CONVERSATION PROMPTS FOR
TALKING ABOUT MENTAL HEALTH WHILE DATING

(Because your truth deserves a seat at the table and if they can't handle it,
they were never built to stay.)

1. "There's something important to me I'd love to share when you feel ready to hold space for it." Soft, respectful, clear. You're not dumping. You're *inviting.*

2. "Mental health is something I take seriously in my life. It's part of who I am, and I've done a lot of work around it. I'd love to talk about that with you sometime." This lets them know this isn't shame, it's self-awareness.

3. "I've had my own journey with anxiety/depression/etc. nothing I expect you to fix, but something I think it's important to be open about as we get to know each other." This frames it as *shared reality*, not a cry for help.

4. "Can I be real with you for a sec? I've dealt with [insert issue] before, and I've learned a lot through it. I always try to be transparent about the things that shaped me." You're not fragile. You're *formidable*. And you're leading with truth.

5. **"Some days I need space, and it's not because I'm upset, it's how I manage my energy and mental health. I'll always communicate with you, but I need someone who can respect that."** No apology. Just boundary. That's *grown*.

6. **"I've learned that when I start dating someone seriously, I need to know they're emotionally safe not perfect, just grounded. Is mental health something you feel comfortable talking about?"** Flip the script. *Let them show you who they are.*

7. **"I'm not looking for someone to fix me. I've done and continue to do that work myself. But I am looking for someone who can hold space for the real me, even when I'm in the hard parts."** If they flinch? They're not your person.

8. **"Just so you know, therapy's a big part of my life. If that's weird for someone, I'd rather know early on."** Normalize it. Make it clear you date *from awareness*, not chaos.

And finally, the quietest flex of all:

9. **"I'm not afraid to talk about the hard stuff. I think it's actually what makes real connection possible. You?"** Simple. Brave. Leveling the playing field. That's your voice.

10. **"Before things go any deeper, I just want to share something personal with you. It's not a red flag, it's just part of my truth. I've had my own mental health journey, and I want to be upfront about it."** You're not warning them. You're *inviting them into your reality* without fear, without apology.

How to read the room without spiraling

(Because intuition is a superpower but spiraling is not a personality trait.)

You *feel* everything. The change in his tone. The shift in his eyes. The way he took 30 minutes longer to text back than usual. You read the pauses between the words louder than the words themselves. And sometimes? You're right. But other times? You're spiraling yourself into a story that doesn't exist. Let's break it down and get your power back.

I. Yes—You're Probably Right. But That's Not the Problem.

First things first: If you're sensing a shift, you're probably not imagining it. But that doesn't mean you need to decode it like a cryptic riddle on a CIA mission. The spiral usually begins here:

"What did I do?"

"Why is he pulling away?"

"Should I say something or will that make it worse?"

"Maybe I'm overreacting…"

"Maybe he's just tired…"

"Maybe I'm the problem."

No, queen. You are not the problem. But your mind trying to solve something that hasn't even been *named* yet? That's the trap.

71

II. Spiraling vs. Observing: Know the Difference

SPIRALING	OBSERVING
Assumes worst-case	Notices change
Personalizes everything	Tracks patterns objectively
Rushes to react	Waits for clarity
Seeks control	Holds self-trust
Clings to reassurance	Asks better questions

You are allowed to notice energy shifts. You are not required to **fix** them.

III. How to Stay in Your Power When the Vibe Changes

1. Hit Pause Before You Interpret. If you feel tension, don't immediately assume it's about you. Ask: *Did I feel good before this moment?* If yes, anchor back to that truth instead of abandoning it for a story.

2. Ask Yourself: Is This New... or Just Familiar? Are you reacting to *this man* or to *every man who's ever gone silent before the crash?* Spirals often come from memory, not the present.

3. Don't Ask Leading Questions for Reassurance
"Are you mad at me?"
"Is something wrong?"
"Are you sure we're okay?"
These questions **leak anxiety** and rarely lead to clarity. Instead, ask: "You feel a little distant, are you okay?" Confident. Direct. No begging.

4. Mirror His Energy, Not His Inconsistency. If he's pulling back, you don't chase. You **hold**. Not as a game. As a standard. Let him bring clarity or create distance. You respond *after.* Not during his fog.

IV. What to Do Instead of Spiral

- **Journal what you're feeling.** Not what you *think* is happening, what you're experiencing in your body.
- **Text a friend, not him.** Say: "I'm feeling a shift and I want to react, but I'm holding off." Let someone talk you off the ledge.
- **Go do something sensory.** Touch water. Walk outside. Move your body. Get back in *your* energy.
- **Name the fear beneath the feeling.** Are you afraid he's losing interest? About to ghost? About to reject you? Call it out. Most spirals die in direct sunlight.
- **Don't check on AWDTSG.** We live in a pick me world, where women are desperate and want to be heard. So, if you do look take criticism with a gain of salt. If he's not married, not an abuser, drug addict, or STD spreader, see at least if you vibe.

V. If You Need to Say Something, Say This

You don't need a script, but if you're going to speak, do it from center, not panic. Try: "Hey, I noticed a shift in your energy and just wanted to check in. No pressure just want to be clear with each other."

Or: "You seem a little off, if there's something I need to know, I'd rather hear it directly."

"I value directness over guessing games. Let me know if you need space, but don't leave me decoding silence."

If that scares him off? **He was never emotionally available.** He just knew how to flirt.

Final Word: You are not needy for noticing. You are not dramatic for feeling. You are not "too much" for naming energy. But your intuition deserves a companion called discernment. And your power lives in observation, not obsession. You don't need to read every room perfectly. You just need to know when the room isn't worth staying in.

Dating and Social Pressure

Balancing Expectations (Without Losing Your Damn Soul)

Dating today is basically a Hunger Games arena. Everyone has an opinion about how you should look, when you should settle down, how you should act, and what milestone you should have hit preferably yesterday.

Here's the truth:

- You don't owe anyone a damn thing.
- You are not a Build-A-Bride.
- You are not late to anything.
- You are right on time for your own damn life.

Here's how to slam the brakes on the bullshit and take your power back:

1. Know Your Own Voice Before Everyone Else Drowns It Out. Before you let your mom, your friends, your coworker's divorce lawyer, and TikTok tell you what to want figure out what *you* want. *Loudly.*

2. Stop Using Society's Timeline as a Weapon Against Yourself. You are not "behind." You are not "failing." You're not a carton of milk with an expiration date stamped on your forehead.

3. Relationship Milestones Are Not a Checklist. Boyfriend by 26. Married by 28. Kids by 30. Who made these rules? Burn the checklist. Live the life.

4. Communicate Like a Grown-Ass Human, Not a Mind-Reader. No more silent stewing. No more hoping they'll "just know." Speak your expectations. Set your standards. Clarify your boundaries.

5. If It Feels Like You're Settling, You Are. If you're convincing yourself it's "good enough" because you're "running out of time" STOP. You're not "building a future." You're building a regret.

6. Other People's Happy Pictures Are 90% Lies. They're posting the curated highlight reel. You're living the messy, beautiful, real thing. Comparison is delusion. Trust me. Story time: I have this friend from high school, who is constantly posting how amazing his wife is and how great his family is and he loves his wife, blah, blah, blah. I asked my one girlfriend about him for something else and she said she blocked him, because he kept trying to sleep with her, yes, while in his ever-so happy marriage.

7. Take the Damn Pressure Off Dating. Your next date doesn't have to be your husband. It doesn't have to be a fairytale. It doesn't even have to be great. It just has to be *real*.

8. Your Single Years Aren't a Waiting Room for "Real Life." This IS your real life. If you're holding your breath until you're coupled up, exhale. LIVE. *Now*.

9. Being Picky Isn't a Crime. You're allowed to have standards that make other people uncomfortable. You're allowed to want it all. Screw anyone who tells you to "lower your expectations."

10. Find Your Inner "F*ck It" Energy. Seriously. Some days, the best thing you can do is pour a glass of wine, throw your phone across the room, and say "f*ck it" to every voice trying to run your love life but their own.

11. Protect Your Mental Energy Like It's a Rare Diamond. Not every comment deserves a response. Not every "when are you getting married?" deserves your emotional labor. Smile. Shrug. Protect your peace.

12. Stop Asking for Relationship Advice from Miserable People. If their love life looks like a dumpster fire, maybe don't take notes.

13. Remember: They're Projecting Their Own Panic. When people pressure you, it's rarely about you. It's about their own fears, their own regrets, their own timelines that didn't go to plan. Not your problem.

14. Redefine "Success" in Dating. Success isn't getting cuffed fast. Success is staying true to yourself, keeping your peace, and refusing to let the world rush you into a miserable life.

15. Choose Freedom Over Fear Every Single Time. Freedom to choose your timeline. Freedom to change your mind. Freedom to walk away from what doesn't feel like peace. That's the flex. That's the win.

Social Pressure Detox:
5 Savage Reality Checks for When You Feel Like You're "Behind"

Because you're not "behind" you're just **listening to too many idiots.** Next time you feel that creeping panic, run these questions:

1. Whose Timeline Am I Actually Following? Mine or Someone Else's?
(*If it's not yours, burn it. Immediately.*)

2. Would I Even Want What They're Pressuring Me to Chase?

(Marriage, kids, relationship, whatever. If your gut doesn't light up, it's not your dream.)

3. Who's Actually Winning Here: The One Who Settled Fast or The One Who Waited for Real?

(Check receipts. Most of the people who "got there first" are miserable as hell.)

4. If I Had Zero External Pressure, What Would I Choose?

(If no one could see or judge you, what would your love life look like? THAT'S your real compass.)

5. Am I Building a Life I'm Proud of? With or Without a Plus One?

(Because if the answer's yes, you've already won.)

The Mindset Reset: Complete.

You don't just date differently after this. **You exist differently.** You vibrate differently. You hold yourself differently. You walk into every room, every date, every decision with a new compass, **your own.**

You are no longer available for:

- Confusion.
- Half-effort.
- Self-betrayal.
- Almosts.
- Delays in your destiny.

You are not "hoping" anymore. You are not "waiting" anymore. You are leading. This first stage was about *mindset realignment* so the next stages can actually land inside the powerhouse you've become. Because now? You're not looking for someone to choose you. You're choosing your own damn life and anyone who wants a seat better come ready.

The Magnetic Blueprint:
Manifestation, Energy & Soul Strategy

The Energy Shift – How to Become the One Who's Chosen
(Without Lowering Your Standards or Begging for It)

There's a moment where the girl who's always chasing, doubting, settling, and waiting...becomes the woman everyone else is chasing, admiring, and trying to lock down. It's not magic. It's not luck. It's an energy shift. And once you flip that switch? You'll never date the same way again.

Step One: You Master the Art of Unbothered
Someone ghosts? Your response isn't a meltdown. It's: "Thank you for eliminating yourself early, king." Someone plays games? Gone. Someone can't commit? Gone. You're not panicking over losing someone who already showed you they couldn't handle you. You bless and block with grace and you NEVER chase energy that's running from itself.

Step Two: You Stay Soft, But Watch Carefully
Being high-value isn't about being cold, hard, or "proving you don't need anyone." It's about being warm but observant. You give love freely but you stop trying to earn it from people who can't even show up. You stay soft without letting people walk through you like a doormat.

Step Three: You Make Peace with the Fact That Not Everyone Will Choose You
And that's a GOOD thing. Because if everyone could access you, you wouldn't be rare. You only need one right person to recognize you. Not the whole damn city.

The REAL Energy Shift Looks Like This:
- You walk away from "almost" relationships without writing 10-page text essays.
- You spend more time enjoying your own company than worrying about someone else's opinion.
- You realize "being chosen" isn't about being better, it's about being aligned.
- You glow different because you know no man, no app, no text can make or break your worth.

The Difference Between High Standards and Being Unrealistic
(Because "He Must Have a Six-Pack and Heal My Inner Child"
Is Not a Realistic Dating Plan)

When you level up your energy, raise your standards, and start acting like the damn prize you are, you're going to attract better. But you also need to make sure you're building a throne, not an electric fence no one can climb. There's a difference between being high-value and being delusional. Let's break it down.

High Standards Look Like This:

- Wants to actually know you — not just hook up.
- Communicates clearly — no games, no confusion, no psychic skills required.
- Respects your boundaries — and doesn't throw a tantrum when you say no.
- Values loyalty, kindness, effort, consistency — not just "vibes" and "good mornings."
- Actually has a life, goals, and emotional intelligence — because you're not building a man from scratch at this big age.

Unrealistic Expectations Look Like This:

- Must be 6'4", billionaire, Olympic athlete, and part-time therapist.
- Needs to respond to every text within three minutes or you spiral into a trauma loop.
- Expects them to "just know" what you're thinking without ever saying it out loud.
- Demands they never trigger any insecurity in you, ever! Because you don't want to actually work on your healing.
- Believes your soulmate will just magically appear at your door with a ring, a house, a healing crystal, and no baggage whatsoever.

Here's the Savage Reality:

- High standards protect your peace.
- Unrealistic standards protect your loneliness. *(And you can dress it up however you want, but that's the truth.)*

How to Check Yourself: Before you dump someone because they didn't plan the world's most magical date in week two, ask yourself: **"Is this a real standard or is this a fantasy designed to keep me safe from vulnerability?"** Real standards are about character, not cosmetics. Real standards are about energy, effort, and alignment: not abs, yachts, and TikTok love story reenactments.

Signs You're Finally Dating from Secure Energy

(Because Chaos Is Exhausting and Real Peace Is the Real Flex)

You know you're shifting into your power when dating doesn't feel like surviving anymore, it feels like choosing. When you date from secure energy, everything hits different. You're not chasing. You're not guessing. You're not spiraling over people who couldn't even tell you their middle name. You're moving like a woman who knows she's the table and the damn feast.

- **You let people show you who they are and believe them.** No more potential. No more fantasy league boyfriends. If they're inconsistent, lazy, or avoidant, you don't make excuses, you make exits.
- **You don't try to force it.** You know chemistry without effort is possible but *compatibility without effort* is not. If it's not mutual, easy, and building naturally, you'd rather be at home with your wine and your face mask than wasting time.
- **You're not afraid to lose someone.** You don't shrink yourself to keep them. You don't abandon your standards to impress them. If they leave, that's not your tragedy, it's their loss.
- **You speak your needs calmly not like you're setting off a fire alarm.** You say what you need without the fear of scaring them away. If they run because you expressed a boundary? Good. Let the trash take itself out.

- **You're not obsessed with labels. You're obsessed with actions.** A title means nothing if the behavior isn't backing it up. You don't just want to be "his girlfriend" you want to be consistently loved, respected, and prioritized.
- **You don't take rejection personally.** You're not everyone's flavor. Neither is champagne, and you don't see Dom Pérignon crying about it.
- **You glow different.** You don't even notice how hot you look, because you're too busy living your life, loving yourself, and not giving a damn about who's watching. (Which ironically makes you even hotter. Funny how that works.)

Final Word: When you date from secure energy, you don't just find better people, you become the person you've always been looking for. And from that place? You don't "get lucky" in love. You attract what you already are. Keep going, light. You're closer than you think.

Building an Unshakeable Dating Mindset

(So... You Stop Crumbling Every Time Someone Texts "Hey" and Disappears)
You can have all the red flag checklists, the best profile pics, the funniest opening lines, but if your mindset is weak, you will fold every damn time. Dating will test you. Your energy. Your standards. Your emotional stamina. If you don't have a steel-trap mindset, you'll start:
- Accepting less because you're tired.
- Compromising too soon because you're lonely.
- Letting anxiety dictate your worth because some guy didn't text back fast enough.

Not anymore. Here's how you build a dating mindset so unshakeable, it would take an act of God to throw you off:

1. Stop Future-Tripping. Your job on a first date isn't to decide if he's husband material. It's to decide if you even want a second coffee. *Stay present or you'll keep falling for potential instead of reality.*

2. Trust Energy, Not Excuses. If someone makes you feel unsure, anxious, unsafe, or like you're chasing? That's all the information you need. Energy doesn't lie. People do. If the vibe is off, honor it. No more talking yourself out of your own intuition.

3. Your Standards Are Non-Negotiable. They are not situational. They are not flexible because "he's cute" or "he's had a hard life." If he doesn't meet the bar, he doesn't get the girl. No exceptions. No emotional coupons.

What to Do When You Feel Discouraged

(Because Sometimes You Just Want to Throw Your Phone into the Ocean)
Let's be honest: **Dating can feel like emotional CrossFit.** Swipe. Hope. Ghost. Repeat. It's easy to get tired, jaded, or ready to fake your death and move to a cabin in the woods.

But hear me right now: Discouragement is a stop, not a sentence. You're allowed to feel it. You're NOT allowed to live there. Here's how you climb out of the discouragement pit before it swallows you whole:

1. Take a Beat. Not a Forever Break. Feeling burnt out? Take a week off. Delete the apps for a minute. Focus on your own glow-up. But don't make some grand "I'm never dating again" declaration. That's just your wounded ego talking. Let yourself rest not quit.

2. Reframe the "Failures." Every date that didn't work out wasn't a failure. It was a filter. Another wrong one eliminated. Another step closer to someone who actually matches your energy. Not wasted time. Training.

3. Protect Your Heart Without Hardening It. You can be smart without being cynical. You can be guarded without being made of concrete. **You are allowed to be hopeful; you just don't have to be naive.** Hope is your superpower. Cynicism is just fear wearing a leather jacket.

4. Cut the "I'm the Problem" Spiral. When dating gets discouraging, it's easy to turn on yourself:
- "Maybe I'm too picky."
- "Maybe I'm not good enough."
- "Maybe I should just lower my standards."

NO. STOP. IMMEDIATELY. You are not asking for too much. You're just noticing that most people can't deliver what they're pretending to offer. That's not your flaw, that's your discernment working.

5. Find Joy Outside of Dating. You cannot let dating be your only dopamine source. Fill your life with friends, hobbies, passions, self-care rituals. When your life is already full? **Dating is just an enhancement not your only outlet for happiness.** This is how you stop feeling desperate. This is how you date from overflow instead of starvation.

When love becomes the center of your world, every text, pause, or disappointment hits harder than it should. The real shift happens when your life is already full: full of plans, curiosity, experiences, and joy that exist *with or without* a partner. That's why building a life outside of dating matters. *A Single Girl's Ultimate Bucket List* and *Bucket List* were created for exactly this reason, featuring over 10,000 ideas to help you fill your days with adventure, creativity, connection, and momentum. When your life is rich on its own, dating stops feeling desperate and starts feeling optional, an enhancement, not a lifeline.

https://yourdatingunexpert.com/buy-therapy

Affirmations That Actually Work
*(Because the Right Words Rewire Your Brain and
the Wrong Ones Keep You Stuck in Dating Hell)*

Affirmations aren't magic spells. They're mental reprogramming. Every time you say one, you're either:
- Strengthening your self-worth,
- Shifting your dating energy,
- Or preparing your nervous system to receive actual love without self-sabotage.

Let's get you some affirmations that actually DO something.

Dating Standards + Boundaries Affirmations
(Because Queens Don't Beg, They Decide.)
1. **"I set the tone for how I'm treated."**
   (If you don't set the standard, they'll set it for you and you won't like the discount version.)
2. **"No is my protection word, not a bad word."**
   (If you can't say no, you can't protect your peace.)

Healing From the Past Affirmations
(Because You Can't Build a Castle While You're Still Crying in the Wreckage)
3. **"I release what broke me without letting it define me."**
   (It's part of your story not your whole story.)
4. **"I bless the lessons and block the bullshit."**
   (No bitterness, no baggage, just boundaries.)

Opening to Love Affirmations
(Because You Can't Call In Real Love with a Barricade Around Your Heart)
5. **"I am safe to open my heart again."**
   (You are not the same woman who got hurt before, you're wiser now.)
6. **"I attract healthy, available love because I am healthy and available to myself."**
   (Like attracts like. Always.)
7. **"It is safe for me to trust myself and my intuition."**
   (When you trust YOU, you don't fear them.)

Unshakeable Confidence Affirmations
(Because You're Not the Backup Plan, You're the Whole Damn Upgrade)
8. **"I am unforgettable because I am undeniable."**
   (Real energy imprints. You don't have to force it.)
9. **"I don't compete where I don't compare."**
   (There is no competition when you're in your own damn lane.)
10. **"I bring the table, the feast, and the damn wine."**
    (You're not asking for a seat. You are the invitation.)

Receiving Healthy Love Affirmations
(Because You Deserve More Than Just Being Chosen, You Deserve to Be Cherished)

11. **"I am ready to receive love that feels safe, steady, and real."**
    (You're done chasing highs. You're here for peace.)
12. **"I am magnetic to emotionally available, loving partners."**
    (You don't attract what you want, you attract what you ARE.)
13. **"It is safe for me to fully be seen and still be loved."**
    (You don't have to hide parts of yourself to be worthy.)

Emotional Resilience Affirmations
(Because Dating Is for Grown Women, Not Glass Dolls)

14. **"I bend. I don't break."**
    (A setback isn't a sentence.)
15. **"Every experience grows my wisdom, not my bitterness."**
    (Lesson or blessing, either way, you win.)
16. **"Everything meant for me is already on its way."**
    (Relax. It's handled.)

Dating Sanity Reminders
(Because You're Gonna Need a Battle Cry Sometimes)

17. **"I can be disappointed and still not settle."**
    (Pain is not permission to lower the bar.)
18. **"One bad experience doesn't define the entire journey."**
    (You don't stop traveling because of one shitty flight.)
19. **"I trust divine timing over my own impatience."**
    (The universe knows what you're ready for.)

Endgame Queen Energy Affirmations
(For When You Remember Who the F You Are)

20. **"My love is a privilege, not a punishment."**
    (You are the blessing. Full stop.)
21. **"I don't need everyone. I just need the right one."**
    (Quality over quantity, always.)
22. **"I am loved, chosen, and safe, even when I'm alone."**
    (Your worth is not on layaway.)

If these affirmations hit, imagine having **all 101** in one place: categorized, printable, and ready for daily use. The full *101 Dating Affirmations That Actually Work* is designed as a standalone reprogramming tool you can return to anytime your confidence wobbles, your standards slip, or dating starts messing with your head.

Scan below to upgrade your mindset and lock this energy in for good.

https://www.etsy.com/listing/4430592752/101-dating-affirmations-that-actually

Manifestation Techniques No One Talks About

(Because You're Not Just Dreaming It, You're Commanding It.)

Everyone loves to talk about manifestation like it's this glittery, Pinterest-board exercise:
- "Light a candle."
- "Write your list."
- "Visualize your dream man while whispering affirmations to the moon."

Cute. Necessary? Maybe. Sufficient? Not even close. Real manifestation, the kind that bends your reality, requires two things:
- A complete energy shift.
- And actions that actually align with that energy, even before the results show up.

Want the relationship, the life, the peace you're craving? You have to move differently. Think differently. Choose differently. Here's what no one tells you, but I will:

1. You Have to Stop Manifesting from Your Wounds. If you're asking for money because you feel scared? If you're manifesting a man to "prove" you're worthy? You're not manifesting. You're bargaining from your wounds. And guess what? The universe reads energy, not words. If your energy screams "I'm not enough," you'll attract lessons that reflect that, not blessings. Shift first. Call it in second.

2. You Have to Embody It Before You See It. You don't manifest love by crying every night and hoping it saves you. You manifest love by becoming the loved woman you want to be. Not someday. Not after he shows up. NOW.
- Walk like you're already adored.
- Talk like you're already chosen.
- Make decisions like your future partner is already watching.

3. You Must Close Open Loops. Still stalking your ex's page? Still sleeping with people you know damn well are bad for you? You're telling the universe you're not ready. Manifestation requires energetic clarity. No confusion. No "just in case" options. No half-open doors you refuse to close. You can't call in a soulmate while holding hands with your soul-tie.

4. You Must Act Before It's Logical. Manifestation often looks crazy to the untrained eye.
- Investing in yourself when you don't have "proof" it will work.
- Saying no to a decent guy because you know he's not the one.
- Moving cities, ending friendships, upgrading your life for a future you haven't "seen" yet.

You must move based on your inner knowing not external validation. Leap first. Net appears second.

5. You Must Become Impossible to Shake. The second you set a real manifestation intention, life will test you. You will get breadcrumb offers. You will get almost-rights. You will get triggered by loneliness, fear, ego. Your job? Stay. Unshakeable. No doubting. No questioning if you're crazy. No "maybe I should just settle because I'm tired." The ones who manifest aren't the ones who got lucky. They're the ones who refused to lower their frequency.

6. You Must Release Timelines. Clutching a clock is one of the fastest ways to block your blessings.

- "It has to happen by June."
- "If it doesn't happen by my birthday, I'm giving up."
- "It better come fast or it means it's not working."

That's not manifestation. That's emotional hostage negotiation. Surrender the when. Surrender the how. Hold the vision anyway. Trust the delay is always for your upgrade.

7. You Must Be Willing to Lose Everything Not Aligned. Here's the part nobody tells you because it's brutal:

- You will lose people.
- You will lose jobs.
- You will lose comfort zones.

Because you cannot live a new reality while clinging to the old one. When the wrong things fall away, celebrate. The universe is clearing the runway. Get excited, not scared.

10 Things to Start Doing Today to Become a Manifestation Magnet

(Because Reading About It Is Cute, Doing It Is Where the Power Lives.)

1. **Clean out one toxic connection immediately.**
   (Dead energy clogs blessings. Cut the cord. Now.)
2. **Upgrade your environment by 10%.**
   (Make your world reflect the life you're manifesting even if it's just changing your phone background.)
3. **Stop complaining for 24 hours.**
   (Every complaint is an energy leak. Plug the damn hole.)
4. **Move your body like you're already living your dream life.**
   (Your nervous system needs to FEEL it before it sees it.)
5. **Unfollow one account that makes you feel small.**
   (Comparison kills magnetic energy. Protect your mental garden.)
6. **Speak one "delusional" affirmation out loud like it's already true.**
   (If it doesn't scare you a little, it's not big enough.)
7. **Take one scary action that future-you would do without hesitation.**
   (Book the trip. Apply for the thing. Delete the situationship.)
8. **Spend 10 minutes visualizing your life already done and feeling it fully.**
   (Feeling is the Wi-Fi password to manifestation. Access granted.)
9. **Write down what you want in the present tense not "I want," but "I have."**
   (Wanting energy attracts more wanting. HAVING energy attracts more having.)
10. **Every time you catch yourself doubting, smile and say: "It's already mine."**
   (Nothing fcks with a woman who truly believes in herself.)

Final Energy Blast: You don't manifest by hoping. You don't manifest by begging. You manifest by **becoming** the version of yourself who already has everything she ever prayed for. The sooner you act like her, the sooner you meet her. And trust me, she's a bad bitch.

Self-Trust: Your New Dating Compass
(Because No Oracle, No TikTok Tarot Reader,
No Best Friend Knows Better Than You.)

Here's the truth no one tells you: **Dating is not a game of guessing. It's a game of listening to yourself.** If you don't trust yourself, it doesn't matter how many strategies you memorize, how many "red flag" lists you read, or how many dating coaches you pay $5,000 to "heal your inner child." You will always be outsourcing your own damn wisdom. You'll be texting your friends to decode every "wyd" text. You'll be Googling "Is he losing interest???" after two hours of no reply. You'll be convincing yourself to stay just because "maybe it's just my trauma."

Girl, stop.

You know. You *always* know. The real work? Is building the spine to trust it.

Why Self-Trust Is Your New Dating Compass:

1. Because Your Nervous System Speaks Before Your Brain Does. Ever felt your stomach twist around someone and then tried to rationalize it away? Ever felt calm and grounded with someone without knowing why? That's your compass. That's your body already decoding what your mind is too scared to see. Stop needing a 48-slide PowerPoint presentation from the universe. Start trusting the first whisper.

2. Because If You Can't Trust Yourself, You'll Always Trust the Wrong People. If you don't anchor inside yourself, you'll be blown around by whatever energy hits you next.
- Gaslighters will sound convincing.
- Lovebombers will feel like soulmates.
- Walking red flags will seem "not that bad if I just squint."

Self-trust is the difference between falling for potential and choosing reality.

3. Because Your Intuition Is Always Quicker Than Your Wounds. Fear screams. Trauma begs. Intuition just calmly states the truth. It's never frantic. It's never desperate. It doesn't explain itself. It simply says: yes or no and leaves it up to you whether you'll honor it.

How to Start Building Unbreakable Self-Trust Today:

1. **Stop Polling Your Friends Before You Trust Your Own Gut.**
   (Their advice is based on their wounds not your path.)
2. **Practice Making Micro-Decisions Without Second-Guessing.**
   (What to wear. What to eat. Who to text back. Own the choice.)
3. **When You Feel "Off" About Someone, Believe It the First Time.**
   (You don't owe second chances to weird energy.)
4. **Write Down Times You Knew and Were Right.**
   (Stack your proof until you can't gaslight yourself anymore.)
5. **Treat Every Date Like an Observation Not an Evaluation of Your Worth.**
   (You're studying THEM. Not begging for THEM to validate YOU.)

Final Word: Your intuition isn't broken. Your picker isn't broken. Your self-trust muscle is just underdeveloped and that's fixable as hell. You don't need five more signs. You don't need him to act worse before you "get it." You need one thing: The decision that your peace matters more than potential.

That your body knows before your ego catches up. That your worth is not up for debate even in your own mind. You are the compass. You are the destination. And when you move like it? The world bends to meet you there.

Quick Self-Check: Are You Trusting Yourself or Outsourcing Again?

(No Judgment, Just Radical Self-Awareness.)

Answer each question brutally honestly:

✅ = I'm solid.

✖ = Uh oh...I might be betraying myself.

1. When something feels "off" with someone, do I trust it the first time or do I wait for proof?

✅ I trust my gut and adjust immediately.

✖ I wait until they completely wreck me before admitting I was right.

2. Do I ask my friends to interpret texts for me instead of asking myself how I feel about it?

✅ I check in with myself first, not the group chat.

✖ I basically run a dating detective agency with my friends on speed dial.

3. When I feel uncomfortable on a date, do I politely excuse myself or force myself to stay longer to "be nice?"

✅ I leave. My safety > their ego.

✖ I sit there hating every second and then blame myself later.

4. When someone's words and actions don't match, do I listen to their behavior — or their excuses?

✅ I believe patterns, not promises.

✖ I collect red flags like they're f*cking Pokémon cards.

5. Am I dating to see if I even like them or to prove I'm lovable?

✅ I know I'm lovable already. They're the ones auditioning.

✖ I'm performing like it's the Olympics just to get a damn rose.

Scoring Reality Check:

- **5 ✅s:** You're a self-trust sniper. Savage. Sacred. Unstoppable.
- **3–4 ✅s:** You're close! Tweak your habits and you're in queen territory.
- **1–2 ✅s:** Baby, we gotta rebuild the foundation. (Good news: you're here now and now is when it changes.)

Micro-Manifestation Steps

Daily Moves That Shift Your Frequency Toward Real Love

This isn't a vision board. This is vibrational warfare. You don't just 'attract' love, you prep your field for a fcking arrival.

1. **Make Your Bed Like He's Coming Over Tonight.** Clean sheets, candles lit, sexy AF pajamas. Not for him, for the *readiness*.

2. **Delete His Number and Smile While Doing It.** The universe won't send the new while you're still texting the old.

3. **Make a Playlist Called "Love Is Inevitable."** Only songs that make you feel soft, powerful, and already held. Because you know I love me a good playlist, so here's another. This playlist is for trusting the timing, lifting your gaze, and remembering that good things don't need to be chased to arrive. https://open.spotify.com/playlist/5fXuqPfEVfTGFFexncP5T1?si=YT04Oq1ITXOBcu7vMq3 dUg

4. **Clean Out Your Underwear Drawer.** Trash anything with holes, ghosts, or regret. Make space for worship.

5. **Say This Before Every Swipe:** "I'm not here to chase. I'm here to attract the one who recognizes me."

6. **Don't Just Journal. Channel.** Write letters from your future partner. Let him speak through your pen. Then read it back like gospel.

7. **Touch Yourself Like Someone's Praying They Could.** Set the standard for reverence. The body holds memory, start building one.

8. **Leave One Night a Week Open for the Unexpected.** No plans. No agenda. Just you, dressed like a miracle, in case life gets brave.

9. **Stop Talking to Men Who Leave You Confused.** Confusion isn't chemistry. It's nervous system damage. Pull the plug.

10. **Turn Off the Noise.** No dating advice for one week. No YouTube tarot. Just your body, your breath, and your knowing.

11. **Write "Taken" on a Sticky Note. Put It on Your Mirror.** Not because you are. Because you *will be*. Let the future loop in.

12. **Say This Before You Leave the House:** "May I be noticed by the ones who know how to hold me."

13. **Make Eye Contact with Three Strangers Today.** Then smile like you know a secret. You're not waiting. You're *broadcasting*.

14. **Burn One Old Love Letter or Screenshot.** Let the past watch you set it on fire. Ritual matters.

15. **Every Time You Catch Yourself Wishing, Shift to Receiving.** Say: "It's already mine. I'm just meeting it on the way."

16. **Watch a Romantic Movie Without Bitterness.** Feel the love, not the lack. Let it warm your cells. That's prep, not pain. Of course, by now, you should know I am a Virgo and love lists, so here are my favorite romance movies for your viewing pleasure. These come from my amazing book *A Single Girl's Guide to Movies*. And, yes, I flipping love classic movies, Cary Grant is my favorite. https://yourdatingunexpert.com/dating-survival-bible-therapy#dating-survival-movie-canon

17. **Take One Photo a Week That Makes You Feel Chosen.** Not hot. Not liked. *Chosen.* The difference is everything.

If these micro-moves resonated with you, there's a deeper version waiting. **Love Is Already On Its Way** expands this section into a full, calming checklist you can return to anytime you feel stuck, restless, or tempted to chase what isn't aligned. It's designed to help you shift your energy without overthinking, emotional labor, or pressure, just quiet, confident preparation. Scan the QR code below to access the full checklist and keep this momentum going. No forcing. No spiraling. Just alignment.
https://www.etsy.com/listing/4430602671/love-is-already-on-its-way-micro

Secrets to Finding the One They've Kept Hidden

(Because "Just Keep Swiping" Was Never the Plan.)

Most dating advice is built for the surface world. Swipe harder. Fix your profile.

"Put yourself out there!"

Smile more. Settle faster. Stay busy. Stay available. None of it touches the truth. None of it unlocks the soul-level connection you're craving. Because the truth about finding "the One" is something they've buried. Hidden behind fear, consumerism, wounded masculine systems, and shallow timelines. But not today. Today you get the real codes.

1. You Don't Find "the One." You Collapse Time to Meet Them

You don't "search harder."

You don't "get luckier."

You don't "try more apps."

You meet them at the timeline where you are already her. The woman who stopped living halfway. The woman who stopped doubting her own glow. The woman who radiates certainty, not desperation.

2. You Are the Portal, Not the Passenger

You're the portal. You are the vibrational doorway through which the entire frequency of your next life flows in. And "the One?" He doesn't drag you across a finish line. He doesn't "save you." He's drawn through the portal you built when you healed, stood still, and remembered who you are. You magnetize him by becoming the energetic signature of the life you actually deserve not the one you were settling for.

3. You Cannot Find Them While Begging Half-Loves to Love You

There's no space for "the One" when you're renting out your soul for pennies.

- "Situationships" rob your signal.
- "Almosts" block your alignment.
- "Good on paper but no soul connection" drains your timeline.

You have to starve the old energy to feed the new. You have to clear the clutter. Close the door. And sit in the sacred silence, long enough for real love to find a wide-open path to you. Half-loves are the toll booth. You stop paying the toll, the road clears.

4. Your Soul Already Recognizes Them but Your Ego Might Block It

Finding "the One" isn't about rational boxes. It's about *resonance*. It's about *remembering*. You'll know them because:

- You feel peaceful, not panicked.
- Your heart expands, not contracts.
- Your intuition whispers "yes" without a presentation deck.

But if your ego is screaming: "He must look like THIS," or "It must happen exactly like THIS," you'll walk past the very person you've already met 1000 times in your dreams. Surrender the checklist. Follow the resonance.

5. True Love Is a Mirror and It Will Terrify Your Wounds Before It Heals You

Here's the part nobody tells you: **Meeting "the One" doesn't instantly feel like floating on a cloud.**

It often feels like:

- "Holy shit, can I actually receive this?"
- "Is this real or am I making it up?"
- "Am I allowed to be this happy?"

Because real love will:
- Terrify the part of you that thought you had to earn it.
- Trigger the part of you that still feels unworthy.
- Awaken the part of you that still fears abandonment.

And you will have to choose it. Again and again and again. Until choosing it feels safer than sabotaging it. The One isn't just your reward. He's your mirror. He's your reflection of everything you finally believed you deserved.

You will meet the One when you become the woman who no longer *questions if she deserves it*. And when you do? It won't feel frantic. It won't feel confusing. It won't feel like negotiating. It will feel like coming home to yourself through them. And there will be peace. Not because they gave it to you. But because you built it inside yourself first. And THAT is what they never wanted you to know.

Signs You're Actually Close to Meeting the One
(Not Just Manifesting Another Lesson)
(Because You Deserve to Know When It's the Real Deal,
Not Just Another Pop Quiz from the Universe.)

1. **You'd rather be alone than almost-loved.** *You're not lonely. You're elevated. There's a difference and you can FEEL it now.*
2. **You stopped begging the universe and started trusting it.** *No more frantic midnight affirmations. No more vision boards coated in desperation. You just KNOW.*
3. **Your life already feels full, even before anyone new enters.** *Love won't complete you. It'll enhance an already banging life you built yourself.*
4. **The old temptations stop tempting you.** *The two a.m. texts don't even phase you anymore. You don't crave half-effort crumbs when you're baking full loaves for yourself.*
5. **You've made peace with past relationships without needing an apology.** *Forgiveness became freedom. Bitterness burned off. Space has finally been cleared.*
6. **You're grounded in your standards but open in your heart.** *You're not rigid. You're radiant. Big difference.*
7. **You're no longer asking "What if they don't like me?" you're asking "Do I even like them?"** *Shift. Activated. Power. Unlocked.*
8. **You feel a strange, quiet excitement in your chest like you're standing at the edge of something beautiful.** *That's not imagination. That's alignment.*

Final Reminder: When you're close to finding the One, you stop chasing time, people, or validation. You anchor into your soul, you open your palms to the sky, and you whisper: "I trust you. I trust me. I trust love. And I'm ready whenever it's ready for me."

And the whole universe shifts to meet you there.

Energy Tricks

"You don't need to chase love.
You need to become the kind of vibration that makes it crawl to you like it's starving."
—Your Dating UnExpert

1. Cord Snapping Ritual (Break That Invisible Sh*t). Still dreaming about your ex? Still feeling him during sex with someone else? That's a cord. Take a salt bath. Say his full name. Visualize a thick energetic cord between your belly and his. Then? Slice it clean with your hand and say: "I call all my power back. I release all energy that is not mine." Then rinse under cold water. He'll feel it. You'll feel it more.

Energy Shift: Clear channel. No haunting frequencies. You're fresh, magnetic, unbound.

2. Aura Mirroring for Manipulation Detection. Wanna know who's fake? Mirror their body posture subtly and watch what happens. If their aura reacts with unease or shift, they're masking. If they lean in more? You've got trust.

Energy Shift: Aura mirroring triggers unconscious nervous system alignment. It's pure primal data.

3. Vaginal Memory Detox. Your yoni is a literal energy storage vault. Every man who's been inside you has left an energetic imprint. Want to cleanse it? Steam with herbs (mugwort, rosemary, rose), journal their names, and consciously say: "I release every energetic residue stored in my womb. This is my sanctuary. No old frequency may remain."

Energy Shift: You stop attracting similar men when your body stops broadcasting their residue.

4. Energetic Business Card Drop. Before a date or night out, stand tall and say: "May every soul aligned with my growth feel me walk in the room." Visualize gold energy beaming from your crown down to your feet. Then picture a thousand golden business cards flying off you into the air, each with your vibe encoded. You're not chasing. You're summoning.

Energy Shift: You pre-vibrate your presence into the space before you even arrive.

5. The 8-Second Eye Lock. Hold eye contact for eight full seconds, past the comfort zone. No smile. No talking. If they look away first, you're in control. If they lean in? They're hooked. If they smirk? They're cocky, test them.

Energy Shift: Eye contact is a psychic handshake. Eight seconds turns it into a soul scan.

6. The Timeline Command. Before bed, whisper: "I activate the highest possible timeline for love. May what is not aligned fall away with ease." Then surrender. This works faster than affirmations because you're not telling the universe *what* to bring. You're commanding the *version of you* who already has it to wake up.

Energy Shift: Timeline jumping + surrender = rapid results and peace.

7. Mirror Water Ritual. Get a small bowl of water. Stare into it like a mirror. See yourself how they would see you on your best day: mysterious, magnetic, untouchable. Whisper: "I am the fantasy they don't admit they crave." Then toss the water out your front door. Don't look back.

Energy Shift: Water amplifies intention. Mirror + emotion = broadcast.

8. Heart Lock Reset. Ever get a weird gut pull to someone who treats you like garbage? That's an energetic "lock" your heart's been hijacked. Write their name on paper. Burn it in a bowl with cloves and salt. Say: "This story ends now. I revoke consent." Flush the ashes. Cleanse the room. Go take a shower like a baptism.

Energy Shift: You just severed a soul contract. No contact required.

9. The Siren Walk. Before you enter a room, pause. Visualize your aura expanding five feet out: golden, fluid, slow. Now walk in like you're underwater. Head high. Shoulders back. Smile like you know something they never will. Say nothing first. Let the silence serve you.

Energy Shift: You're not chasing energy. You *are* the shift in energy.

10. Orgasm Manifestation (Properly Done). Most women waste their orgasm on men who don't deserve it or thoughts that don't serve them. Next time you're alone, think about the feeling of finally being met. Not a face. A frequency. Right at climax, say in your mind: "I receive. I'm ready. Bring him to me." Then sleep. Let it work while you rest.

Energy Shift: You collapse timelines through cellular surrender.

11. Dream Invasion Technique. Want someone to dream about you? Right before sleep, write their full name on paper. Whisper: "See me in the in-between." Put the paper under your pillow. Don't reach out to them for three days. Just let it bake. You'll know it worked when they watch your story or randomly check in. You entered the dream field.

Energy Shift: The subconscious is where real seduction begins.

12. Third Eye Triangle. Walk into a date or a room where you want to dominate the space. Don't look them directly in the eyes. Instead, hold your gaze on the spot between their brows. The third eye. They won't know why, but they'll feel *seen*. Then drop your gaze to their mouth. Pause. Then finally meet their eyes. You just psychically undressed them and made them wonder if you're real.

Energy Shift: That's not eye contact. That's hypnotic programming.

13. The Lip Bite Hex. Only do this once. When they say something *slightly* bold or flirty, hold eye contact and bite your bottom lip very slowly... then look away like it was nothing. You just dropped a memory they'll replay for the rest of the week. You gave them hunger, then took the meal away.

Energy Shift: One gesture. Infinite loops in their mind.

14. The "Who TF Is She?" Trick. Right before you post a selfie or walk into a place he'll be, sit down and whisper: "May everyone feel confused by my glow." Then visualize people seeing you and immediately second-guessing their life choices. Then walk in/post as if you've never known rejection.

Energy Shift: You're transmitting quantum-level disorientation. And he's not immune.

15. Soul-Tagging with Scent. Wear a very specific scent. One that isn't trending, isn't common, and that you only wear when you're in your power. Dab a little on the back of your neck and behind your knees (not just your wrists). Then walk by him. He'll smell it for weeks. Even in dreams. Even in other women. And he won't know why.

Energy Shift: You just installed yourself in his subconscious through scent memory. Welcome to psychic fragrance warfare.

16. Timeline Disruption through Style. Stop dressing how you think you're "supposed to." Dress like the woman he hasn't met yet, but won't forget. Disrupt his reality. Velvet in July. Leather in church. A red lip at Whole Foods. A silk dress barefoot. You want him to think, "Who *was* that?" not "She was cute."

Energy Shift: You rupture pattern recognition. Now you're imprinted.

17. Astral Withdrawal. If you've been *thinking* about him too much, stop. Not by force by detachment. Say: "I call back all fragments of my soul that have been leaking into others without consent." Visualize yourself zipping up your aura like armor. Go silent. You don't need to block him. You need to starve the tether.

Energy Shift: You become energetically unavailable... and that makes them panic.

18. Magnetic Field Amplifier. Before a first date, orgasm. But don't think about *him*. Think about how you want to feel around him: safe, powerful, desired, in control. Let that frequency *burn into your aura*. Then walk in like a goddess who's already satisfied.

Energy Shift: You radiate "I don't need you, but I *chose* to show up." That's irresistible.

19. Energetic Rebranding Ritual. Light a candle. Write a short sentence about how you *used to be in love*. Then cross it out and write how you love now: "I don't wait. I attract." Burn the paper. Say: "I am no longer that girl. She was the warm-up act." Then step into your f*cking life.

Energy Shift: You cut contracts with your old self. That's what opens the door. Let's burn the veil down, queen.

20. Quantum Mirror Leap. Stand in front of the mirror. Look dead into your own eyes. Say: "I no longer seek him. I *am* him." Not because you want to become masculine. But because when you become your own divine masculine, the match arrives. Then walk away like the timeline already shifted. Because it has.

Energy Shift: You stop vibrating in longing. You start vibrating in arrival.

21. Command from the Crown. Your crown chakra is a satellite dish. Most women don't use it. Before a date or night out, sit still. Say: "I call forth all soul matches who are ready for real love. Let my crown only open to the ones who see me." Touch the top of your head and pull energy upward. Then go out. Don't look for him. He'll feel you first.

Energy Shift: You're not calling in men. You're activating allies.

22. Glamour Layering. You're not dressing for the male gaze. You're dressing for the *energetic illusion*. Layer your outfit with intention:
- Undergarments = protection
- Skin = seduction
- Outerwear = mystery
- Scent = seal the spell
Walk into the room as a walking enchantment.
Energy Shift: You are no longer a body. You're a mirage with purpose.

23. Touch Deprivation Reversal. Miss him? Crave his touch? You don't need him back. You need touch frequency restored. Lie on your bed. Rub lotion over your entire body like he used to. But this time, say: "I'm the one who touches me now." Repeat until the craving fades. You don't need to break no-contact. You needed to *replace the signal*.

Energy Shift: You stop feeling abandoned. You feel whole again.

24. Energetic Fame Activation. Want to go viral? Want to become unforgettable? Say this before every post, photo, date, or appearance: "May my frequency be felt by those I've been sent to activate." You're not performing anymore. You're *broadcasting*. Walk like you're a prophecy. Post like you're code. Let them try to look away.

Energy Shift: You shift from content creator to transmitter of frequency.

25. The Full Shutdown. If you really want to reset your field, shut it all down. No texts. No social. No stories. No calls. No posting. Just disappear for 3–5 days while you fully recharge, grieve, recalibrate. When you return, do not explain. Do not overcompensate. Let the mystery speak for itself.

Energy Shift: You stop being predictable. You become myth.

Mindfulness Practices for Dating

Mindfulness isn't some woo-woo add-on to your dating life. It's the armor, the sword, and the intuition upgrade you need to not get dragged through emotional sewage disguised as "romance." If you want love, *real* love, you have to stay **awake** while the world tries to knock you unconscious.

Here's how:

1. Come Home to Your Body Before You Hand It to Anyone Else. Before the date. Before the kiss. Before the "wyd" text. Your body knows before your brain does. Tune in. Trust it.

2. Breathe Before You Text Back. One breath. That's all it takes to shift from desperation to dominion. You don't text from panic. You text from *power.*

3. Observe. Don't Absorb. Stay curious, not clingy. Watch their patterns, not their promises. The second you stop "hoping" and start *seeing*, you start choosing.

4. Anchor Into Reality. Not Potential. Potential is an IOU that may never cash. Reality is what's standing in front of you right now. If he's not showing up, he's not your future.

5. Let Silence Protect Your Peace. You don't need closure. You don't need answers. You need peace and peace answers everything.

6. Center Yourself After Every Encounter. You are your own home base. Not him. Not his goodnight texts. Not his Spotify playlists that he "made just for you." *Come back to yourself after every date. No exceptions.*

7. Set Intentions, Not Expectations. Intentions keep you grounded. Expectations set you up for spirals. Go into every connection knowing who *you* are and what *you* bring not betting on what they'll do.

8. Detach from Outcomes. Attach to Your Standards. You can want love *without* needing it from a specific person. You can show up open *without* selling yourself short. Standards don't bend because you're lonely. They bend because you forget you're the prize.

9. Notice When You're High Off Fantasy Instead of Facts. That's not a soulmate connection you're feeling after two dates. That's serotonin, attachment wounds, and childhood fairy tales doing a keg stand in your subconscious. Date with your heart open and your eyes even wider.

10. Hold Your Inner Child's Hand on Every Date. You're not just dating for the woman you are now. You're dating for the girl you used to be: the one who believed in magic, trust, and good endings. Protect her. Honor her. Don't hand her over to someone who doesn't deserve her.

The Mindful Dating Manifesto

I do not chase.

I attract but only what *matches my worth.*

I do not confuse butterflies with warnings.

I trust my body to tell me the truth before my mind makes excuses.

I am not desperate for connection.

I *am* the connection to my peace, my standards, my sacred fire.

I am not here to perform for love.

I am here to be seen, chosen, honored or not at all.

I do not bend my standards to fit into broken rooms.

I do not betray myself to win temporary affection.

I do not negotiate with red flags.

I do not wait for crumbs from anyone who would feast elsewhere.

I know that my energy is a *privilege,* not a consolation prize.

I know that my softness is sacred, not a weakness to be weaponized.

I know that walking away when I am not met is not loss, it is victory.

I let distance reveal the truth.

I am patient with love.

I am ruthless with disrespect.

I am kind to myself in every season.

I do not abandon myself for anyone.

Not this time.

Not ever again.

I am the love I have been waiting for.

Everything else is a bonus.

THIS is how you stay awake.

THIS is how you is how you stop abandoning yourself.

THIS is how you make them *remember who the f*ck they are.

Sacred Reminder: *"If I have to leave myself behind to keep you, you were never mine to begin with."*

Here are a few more **bonus options** depending on the energy you want:

     "My peace is not up for negotiation."

     "I will not beg for what I was born worthy of."

     "I trust what leaves. I honor what stays. I remain whole either way."

     "Love doesn't require self-abandonment. Chaos does."

MINDFUL DATING AFFIRMATIONS

(Say these until you don't just believe them, you become them.)

◆ "I trust my gut louder than I trust their words."

◆ "I choose peace over potential every single time."

◆ "If loving you costs me myself, the price is too high."

◆ "I release what confuses me. I welcome what calms me."

◆ "My worth isn't built in your hands. It's anchored in my soul."

◆ "I don't chase energy that has to be convinced to see me."

◆ "No response is a response. No effort is an answer."

◆ "I am allowed to leave any table where I am no longer fed."

◆ "The right love will not ask me to bleed to prove I am worthy."

◆ "I do not date to fill a void. I date to share an overflow."

◆ "I am not for the faint-hearted. I am for the fully awake."

Mic Drop Line (optional to close the page): *"I am the storm and the stillness. Whoever comes to me must know how to weather both."*

The Mindful Dating Ritual

(How to Protect Your Energy Before, During, and After Any Date)

Pre-Date Power Cleanse:

- **Ground Yourself:** Stand barefoot (or just close your eyes) for 30 seconds. Feel your energy sink into the earth. *You are rooted. You are safe. You are enough.*
- **Set Your Intentions:** Say this out loud (or in your head if you're in a rush):
  - *"I am open to connection, not confusion. I am here to observe, not absorb. I will not abandon myself, no matter how this goes."*
- **Seal Your Energy Field:** Visualize yourself wrapped in golden light. Nothing gets in unless you invite it. (Yes, this sounds a little witchy. It also works.)

During the Date:

- **Stay in Curiosity Mode:** Pretend you're a calm investigator gathering intel, *not* a Disney princess waiting to be chosen.
- **Check Your Body Signals:** Tension = pay attention. Ease = explore further. If you find yourself holding your breath, forcing smiles, or shrinking? *You're not imagining it. Get real.*

Post-Date Sacred Reset:

- **No Immediate Overthinking:** You are NOT allowed to mentally plan your wedding or your escape route in the first 30 minutes after a date. *You are allowed to just exist.*
- **Three-Question Reality Check:** Instead of spiraling, ask yourself:
  - How did I feel *in my body* around them?
  - Did I feel more *like myself* or less?
  - Did their energy expand me or drain me?

- **Release the Outcome:** Say this: *"If it's for me, it will stay. If it's not, it will leave. Either way, I am whole."* Then go live your badass life. The date is over. You are still everything.

Final Word: You don't need luck. You don't need signs. **You ARE the love. You ARE the storm.** Anyone meeting you on this journey is just a bonus. Never the source.

Mindful Date Power Checklist

(Did I stay rooted in my worth today? Check yourself before you wreck yourself.)

- ✓ **I checked in with my body before the date.** (Trust the whisper. It never lies.)
- ✓ **I set an intention not an expectation.** (Showed up open, not desperate.)
- ✓ **I stayed curious not attached.** (Observed without absorbing.)
- ✓ **I breathed before I reacted.** (Texts, looks, comments, nothing pulled me out of my center.)
- ✓ **I stayed rooted in my standards.** (No bending. No chasing.)
- ✓ **I didn't make it about me if things felt off.** (Their energy is their responsibility not my reflection.)
- ✓ **I returned to myself after the date.** (Reflected without spiraling.)

Closing Reminder: "The date didn't define me. It revealed me. And baby, I loved what I saw."

POST-DATE MANTRAS

(Repeat these in your head or out loud in the Uber ride home, like the boss you are.)

- ◆ "Their energy is information. Not a verdict on my worth."
- ◆ "If it's right, it won't feel like chasing."
- ◆ "Confusion is a no. Clarity is a yes."
- ◆ "I didn't come here to be chosen. I came here to choose."
- ◆ "No matter what happens next, I am already complete."

Mic-Drop Affirmation (optional to close this section): *"The date ended. My magic didn't."*

Emotional Intelligence & Inner Tools

The Emotional Risk Scale

Here's a savage truth no one talks about: Dating is a risk sport. Like skydiving, except no helmet, no parachute, and the "instructors" are mostly drunk, bitter, or lying about their height. You are *always* taking an emotional risk when you put yourself out there but not all risks are created equal. That's why you need an Emotional Risk Scale: your personal bullshit barometer to measure *what level of emotional investment* you're actually making before you start spiraling over some guy who said he "loves your vibe" after two tequila sodas.

Think of it like this:
Level 1 Risk: You matched on an app. You chatted a few times. You haven't even met yet.
Reality Check: You are investing *zero* real emotional energy. If he ghosts, it's not a betrayal, it's a *favor*.

Level 3 Risk: You've gone on a few dates. You like him, *but* you don't know his middle name, if he pays taxes, or if he has a mattress on a frame.
Reality Check: Curiosity is fine. Attachment is premature. Manage your expectations like a boss.

Level 5 Risk: You've been dating consistently. He's met your friends. You know his coffee order *and* his pet's name.
Reality Check: It's okay to feel hopeful, but stay anchored. You're still gathering *data*, not building castles in the sky.

Level 7 Risk: You're emotionally invested. You're talking about trips, future plans, and maybe even exclusive titles.
Reality Check: Now you're on the real playing field. Emotional investment = vulnerability. Keep your standards high and your eyes wide open.

Level 10 Risk: You're in a full-blown relationship. He's seen you ugly cry and you know his mom's drama.
Reality Check: You're allowed to love hard but you *still* don't abandon your self-worth at the door. Ever.

Why the Emotional Risk Scale Matters: Because *most dating pain* comes from misjudging the level of risk you're actually at. You treat a random Bumble match like he's your future husband? You're gonna bleed over a paper cut and call it surgery. You give your whole heart to someone still operating at Level 2 Energy? You're setting yourself up for emotional foreclosure.

Knowing your emotional risk level is self-protection not cynicism. It's about matching your investment to the reality in front of you, *not* the fantasy in your head. This is how you stay powerful. This is how you stay free. You're not closing yourself off to love, you're closing yourself off to delusion.

The Chemistry Check Quiz

(Part 1: The Prep → Section 2: Emotional Intelligence & Inner Tools)

Listen up: Chemistry is the biggest scam in dating if you don't know how to *check it* properly. It's how people end up "in love" with a dude who can't even text back sober. Real chemistry isn't just butterflies, adrenaline, and lust. That's hormones. That's your trauma bonds doing a sexy little cha-cha.

So, here's your **Chemistry Check Quiz:** Before you decide this person is your soulmate based on one great night out and a heavy make-out sesh in their car, ask yourself these five savage questions:

1. Do I actually feel *seen* by this person or just *wanted*?
- Lust makes you feel wanted.
- Love makes you feel *seen*.

(If you can't tell the difference yet, you're not ready to pick your life partner.)

2. Can I breathe around them, or am I performing for approval?
- Chemistry without peace is just anxiety dressed up in a crop top.
- If you're working overtime to seem "cool," "chill," "low-maintenance," or "hot enough" that's not chemistry. That's survival mode.

3. Do they *listen* when I talk, or do they just wait to talk about themselves?
- Connection is a two-way street.
- If you feel like you're being interviewed for the privilege of their time, **run**.

4. Is our physical chemistry rooted in actual connection or just horniness?
- Look, no judgment — *horny is human*.
- But building a relationship off the back of two tequila shots and a blackout is like building a house on quicksand. Good luck with that.

5. Does this energy feel *expansive* or *contracting*?
- Real chemistry makes you feel lighter, freer, more yourself.
- Trauma chemistry makes you feel addicted, anxious, desperate, and never "enough." **(Big difference.)**

Your Final Score:
- **Mostly YES answers** → You're probably vibing with someone real. Proceed with hope and standards intact.
- **Mostly NO answers** → Congratulations, babe. You just saved yourself six months of heartbreak and eating Nutella out of the jar at two a.m.

Bottom Line: You don't just want chemistry. You want *aligned chemistry*. The kind that doesn't burn you alive trying to keep the fire going. If it's real, it won't feel like a game. If it's real, you won't have to fight yourself to keep it. Chemistry that costs you your peace is just chaos with good lighting.

Recognizing Cognitive Biases in Dating

You're not crazy, you're human. And being human means your brain is full of glitches that mess with your ability to see people clearly. They're called cognitive biases and if you don't catch them fast, they will wreck your dating life harder than your ex did.

Dating isn't just about finding the right person. It's about fighting your own brain long enough to recognize who that person actually *is*. Here are the biggest biases that screw us over (and how to slap them back into place before they destroy your standards):

1. The Halo Effect
What it is: You notice *one* amazing thing about them: they're hot, they're charming, they volunteer at the animal shelter and now your brain paints the rest of them with the same golden brush.
Reality Check: Just because he looks good holding a puppy doesn't mean he's emotionally available, self-aware, or capable of healthy love. Hot + Kind Gesture ≠ Husband Material. Stay sharp.

2. Confirmation Bias
What it is: Once you decide you like someone, your brain only sees the evidence that supports it and conveniently ignores every red flag waving in your face like an Olympic ceremony.
Reality Check: If you have to keep "finding reasons" to justify their shitty behavior, you're not falling in love, you're falling into delusion.

3. Sunk Cost Fallacy
What it is: You've already put in time, energy, maybe even feelings, so even when it's clearly not working, you stay because you don't want to "waste" what you've invested.
Reality Check: Staying longer doesn't make it work. It just makes you lose even *more* time. Cut your losses like a boss. Walking away isn't failure, it's flexing.

4. Recency Bias
What it is: They just did something sweet, finally texted back, finally planned a real date, so you forget the previous five weeks of inconsistency and disappointment.
Reality Check: A recent good moment doesn't erase a bad pattern. Look at the *total trend*, not just the last text.

5. Scarcity Bias
What it is: You believe this person is "your last shot" that there's no one else out there who will vibe with you, get you, want you.
Reality Check: Scarcity is a LIE. There are *millions* of people you could connect with. A good partner isn't rare, your self-worth is just rare in a world that preys on insecurity.

Bottom Line: If you don't recognize your cognitive biases, you'll keep handing the crown to people who don't even deserve a plastic tiara. Your brain wants shortcuts. Your heart deserves better. Catch yourself. Check yourself. And if necessary? Wreck yourself *before* someone else does.

Mic Drop Line (optional for under the cheat sheet): *"If your brain's lying to you, it's your job to slap it with the truth."*

Dating and Body Language:
Understanding Non-Verbal Cues

(So, You Don't Get Played)

Words are cute. But energy doesn't lie. Body language doesn't lie. Vibes don't lie. A man can tell you he's into you all day but if his body is checked out, closed off, or showing hidden aggression? Believe the body over the words. Always. Learning how to read non-verbal cues isn't just a skill. It's survival. It's power. It's how you stop falling for men who sell fairy tales with their mouths while their bodies scream *disinterest, deception,* or *danger.* You can check out my body language game earlier in the book.

Here's what you need to watch and what it really means:

1. Eye Contact: Real Ones Lock In, Fakes Look Everywhere Else. If he's locked in on you with relaxed, easy eye contact? Good sign. If he's looking over your head, at his phone, or around the room every five seconds? He's shopping for better options.

2. Smiling: Watch for Real vs. Fake. A genuine smile reaches the eyes. Crinkles, warmth, ease. A fake smile is all mouth and dead fish eyes. (*You're not crazy. You're catching the glitch.*)

3. Facial Expressions: Micro-Reactions Expose Everything. Look for flashes of disgust, contempt, or boredom when you talk. (If he sneers even once? Believe it. That's the real him slipping out.)

4. Posture: Relaxed Interest vs. Defensive Withdrawal. Leaning slightly toward you? Good. Sitting rigid, arms crossed, leaning away? Closed off. Guarded. Defensive.

5. Gestures: Big, Open, Loose = Attraction. Tight, jerky, self-soothing gestures (rubbing neck, tapping feet, clenching fists)? He's either lying, uncomfortable, or wishing he was somewhere else.

6. Touch: Light, Respectful Touches Build Connection. Creepy Grabs Break It. If he's brushing your arm naturally? Green flag. If he's pawing at you aggressively? Red flag. Immediate disqualification.

7. Mirroring: If He's into You, He'll Start Copying You Without Realizing It. Same posture. Same tone. Same energy. Mirroring isn't a conscious move, it's instinctual when chemistry is real.

8. Proximity: Closer = Comfort. Distance = Disinterest. Is he finding reasons to sit close, lean in, walk alongside you? Good. Is he leaving three chairs between you at the bar? **Girl.**

9. Fidgeting: Some Nerves Are Cute. Some Are Red Alarms. A little nervous fidgeting? Human. Constant twitching, tapping, looking like he's about to bolt? Emotional unavailability loading...

10. Hands and Feet: They Point Where the Heart Wants to Go. Subconsciously, people's feet and hands face where they want to go. If his feet and body are always aimed toward you? Good. If they're aimed at the door? Even better for you to leave.

11. Head Tilts: The Subtle Sign He's Actually Engaged. Tilting the head slightly when you speak = curious, attentive, interested. No tilt = auto-pilot. (*Or calculating how fast he can ghost after dessert.*)

12. Sudden Energy Shifts: Your Cue to Check Out. If the vibe suddenly drops: he pulls back, gets colder, withdraws without explanation, don't explain it away. Notice it. Move accordingly.

13. Slow Blinking: Massive Clue He's Over It. Rapid blinking = excitement. Slow, heavy blinking while you talk = he's done. He's mentally planning his escape.

14. Gut Overrules All. If your gut says something feels "off" even if his mouth is saying all the right things? TRUST YOUR BODY FIRST. YOUR BODY KNOWS.

Body Language Survival Gut Check:
5 Brutal Questions to Spot the Truth Before You Fall

Because if you don't watch his body when your energy shifts, you might miss the biggest warning signs of your life.

1. How does he react when I lean back and slow down? *If he leans in harder to reconnect, good. If he retreats, checks his phone, or looks bored, he was only chasing the chase, not you.*

2. What happens when I break eye contact first? If he tries to pull you back with his eyes, he's locked in. If he immediately disengages, he was never that interested, he was just responding to being seen.

3. Does his energy stay consistent or does it spike and crash? *Steady attention = real interest. Spiky hot/cold = trauma bond energy. Run.*

4. When I assert a boundary, does his body stiffen, shift, or relax? *Respectful men soften when you show strength. Controllers get stiff, defensive, or withdraw when they realize they can't manipulate you.*

5. Does he *light up* around me or does he just seem to enjoy being admired? True chemistry makes *both* people light up. If he only glows when you're fawning over him and dims when you're centered on yourself: *girl, that's a narcissist snack, not a soulmate.*

Final Word: You're not just reading him. You're watching him react to YOU. That's the real test. Watch what happens when you pull back. Watch what happens when you shine brighter. Watch what happens when you stop performing. **Their body will answer before their mouth ever gets a chance to lie. Believe it.**

Power Prep Before a Date

First Date Power Moves

(Because you're not auditioning. You're evaluating.)

First dates aren't just "let's see if they like me."

First dates are combat missions where you gather intelligence, protect your kingdom, and keep your crown polished the entire time. No more hoping they pick you. No more losing yourself trying to impress them. You walk in knowing: they're lucky to even be sitting across from you.

Section 1: The Arrival Game

1. Arrive Five Minutes Late: Calm, Collected, Unbothered. Not rudely late. *Powerfully late.* You're on your time. They'll feel the difference the second you walk in. You're not waiting around for approval.

2. Own Your Entrance. Walk in like you already know everyone is watching you even if nobody is. Chin up. Shoulders back. Easy, slow steps. *Presence before words. Mystery before access.*

3. Never Wait Inside for Them. If you get there first, wait outside or at the bar not awkwardly sitting there looking nervous. You are not a sad puppy in a coffee shop. You are a limited-edition event.

MANTRA: *You're not arriving. You're entering.*

Section 2: Conversational Power Moves

4. Ask One Disruptive Question. Not "So what do you do?" like a LinkedIn zombie. Ask something raw, unexpected, playful. Examples:

- "What's something you're secretly proud of but never brag about?"
- "If we had to rob a bank tonight, what would your role be?"
- "What's one dream you haven't admitted out loud yet?"

Shake their brain. Watch how they respond.

5. Answer Deep but Not Full-Disclosure. You're real. You're honest. But you don't trauma-dump or overshare. You give them just *enough* to feel intrigued and save the soul-level stories for those who *earn* them.

6. Flip the Script. Evaluate Them. You're not there to "pass their test." You're running the interview. Subtle mindset switch = total power shift. Examples:

- Instead of "I hope he likes me," think: *"Is he aligned with the life I'm building?"*

Section 3: Energy Power Moves

7. Stay Relaxed, Not Rushed. No fidgeting. No chugging your drink. No laughing too hard at bad jokes. Slow movements. Calm energy. The more relaxed you are, the more they'll lean into *your* pace.

8. Own Your Yes and Your No. If you like something, say it. If you don't, *also* say it. No polite pretending. Realness is 10x sexier than bland agreeableness.

9. Micro-Flirt Without Over-giving. You don't need to be a giggling flirt machine. One glance. One slow smile. One subtle touch to the arm (if you *feel* it). Less is more. Mystery leaves them dying for more.

Section 4: Exit Strategy Power Moves

10. Leave First If You Feel the Vibe Is Off. You don't owe anyone your time because you "feel bad." If the energy isn't it, stand up, smile, say, *"Thank you for meeting. I'm going to head out."* Period. Zero drama. Ultimate flex.

11. End the Night Before It Gets Stale. Even if you're having fun, leave *a little early*. Cut the night at the *peak*, not after the energy fades. Leave them *wanting more*, not wishing they'd ended it an hour earlier.

12. No "Where This Is Going" Conversations. The first date is NOT the time to talk about exclusivity, marriage, babies, or TikTok-famous relationships. You are the moment. Not the mortgage planner. Let the mystery live another day.

13. Always have a soft exit plan ready. If the date tanks: "This has been interesting but I have an early morning. Thanks for meeting up." No drama. No excuses. Just sovereignty.

Section 5: Post-Date Power Moves

14. No Play-by-Play Recaps with Friends. Gushing for two hours over a first date binds you to a fantasy. One quick summary is fine. Then go live your life.

15. Don't Text First Unless You Damn Well Feel Like It. You *can* text if you want. You *don't have to* text to seem polite. Move how you feel not how you're trained to "be nice."

16. Recenter Yourself Before Deciding Anything. Whether it was electric or awkward, you recenter first. Journal. Meditate. Move. Get back to you before making it *about them.*

PSYCHOLOGICAL POWER MOVES

1. Show up with a full life already in motion. They should feel like they're lucky you carved out time not like you're available 24/7.

2. Subtly mirror their body language but only when you want to build quick comfort. Mirror = rapport. But *don't overdo it*! You're leading, not chasing.

3. Never immediately compliment their looks. If you compliment, make it about something *unique* they said or did. It tells them you see deeper, and it destabilizes their "I'm hot" autopilot.

4. Hold strategic silence after you answer a question. Silence forces them to lean in, reveal more, and chase the emotional space. Silence is control. Master it.

5. Be the first to introduce mystery. Drop a line like: "I'm not everyone's cup of tea. But I'm somebody's shot of whiskey." Watch them lean forward. Curiosity is power.

PHYSICAL PRESENCE MOVES

6. Control your blink rate and breathing pace. Slow blinks and deep breathing = extreme calm energy = *subliminal dominance.* High anxiety energy reads as low value. Calm = magnetism.

7. Take up more physical space confidently, not aggressively. Drape your arm lightly on the back of your chair. Cross one knee over the other. Subtle body expansion = unconscious "alpha" cue.

8. If you do a toast, *let them lean toward you*. Make them close the gap. Not you. You're the gravity in the room.

CONVERSATION DOMINANCE MOVES

9. Lead the frame early. Ex: *"I was actually excited for this. It's rare to meet someone who seems halfway interesting."*
--> playful, confident, you're setting the tone.

10. Make them laugh first, but not at yourself. Never self-deprecate on a first date. Laugh at life, not at yourself. Confidence over clowning.

11. Plant one offhand comment that implies future plans without being needy. Ex: *"You seem like the type who'd be down for an actual adventure. But we'll see if you survive tonight first."* --> sets a future anchor without pressure.

EMOTIONAL MASTERY MOVES

12. Don't trauma-bond on the first date. No sad backstories. No "my ex was the worst." You stay in the light. You leave your shadows sacred.

13. Laugh freely but don't emotionally invest yet. Fun = open heart. Attachment = closed eyes. There's a difference. Know it.

14. Accept compliments effortlessly. No blushing, no "omg stop," no deflecting. Say: *"Thank you."* Smile. Move on. Confidence. Locked.

15. Check in with YOURSELF during the date, not just with them. Mid-date, quietly ask: "How do I feel in my body right now? Expanding or shrinking?" Your body always knows before your brain rationalizes.

SAVAGE SECRET POWER MOVES (Most People Never Think Of)

19. Set one conversational boundary if needed instantly. Ex: *"I don't joke about that."* or *"Not my vibe."* One line. Instant boundary. Instant upgrade in their mind.

20. Let them initiate the next move. If they want a second date, let them *say it*. Let them *earn it*. The more they invest, the more attached they become.

21. Smile once you're leaving not just when you're arriving. It leaves a lasting final imprint of warmth + mystery. (Trust: *Last impressions beat first impressions.*)

Final Word: First dates aren't about "winning them over." First dates are about protecting your empire. You are the event. You are the prize. You are the *main character in the story they'll never forget whether you choose them or not.*

First Date Power Moves Manifesto

I do not shrink to fit the room. The room expands because I entered it.

I do not audition for affection. I observe who is worthy of my time.

I do not rush to impress. I let curiosity chase me.

I do not explain my standards. I embody them: effortlessly, unapologetically, completely.

I do not attach to potential. I anchor myself in reality and honor my intuition above all noise.

I am not here to beg for connection. I am connection.

I do not overstay my presence.

I leave them wondering not wondering why I stayed.

I walk into every first date as the event, the elevation, the storm, and the calm after.

I am the prize. I am the peace. I am the revolution.

Whoever sits across from me?

They're the ones getting evaluated.

And I do it all without rushing, without folding, without forgetting who the f*ck I am.

Dating Etiquette

(How to show up like someone who respects themselves, respects others, and isn't here to play small.)

Dating etiquette isn't about being rigid, fake, or stuck in some outdated gender role script. It's about showing up with energy that says: *I value your time, and mine.* It's how we build trust before a single word is spoken.

Yes, things have changed but good behavior, emotional awareness, and basic social grace will never go out of style. These aren't "rules." They're the *baseline* for anyone who wants to date with clarity, confidence, and connection.

1. Show Up on Time. Being late without a heads-up isn't quirky or mysterious, it's disrespectful. If you can't be on time, communicate it early and own it. Punctuality tells someone you value their energy before they even meet you. There is the five-minute rule. If he's late, fucking leave, he has intimacy issues.

2. Dress Like You Thought About It. You don't need to be red-carpet ready, but show up looking like you gave a damn. Wear something that makes *you* feel confident and present. Not for them. For the energy you're bringing into the space.

3. Smell Good, Be Clean, No Excuses. If you're going on a date and haven't handled your breath, your hygiene, or your basic grooming, don't go. Respect starts with how you show up physically. It's not superficial, it's sensory consideration.

4. Don't Be on Your Phone Like It's a Third Wheel. Unless you're a surgeon or on-call for the Pentagon, put your phone away. If you *must* check something, say so. Otherwise, give your date the same attention you'd want if you were speaking your truth.

5. Ask Real Questions and Actually Listen. This isn't an interview. This is about presence. Nod. React. Be curious. The goal isn't to impress, it's to connect. And nothing is sexier than someone who's *genuinely* paying attention.

6. Respect Boundaries Without Making It Awkward. Don't touch unless there's clear comfort. Don't fish for trauma. Don't make assumptions. If you're not sure what someone's comfortable with, ask. Consent is hot. Clarity is hotter.

7. Check Your Tone and Attitude. Sarcasm isn't a personality. Negging isn't flirting. And bitterness isn't edge, it's unresolved pain. Be kind. Be real. Be emotionally safe to sit across from.

8. Be Generous, Not Performative, When It Comes to the Check. Who pays? Whoever *offers* with clarity and good intent. That said—if you invited someone, you pay. If you're not sure, offer to split or say, "Can I get this one?" Don't turn generosity into a control move. It's a vibe check, not a transaction.

9. Know Basic Dining Behavior. You don't need to be royal but please:

- Don't talk with your mouth full
- Don't trash the staff
- Don't scroll the menu like it's your phone This isn't about being prim, it's about being present and gracious.

10. Follow Up Like an Adult. If you liked them, say so. If you didn't, say that too, but *kindly*. Ghosting isn't edgy. It's lazy. And the truth is: "Thanks for the date. I'm not feeling a strong romantic connection, but I really appreciated our time" is easy, respectful, and rare.

11. Don't Trauma-Dump to Bond. Honesty is great. Oversharing to create false intimacy is not. Build the foundation before you burn it. Let depth unfold instead of dropping your emotional résumé on date one.

12. Show Gratitude and Appreciation. Thank them for showing up. Compliment their energy, their vibe, their laugh. Even if you don't want to see them again, acknowledge the effort. We're all human. We all want to feel seen.

13. Be Yourself but Be Your *Intentional* Self. "Just be yourself" doesn't mean no self-awareness. Bring your truth, your weird, your authenticity but also bring your best energy. People don't fall for perfection. They fall for presence.

14. Don't Bring the Ghosts of Exes Past. Mentioning your ex once? Fine. Name-dropping them in every other story? Trauma talking. If you're not emotionally available, don't fake it. Your date deserves *presence*, not comparison.

15. Gauge Chemistry Without Forcing It. If it's not flowing, don't fake it. You're not there to impress your way into a second date, you're there to see if there's actual resonance. If there's a vibe, cool. If not, *cooler* to notice that and move on without pressure.

16. Read the Room. Match Their Energy Without Mimicking It. Are they shy? Give them warmth. Are they direct? Meet them there. But don't morph into who you think they want. Energy-matching is respectful. People-pleasing is self-abandonment.

17. Avoid Overscheduling a Marathon Date. You don't need eight hours and three locations to connect. Over-planning puts pressure on chemistry that might not be there. Start simple. Let it build naturally. Leave space to *want* more, not just survive the whole night.

18. Know When to End the Date Gracefully. Whether it's magical or a mismatch, how you leave matters. Don't linger in awkward energy. If it's great: "I've really enjoyed this. Let's do it again."

If it's not: "Thanks for meeting up. I appreciated your time."

Be kind. Be clear. Be done.

POST-DATE REFLECTION CHECKLIST
(Because how you feel after the date is just as important as how you felt during it.)

- Did I feel like I could be myself?
- Did I enjoy their company or just enjoy being wanted?
- Was there real conversation or just entertainment?
- Did they make me feel seen, safe, respected?
- Did I feel energized, neutral, or drained afterward?
- Would I want to spend time with them again if sex, status, or chemistry were off the table?
- Was I chasing their approval or assessing compatibility?

What Not to Do on a Date

(And How Not to Get a Second Date)

Look, I get it. The date's going well, the drinks are flowing, and suddenly you're spilling more than just your cocktail. But here's the deal: oversharing is the fastest way to tank something that had potential. Unless you're purposely trying to self-sabotage (been there, no judgment), these are the things that need to stay locked up on date one.

1. Your Body Count. Nope. Absolutely not. This is not the time, nor the place. The second you bring up how many people you've slept with, your date is going to picture it, *all of it*, and now they're distracted trying to decide if you're a prude or a walking STD. There is no winning with this question. It's either "too low" and they'll question your experience or "too high" and they'll question your judgment. Just keep it sexy and mysterious. Your number is nobody's business.

2. Your Baby Fever. Unless you already have kids and need to discuss logistics, do *not* launch into your egg countdown or how you're dying to name your daughter Luna. I don't care if your ovaries are practically screaming, *save it*. Talking about kids too early makes it seem like you're just looking for a donor with a pulse. It's not that you can't want a family just don't act like you've already picked out your future baby daddy while the appetizer's still on the table.

3. Your Salary or Stuff. Whether you make six figures or just bought a Birkin, zip it. Bragging about your income or flashing your wealth is tacky and honestly, dangerous. You don't know this person yet. And if they *are* a gold digger, congrats, you just made their night. Let them get to know your soul before you show them your assets.

4. Your Ex (in any capacity). No, no, and hell no. The moment you start talking about your ex, even if it's "just a funny story" you've opened the portal. Nothing screams "I'm not over it" louder than an ex-monologue on date one. Don't bash them. Don't praise them. Don't *mention* them. If they come up, keep it neutral and move on. This isn't a retrospective. It's a *new* date. Act like it.

5. Their Outfit (Unless It's a Compliment). I don't care if he's wearing square-toe shoes or if her makeup is giving '90s Myspace, shut your mouth. You're not on "What Not to Wear." Even a backhanded comment that sounds "playful" can come across as judgmental AF. First date rule: compliments only. Save the roast for the third date, minimum.

6. Your Mental Health Diagnoses. This one is delicate. We're all working on something. But don't trauma-dump your entire DSM-5 file before dessert. Let trust build before you drop the heavy stuff. Protect your story *and* your energy.

7. Your Stalking Habits. We've all done the deep dive: the IG scroll, the Venmo search, the LinkedIn sneak, and maybe even a little "Are We Dating the Same Guy." But don't *admit* it on the first date. Laughing about how you found their mom's Facebook before even meeting? You think it's cute. It's not.

8. Your Job Misery or Life Burnout. If all you do is complain about your boss, your coworkers, your commute, your family drama, *girl, are you okay?* You don't need to fake joy, but don't be a walking Yelp review of your own life.

9. Your Timeline for Marriage. You can want forever, but don't walk into the first date talking about venues, rings, and the name of your future dog together. That's not romantic, it's terrifying.

10. Bring the Vibe of a DMV Line. If you're cold, boring, monotone, or treating the date like a chore, *don't act surprised when they ghost you like it's their civic duty.* Energy matters. Bring some.

11. Order Like a Dictator, Tip Like a Criminal. Barking at the waiter and leaving $2 on a $68 check? Congrats, you've just given your date the ick and a dinner story they'll be telling for *years.*

12. Try to Win a Debate They Never Asked For. If you start arguing about politics, astrology, or whether pineapple belongs on pizza and act smug about it, you're not charming. You're exhausting. Not a vibe.

13. Act Like They Should Be Grateful to Be There. This one's for the delusional. If you spend the whole date hyping yourself up while ignoring their presence like you're interviewing fans, just date a mirror.

14. Flex in All the Wrong Ways. Talking about your crypto gains, your "network," or how many people DM you? It's not hot. It's giving *insecurity in designer shoes.*

15. Make It Weirdly Transactional. If you're keeping score, asking "Who's paying?" like it's a test, or acting like dinner = entitlement… congratulations, you're now the reason people write dating rants on Reddit.

16. Talk Like You Already Own Them. "You're the kind of guy I could hub." Girl, you just met. Keep it cute. You don't even know his middle name, or shouldn't at this point.

17. Drop the Ball on the Follow-Up. You had a great time. So you… vanish? No text, no call, no signal you're alive? People don't chase anymore. They delete.

18. Act Like You're Doing Them a Favor. You showed up, not descended from the heavens. Arrogance is not a flex, it's a repellant. Humility? Now *that's* hot.

19. Interrupt Like It's a Sport. You know what's sexier than talking? Listening. Let them finish a damn sentence without turning the date into your own monologue.

20. Try to Fast-Track the Intimacy. If you're pushing physical before there's emotional, don't be surprised when the vibe evaporates. Respect is never optional.

21. Treat Them Like a Placeholder. Asking "So what do you bring to the table?" like you're Shark Tank? You're not Mark Cuban. Relax.

22. Drop Your Standards on the Table. Listing your "non-negotiables" like you're reading from a manifesto? This isn't LinkedIn. Chill out.

23. Treat Their Vulnerability Like a Punchline. If they open up and you mock, belittle, or brush it off, you're not edgy. You're just an emotional liability.

24. Play the "I Don't Date Much" Game. If you use fake innocence as a cover for awkwardness, it's not endearing, it's confusing. Own your experience, whatever it is.

25. Get Passive-Aggressive About Rejection. If they're not into you, don't get salty. Don't neg them. Don't spiral. Just take the L with grace and move on.

26. Make Zero Eye Contact. If you're looking everywhere but at them, they're gonna assume you'd rather be *anywhere* else. Eye contact is intimacy 101.

Bottom line? If you made it to a first date, don't self-sabotage like it's your kink. The goal isn't to win. It's to connect. If you're playing games, being shady, or bringing zero effort, just admit you're not ready and stay on the sidelines until you are.

Don't Play Interviewer or Therapist

It's a date, not a job interview and you're not licensed.

There is a *very* fine line between being curious and being exhausting. And some of y'all are crossing it like you're prepping for a feature story in The New York Times. If your first date feels like an interrogation: "Where do you see yourself in five years?" "What's your attachment style?" "What's your biggest fear in relationships?" *congrats,* you've just turned a potential connection into a one-man TED Talk with zero romance.

You're allowed to ask questions. Obviously. That's how humans get to know each other. But questions should feel like a *conversation,* not a pop quiz with bonus trauma points. Same goes for trying to play therapist. If your date mentions something heavy, like a divorce, a loss, or a personal struggle, don't launch into "Well, what have you done to heal that?" You're not their healer, babe. You're someone they just met at an overpriced wine bar. Stay in your lane. This includes (but is not limited to):

- Saying "That sounds like unresolved trauma"
- Offering unsolicited advice or spiritual bypassing
- Turning every topic into a life lesson
- Acting like a walking Instagram meme account

Want to show you're thoughtful and emotionally intelligent? Listen. Be present. Ask a good follow-up. And know when to *not* make it deep. Flirting is not a diagnostic tool. Repeat after me: *You are not licensed. You are not certified. You are not Dr. Phil.* You're on a date. Act like it.

Don't Get Wasted

It's a first date, not your cousin's bachelorette party.

Listen, a drink or two to loosen up? Totally fair. Liquid courage is a real thing and sometimes necessary. But there's a very thin line between "fun and flirty" and "slurring your words while trauma-dumping in a bar bathroom."

There is nothing cute about losing your filter, oversharing every sad breakup story you've ever had, or aggressively flirting with the bartender mid-date. And no, being "a fun drunk" does *not* make it better. Red flags include:

- Talking way louder than you think you are
- Ordering a double before the server finishes asking what you want
- Turning every conversation into a sexual innuendo
- Crying, raging, or suddenly texting your ex mid-date (yes, it happens)

Why does it matter? Because alcohol blurs perception and when you're trying to get to know someone *clearly,* the last thing you need is tequila goggles telling you they're "actually kinda sweet." No. He's still a walking ick. You're just two martinis deep. Keep it classy, keep it conscious, and for the love of sobriety *pace yourself.*

Don't Pretend to Be Someone You're Not

Spoiler alert: they'll find out eventually and it won't be cute.

On a first date, the temptation to "brand" yourself is strong. You want to come across cool, interesting, sexy, funny, adventurous, down-to-earth, and also probably like you just casually fell into this outfit (that took you three hours to perfect).

But pretending to like football when you don't even know how many players are on the field? Saying you're "totally spontaneous" when you pre-schedule your bathroom breaks? Telling him you "love camping" when you can't sleep without silk pillowcases? Girl, *why?*

Every time you water down who you are just to seem more appealing, you're building a connection on fiction. And fiction never lasts.

Do *not*:

- Pretend you're busier than you are to seem in-demand
- Downplay your success to stroke their ego
- Act like you're emotionally detached when you're actually a raging romantic
- Say "I'm totally chill" when you know damn well you spiral if someone leaves you on read

This also goes for the "cool girl" act. The one where you laugh off things that bother you, avoid asking for clarity, and pretend to be unfazed because you don't want to scare them off. You know what's scarier? Waking up in a relationship where you can't even be yourself.

First dates are not auditions for who you *think* they want. They're filters to find someone who actually wants *you*. So be yourself: the messy, funny, layered, intuitive, imperfect, incredible version. The right one will vibe with it. The wrong one will bounce. And either way? You win.

Don't Come in Jaded or Guarded AF
If you've already decided dating sucks, it will.

We get it. You've been ghosted. Lovebombed. Gaslit. Watched situationships crash and burn faster than your last eyebrow wax. You've got receipts, trauma, stories, and a psychic that swore 2023 was your year. But here's the hard truth: *If you show up guarded, bitter, and convinced it's all doomed… you're setting the date on fire before it even begins.*

And that "IDGAF" energy? Not mysterious. Not sexy. Not powerful. It reads like someone who's been hurt so many times they can't tell the difference between intuition and fear anymore. You don't have to pretend you're perfect. You don't have to fake optimism if you've been through hell. But if the words "all men suck," "I hate dating," or "I'm probably wasting my time" come out of your mouth within the first ten minutes, congratulations, you've just put a brick wall between you and the one person trying to get to know you.

Here's what it looks like:
- Preemptively calling out red flags before they even show up
- Making sarcastic comments about how dating is a joke
- Mentioning that you're only here because your friend made you
- Acting disinterested as a form of protection

I'm not saying you have to be sunshine and butterflies. But if you're too guarded to even let someone *try,* then take a breath. Heal a little more. And come back when you can sit across from someone without making them pay for what the last idiot did. Because real connection can't grow in a space filled with barbed wire. You have to risk a little hope. And if that feels impossible, you might not be ready. And that's okay too.

Don't Jump Ahead 12 Steps
It's a first date, not your wedding Pinterest board.

Listen, it's one thing to know what you want. It's another to treat your date like they've already passed the background check, met your therapist, and are being groomed to be your life partner and we just sat down.

This includes:
- Talking about your wedding "vibe" (unless they ask, which they won't)
- Dropping "when we have kids" mid-sentence like you didn't rehearse it

114

- Making jokes about "our future" that don't sound like jokes
- Telling them your lease ends soon and casually floating cohabitation (ma'am...)
- Saving their name in your phone as "Husband Material" after date one

When you project a whole-ass future onto someone you just met, it's not manifesting. It's manic. And it's not fair to them *or* to you. First dates should feel like a spark, not a strategy session. There's no "timeline" if you haven't even built trust. And just because you're ready doesn't mean *they* are or that they should be. Let it breathe. Stay curious. And don't audition people for a role they haven't even said they want. That's not dating that's casting.

The UnExpert Blacklist: Dating Crimes That'll Get You Ghosted
Because sometimes it's not "the apps." Sometimes it's just... you.

Let's be real, first impressions matter. And while dating isn't about being perfect, it *is* about not making people regret shaving for you. Here's the UnExpert guide to what *not* to do unless you want to be a cautionary tale in someone's group chat.

1. Main Character Syndrome. If you dominate the convo like it's a TED Talk about *you*, congrats, you've just turned a date into an unsolicited podcast. Ask a damn question. Listen. Let them finish a sentence without hijacking it. We get it. You've got stories. But if you turn every topic into a monologue about your life, your accomplishments, or your opinions on polyamory... congrats, you're the walking definition of emotionally unavailable. Shut up and *listen*.

2. Rude Vibes Are Loud AF. Being short with the server, rolling your eyes, or acting like the world owes you something? Yikes. If you're rude to anyone on the date, you've just given a sneak peek of how you'll treat *them* later.

3. Buzzkill Topics Too Soon. Politics, religion, and your ex named Kyle who "still messages sometimes" maybe save that for, I don't know, *not* date one?

4. Negative Nancy with a Side of Complaints. The food sucks. Work sucks. Life sucks. Cool, but *why are you here?* No one's expecting toxic positivity, but if your vibe is "life is pain," don't be shocked when they peace out mid–Caesar salad.

5. The Creep Rush. Trying to escalate things way too fast? Read the room. If you're inching closer like a cartoon villain while she's subtly leaning away, stop. No one's here to be pressured into a plot twist.

6. Walking Apology. Confidence is sexy. Constantly putting yourself down is not vulnerability, it's emotional babysitting. Own your weird. Don't make your date talk you into liking yourself.

7. Fake It Till You... Get Blocked. Lying about your height, your age, your job, or your relationship status? You're not "manifesting" you're catfishing. Nothing kills a vibe faster than realizing you're dating a walking résumé lie.

Bonus "WTF Are You Doing?" First Date Don'ts:

Don't Trauma-Bond Over Shared Hatred. Bonding over hating dating apps, people from your hometown, or society as a whole? Yeah, it *feels* like connection… but it's trauma-fueled chaos. Find common ground in what you love, not just what you both hate.

Don't Flirt with Other People While You're on the Date. This includes the bartender, your server, or anyone else who looks vaguely attractive. You're not "just being friendly." You're giving emotionally unavailable with a side of red flag. Focus, babe.

Don't Overshare Your Digestive Issues, Your Ex's Kinks, or Your Weird Medical History. Some of y'all are out here talking about your IBS, toe fungus, or how your ex liked to be pegged within the first hour. NO. Just… NO. You can be vulnerable *without being repulsive.*

Don't Make It a Content Opportunity. If you start taking videos, snapping selfies, or filming your meal for TikTok, your date is not on a date, they're a background extra in your personal highlight reel. Unless they're filming with you, *put the damn phone away.*

Don't Try to "Fix" Them Already. You're not here to change their wardrobe, solve their anxiety, or tell them what kind of girl they should be dating (Spoiler: it's not you if you're already trying to fix them). This is a date, not a personal development seminar.

Digital Communication Etiquette
(The fine art of not looking unhinged on the internet)

You're Not Just a Vibe, You're a Brand

Every digital interaction is either building your value or draining it. I don't care how hot your profile pic is, if your messages scream "emotionally chaotic finger-vomiter," the only thing getting ghosted is your dignity.

Here's your new mantra: *My digital presence is an extension of my self-worth.* Now let's act like it.

When to Respond (And When to Go Outside Instead)
1. **Don't reward mediocrity.** If a man opens with "hey" and you reply with a paragraph, I want you to go outside, touch grass, and then write "I deserve better" on your mirror with lipstick.
2. **Response times are power moves.** Always mirror energy. He waits 10 hours? You wait 12. And no, you're not "playing games" you're signaling *you're busy and booked* (even if you're just binging true crime in sweatpants).
3. **Never text first if you're mad.** You're not here to emotionally self-harm via iMessage. Step away from the screen and call a friend, not the man who triggered you.

What to Say (and Not Say) If You Want to Keep Your Crown
- **Things to talk about early:** Fun plans. Petty gripes. Life ambitions. Sarcastic hot takes. Banter is foreplay.
- **Things to *never* talk about early:** Your trauma dump. Your ex. His ex. His childhood unless you're actually qualified in clinical psychology.
- **Don't perform pain to build intimacy.** He is not your journal. Save the vulnerability for when someone's actually earned a backstage pass to your soul.

How to Spot Trash Texts (And Burn the Bin)

Here's a short list of what to block without hesitation:
- "U up?" — Block.
- "I'm not really looking for anything serious rn" — Block and say thank you for pre-disqualifying yourself.
- "You're not like other girls." — Vomit, then block.
- Anything with the word "submissive" unless you're literally on a kink app.
- Lovebombing texts in the first week? BLOCK. (Then screenshot for your group chat.)

Reminder: You don't owe anyone closure, kindness, or a second chance to confuse you.

Power Moves in Digital Presentation
- **Your bio should filter, not attract.** This is not a job interview, it's a velvet rope. Write it like a bouncer who knows her worth.
- **Use real photos that say "main character," not "backup dancer."** Don't overfilter, and don't pretend you hike if you haven't seen the sun in three months. Be *you*, but like the version of you who got enough sleep and knows how to hold a boundary.

117

- **Don't overshare in text.** Save the chaos for your close friends' IG story. Maintain an air of mystique. If he knows your whole life before date one, you've already emotionally strip-teased.

How to Handle the Inevitable Fade

- **If he stops responding, he did you a favor.** Don't double text. Don't spiral. Don't send that "Just wondering if I said something wrong?" message. You're not a glitch. He just doesn't have the capacity to handle you.
- **Block if needed, mute if strategic.** If seeing him online makes you want to rip your face off, block him. If you're petty and thriving, mute him and let him wonder why you're glowing.

Bonus: The "Should I Reply?" Checklist

Ask yourself:

- Would a woman who knows she's the prize respond to this?
- Will I regret this message tomorrow?
- Am I feeling powerful, or am I emotionally spiraling with thumbs?

If it's not from your queen energy, delete and re-read this chapter.

The Three-Message Rule. You're allowed to send three messages max without a reply before you look unhinged. That's it. Three is your dignity limit. After that, you're not flirting, you're performing unpaid emotional labor.

> *"Hey...?"*
> *"Just checking in..."*
> *"Guess you're busy 😅"*

NO. Never again. Delete, regroup, block if necessary.

Don't FBI Yourself into a Fantasy. Stop stalking every girl who likes his post. Stop rewatching his story views. You're not a detective, you're a goddess. The second you start strategizing your self-worth based on his digital behavior, you've already lost the game. Unplug. Take a bath. Start a soft-block cleanse.

Your Phone Is Not Your Worth Mirror. If a man doesn't text you back, that's not a reflection of you. That's a reflection of *his bandwidth, his priorities,* and probably his attachment style he never healed from middle school. **Remember:** Absence of a response is still a response.

Don't Haunt Your Own Feed. If you have to keep checking your own stories to see if he viewed them, *archive it.* Posting things *for* him is energy leeching disguised as empowerment. We don't post to prove we're fine, we *be* fine. Post because you're glowing, not because you're baiting.

Dating App Swipes: Detox Rules

- **Set a timer.** You are not meant to scroll for two hours. Swipe like a sniper, not a zombie.
- **Don't use it when you're lonely, bored, or bleeding.** Hormones make everyone look like a husband.
- **If you wouldn't say "hi" in person, don't match.** You're not here for quantity, you're here for caliber.

Don't Leave a Paper Trail of Desperation. Delete old thirsty texts. Archive sad DM convos. Stop rereading what you *wish* it had turned into. You're not writing a novel, you're writing a new standard for your future. But I write the novels. I keep them, so you don't have to.

Golden Rule of Digital Communication: If it wouldn't feel good to re-read tomorrow, don't send it today.

Dating Survival Bible: Digital Communication Etiquette Checklist
(A.K.A. The "Stop Embarrassing Yourself" List)

✅ BEFORE YOU TEXT:
- Am I texting from confidence, or from a spiral?
- Am I matching his effort, or trying to force energy?
- Will I cringe tomorrow reading this?
- Is this text adding value or asking for validation?

✅ WHEN TO RESPOND:
- He gave effort, attention, and a full sentence? Sure.
- He sent "hey," "wyd," or any lowercase garbage? Ignore.
- He disappears and resurfaces? Respond only if you're bored **and** spiritually grounded.

✅ WHEN TO NOT ENGAGE:
- You're bored, anxious, or ovulating. Put the phone down.
- He's breadcrumbing with compliments but no plans.
- You're tempted to send a novel or voice note to "explain how you feel."

✅ PRESENTATION MATTERS:
- Is my bio filtering out trash or attracting it?
- Are my photos recent, real, and high-vibe?
- Would I date the person I appear to be online?

✅ BOUNDARIES & DETOX:
- Am I checking his story views more than twice a day?
- Am I using dating apps like a junkie or like a queen?
- Did I archive the convos that no longer serve me?
- Do I need a 7-day block cleanse to reset my energy?

Online Dating Safety

(Because he might not just ghost you, he might be married. Or fake. Or both.)

This chapter is not here to scare you. It's here to **awaken the badass investigator inside you** that's been screaming, "Something feels off," while your libido hit swipe right.

How to Spot a Fake Profile (Before You Catch a Scam or a STD)
The Signs:

1. **They want to move off-app immediately.** The "let's talk on WhatsApp" guy is 92% scammer, 8% married. The only thing you should be moving is your finger back to swipe left.
2. **Only one photo or all studio-level shots.** Unless he's a legit model (in which case he's DMing his agent, not you), this is fake energy.
3. **Weird grammar or robotic messages.** No one says "Hello dear, I'm looking for a serious woman to spoil with loyalty." Unless they're a catfishing bot or your mom's prayer circle friend pretending to be Idris Elba.
4. **Avoids answering questions directly.** You ask where he's from, he says "I've lived many places." Sir, this is not a riddle. It's a safety screening.
5. **Too hot to be true, and "working overseas."** If he says he's an oil rig engineer, army general, crypto trader in Dubai, or "self-made CEO in Belgium," run. Or better yet, reverse image search his lying face.

Reverse Image Search Like a Queen
- Screenshot his photo.
- Go to images.google.com
- Click the camera icon and upload the pic.
- If his face shows up in 12 LinkedIn profiles and a Russian modeling site, congrats, you just avoided becoming a Netflix documentary.

How to Handle Red Flags IRL
- **He gets defensive when you set boundaries?** Block, unmatch, and journal about your queen energy.
- **He talks down to you, touches without consent, or gives creepy vibes?** Leave. Loudly. You don't owe politeness to predators.

What Not to Share Until You're Sure
- Your last name
- Your exact home or work location
- Your daily routine
- Your travel plans
- Your financial info or career salary details
- Photos of your kids, home interior, or car license plate

The "Gut Check" Test

If your body feels tense, your gut is uneasy, and your brain is doing mental gymnastics to excuse his behavior, that's your nervous system saying RUN. You're not crazy. You're intuitive. *Listen.*

Bonus Section: Don't Be Embarrassed. Be Empowered

If you've been duped before, it doesn't mean you're dumb, it means you're human. Scammers are professional manipulators. And sometimes even the real ones turn out to be fake in other ways. The more we talk about it, the less power shame has.

Dating Survival Bible: First Date Safety Checklist

This isn't paranoia. This is strategy.

PREP BEFORE YOU GO

- **Run a basic vibe scan.** Have you Googled him? Cross-checked his name, job, and photos? If not, do it.
- **Screenshot his dating profile.** Save it in case he unmatches later.
- **Tell a trusted friend the details.** Who, where, when and send a screenshot.
- **Set a check-in timer.** Have someone text or call you during the date as a gut-check moment or exit plan.

LOGISTICS THAT PROTECT YOU

- **Meet in public.** No exceptions. Restaurants, coffee shops, bookstores. Not his house. Not yours.
- **Drive yourself.** Or rideshare solo. You need the power to leave.
- **Use your own phone for contact.** Don't give out your number if you're uncomfortable. Use the app's chat or a burner number (Google Voice is free).
- **Plan your exit before you get there.** Know how to bail, where to go, and who to call if things feel off.

IN-PERSON RED FLAGS TO WATCH FOR

- He changes the location last minute to somewhere private or sketchy.
- He pushes you to drink more than you want.
- He invades your personal space early and often.
- He gets weirdly irritated when you say "no" to anything.
- He pressures you to leave the public area or go to a second location.

If any of these show up, **leave. No guilt. No explanation needed.**

BOUNDARIES TO MAINTAIN

- Don't overshare personal details until you feel safe.
- Don't get drunk. One drink max until you've built trust.
- Don't go home with them, even if the date feels "amazing."
  Great manipulators often feel like soulmates. Wait and observe.

BACKUP MOVES

- Keep your phone charged and on loud.
- Have a safety code word with a friend. One word and they know to come get you or call for help.
- Carry pepper spray, a safety keychain, or whatever makes you feel powerful, not paranoid, *prepared.*

LAST RULE: Trust your gut, not the story you're trying to write. If you feel off, don't explain it, *act on it.*

Dealing with Rejection

*(Or: How to stop crying over clowns and
start walking like the main character you actually are.)*

Let's get one thing straight: rejection *hurts.* Even when you "weren't that into them." Even when you *knew* they weren't your match. It still sucks. Because it stirs up old stories. Old wounds. The teenage version of you who just wanted to be chosen.

But here's the truth they don't teach you: **Rejection isn't a loss. It's a damn filter.** It's life's way of saying: *Not him. Not now. Not at that level. Reroute, babe, we've got bigger plans.* So, grab your confidence. Pull your worth back off the floor. And read this when you're tempted to spiral over a man who couldn't even spell the word "emotional availability."

1. Feel the Hit. Then Stop Letting It Define You. Cry. Cuss. Journal. Punch a pillow if you have to. But *don't* turn this moment into a full-blown identity crisis. You didn't get rejected because you're unlovable. You got rejected because something misaligned and *that's data, not a death sentence.*

2. Do NOT Internalize Someone Else's Limitations. He said he "wasn't ready." Translation? He's not emotionally available and didn't want to admit it. That has *nothing* to do with how incredible you are. Never let someone's inability to choose you convince you you're unworthy of being chosen.

3. Block the Fantasy, Not the Person. The version of him you built in your head after three good dates and an unexpected forehead kiss. That's what's got you spiraling. So cut the daydream off where it started and get real.

4. Get Petty... Productively. Let yourself be dramatic for 24 hours max:
- "I hope he marries someone who talks during movies."
- "I hope he gets ghosted by his therapist."

Then snap out of it and go upgrade your life so hard it makes his rejection look like a *favor.*

5. Turn the Mirror Around. Instead of obsessing over what you could've done differently, ask: "Was I ignoring red flags to chase the high?" Half the time we're not heartbroken, we're just embarrassed we settled *again.*

6. Zoom the Hell Out. One person not choosing you doesn't mean "no one will." It means *he won't.* And that's great news because your person? Doesn't fumble you. Doesn't fear depth. Doesn't disappear when things get real. He leans in. And you weren't going to meet him if you kept playing small for this one.

7. Protect Your Energy Like It's Gold. Because It Is. Rejection hurts more when you're already low on energy. So go refill:
- Move your body.
- Text your savage group chat.
- Eat something nourishing.

Do not let the loss of one man deplete *every version of your power.*

8. Say Thank You (Even If You Still Want to Key His Car). Say it out loud if you have to:

- "Thank you for not wasting more of my time."
- "Thank you for showing me what I *won't* accept again."
- "Thank you for leaving so the real one can find me."

Gratitude doesn't mean approval. It means you're ready to *elevate*.

9. Write a "She's Gonna Be Fine" List. List everything you're proud of. Everything you're healing. Everything you bring to the table that has *nothing* to do with who's sitting across from it. Remind yourself: *You were whole before he got here. You'll be legendary after he leaves.*

10. Let Rejection Build Your Boundaries, Not Your Walls. Use this moment to get *clearer*, not colder. Ask:

- What signs did I ignore?
- Where did I abandon myself to stay in this?
- What would I do differently next time?

That's called evolution, babe. Don't close your heart, *sharpen it.*

Final word: Rejection isn't the universe punishing you. It's the universe *redirecting you toward your standard.* And you're not here to grovel for breadcrumbs. You're here to create a love that's as deep, steady, and radiant as you are. Take the L. Fix your crown. And walk away like a woman who finally realized: **He didn't reject you. He released you.**

BAD BITCH JOURNAL PROMPTS
FOR REJECTION RECOVERY

(So you never again confuse being dismissed with being undeserving.)

Write these in all caps if you need to. Write them in lipstick. Write them on the back of his excuses. But *don't stop writing until you feel like you again.*

1. What did I make his rejection *mean* about me and what's the truth that actually lives beneath that story? Write both. Burn the first one. Keep the second on your mirror.

2. Where in my life have I abandoned myself just to keep someone else comfortable? Now ask: what would it look like if I never did that again?

3. What are three things I bring to a relationship that are so rare, they should be considered sacred? And if you say "loyalty," you better follow it with *"to the right people, from now on."*

4. What version of me am I being invited to step into now that this man is no longer in my life? This isn't about who he didn't want. This is about who *you're about to become.*

5. What part of me is still asking to be chosen and how can I choose her myself, fully, today? Write the love letter to *her*. Not him. Not the fantasy. Just the version of you that still needs your own damn devotion.

6. If I never saw his face again, what would I do with all the energy I wasted wondering what I did wrong? That's your next chapter. That's your power source. Go build the life he was never built to hold.

7. What is the standard now? Post-rejection. Post-realization. Post-breakdown. Write the new rulebook. Minimum requirements. Red flag detectors. Emotional safety musts. Write it like a contract with yourself.

8. Who am I when I'm not waiting to be validated? Who am I when I'm fully in my worth? Describe *her*. She's not gone. She's just buried under someone else's silence.

9. What would I tell my best friend if she was blaming herself for being rejected by someone clearly not built for her capacity? Now go say it to yourself louder.

10. How would my life change if I believed I was the f*cking prize every single day? Write the answer. Then start living it.

Final prompt (pin this one forever): What does it mean to be unf*ckwithable when it comes to love? Define it. Become it. Repeat it until your soul memorizes it.

Dating as an Introvert

(Because small talk is your nightmare,
and pretending to enjoy loud group dates is officially off the table.)

Introverts don't date like everyone else. You're not here to "just put yourself out there" and have a million meaningless conversations. You're here for *depth*. For *presence*. For something that doesn't drain the life out of you just to say you're trying. This chapter is your permission slip to stop performing like an extrovert and start dating in a way that *actually works for your nervous system*. You don't need to be louder to be loveable. You just need to be *you*, without apology.

1. Be Unapologetically Selective. You're not picky. You're *efficient*. You don't need 30 dates. You need *one aligned connection*. Own that. Your energy is sacred. Stop wasting it trying to "give everyone a chance" when your intuition already said no.

2. Lead With What You Actually Love. Skip the generic "so what do you do?" icebreakers. Start with what lights you up. Whether it's books, plants, gaming, documentaries, or dog memes. Talk about what matters to you. That's how you attract *your people*.

3. Pick Date Settings That Feel Safe, Not Draining. You don't have to agree to a crowded bar just because they suggested it. Meet for a walk, a quiet coffee, or something low-pressure. Your environment matters, set yourself up to *thrive*, not survive.

4. Use Dating Apps That Don't Exhaust You. Swipe culture is not built for depth. Choose platforms that prioritize real profiles, real prompts, and people looking for connection, not chaos. And take breaks when it starts feeling like a chore.

5. Protect Your Recharge Time Like It's Sacred. Introverts need alone time like oxygen. Block out post-date recovery time on your calendar *in advance*. Rest is not optional. It's your reset button.

6. Ask the Questions That Actually Matter. You hate small talk anyway so go deep, early. Try:
*   "What's something that's shaped how you love?"
*   "What does emotional safety look like to you?"
Lead with curiosity, not performance.

7. Be Honest About Your Bandwidth. You don't have to explain why you need a night in. You just have to say: "I recharge best with some solo time. I'll text you tomorrow, but I need to decompress tonight." If they don't respect that, they're not your person.

8. Practice Soft Boundaries, Not Walls. You don't need to overshare to prove you're emotionally available but you do need to let people in slowly. Let them earn the deeper layers. That's not withholding, that's wisdom.

9. Take the Pressure Off "Chemistry" on the First Date. You probably won't be at your most charming right away and that's okay. Introverts warm up with trust. Don't write someone off just because sparks didn't fly instantly. Let it *build.*

10. Say No to Plans Without the Guilt Spiral. You're allowed to cancel, decline, or reschedule. Your job isn't to manage other people's disappointment, it's to protect your own energy. If the vibe feels off, trust that and stay home.

11. Treat Social Events Like Missions, Not Marathons. Show up, engage with intention, then *bounce when your social battery hits red.* You're not failing. You're navigating like someone who *knows themselves.* That's power.

12. Have a Dating Support Buddy. Find that one friend who gets your introvert soul. Vent to them. Debrief after dates. Ask them to hype you up when you need to be social. Introverts aren't antisocial, we just need our *safe people.*

13. Be Patient with Your Process. You're not behind. You're just intentional. Don't let extroverted timelines rush you. When you date from *alignment* instead of urgency, the connection lasts longer and feels way better.

14. Take Breaks Without Quitting. Dating doesn't have to be constant. Let yourself take intentional pauses. Clean out the apps. Reconnect to yourself. Come back when it feels like curiosity not obligation.

15. Own That You're a F*cking Catch. Quiet Doesn't Mean Less. Stop thinking you need to be "more outgoing" to be attractive. Some of the deepest, most magnetic people on the planet are introverts. Your presence is powerful. Your mind is electric. Your quiet is not a flaw, it's your *filter.*

INTROVERT POWER AFFIRMATIONS

(Repeat these until you never apologize for your quiet strength again.)

1. "My quiet is magnetic. I draw people who value depth and genuine connection."
2. "I honor my need for solitude; it's where my power recharges and clarity returns."
3. "My introversion is not a flaw, it's my built-in filter for authentic relationships."
4. "I am allowed to protect my energy unapologetically. My social battery is sacred."
5. "I choose to date from alignment, not urgency. I trust my timing and my process."
6. "My voice matters, even when it's quiet. My presence is felt, even in stillness."
7. "I am not responsible for other people's comfort when I assert my boundaries."
8. "The right people make me feel safe, not drained. I accept nothing less."
9. "I am deeply worthy of love that respects my rhythm and honors my pace."
10. "I never have to change who I am to attract the love I desire. My authenticity is enough."

REFLECTION PROMPTS FOR INTROVERTED DATERS

(Because dating doesn't have to drain you, it can actually deepen you.)

Grab your journal, get comfy, and answer honestly. This is how you recalibrate, recharge, and reclaim dating as a powerful experience for your introverted soul.

1. **When do I feel most comfortable and myself on dates?** *What settings, people, or conversations let me drop the mask and just breathe?*

2. **What boundary do I often ignore just to avoid appearing difficult or withdrawn?** *And how would my dating life change if I protected that boundary fiercely?*

3. **How would it feel if I never again apologized for needing alone time or quiet space?** *What would change in my confidence, my energy, and my relationships?*

4. **Who am I when I'm fully honoring my introversion in dating?** *Describe this unapologetic, confident, at-peace version of yourself.*

5. **What kind of relationship or partner would allow my introverted qualities to shine, not shrink?** *Be specific: what traits, habits, or approaches would honor me deeply?*

6. **What stories have I told myself about needing to be "more extroverted" to be desirable?** *And what's the deeper truth beneath that lie?*

7. **When have I ignored my intuition or energy signals and forced myself into dating situations?** *What was my body trying to tell me? How can I honor that in the future?*

8. **How do I feel after a genuinely aligned date versus a forced, draining one?** *Describe the difference clearly, let this guide future choices.*

9. **What small actions can I take to ensure my dating process feels aligned, sustainable, and emotionally healthy?** *Scheduling alone time after dates? Saying no more often? Choosing specific date types?*

10. **What permission slip do I need to write myself right now, as an introverted dater?** *Literally write it down. Pin it to your mirror.*

DATING AS AN EXTROVERT

(Because your social battery never dies, and you're here to date in full technicolor.)

As an extrovert, you move through life at a different frequency. You live for connection, thrive on energy, and show up bigger, louder, and more confidently than most. Your social vibe is your superpower, but it can also bulldoze someone if you're not careful. This guide is your emotional permission slip to shine your light without blinding your dates, attract aligned energy without sacrificing your own, and enjoy dating as the bold, badass, lovable extrovert you are.

1. Lean into Your Social Superpower. Your confidence is electric. Use it. Approach first, ask questions, and charm effortlessly. People adore your boldness. Own it and never shrink to make someone else comfortable.

2. But, Seriously, Listen More Than You Talk. I know you love telling stories. Just remember, the sexiest thing an extrovert can do is pause, listen deeply, and genuinely take in someone else's energy. Connection deepens in those quiet moments.

3. Plan Dates That Match Your Spark. Ditch boring dinners and go for interactive dates: concerts, dancing, art classes, trivia nights, or spontaneous road trips. Life is too short for dull, awkward small talk. Your extroverted soul deserves excitement.

4. Balance Your Group Energy with One-on-One Intimacy. Yes, you love your crew, your network, your party squad, but build in meaningful solo time. Deep bonds happen privately; intimacy grows quietly. Make sure your partner feels special, not lost in your social whirlwind.

5. Respect Introverts (Without Feeling Stifled). You're an extrovert dating an introvert? Great. Give them room to breathe. Invite without pressure, and respect their downtime. Quiet people have rich inner worlds, don't miss out because you're busy dominating conversations.

6. Never Apologize for Your Enthusiasm. Stop saying sorry for being "too much." Your passion, your humor, your storytelling? That's your magic. The right person isn't overwhelmed by your presence. They're energized by it.

7. Match Their Pace, Don't Drag Them Along. If you're dating someone quieter, match their emotional tempo. Draw them out gently. Let them ease into your world at their own speed. Don't force them into your spotlight before they're ready.

8. Handle Rejection Like a Boss. Yes, you put yourself out there more than most, which means more potential "no's." So what? Your confidence is your armor. Rejection is just life's way of clearing out the wrong matches faster.

9. Expand and Blend Your Circles. Introduce your date to your social crew, and get to know theirs. Shared friendships amplify your connections. Just make sure your partner feels included, not overshadowed, when entering your extroverted universe.

10. Practice Social Awareness and Emotional Intelligence. Your personality can fill a stadium. But always read the room. Know when to shine and when to soften. Emotional intelligence makes extroverts unstoppable not just entertaining.

11. Champion Their Quieter Dreams. Your introverted partner loves solitude or quieter passions? Celebrate that. Show up for their interests the way you want them to show up for yours. Your enthusiasm, when aimed at them, makes your partner feel deeply seen and appreciated.

12. Avoid Oversharing for False Intimacy. Extroverts sometimes mistake openness for instant closeness. Vulnerability should grow naturally, not spill out like confetti. Share yourself authentically, yes, but let intimacy unfold slowly, intentionally.

13. Protect Your Energy. Even Extroverts Need Recharge. You run on high octane, but burnout is real. Schedule occasional downtime to avoid emotional crashes. Extroverts recharge through meaningful connection, but make sure you rest before you burn out.

14. Let Your Heart Be as Bold as Your Personality. Express your feelings openly. Say "I'm into you," "I want to see you again," or "This matters to me." Your willingness to be emotionally clear gives others permission to drop their guard too.

15. Remember: You're the Party Not the Performer. Your extroverted charm is intoxicating, but you don't always have to entertain. True love means someone sees you behind the charisma, your quieter, deeper layers. Let yourself be fully known not just loudly loved.

Final mic-drop moment: You don't need to tone yourself down. You just need someone who can match your energy or quietly anchor it. Either way, your full-force extroverted magic deserves to be celebrated, never censored.

EXTROVERT POWER AFFIRMATIONS

(Because your boldness deserves to be celebrated, never dimmed.)

1. "My energy is magnetic. I effortlessly attract people who match my enthusiasm and joy."
2. "I never apologize for showing up fully. My personality is my power, and my boldness is beautiful."
3. "I honor my own pace, boundaries, and energy. I thrive socially but protect my inner peace fiercely."
4. "Rejection doesn't define me, it redirects me to people who can handle and honor my brilliance."
5. "I create connections easily, deeply, and authentically. My warmth and openness is a gift."
6. "I deserve love that celebrates my enthusiasm and matches my level of emotional generosity."
7. "My voice is powerful, my presence unforgettable. I never shrink to make others more comfortable."
8. "I effortlessly balance social vibrancy with emotional depth. My relationships flourish because of it."
9. "I attract relationships that value authenticity over performance. I am loved exactly as I am."
10. "I'm worthy of a love as bold, expressive, and passionate as my heart naturally is."

REFLECTION PROMPTS FOR EXTROVERTED DATERS

(To keep your heart open, your energy clear, and your connections meaningful.)

1. **When do I feel most energized and authentic on dates?** *What situations or people amplify my natural spark without draining me?*
2. **What's one way I tend to overwhelm quieter partners unintentionally?** *How can I soften my approach without silencing my spirit?*
3. **What boundaries can I set to better protect my energy even as someone who loves to connect?** *Identify clear practices to recharge and reset.*
4. **What does genuine intimacy look like for me beyond my outgoing personality?** *Who sees beneath my charisma, and how do I know?*
5. **What part of me have I learned to censor or shrink to appear less "intense" or "too much?"** *What permission do I need to fully reclaim that part of myself?*

6. **How do I handle rejection or disappointment differently because of my outgoing nature?** *How can I better manage those feelings without dimming my light?*

7. **In what ways does being an extrovert shape my ideal vision for relationships and love?** *Clearly define the kind of love that matches your big energy.*

8. **How can I make space for my partner's quiet needs while still honoring my own social energy?** *Identify specific strategies to create balance.*

9. **What does emotional safety look like to me as an extrovert?** *Describe what makes you feel truly safe to show your full, unfiltered self.*

10. **How can I recognize a healthy partner who appreciates my extroverted qualities instead of trying to contain them?** *Define clear signals that someone genuinely celebrates you.*

The Role of Physical Attraction

Let's get brutally honest: *Physical attraction matters.* It's the spark that makes you *want* to swipe right, walk over, or double text. But it's also a double-edged sword that can slice you open if you're not careful. Here's the truth no one wants to say out loud:

1. Physical Attraction Is the Gatekeeper Not the Full Experience. Looks might get someone in the door. Character is what keeps them in the damn building.

2. Hot Doesn't Equal Healthy. Being physically gorgeous doesn't guarantee someone is emotionally available, kind, funny, or even remotely interesting. (*Some of the hottest guys are wallpaper with abs.*)

3. Chemistry Is More Than Looks. You can think someone is physically beautiful and still feel absolutely nothing when you're in a room together. Energy >>> aesthetics.

4. Looks Fade. Energy Lingers. No one's six-pack or jawline is going to save a relationship where the conversation is dead and the respect is nonexistent.

5. Your Preferences Might Be Programmed. A lot of what we call "my type" is just social conditioning. Dig deeper. Are you attracted to him or to how you think being with him would *look*?

6. Balance Is the Goal, Not Settling. You deserve both attraction *and* emotional connection. Don't date someone you're not drawn to. But don't worship a hot face while ignoring your own misery, either.

7. Emotional Intimacy Changes Physical Attraction. Someone you didn't feel fireworks for at first can become jaw-droppingly sexy once you see their heart. Give connections a chance to build.

8. Lust Can Be a Liar. That overwhelming physical chemistry? Sometimes it's not love. Sometimes it's your unhealed wounds trying to reenact an old story.

9. Insecurity Can Warp Attraction. Sometimes we only chase people who feel unattainable because we're trying to prove something to ourselves. (*Validation is not love.*)

10. Boring Is the Enemy of Beauty. You can only stare at abs for so long before you realize you're talking to a human white noise machine. If there's no *spark of mind or soul*, it will eventually feel hollow.

11. You're Allowed to Want to Rip Their Clothes Off. Let's be real: you should *want* your partner. Settling for "nice" but no spark is cruel to both of you. Chemistry matters just don't let it blind you.

12. Stop Grading People Like Produce. He's not "an 8." She's not "a six with a good personality." People aren't produce. They are layered, dynamic, and far more complicated than some made-up hotness scale.

13. Real Hotness Is How They Make You Feel. The most magnetic, heart-melting, panty-dropping kind of attraction? It's not just how they look. It's how seen, safe, challenged, and alive you feel when you're with them.

Bottom Line: Physical attraction is important. But without real connection, it's like building a house out of matchsticks, beautiful for a second. Burned down in a heartbeat. Seek the fire that keeps burning long after the first glance fades. Seek the soul beneath the skin. Balance, my friends. Always balance.

Physical Attraction Reality Check:
Are You Choosing with Eyes *and* Soul?

Before you chase the next six-foot-tall heartbreak in sneakers, stop and ask yourself these five questions:

1. Am I attracted to their *energy* or just their face? *Because one gets hotter over time. The other fades fast.*

2. Would I still want them if they lost their looks tomorrow? *Be honest. If the answer is no, you're chasing a fantasy, not a future.*

3. Does our chemistry feel energizing or just addictive? *Healthy attraction fuels you. Trauma bonding exhausts you.*

4. Am I proud of how I feel about myself around them? *Attraction that kills your confidence is not attraction, it's your body warning you to run.*

5. If no one else could see who I'm dating, would I still be excited about them? *If the flex disappears when the audience disappears, it's not real.*

Mislabeling the Moment:
Friend Zone, Gender Codes & What They *Really* Mean

Friend Zone Recovery
(How to Spot It, Handle It, and Not Hate Yourself)

Let me tell you a little story. My girlfriend started dating this guy who was, how do I say this nicely,
100 pounds overweight and living half the year in a different state. (**Fun fact:** For every 40 pounds a man is overweight, he loses about an inch off his penis. Don't get mad at me. That's straight science from my book, *A Single Girl's Guide to Hilarious Facts About Sex You Never Knew.* You're welcome.)

Anyway, she tried. She genuinely had fun with him. But the sexual attraction? Nonexistent. She didn't even need to say it out loud. He could feel it. And because men are predictable as hell, he friend-zoned *her* first just to save himself from the inevitable blow to his ego when she didn't want to sleep with him.

The moral of the story: Friend-zoning isn't always about rejection. Sometimes it's about energy. The unspoken vibe that one or both people can smell from a mile away. And sometimes? It's a mercy killing. For everybody involved.

Here's the savage truth about the Friend Zone and how to survive it with your dignity intact:

1. Don't Make It Weird or You're Proving Them Right. If you turn passive-aggressive, bitter, or "we can never speak again" dramatic, congratulations, you just confirmed why it wasn't a match.

2. Know That Chemistry Isn't Charity. Attraction isn't earned. It's either there or it isn't. (You don't want to be someone's charity project anyway.)

3. If It Hurts Too Much, Walk Away with Your Crown On. No, you're not "weak" for needing space. You're wise. **Your heart isn't a clearance rack item.**

4. Don't Try to "Prove" Your Worthiness After the Fact. If you suddenly start trying to glow up harder, post thirst traps, or become everything they ever said they wanted, **stop.** You're not an unpaid contestant on *The Bachelor.*

5. Sometimes You Friend-Zone Yourself Without Even Knowing It. Energy doesn't lie. If you're treating it like a friendship, being ultra-available, never flirting, never creating tension sometimes you friend-zoned yourself before they ever opened their mouth.

6. Use It as a Flex for Your Growth Game. Being friend-zoned builds emotional resilience. You learn to survive disappointment without shattering your self-worth. You level up.

Friend Zone Survival Gut Check: 5 Brutal Questions to Keep Your Dignity Intact

Because your heart deserves better than hanging around hoping they change their mind.

1. Am I feeling genuinely valued or low-key tolerated? *If it feels like they're "keeping you around" out of politeness, not passion, you already have your answer.*

2. If they called me right now for a "talk about their love life," would I feel honored or low-key humiliated? *If you're their free therapist while they date other people, girl move with dignity, not delusion.*

3. Am I secretly hoping one grand gesture will "make them see me differently?" *Spoiler: It won't. And you shouldn't have to beg to be chosen anyway.*

4. Have they made it 100% clear where I stand but I'm still mentally writing fan fiction? *If you're inventing a fantasy version of them where they "come to their senses" you're stalling your own destiny.*

5. Would I want someone I love to stay in this situation? If you wouldn't want your best friend or sister stuck here, why the hell would you settle for it yourself?

Gender Roles & Dating Stereotypes
Challenge the Script, Not Yourself

Here's the thing nobody wants to admit: Most of what we call "dating rules" are just outdated scripts from a world that doesn't exist anymore. Men pay. Women wait. Men lead. Women smile. Yawn. If you want a real connection, not just a socially approved photo op, you're gonna have to burn some of this old shit to the ground. Here's how you break free without losing your mind:

1. Catch Yourself When You Start Playing a Role. If you're doing something just because "that's what girls are supposed to do" STOP. You're not a character. You're a whole-ass human being.

2. Make the First Move If You Want To. Flirt first. Text first. Ask them out. If they're threatened by a woman who knows what she wants, they were never strong enough for you anyway.

3. Share the Emotional Labor Too. You don't have to do all the emotional heavy lifting. You're not their emotional Sherpa just because you have boobs.

4. Smash Stupid Stereotypes Out Loud. If he's nurturing and emotional? Good. If you're ambitious and blunt? Good. Real power couples aren't carbon copies of old tropes. They're custom-built.

5. Celebrate Each Other's Power, Not Compete Over It. His wins don't diminish you. Your shine doesn't emasculate him. *Big energy matches big energy.*

6. Know the Difference Between Flexibility and Losing Yourself. Being flexible = cool. Twisting yourself into a damn pretzel just to fit someone's idea of "wifey material" = miserable.

7. Audit Your Own Internalized BS. You might be holding outdated beliefs you didn't even realize. (*"He should always..." / "I'm supposed to..."*) Challenge that shit. Rewrite it.

8. Lead By Being Unapologetically You. You don't break stereotypes by giving TikToks about them. You break them by *living out loud*: fully, fiercely, messily, magnificently.

Gender Role Breaker Gut Check:
5 Questions to Snap Out of Outdated Scripts

Because you're not here to live someone else's dusty fairytale.
You're here to build something *real*.

1. Am I doing this because I *want* to or because I think I'm "supposed" to? *If it's guilt-driven, fear-driven, or "good girl"-driven, it's not you. It's programming. Smash it.*

2. If I made the first move, would it make me feel empowered or desperate? *Real queens don't chase. They **choose**. Big difference.*

3. Am I hiding parts of myself to seem more "palatable?" *Are you shrinking your ambition, your voice, your needs? If yes, stop. The right person will fall harder for the full version, not the watered-down one.*

4. Do I believe love requires me to become smaller, quieter, or less demanding? *Because real love **amplifies** you. It never asks you to disappear.*

5. Am I building a relationship that honors both of us fully or just a prettier version of outdated expectations? *Your life isn't a 1950s ad campaign. It's a f**king revolution.*

Final Word: You're not here to fit their mold. You're here to break it. The world doesn't need another Stepford Wife. It needs you: raw, bold, loud, brilliant, alive. Own it. Live it. Lead it.

Dating and Career

(Because your ambition isn't intimidating. It's just incompatible with mediocrity.)

You're not asking for too much. You're asking for a man who doesn't flinch when he realizes you've got sh*t to do. A man who sees your drive, your calendar, your chaos and still wants in. This isn't about slowing down. It's about being strategic with your time, sovereign with your energy, and unshakably clear about the kind of connection that *complements*, not competes with, your empire.

1. Stop Apologizing for Being Busy. You're not "too busy." You're *just booked with purpose.* If a man takes your ambition personally, that's not a miscommunication. It's a misalignment.

2. Make Space. Don't Give Up Your Life. Yes, make time for love. But don't burn down your boundaries to do it. If dating requires you to become less of yourself, you're not dating, you're *shrinking.*

3. Never Date a Man Who Competes with Your Career. If he jokes about you being "married to your job," he's not playful, he's *insecure.* A real man roots for your success like it's his own.

4. Use Your Professional Energy to Filter Faster. Interview questions, but make it dating. "What does your ideal week look like?" "What's your five-year plan?" "How do you show up when you're stressed?" *Clock the answers like you're reviewing a resume.*

5. Be Clear About Your Availability and Stick to It. Don't say "I'll try to squeeze it in." Say, "I'm available Thursday or Sunday, let me know what works." That's not rigid. That's **self-respect.**

6. Prioritize Energy Over Time. It's not about how many hours you have, it's about how *drained* you are. Some weeks you'll have space. Some weeks you won't. Communicate that. Don't force connection when your soul's on 2%.

7. Only Date People Who Support Your Wins Without Feeling Small. If he gets weird when you hit a milestone, walk. Real partners celebrate your glow-up. They don't get quiet when the spotlight's on you.

8. Don't Romanticize the Struggle Dynamic. You've worked too hard to become the emotional or financial ladder for someone else's potential. You're not here to build a man. You're here to *build with* one.

9. Know the Difference Between Busy and Avoidant. He's not too "driven" to communicate, he's just *not prioritizing you.* Ambition isn't an excuse for inconsistency. If he wants to see you, he'll make a plan. Period.

10. Your Career Is Not Your Personality but It's Part of Your Identity. You don't need to tone it down to be "softer." Your ambition is part of your essence. Own it fully. The right man won't just accept it, he'll *fall in love with it.*

11. You're Not Looking for Someone to Complete You, You're Looking for Someone Who Doesn't Get in the Way. You're whole. You're evolving. You're *on fire.* And if love enters the picture? It better *amplify* you not mute you.

FUN CONVERSATION PROMPTS
FOR HIGH-ACHIEVING WOMEN

(Because your ambition is the invite, not the apology.)

You're not dating to be impressed. You're dating to be inspired, met, and matched. Use these to spark real talk fast without sounding like you're handing out a job application.

1. "What's something you're really proud of that you don't talk about enough?" Their face will tell you everything. Confidence without arrogance is the vibe you're hunting for.

2. "If you had a free week with no obligations, how would you spend it?" Does he build? Create? Chill? Chase clout? This will show you where his soul actually lives.

3. "What's your relationship like with your own ambition?" Pay close attention. If he gets defensive, jokes about being lazy, or downplays having goals, you know he can't handle your fire.

4. "What motivates you on days when nothing's going right?" This separates the boys who need instant gratification from the men who can grind without losing heart.

5. "When you think about the future, what's non-negotiable for you?" This checks for alignment. Fast. No vibe-wasting with men who "don't know what they want."

If you want more questions to make you the most interesting woman in the room, I have you covered:
https://www.etsy.com/listing/4414840499/conversation-starter-cards-101-questions

SAVAGE FIRST-DATE FILTERS
FOR WOMEN WHO KNOW THEIR WORTH

*(Because you're not investing another three months
into a man who folds when you shine.)*

Use these quietly not aggressively but mentally *score them* as the date unfolds.

1. How does he react when you talk about something you're passionate about? Is he curious? Does he build on it? Or does he redirect the convo back to himself? *If he's not interested now, he'll resent it later.*

2. Does he compliment your drive or backhand shade it? "You must be soooo busy." "Bet you're intimidating to guys." Anything less than *direct admiration* is a red flag.

3. Does he bring real energy to the table or just show up and expect you to carry the conversation? A man who can't engage with depth on day one isn't going to evolve into someone who suddenly values connection.

4. Does he flinch when you set a boundary about time, work, or personal priorities? This is the litmus test. Right here. If he respects your boundaries with ease, green light. If he jokes, sulks, or challenges it—*exit stage left.*

Dating and Social Media

(Because dating was already a jungle and then we gave everybody Wi-Fi and filters.)

Social media didn't ruin dating. It just exposed everybody's insecurity, performative nonsense, and secret double lives faster. You're not crazy for thinking it's complicated. You're not wrong for wanting clarity, privacy, and realness. Here's what you need to know if you want to date *and survive the algorithm.*

1. If He Won't Post You, It's Not Because He's "Private." It's because he's *undecided.* Privacy protects. Secrecy *hides.*

2. "Likes" Mean Nothing. Consistency Means Everything. He can double-tap your bikini pic but ghost your soul. Watch what he *does*, not what he likes.

3. Dating Apps Are Just Tools, They're Not a Personality Trait. Meeting online doesn't make your story less real. It makes it efficient. Stop shaming yourself for adapting to the century you live in.

4. Digital Flirting Counts as Real Flirting. "Heart eyes" on some girl's selfie every week isn't "harmless." If he wouldn't do it sitting next to you, he doesn't get to do it online either.

5. Couple Content Should Be Real not a PR Campaign. Posting each other out of genuine happiness? Beautiful. Posting each other to prove something to your ex/followers/haters? *Pathetic.*

6. Mutual Friends Don't Guarantee Mutual Values. Just because you have ten Facebook friends in common doesn't mean he's safe. Serial heartbreakers also know how to work LinkedIn.

7. You're Not Competing with Instagram Models. You're Competing with His Maturity. It's not about her body. It's about whether he has the emotional discipline to honor what's real instead of chasing what's available.

8. Relationship Health Isn't Measured by Post Frequency. You can be posted every day and still be disrespected behind DMs. You can be posted never and still be deeply loved. Learn the difference.

9. If You Feel Weird About What He's Doing Online, Don't Gaslight Yourself. Trust your gut. Screenshots don't lie. Energy doesn't either.

10. Not Everyone Deserves Access to Your Private Life. You don't owe the internet updates on who you're dating, when you're fighting, or whether you're thriving. Let real love grow without public commentary.

11. Comparison Will Destroy a Good Thing Before Cheating Ever Could. Their matching pajama photos mean nothing. Focus on the man holding your hand, not the one holding his phone.

12. Social Media Boundaries Need to Be Set Early or You'll End Up Fighting Over Imaginary Rules, Talk about it. What's private? What's public? What's respectful? Handle it before it handles you.

13. Your Relationship Should Feel Better in Real Life Than It Looks Online. If you're happier posting about each other than actually *being* with each other, it's not a relationship, it's a PR stunt with benefits.

HOW TO SPOT RED FLAG vs. GREEN FLAG COUPLES ON SOCIAL MEDIA

(Because your inner FBI agent deserves to be both entertained and educated.)

RED FLAG COUPLES

1. The Overcompensation Olympics. Every post is "my rock," "my king," "I'm so lucky." Meanwhile, she's crying in her car once a week and reposting cheating TikToks. *If you have to say it that loud… it probably isn't that real.*

2. The Soft Launch That Never Becomes a Hard One. You've seen his elbow. His dog. The back of his hoodie. Six months in, she's still hiding him like a dead body in a Netflix series. *He's either married or deeply non-committal. Pick one.*

3. The Constant Breakup-Reunion Loop. They unfollow. Re-follow. Archive. Un-archive. Caption: "Some people are meant to find their way back." Translation: *We're both emotionally addicted and can't afford separate rent.*

4. The "We Travel but Don't Talk" Couple. Greece. Cabo. Turks & Caicos. But never a video of them laughing, talking, or making eye contact. They're not in love, they're in content.

5. The Mismatched Posting Energy. She posts him like he cured cancer. He posts her… *never.* One of them is in a relationship. The other is just tolerating it.

GREEN FLAG COUPLES

1. They Post Sparingly but When They Do, It's Real AF. One candid photo. A short caption. No performative PDA just *presence.* You can feel the peace through the pixels.

2. Their Stories Look Like Friendship First. You see them laughing. Playing. Supporting. Not just kissing under fireworks but *folding laundry, eating tacos, going to Costco. That's the kind of boring every woman should aspire to.*

3. No Passive Aggression, No Subtweeting. They communicate like adults. You never see "some people don't appreciate what they have until it's gone" on her story because she *tells him, not the internet.*

4. They Post Each Other Because They Want to Not Because They're Proving Something. It's not about followers. It's about celebration. There's no quota, no pressure just genuine moments they want to share.

5. No Thirst Traps, No Shady Likes, No Deleted Posts. There's no drama in their digital trail. It's clean. Respectful. Uncomplicated. They act like they're in a relationship *even when no one's watching.*

6. You Don't See Them Online All the Time Because They're Too Busy Being in Love IRL. You remember them every few months and think, "Oh yeah, they're solid." That's the real flex. *Not attention, longevity.*

How to Exit a Bad Date
Without Faking a Family Emergency

When to Call the Whole Thing Off Mid-Date
(And How to Exit Like a Legend)

(Because you don't owe anyone your time just because you ordered drinks.)

There's awkward. There's "eh, maybe." And then there's "I would rather crawl out the bathroom window in heels than sit through another 45 minutes of this." And *that* moment? That's your cue.

I. Signs You Can (and Should) Leave Mid-Date

Let's not overthink it. If you're wondering "Is this rude?" ask this instead: Is he wasting your presence? Leave if:

1. He shows up late, acts like it's no big deal, and doesn't apologize.
2. He orders for you without asking.
3. He talks at you, not to you.
4. He says anything derogatory about women, exes, or "crazy girls."
5. He makes sexual comments that are creepy, not clever.
6. You feel uncomfortable, unsafe, or just… dead inside.
7. You feel yourself shrinking, performing, or trying too hard.
8. He's on his phone more than he's making eye contact.

Reminder: You're not there to make him feel good. You're there to decide if *you* want to see him again. And if the answer is no? Exit.

II. The Art of the Mid-Date Exit (No Emergency Excuse Required)

You don't need a fake call from your "sick aunt" or to pretend your dog just ran away. Here's how to leave with class, clarity, and a little flair.

OPTION 1: The Direct + Polite Disengage

"Hey, I want to be honest. I'm not feeling a spark. You seem great, but I don't want to waste either of our time." Simple. Clean. Unshakable self-respect.

OPTION 2: The Energy Mirror

"I'm picking up that this maybe isn't vibing for either of us. I'm going to head out early, but I wish you all the best." Let him off the hook while still taking the wheel.

OPTION 3: The Calm Power Move

"I'm realizing this isn't a match for me, and I'd rather end the night here than force something that isn't aligned. Take care." That's not rejection. That's emotional maturity. You'll haunt him in a good way.

III. How to Prepare Mentally (So You're Ready to Bounce if Needed)

Before the date:

- **Drive yourself.** Always. Your power is in your escape route.
- **Have a backup plan** for where you'll go after. Friend's house. Solo drinks. Target. Doesn't matter, *you're not going home deflated.*
- **Practice saying it.** Not because you owe an explanation, but because clarity is your flex.

IV. How to Handle Pushback Like a Damn Queen

If he gets defensive, tries to guilt you, or says something like "Wow, really?" you don't argue. You don't over-explain. You don't match the energy. You say: "Yep."

"Still wish you well."

"I know what I want, and I'm honoring that." And then you leave. Without fidgeting. Without apologizing. Without second-guessing.

V. What to Do After You Leave

- Text your best friend: "I left. It was a NOPE."
- Reward yourself. Dessert, music, a walk, a bath, you just reclaimed your time.
- Journal one savage line from the date and add it to your memoir.
- Block or unmatch. You don't need to linger in his universe.
- Remind yourself: *I can always leave. Always. And next time, I'll leave faster.*

Final Word: Leaving a bad date early isn't rude. Staying when your soul is saying "get out" is what drains your magnetism. You don't owe anyone your time just because you were polite enough to show up. You showed up. You assessed. You exited. That's legendary energy. That's main character awareness. That's survival, but sexy.

How to Stay Magnetic When You're Losing Interest

(Because ghosting isn't your brand, but neither is faking it.)

This chapter is for when he's nice… on paper. Checks boxes. Says the right things. Texts back. But your body? Your intuition? Your vibe? Snoozing. You want to *want him.* But the chemistry's drying up like your patience. So how do you stay magnetic without being fake? How do you stay *in your power* when you're halfway out the door?

I. Ask Yourself: Am I Bored... or Triggered?

Sometimes disinterest isn't about *him*, it's about your nervous system.

- Is he too safe, too calm, too available?
- Are you mistaking "peace" for "lack of spark?"

Before you bounce, check this: *Am I actually bored or just not used to being treated well without a side of drama?*

II. How to Stay Present When You're Over It

If you're going to finish the drink, the convo, or the dinner, here's how to do it without shrinking:

- **Shift into observer mode.** Study him. Notice how he talks about people, how he handles awkward silences, how he reacts when the server is slow.
- **Turn the convo deeper.** Ask better questions: "What's something you've never told someone on a date?"
- **Play the energy game.** Test the polarity. Pull back your energy, get playful, see if he meets you in the dance or short-circuits.
- **Stop trying to impress him.** Give yourself permission to be unfiltered. If he can't hang? Exit.

Final Reminder: Sometimes the most attractive thing you can do is not pretend to care. Hold your light. Hold your truth. And if he's not *it*, don't dim for politeness. Let it fizzle, but do it with power.

Are You Actually Compatible... Or Just Infatuated?

(Because one is a connection. The other is a delusion in a trench coat.)

You're obsessed. He feels like a drug. You can't stop thinking about him, checking his socials, replaying what he said under your breath like it was scripture. But... is this real? Or is this just a chemically-induced fantasy built off hot eye contact and one traumatic childhood overlap? Let's find out.

I. The Chemical Trap: Why Infatuation Feels Like Love

Your body is high on:

- **Dopamine** (reward: he texts)
- **Oxytocin** (bonding: he touched your back once)
- **Cortisol** (stress: he disappears)
- **Hope** (the deadliest drug of all)

You're not connecting. You're chasing a feeling you think he can give you again.

II. Compatibility = Alignment. Infatuation = Projection.

Let's break it down:

	Compatibility	**Infatuation**
Core Values	Aligned	Unknown or ignored
Communication	Clear & reciprocal	One-sided or chaotic
Future Plans	Compatible visions	Fantasy-based
Emotional Safety	You feel safe	You feel addicted
Sense of Self	Grounded	Lost in him
Pace	Sustainable	Intense, fast, disorienting

If you don't know his actual values, his stress response, or how he acts when things *aren't* sexy or fun... You're infatuated. Not compatible.

142

III. The Reality Test: Questions to Ground You

1. Can I be fully myself around him?
2. Do I feel safe sharing my truth, even if it's messy?
3. Have we talked about our values and life goals beyond the surface?
4. Does he show up consistently, or do I always feel unsure?
5. Can we disagree without it turning toxic?
6. Do I know how he handles stress or failure?
7. Have we built something slowly or did it go from 0 to soulmates?
8. Would I want a friend I love to be treated the way he treats me?

If most of these feel *off*, you're infatuated. Not doomed. Not broken. Just momentarily high.

Final Word: Compatibility is calm. It's honest. It's clear. It doesn't spike your nervous system and call it magic. So, if you're not sure if he's "the one" or just the *current obsession*. Pause. Breathe. Wait to see how he acts when the high wears off. Because love isn't found in a rush. It's revealed in the quiet consistency that comes next.

Why You Keep Falling for Potential (And How to Stop)

(Because dating a blueprint isn't the same as building a future.)

He *could* be great. He *might* figure it out. He *has* a good heart… somewhere beneath the ghosting, gaslighting, and six-month identity crisis. You see the man he could become if he just got his shit together. **The problem?** That version of him doesn't exist yet. And you've confused the *idea of him* with the man in front of you.

I. Why We Fall for Potential

Let's be brutally honest:

- **You're emotionally intelligent**—you can see depth others miss.
- **You're a natural healer or nurturer**—you want to help him grow.
- **You romanticize effort**—his *trying* makes you feel seen.
- **You're trauma-bonded to inconsistency**—chaos feels like chemistry.
- **You believe in his light**—even when he keeps dimming yours.

You're not broken. You're just wired to believe love means work. And the harder the work, the more real it must be. (It's not.)

II. How to Know You're Dating Potential, Not Reality

Here's how it shows up:

1. **You're constantly defending him to your friends.** "He just needs time." "He's been through a lot." "He's not like this with anyone else."
2. **You find yourself making excuses for his lack of consistency.** Work. Stress. Timing. Mercury in retrograde. Anything but the truth: *He's not showing up.*
3. **You get more emotionally invested when he pulls away.** The less he gives, the more you try. That's not love, it's a nervous system glitch.
4. **You're imagining a future with someone who's not showing up in the present.** You're dating the version of him that only exists in your mind.

III. Why This Keeps You Stuck

Falling for potential keeps you in:

- **Over-functioning mode** — You do all the emotional work.
- **Low-reward relationships** — You're always hoping for a shift that never comes.
- **Self-worth limbo** — You confuse *patience* with *deserving better.*
- **False intimacy** — Struggle becomes your bonding agent instead of actual compatibility.

And meanwhile? You miss out on real men. The ones who don't need to be "fixed" before they can love you.

IV. How to Stop Falling for Potential and Start Attracting Reality

1. **Watch the Pattern, Not the Apology.** People show you who they are. *Believe the patterns*, not the performances.
2. **Ask: Would I Want to Feel Like This Forever?** If this dynamic *never changed* would I be okay? If not, why am I still here?
3. **Stop Mistaking Effort for Alignment.** Trying hard doesn't mean it's right. It just means you're attached.
4. **Ask Yourself: Am I Building a Relationship or Babysitting a Breakdown?** You're not his emotional scaffolding. You're not his muse. You're not a life coach with benefits.
5. **Set a Time Limit for "Maybe."** If you're still unsure after three months of dating someone consistently, it's a no. Uncertainty is clarity in disguise.

V. What Real Compatibility Feels Like (So You Stop Settling for the Draft Version)

- You feel grounded, not anxious
- You trust his actions, not just his words
- You don't have to shrink to keep the peace
- You feel seen *now*, not in some imaginary future
- You feel safe enough to stop performing

Because real love doesn't need a blueprint. **It shows up built.**

Final Word: You don't want potential. You want partnership. You don't want almosts. You want actuals. And until he shows up as the man you deserve, not just the one you imagine, let the fantasy die. The right man won't need you to believe in his future. He'll be ready in the present.

What His First Date Behavior Says About Him

(Because the red flags don't wave, they whisper. Until you listen.)

You already know what you bring. The real question is *who is this man really?* We're going to decode it all: The way he walks in. The way he orders. The eye contact, the interrupting, the bill, the silence, the over-talking, the weird flexes. Everything is data. Let's make you fluent.

I. How He Arrives = How He Shows Up in Life

- **He's late without a heads-up?** Expect poor time management, weak accountability, and emotional delays.
- **He's late but texts ahead to apologize?** Still not ideal, but self-awareness = possible redemption arc.
- **He's on time and looks put together?** He preps. He respects time. He *might* respect you.
- **He shows up rushed, distracted, and already venting?** You're not the date, you're a walking therapist booth.
- **He walks in calm, makes direct eye contact, and greets you like a gentleman?** That's regulated nervous system energy. Green flag.

II. How He Talks = How He Relates

- **He talks non-stop about himself and forgets your name?** You're dating a dude with a god complex.
- **He trauma dumps before the drinks arrive?** He has no boundaries, no self-regulation, and no shame spiraling when you don't text back tomorrow.
- **He asks surface questions only?** He's either boring, emotionally avoidant, or just not that into you.
- **He actually listens, reflects, and asks layered questions?** Emotional intelligence. Presence. You've entered *potential keeper* territory.
- **He interrupts you often or finishes your sentences?** He's either anxious… or doesn't actually value your voice. Pay attention.

III. How He Orders = How He Handles Decision-Making + Control

- **He orders for you without asking?** Run. You're not his daughter. You're not his possession. You're dessert with a pulse.
- **He asks what you want, but lowkey pressures you to get what *he* likes?** Control dressed as charm. It gets worse.
- **He's indecisive and defers everything to you?** Nice guy or no backbone? TBD. But leadership matters.
- **He's assertive, checks in with your preferences, and handles the ordering smoothly?** Balanced. Confident. Doesn't need to dominate to lead.
- **He talks down to the staff?** He'll talk down to you, eventually.

IV. How He Engages = How Safe You'll Feel

- **You feel seen, but not watched. Heard, but not analyzed. Safe, but still lit up.** That's regulation and presence. That's *mature masculine energy.*
- **You feel like you're performing. Like you're being evaluated. Like you need to impress.** That's a walking wound with a hidden scorecard. You'll never win.
- **You feel off but can't explain why.** That's your intuition. You don't need evidence to leave. You just need *a signal*.
- **You feel like yourself. Or more yourself than usual.** That's alignment. Stay curious.

V. How He Ends the Date = How He Handles Closure + Boundaries

- **He pressures you to "come back to his place" or "keep hanging out" despite clear signs you're not into it?** Disrespect masked as "chemistry." He doesn't do boundaries. He does *tests.*
- **He walks you to your car, doesn't push for more, and still expresses interest?** Safe. Sexy. Secure. That's high-value self-restraint. Rare and hot.
- **He ghosts right after a great date?** That wasn't chemistry, it was performance. His attention span expired the second the ego hit wore off.
- **He follows up with clarity and consistency?** This man actually means it. Watch how he *sustains*, not how he starts.

VI. Red Flag First Date Behaviors to Never Excuse

- Keeps checking his phone or texting under the table
- Makes passive aggressive or condescending jokes
- Tries to flex money or status instead of curiosity or respect
- Asks about sex too soon or makes comments about your body early
- Tries to control the vibe, the location, the plan, the schedule without asking what *you* want
- Tells you "You're not like other girls"
- Brags about ghosting or cheating
- Doesn't thank you for your time at the end

If you're collecting yellow flags on Date 1? You're signing up for a red flag parade by Date 3.

Final Word: The first date is the preview. It doesn't get better than what he chooses to show you right now. He's not on his worst behavior. He's giving you his *highlight reel*. So don't fall in love with the good parts. Fall in love with the *full picture* or not at all. Because if you're confused now, you'll be in therapy later. And if you feel safe, seen, and strong from the jump? That's not luck. That's alignment.

PART II
THE PROFILE
CREATING A PRESENCE THEY CAN'T SWIPE PAST

Profile Creation Mastery

How to Make a Dating Profile
(A.K.A. Your Personal Billboard to the Chaotic Dating Universe)

Let's be real: your dating profile is not a diary entry. It's a *teaser trailer*, the best 30 seconds of your movie, not the slow character development scenes. This is the first impression before they ever say "hey." And in a world of emotional unavailability and AI-generated small talk, you need to stand out without sounding like you're auditioning for a reality show.

1. Choose the Right App. First things first: know your playground. Tinder = chaos. Bumble = girlboss energy, with low-effort men though. Hinge = "supposedly" for relationships but still packed with shirtless dudes in fish pics. Facebook Dating might also not be terrible. Pick your poison based on what you're looking for and how much patience you have. Dating app = vibe. Pick accordingly.

2. Pick a Profile Picture That Doesn't Betray You. Your main pic is your first impression. It should scream "Yes, I'm hot AND sane" not blurry, broody, or buried in a group photo from 2017.
- ✓ Face visible
- ✓ Eyes looking at the camera
- ✓ Smile that says *confident, not desperate*

🚫 No sunglasses. No car selfies. No lying about your weight via weird angles. This isn't your LinkedIn headshot, but it's also not your OnlyFans preview. Aim somewhere in between.

3. Write a Bio That Doesn't Make People Swipe Out of Sheer Cringe. Your bio is your elevator pitch: short, spicy, and *so you*. Skip the generic garbage ("Love to laugh and travel"). That's not a personality.
Here's the formula:
- **Be honest.** Talk about what you *actually* like to do on a Sunday. (Spoiler: most men lie about hiking.)
- **Be specific.** "I've read 12 WWII books and can quote *The Office* without blinking." That's more memorable than "I like books and shows."
- **Be playful.** Humor is hot. Deadpan is hotter.

4. Mention the Non-Negotiables (Without Sounding Like a Dictator). Yes, you can say you want someone who's emotionally intelligent, employed, and doesn't think therapy is a scam. Just say it *with grace*. Example: "Looking for someone whose idea of fun doesn't involve ghosting after three great dates."

5. Proofread, Darling. There is nothing more unattractive than "your" instead of "you're." Grammar matters and so does flow. Read it out loud. Does it sound like you? Or does it sound like a guy who says "let's vibe" in every message?

The 5-Photo Formula

(Because one good selfie is not a personality, and seven blurry mirror pics is a cry for help)

Your photos do **80% of the work** on a dating app. Sorry, writers. This is not the place to showcase your poetry unless it's inked on your body and captured under golden hour lighting. So, here's your foolproof, no-regret lineup for profile pics that actually *get* swipes (and not the wrong ones).

1. The Face Shot (Main Pic)

Rule: This is your "Hi, I'm not a catfish" photo.
- ✓ Eye contact
- ✓ Natural lighting
- ✓ Solo shot (aka no cropped exes, friend groups, or your mom)
- ✓ No filters. You're already hot. Let them deal with it.

Pro tip: A smile is 10x more effective than a pout.

2. The Full Body

Let's just get this out of the way, they're going to stalk your body. So beat them to it and own it with confidence.
- ✓ Candid or posed, just don't be stiff.
- ✓ Outfit = flattering but true to you.
- ✓ NO GYM MIRROR PICS. You are not a fitness bro.

Confidence is hot. Desperation disguised as flexing? Not so much.

3. The Vibe Shot

This is your aesthetic. Your "this is what I do when I'm not swiping on weirdos" photo.
- ✓ You on vacation
- ✓ You at a concert
- ✓ You with your dog, but make it editorial

Let them see your lifestyle, not your laundry pile.

4. The Social Shot

One group pic max. Just one. And ONLY if:
- ✓ You are the clear standout
- ✓ No one in the photo is hotter than you
- ✓ No frat party chaos or drunk bathroom selfies

Think *polished social butterfly*, not *Bachelor reject on night one*.

5. The Curveball

This one seals the deal. Weird, bold, meme-worthy, or just straight-up hilarious.

- ✓ You dressed as a chicken on Halloween
- ✓ You holding a "Swipe right or regret it forever" sign
- ✓ A pic that makes someone message just to say "WTF I love this"

This is your invitation to be memorable. Don't be afraid to *lean in to your brand of weird*.

How to Take the Perfect Photos

(Because your face deserves better than a grainy bathroom selfie from 2018)

You don't need a full glam team or a DSLR to look like a catch. You just need some intention, some lighting, and a little bit of "I know I'm the moment" energy. Let's break it down. Here's how to actually take dating profile photos that stop thumbs, spark DMs, and make men wonder why they ever fumbled a woman like you.

1. Know Your Light. Natural light is your best friend. Artificial light will betray you faster than a man who says, "I'm just not ready for a relationship," after he just slept with you and told you, you were his for sure forever. Stand near a window. Aim for that golden hour glow just before sunset. Cloudy days? Even better. Diffused light smooths everything out without washing you out. Never stand directly under a ceiling light. That's not contour, it's a crime.

2. Use the Back Camera. Always. Selfies are fine for your Instagram Story, but they do nothing for your dating profile unless you want to attract men who are also posting gym mirror thirst traps. Set up a tripod or balance your phone on a windowsill, shelf, or stack of books. Use the timer or voice activation. You're resourceful. Make it happen.

3. Don't Pose. Move. The trick to looking effortless is actually being a little unhinged behind the scenes. Take 50 photos while you move. Walk, laugh, turn around, touch your hair, fix your collar. Movement gives you options. Stiff posing gives you LinkedIn energy. Candid always wins. Especially when it's fake candid. We don't care. It looks great.

4. Wear Something That Feels Like Power. Don't wear what you *think* is hot. Wear what makes you feel like you own the room, even if it's just your hallway. Pick outfits you already know you look good in. If you're uncomfortable, it will show. If you're pulling your dress down or adjusting your top every five seconds, it's not the one. And yes, wear the damn heels if you want. You don't need an occasion. You are the occasion.

5. Backgrounds Matter. You are not the main character in a messy bathroom. Clean the scene. Solid color walls. Cool textures. Rooftops. Sunsets. City streets. Anywhere that makes you look like you *do things*. Avoid photos in dirty rooms, chaotic cars, or cluttered spaces. You're not selling your laundry basket, you're selling a vibe.

6. Practice Until You Nail It. Yes, it will feel weird at first. Yes, you'll feel ridiculous. Do it anyway. Take test shots. Review. Adjust. Try again. This is not vanity. This is marketing. You are curating your highlight reel. The right photos will do half the work for you. The wrong ones will bury your potential under bad lighting and weird angles.

7. Show Range. Soft, sexy, confident, cozy. Your photos should tell a story with chapters. One glam. One casual. One playful. One "look at me living my life without begging for your attention." If your vibe is "choose your fighter," make sure they see all the modes.

8. Use Props Strategically. Coffee mug? Power move. Dog? Weaponized cuteness. Book, drink, plant, or pastry? All gold. Props humanize you and make the photo feel real, not curated for the algorithm. Just don't let the prop outshine the main character. You.

9. Edit Lightly (If at All). You're hot. Don't blur that fact into oblivion. Adjust lighting and color, not your nose. No cartoon filters, no puppy ears, and no plastic skin. People should recognize you in real life and think you look even better.

10. Audit Like a Savage. Look at every photo and ask:
- Would I swipe on this person?
- Does this photo start a conversation or stop it?
- Does this photo make me look like I *get it*?

If the answer isn't yes, delete it and try again. You're not settling in dating. Don't settle on photos either.

Bio Blueprint

(Because "I like food and travel" is not a personality, it's a Yelp review)

Your bio is the trailer. Not the plot. Not the trauma backstory. Just enough intrigue to hook them, enough spice to keep them curious, and enough *you* to weed out the emotionally bankrupt before they even say "hey." So how do you write a killer dating bio that doesn't scream "I copy-pasted this from someone hotter than me?"

Let's break it down:

1. Hook Them in the First Line. Think of your opener like a pick-up line for *yourself*.
- "Emotionally stable-ish. Snacks always on hand."
- "Can parallel park and pick the restaurant."
- "Looking for someone to split fries and overanalyze movies with."
- "Professional vibe curator. Amateur flirt."
- "I make great playlists and even better first impressions."
- "I take my coffee strong and my connections genuine."
- "Let's pretend we met because of fate, not an algorithm."
- "Looking for someone who laughs easily and orders dessert."
- "I'm the friend who plans the trip and remembers birthdays."
- "Equal parts curious, kind, and sarcastic."
- "Not perfect, but excellent company."
- "Big on communication, bigger on tacos."
- "Main character energy, supporting character humility."

Be weird. Be witty. Be self-aware. First line = make them **stay**.

2. Say What You Actually Like (Not What You Think Sounds Cool). No more: "I like going out *and* staying in." Congratulations, you exist. Do this instead:

- "Currently obsessed with dark documentaries and overpriced oat milk lattes."
- "If you know a better snack than kettle popcorn, I'm listening."
- "Dog person. Plant killer."

If your bio makes your best friend laugh out loud, you're doing it right.

3. Add a Power Line (Close Strong). End with something confident, flirtatious, or just straight-up iconic.

- "Better in person."
- "I dare you to keep up."
- "Swipe right. You'll need the story for your memoir."

Don't:

- Trauma dump
- List your height requirement like it's a résumé credential
- Complain
- Say "I'm bad at this" (then *don't* be bad at it)

Do:

- Be bold
- Be funny
- Be direct
- Be a walking vibe

Dating Profile Prompts to Use

(Because "pineapple on pizza" isn't the personality flex you think it is)

The Flirty & Bold

For when you want to sound fun, confident, and like you definitely get hit on at Whole Foods:

Prompt: The way to win me over is...

- Make me laugh until I snort, then hand me fries without asking.
- Tell me your deepest childhood wound, but, like, make it flirty.
- Show up with snacks, opinions, and an emotionally secure attachment style.

Prompt: Dating me is like...

- Free therapy, but with better outfits.
- A rollercoaster: thrilling, occasionally terrifying, never boring.
- Like your favorite playlist. You'll want it on repeat, then miss it when it's gone.

Prompt: Let's make sure we...

- Never pretend brunch isn't a core love language.
- Have at least one "we're unwell for this" inside joke by week two.
- End up in a spontaneous road trip that becomes a core memory.

The Funny & Unhinged

For unfiltered babes with chaotic good energy:

Prompt: I'll fall for you if...

- You don't say "we're vibing" after three texts.
- You pronounce "charcuterie" like you mean it.
- You can explain taxes to me like I'm five.

Prompt: Together we can...

- Ruin a dinner party with our unsolicited opinions.
- Start a podcast, then immediately abandon it.
- Pretend we're engaged so people stop asking why we're single.

Prompt: My simple pleasures...

- Watching true crime to fall asleep (yes, I know how that sounds).
- Cancelled plans.
- Men in hoodies. But like, the right kind of hoodie.

The Smart & Sassy

For the brainy, bookish, self-aware babes:

Prompt: A fact about me that surprises people...

- I once ghosted someone during Mercury retrograde. I had no choice.
- I make a mean risotto but still Google "how long to boil eggs."
- I've cried during a commercial. More than once. Don't test me.

Prompt: I get along best with people who...

- Know the difference between "you're" and "your" and use it against people.
- Believe ghosting should be punishable by community service.
- Send memes as love language.

Prompt: The hallmark of a good relationship is...

- Laughing in sync at dumb stuff.
- Deep talks > small talk.
- Feeling safe, seen, and still wildly attracted to each other.

The Deep, Soulful, Still-Hot Girl Answers

For when you're in your *"I've done the work"* era:

Prompt: I'm looking for...

- Something rooted in trust, laughter, and mutual hype.
- Someone who isn't afraid to show up honestly and let it get real.
- A connection that doesn't just feel good, it *grows* good.

Prompt: A life goal of mine...

- To heal generational wounds and still make time for dessert.
- To love someone without losing myself.
- To build something better than my parents ever saw.

Prompt: A shower thought I recently had...
- What if we're not healing, just remembering who we were before they broke us?
- What if the green flags feel boring because we were trained to chase chaos?
- Do penguins have soulmates and I'm still out here getting ghosted?

Soft Girl Era Prompts
Because vulnerability is a flex and being soft doesn't mean being naïve.

Prompt: I feel most myself when...
- I'm dancing in my kitchen to 90s R&B in sweatpants and a face mask.
- I'm with someone who sees through the strong front and chooses to stay.
- I'm safe enough to be a little unhinged and a lot of heart.

Prompt: The key to my heart is...
- Emotional availability. And snacks.
- Being intentional with your words, not just your attention span.
- Matching energy and texting back without games.

UNEXPERT ADVICE: As always you know I got more prompts coming at you fast and hard. Here is another 101 list if you dare. https://www.etsy.com/listing/4431247725/101-dating-app-prompt-answers-that

Swipe-Right Profile Hacks
*(How to Beat the Algorithm, Filter Out the Duds,
and Attract Men Who Deserve to Breathe Your Air)*

If dating apps are a game, we're not here to *play*. We're here to *win*. These hacks are your unfair advantage. Welcome to the high-level tactics that turn "meh" matches into "why is this man obsessed with me?" reactions. Let's make your profile swipe-proof.

1. Include One Conversation-Starter Photo. Hold something weird. Wear something bold. Be somewhere cool. You want someone to message you with more than "hey." A curiosity photo makes them work a little harder, which is *exactly* what you want. Examples:
- A dramatic travel pic
- You holding a giant dessert
- You in a Halloween costume that raises questions

2. Write One Line That Feels Like a Dare. Not aggressive. Not performative. Just slightly unhinged in a way that makes people *have* to respond. Examples:
- "I'll fall in love with you if you know the best Trader Joe's snack. Go."
- "Convince me why brunch isn't a scam. I dare you."
- "If you've made it this far, send me your hottest take."

3. Keep the Bio Short, but Memorable. Think of it like a teaser trailer: three lines MAX. Say something unexpected, throw in a line that shows wit, and end with a strong hook.

Bad bio: "Just a girl who loves wine, travel, and her dog."

Better: "Marketing witch. Dog's a better judge of character than me. I like my men how I like my coffee: consistent and hot."

4. Build a Profile That Feels Like a Mood, Not a Résumé. You're not listing your qualifications for a role in someone else's life. You're curating a *vibe* that makes the right person feel like they stumbled into the beginning of something they'll tell their friends about. How to do it:

- All photos feel cohesive (colors, energy, setting)
- Prompts that sound like one voice, yours
- No over-explaining. Let them lean in and ask

Your goal isn't to be liked by everyone. It's to magnetize the few who get it.

5. Set the Tone for the Type of Connection You Want. Men mirror energy. So don't post like you're trying to get attention, post like you already *have it*. That subtle shift changes everything. If you want playfulness, show it. If you want emotional depth, hint at it. If you want something serious, carry yourself like someone who won't waste time on small talk with a boy who "doesn't believe in labels." Whatever you model, you attract. And if they don't rise to the energy you're serving? That's not your loss. It's their missed plot twist.

Why Men Swipe Left
(And Why You Should Care If You Actually Want to Date a Good Guy)

This is where I tell you what the good guys swipe left on. This isn't coming from player energy, toxic bro podcasts, or the guy who sends six "wyd" texts in a row. This is a comprehensive list I got straight from my trusted guy friends and some genuinely amazing guys I dated that didn't work out but who are the type of men you want to swipe right on you. These are the men you should be dating. It's actually not that long of a list whereas the women's swipe-left list for men could be endless, lol.

What Makes Good Guys Swipe Left:

1. **All photos are ridiculously filtered. Every single one.** Not one is actually of you, just a filtered cartoon version of you, deep AI pics of you, and the no pores look. This was unanimous with every man I surveyed: If there isn't at least one real, unfiltered photo of you, they immediately swipe left because they think you're a catfish.

2. **If you don't have any pictures with friends and just have selfies.** That screams isolation, insecurity, or narcissism. None of which are giving soulmate energy. You don't need a bachelorette party group shot, but throw in ONE normal photo with actual human beings to show you exist outside your bathroom mirror.

3. **If you list a fantasy guy in your profile.** You know the list: "Self-aware, ambitious, not intimidated by independence." (Direct quote from a good guy: "This woman

sounds exhausting.") Don't be exhausting. You're not ordering a custom boyfriend off Amazon Prime.

4. **If you have politics in your profile or any political slogans/acronyms.** Swipe left. You can quietly list your political affiliation if it's a dealbreaker, fine. But ranting? Exhausting. If they align with your views, they are already on the same page.

5. **Alcohol photos.** If every photo has a drink in your hand, they wonder if you're a party girl who lives at happy hour. One photo at an event? Fine. Half your profile looking like an open bar promo? Not so much. (Also, why is every drink always massive?)

6. **Totally posed Instagram photos.** "Like she's posing with an ostentatious dress on the French Riviera or some bullshit that screams materialistic." actual quote. Look hot, absolutely. But if every photo looks like a Vogue spread curated within an inch of your life, they're swiping left.

7. **Girls who don't smile in pics.** Stop sucking in your cheekbones and trying to look seductive in every single photo. You look like you're in a hostage video. Smile. You'll still look hot but now you'll also look like someone they actually want to spend time with.

8. **A bio that talks about everything you don't want in a man.** Oh, you're tired of liars, cheaters, and broke guys? SO IS EVERYONE. Nobody wants to swipe on a bio that feels like walking into a courtroom. Fun and flirty, people. Rainbows and butterflies. Rainbows and butterflies.

9. **If your whole profile just feels like too much.** Harder to define but it came up a LOT. It's the energy of "I've been hurt and I'm already mad at you for it." If your profile reads like a warning label ("Don't waste my time unless you're serious!"), good men swipe left. High standards are sexy. A built-in resentment vibe? Not so much.

Final Word: Good guys don't expect you to be perfect. But they do want to feel like dating you would be fun, not like entering a landmine field with a checklist and a timer strapped to their back. Your photos and bio should say: "I'm happy, confident, and ready to meet someone amazing." Not: "I'm still emotionally bleeding out, but thanks for playing."

The Algorithm Game:
How to Outsmart the Machine

How Dating App Algorithms Actually Predict Romantic Desire
(And Why It's All a Hot Mess)

Let's get real. Online dating isn't about finding "the one." It's more like digital roulette with a side of wishful thinking. But buried inside all that swiping, ghosting, and algorithmic chaos? Some juicy insights about how desire actually works. Welcome to the real guts of Algorithm Secrets.

Matt Taylor: The Guy Who Finished Tinder

Once upon a chaotic night, a dude named Matt Taylor ran a bot that swiped right on 25,000 profiles. No, that's not a typo. He brute-forced the entire app and ended up with nine matches. One of them, Cherie, agreed to a date. They hit it off. They got married. Wild, right?

But you can't do this anymore. Tinder caught on and updated the algorithm to penalize the swipe-everything crowd. Because, shocker, if you swipe right on everyone, the app knows you're either desperate or cheating the system.

Still, this stunt tells us something: people don't trust the algorithm. We want love, but we also want control. So instead of relying on a "matchmaker bot," some of us try to out-hack the matrix.

The Algorithm Illusion

Apps promise they can predict who we'll fall for. Fill out a few quizzes, let the algorithm crunch your "upbeat personality" with their "dog dad energy," and boom, soulmates. But here's the catch: those algorithms? Locked behind corporate doors like top-secret recipes. No one outside the company can actually verify if they work.

So, scientists like Dr. Samantha Joel had to get scrappy. She and her team built their own prediction model. Over 100 traits and preferences, plus speed-dating sessions, to try and figure out what sparks romantic interest. They measured two things:

- **Actor Desire**: How much did you like others on average?
- **Partner Desire**: How much did others like you?

They subtracted attraction and choosiness to measure pure *compatibility*... and guess what? The algorithm bombed. It predicted less than nothing. It was statistically worse than flipping a coin. Joel summed it up: "People don't fall in love with data points. They fall in love with vibes."

Why Algorithms Fail (and Humans Are Complicated AF)

It turns out, you can't predict chemistry on paper. You might want someone "funny," but your sense of humor might not match theirs. You say you want tall, dark, and ambitious, and then fall for a short guy who makes you laugh until you snort at brunch.

So, what do we actually do? We say we have deal-breakers... then ignore them. In another study, Joel showed participants dating profiles that hit their red-flag list (smokes, too religious, whatever). Seventy-four percent of people who thought they had a shot still agreed to the date. Why? Because we're not that picky. Or at least, not as picky as we think.

The House of Preferences (aka Dating Tetris)

Dr. Daniel Conroy-Beam had a different idea. He imagined your ideal partner as a spot in a house. Every quality: kindness, looks, humor, etc. is a direction in the house. The closer a potential match is to your "ideal corner," the better your romantic interest.

It worked. Sort of. The biggest issue? People don't rank their preferences the same way. Your 10/10 in "kindness" might be my 6/10 in "sex appeal." And let's be honest, half of us are judging based on vibes and eye contact anyway.

The Matchmaking Spectrum

On one side, you've got eHarmony and Match.com. They hit you with 150-question surveys and brag about their machine learning. Rachael Lloyd, eHarmony's in-house relationship guru, says they focus on "core values," not just chemistry.

But over on the other side? Apps like Tinder and Bumble say, "We're not asking questions. We're showing faces. You tell us what you like." And according to Joel, that might actually work better. Real-time feedback > wishful thinking.

Bonus stat: Men who rate themselves as average (like 5/10) do *just* as well as guys who say they're 10s. Women aren't buying the hype. They want something real.

So... Can Algorithms Actually Predict Love?

Maybe a little. But probably not in the way we think. Real attraction can't be boxed into a checklist. We have moods, trauma, energy, and instinct. We override our own rules for people who spark something in us. Still, if you want to increase your chances:

- Be open-minded.
- Show some damn kindness.
- And maybe don't trust an app to do all the work.

Because no matter how sexy the tech gets, dating is still human. And that, babe, is your algorithm reality check. Welcome to the jungle.

How to Beat the Algorithm

Think dating app algorithms are just there to serve you a curated buffet of hotties? Think again. These systems are coded to serve *the platform* not you. But don't worry. I've cracked the code so you can stop being a pawn and start playing to win. Here's how to outsmart the algorithm and make it work for you:

1. Stop Swiping Right on Everyone. Apps like Tinder penalize users who swipe right too often. It's called the *desirability score* (unofficially, of course). Mass-swiping lowers your score and pushes you further down the deck. Swipe intentionally. Let the algorithm know you're selective.

2. Don't Ghost (The Algorithm Notices). When you match with someone and don't message, it signals disinterest and that affects who gets shown to you. If you're not into a match, unmatch instead of ghosting. Clean behavior = higher score.

3. Use the App Consistently. Apps reward users who log in regularly and engage. Use it daily for 10-15 minutes instead of long binge sessions. That way, you train the algorithm to push you up in the queue.

4. Don't Be Too Hot (Yes, Really). Profiles that look fake or professionally modeled can be flagged as bots or catfish. You want to look amazing, but human. Think: confident friend at brunch, not influencer at a red-carpet event.

5. Message Fast, Message Thoughtfully. Once you match, message quickly. The app tracks how fast you engage and how long conversations last. Higher engagement = higher ranking.

6. Location Hack: Change Your City Before You Travel. Going to Miami next week? Change your location 48 hours in advance. It boosts you in the "new user" stack in that city and gives you fresh reach before you even land.

7. Say Yes to Video Prompts (Even If It Feels Cringe). Apps like Hinge and Bumble push profiles with video content more often. It shows effort and authenticity, two things the algorithm loves to show off.

8. Avoid Linking Instagram or Spotify (Unless It Adds Value). Contrary to popular belief, linking these doesn't help unless the content is strong. If your last IG post was from 2019, or your Spotify is all Kidz Bop, you're better off skipping it.

9. Be One of the First to Like Someone. When you're one of the first likes on a new profile, you get algorithmic bonus points. Apps want to show users quick engagement. Be fast, not thirsty.

10. Answer the Damn Prompts. Blank bios are algorithmic death. Fill out your prompts with witty, insightful, or funny answers. You don't have to bare your soul just show you've got one.

11. Profile Boosts Are Strategic Not Random. If you're going to buy a boost, do it on Sunday nights (most active time) or right before a holiday/event weekend. That's when the traffic is hottest. Weekday evenings (especially Tuesday/Wednesday), and right before major holidays are also the best. The more people are online, the more visibility you get.

12. Let the App Learn You (Then Break the Pattern). Apps learn your type. Throw in the occasional curveball like liking someone totally outside your usual preference to shake up your algorithm bubble. It resets your stack and increases your visibility. Also, switching up your photo order is a huge plus. This tricks the algorithm into thinking it's a fresh profile and gives you another bump in visibility.

13. Boost After Bio Changes. Just updated your profile? Use a boost immediately after. New content + boost = algorithm cocktail that shoots your profile to the top of the stack.

14. Use Every Feature Offered. Hinge polls, Bumble questions, Tinder gifs, if there's a feature, use it. Apps favor users who explore all their bells and whistles. Full-suite users get full-stack visibility.

15. Be Conversational in Your Prompts. The algorithm favors profiles that *receive* responses. So, write prompts like a conversation starter, not a statement. Think "Convince me to…" or "Two truths and a lie…" versus "I like long walks on the beach."

16. Reply with Substance, Not Just Emojis. The app tracks the length and depth of your convos. Short, low-effort replies = low engagement scores. Be playful, be bold, be you in full sentences.

17. Don't Use Filtered Photos. Apps are cracking down on face filters and beauty editing. They flag heavy edits, which can drop your profile's trust score. Show your real glow, not a Paris-filter mirage.

UNEXPERT TAKEAWAY

The algorithm doesn't care about your feelings. It cares about your patterns. Learn how to play *it*, or you'll keep getting fed lukewarm "maybes" instead of red-hot "hell yes" connections. This isn't just dating. It's data. So don't just swipe smart, swipe like a savage who knows the system.

BONUS SECTION: Algorithm Secrets (Extended Cut)

Shadowbanning Is Real. Here's How to Know. No one talks about it, but if your once fire profile suddenly goes ice cold? The app may have quietly buried you.

Red Flags You've Been Shadowbanned:
- You stop getting matches altogether even with good photos and bio
- No replies, even with clever messages
- Boosts do nothing
- New users never seem to see your profile

What to Do: Delete the app completely. Wait seven full days. When you come back:
- Use new photos
- Rewrite your bio (even slightly)
- Limit swipes for the first 48 hours
- Re-engage slowly to rebuild trust

This is your dating app resurrection ritual. Because no, babe, you're not undateable. You were just buried alive by the code.

The Hidden Desirability Score (Aka The Elo Score Theory)

Think of it like Tinder Chess. Every swipe, ghost, or ignored message affects your "score."
1. If hot people like you and you respond? Your score goes up.
2. If you mass swipe, ghost often, or match with low-engagement users? You drop. It's savage. It's invisible. It's real.

160

Hack the Score:

- Swipe selectively
- Respond quickly
- Unmatch, don't ghost
- Limit matches to 3–5 per day for a week to signal quality control

You're not gaming the system. You're **training it to know your worth**.

Paid Users See You First

If a man pays for premium, the algorithm gives him a red-carpet experience. But that means he's getting shown to you first, especially if you're high-engagement. Don't confuse quantity with quality. You're not attracting more men. You're just appearing at the top of the shopping cart for those who paid extra. *Translation:* That hot flood of "new likes?" Might be sponsored.

How to Become Algorithm-Proof

Let's strip this to the bone. An algorithm-proof woman:

- Has a full life offline
- Treats dating apps like one tool, not her destiny
- Prioritizes energy over looks
- Knows when to reset, rebuild, or vanish
- Never begs the system for love, she uses it to filter noise

The most magnetic dating strategy isn't a photo. It's *not giving a damn if the app likes you back.*

The App Overload

Best Dating Apps

Tired of swiping like it's a full-time job only to match with emotionally unavailable crypto bros or spiritual gaslighters with "sapiosexual" in their bios? Welcome to the real list. This is the no-BS guide to the best dating apps in 2025. the ones that are actually worth your time, sanity, and screenshots. Most have free versions, but if you want to unlock their full power (and get past the emotional support bots), a paid tier might be your move.

The Dating App Survival Map

(For Women Who Want to Know What They're Actually Getting Into)

You're not choosing an app, you're choosing an energy field. Each platform has its own vibe, its own risks, and its own success stories (or horror stories). So, let's decode the top apps like the FBI meets your group chat.

App Name	Energy Level	Goal Vibe	Red Flag Risk	Best For	Proceed If...
Hinge	Balanced & Thoughtful	Dating with potential	Low–Medium	Women who want convo + chemistry	You want effort, but not homework
Bumble	Confident & Clean	Semi-serious dating, flirty edge	Medium	Women who lead, love texting first	You're fine making the first move
Tinder	Chaotic & Fast	Hookups or surprise connections	High	Women who can spot BS in 3 messages	You want fun, not forever (yet)
The League	High-Achiever Vibes	Selective, curated dating	Low–Medium	Women who date like it's a résumé	You love ambition & slow-burn energy

Raya	Bougie & Elitist	Artsy flings, soft networking	Medium–High	Women who want a vibe more than a ring	You're a hot creative with options
Coffee Meets Bagel	Calm & Minimalist	Long-term dating, light effort	Low	Women who are burnt out but still hopeful	You want quality without overload
Facebook Dating	Random but Real-ish	Low-key dating, mutual friends	Medium	Women who don't mind nostalgia energy	You're already on FB and curious

LEGEND:

> **Energy Level** = the overall *emotional tone* of the app.
>
> **Goal Vibe** = what most users are looking for *based on behavior, not bios.*
>
> **Red Flag Risk** = likelihood of ghosting, weirdos, or wasting your time.
>
> **Best For** = the kind of woman who'll thrive here.
>
> **Proceed If...** = your gut-check green light.

UnExpert Pro Tips:

- **Hinge** has the *most successful relationships* reported in the last few years, hands down.
- **Bumble** attracts men who respect initiative but ghosting still happens. Also, this is the lazy man's app for obvious reasons.
- **Tinder** can work, but it's survival of the emotionally fittest.
- **Coffee Meets Bagel** is a great detox app after Tinder burnout.
- **The League** gives "slow burn" but they better be hot or ambitious, because it's not fast.
- **Raya** is better for "story value" than soulmates. Like "OMG, I matched with Joshua Jackson." True story, my gf. I matched with Terrell Owens on The League. LOL, good times. Living in LA…

UnExpert Commentary: The app you choose isn't just about features, it's about energy. What vibe are you bringing? Looking for something fun, serious, casual, chaotic? Match the app to your *intention.* Just don't use all ten at once unless you want to burn out and start trauma bonding with chatbots. Now that we've upgraded your dating toolbox, the real game begins: learning how to *actually* use these apps without losing your mind. That's next. And, of course, as we all know, men are very much on all of them simultaneously. So, if you join one, you will be fine.

Sarah Melland
Worst Dating Apps
(The ones that should come with a trigger warning, a tetanus shot,
and an emotional support animal)

Some of these were always bad. Some used to be decent and just *gave up.* Either way, if you're on one of these, I'm gonna need you to log out, sage your phone, and re-evaluate your self-worth. This is the real rundown from sketchy privacy issues to red-flag central casting. Swipe at your own risk.

1. Ashley Madison
Tagline: Where morals go to die.
This app was *literally* built for cheating. Like, that's the brand. It's not "find your soulmate" it's "find your midlife crisis." Then it got hacked, leaked everyone's dirty secrets, and somehow still exists. Why? No one knows.

2. Zoosk
Tagline: Fake profiles, real disappointment.
Spammy notifications, aggressive upsells, and more bots than an Amazon review section. Oh, and good luck canceling your subscription, you'll need a tech support exorcism.

3. MocoSpace
Tagline: It's giving MySpace, but make it worse.
This app still exists. Why? Who knows. Feels more like a virtual flea market for scammers than anything remotely romantic. Most people don't even realize it's a dating app. You shouldn't either.

4. Blendr
Tagline: Like Grindr... but no one asked.
This app is basically a less successful Tinder clone that somehow makes everyone look shady. Location-based hookups? Sure. But the vibe is so off, you'll feel like you're meeting in a motel parking lot even if it's a coffee shop.

5. Paktor
Tagline: All looks, no substance.
Paktor is like a beauty pageant in swipe form, if you're not model-level hot, don't bother. The matching feels shallow and a bit soulless. If you're trying to date, this one's more like a digital thirst trap arena.

6. Plenty of Fish (POF)
Tagline: There's a reason it's called plenty of fish. None are good.
POF has become the chaotic dollar store of dating apps. It's free, flooded with spam, and feels like a Craigslist missed connections section. There might be some good ones, but you'll need to dig through a lot of trash to find them.

7. Badoo

Tagline: Where red flags are part of the onboarding process.

This one looks sleek but gives off serious scammer energy. It's overloaded with questionable profiles, vague location data, and thirsty dudes sending voice notes. I think we have already talked about how I feel about voice notes, if not just wait, it's coming, lol.

8. Clover

Tagline: Like Hinge and Tinder had an identity crisis.

Clover promises everything but delivers nothing. Video dating, scheduling, personality quizzes and yet no one's on it. If a dating app feels like a ghost town, it's probably for a reason.

9. eHarmony (in 2025)

Tagline: For people who still own landlines.

Once iconic, now outdated and overpriced. Feels like it's trying to sell you a timeshare *and* a marriage at the same time. If your goal is to find love *very slowly*, and only after filling out 500 personality questions, be my guest.

10. Happn

Tagline: Missed connection energy, but creepy.

In theory, it matches you with people you've crossed paths with IRL. In reality, it's like a GPS tracker for people you didn't even notice walking past you. Gives serious stalker vibes. No thanks.

HONORABLE MENTION:

Luxy — for people who want to date rich but forgot how to be interesting.

SilverSingles — great for 60+, but if you're in your 30s… run. Unless maybe you want a suga daddy, but I'm guessing you aren't going to find it on this app.

Weird Dating Apps

(Yes, these are real. No, I don't know how they got funded either.)

Dating is hard enough. Add in cats, vampires, truckers, salads, and adult babies, and suddenly you're not just single, you're in *another dimension*. Whether you're morbidly curious, dangerously bored, or just want to see how weird it gets, here's your UnExpert-approved walk through the wildest corners of the internet's dating underworld.

PURRsonals.com

If you're a cat person and only want to date other cat people, here's your litter box. But don't act shocked when your first date brings a laser pointer and asks if you sleep with your cat in the bed. (Spoiler: they do.)

GolfMates.com

For the polo-wearing couples who like their hobbies *expensive and deeply unrelatable*. If "18 holes and no personality" is your dream date, tee up.

Cupidtino.com

This site is for Apple cult members. Yes, if your top love language is "AirDrop me your heart," this is where you belong. If your number one non-negotiable is Apple loyalty... please go here.

SinglesWithFoodAllergies.com

If you're deathly allergic to peanuts and want someone who understands the fear of accidental hummus, congrats, there's a website for that.

BeautifulPeople.com

You literally have to be *voted in* by the already "beautiful" users. So, if you enjoy vanity, rejection, and a dating pool full of mirror-gazing self-lovers, jump in. Bonus: 80% of applicants get rejected, so you're not alone.

StachePassions.com

People who have mustaches. People who love mustaches. That's it. If your kink is facial hair, this is your Mecca. If not... maybe skip.

GK2GK.com

Dungeons & Dragons. World of Warcraft. Magic: The Gathering. This is the realm of full-blown fantasy immersion. If you've ever fallen for an elf in a chatroom, this is your shot at redemption.

PositiveSingles.com

Honestly, this one is admirable. A safe, respectful space for people living with STDs to date transparently. No shade just facts. Not weird. Just niche.

IvyDate.com

Supposedly for Ivy League grads, but it gives major "my parents still pay my rent" energy. High IQ? Maybe. High compatibility? Not guaranteed.

FarmersOnly.com

Where cowboys, cowgirls, and anyone with a tractor fetish unite. But don't get your hopes up, not every farmer looks like a Bachelor contestant.

TrekPassions.com

Star Trek, Star Wars, Battlestar, Firefly: this is your star map to love. If you've ever whispered "I'd go to warp speed for you," boldly go.

SaladMatch.com

Just salad. That's it. If you've ever bonded over croutons and arugula, this is your romaine soulmate portal.

SeaCaptainDate.com

Yes, it's real. Yes, there's a video. Yes, it looks like a recruitment ad for lonely mariners. If you dream of beardy men screaming "Ahoy!" in their sleep, full speed ahead.

18WheelSingles.com

For truckers and the people who want to date them. If a CB radio turns you on and you think truck stop snacks are romantic, roll on through.

NaturistPassions.com

For nudists. Full-stop. There's no profile pic, just… hope and gravity. Probably an older crowd. Possibly leathery.

AltaSphere.com/Dating

For singles who *really* like Ayn Rand. Like… a lot. If your dream date is a 3-hour lecture on objectivism, this one's for you. For everyone else, no.

SugarDaddyForMe.com

This is not what I call SAIF (Single, Attractive, Intelligent, Female) energy. This is the *opposite* of SAIF energy. It's transactional, weird, and 98% of the men on here are broke liars pretending to be rich. If you want a real sugar daddy, go to a steakhouse, not this site.

Meet-An-Inmate.com

People dating people *in prison*. Not post-prison. *In* prison. I have no words. Just questions.

FindYourFaceMate.com

A dating site that matches people who look like each other.

Pounced.com

A furry dating site. Do I know exactly what that means? No. Do I want to Google it? Also, no.

MyFreeImplants.com

Where men can donate to fund a woman's breast implants in hopes she falls in love with them. If that sounds like a solid plan to you, we need to talk.

VampirePassions.com

For people who think they're vampires or want to date someone who drinks blood for fun. Not goth. Not Twilight. Just... yikes.

DiaperMates.com

Adult babies and the people who want to date them. I'm not even going to unpack this. Just know it exists. And that's enough.

VeggieDate.org

For vegans and vegetarians who can't bear the thought of dating a meat-eater. If your ideal partner is a tofu-loving sandal-wearer with flaxseed breath, namaste.

ClownDating.com

Clowns. Literally clowns. No metaphor here. If the idea of face paint, squeaky noses, and balloon animals gets your heart racing, you've found your people.

Honorable Mentions from the "Apps That Shouldn't Exist" List:

- **Bristlr** – For people who love beards way too much
- **Hater** – Matching based on shared dislikes. Toxic but fun.
- **Feeld (formerly 3nder)** – The open-relationship, poly-curious, "we're exploring" zone
- **Tudder** – Not for people. For *cows*. Yes, *literally cows*.

UnExpert Final Word: Would I try one of these just for the story? Yes. Would I stay? Absolutely not. Swipe smart, laugh often, and remember: if it feels like a bad idea… it probably is.

QUIZ: Which Weird Dating Site Would You Accidentally Join?

(Because sometimes you're just one bad day away from signing up for ClownDating.com)

Answer honestly. Or don't. Either way, the results will haunt you.

1. Your love language is:
A) Free stuff and validation
B) Shared trauma and late-night Wikipedia rabbit holes
C) Mutual weirdness and hyper-specific hobbies
D) Talking about your cat like it's your child
E) Full nudity, obviously

2. Your ideal date includes:
A) Being paid to exist
B) Sword fighting (emotional or literal)
C) A picnic with tofu and wildflower readings
D) Matching outfits with your pet
E) A long-haul truck stop and two Red Bulls

3. What turns you off the most?
A) Broke men pretending to be rich
B) People who chew loudly
C) Anyone who thinks Dungeons & Dragons is "just a game"
D) Carnivores
E) Clothing

4. Your kink is closest to:
A) Capitalism
B) Cosplay
C) Judgment-free emotional support
D) Fiber-rich diets
E) Mustaches

5. You've been single too long. What's your sign to join a weird app?

A) Your therapist gives up

B) Your last situationship ghosted you *and* kept your hoodie

C) You accidentally said "I love you" to your Instacart driver

D) You cried watching a dog food commercial

E) You're just… open to the experience

RESULTS:

Mostly A's: MyFreeImplants.com

You're here for the attention, the perks, and possibly a free boob job. You know your worth and apparently, it has a price tag.

Mostly B's: GK2GK or VampirePassions

You're deep. Like, "wrote a fanfic at 3AM" deep. You want someone who understands your favorite lore and won't question the altar in your closet.

Mostly C's: VeggieDate or SaladMatch

You're a crunchy soul who's just looking for someone to match your energy and your diet. You've definitely dated a kombucha brewer and cried about it.

Mostly D's: Purrsonals or FindYourFaceMate

Your love life is deeply personal… and maybe a little delusional. You're looking for someone just like you or your pet. Or both. Which is… concerning.

Mostly E's: NaturistPassions or 18WheelSingles

You live for the plot twist. You're open-minded, unbothered, and a little dangerous. You could fall in love at a truck stop or a nudist colony and somehow *make it work*.

PART III
THE GAME
NAVIGATING THE WILD

Opening Moves

Swipe Left Profiles

Dating apps are all the craze and incredibly time-consuming if not done correctly. So, I have written down how to spot an asshole from a mile away and swipe left. This should save you a few hours of heartache wanting to give up because they aren't hitting you back. This does not account for the automatic swipe lefts on their profile such as political affiliation, children, height, if they do drugs, smoke. Those kinds of things would be your own personal preference. These are universal red flags that should be avoided at all costs.

1. Excessive gym photos. You know the one I am talking about. The one where they are holding the phone in front of them and taking a mirror pic. Pushing their arm muscles into their chest.
2. Guys with no real profile. They just filled out the basics, i.e., just pictures.
3. Here is a quick tip I found out about guys and their height: they lie. If a guy says he is 6', you need to deduct two inches. Sometimes four. Most likely the latter, as I have found out. If a guy says he is 5'11", he is absolutely lying because almost all guys who are 5'11" will round up to 6' as they think they are when they wake up and/or with their shoes on.
4. When guys do duck face in a photo, I tend to swipe left immediately. No guy should ever, and I mean ever, do duck face. Women can get away with it occasionally, but never a man. Also, peace signs, that is another no-no to stay away from. A peace sign with a duck face? Guurrrllll, fucking run!
5. When a guy just got out of a shower and is just wearing a towel photo. I find that a little douchey. Most good men wouldn't do that. Or too many selfies in general.
6. Excessive drinking photos. If in every photo he has a drink, there is a good chance he is going out every night.
7. Guys who spam you with the same message they write to every matched girl. They are usually in book form and sound completely generic. For Example: Hi Sarah, you seem really compatible. Let's connect, maybe go dancing one of these weekends? I'm there occasionally for work. Blah, blah, blah about where I live, but with the right person I will relocate. I don't see the distance as a big problem, if it is true love, we'll find a way to get in the same city. What do you do on weekends? I dance salsa and bachata weekly as a fun way to stay fit. Ever been? I'm athletic type, healthy eater, 6'1, own a business. Send me a text? Or tell me your cell and I'll call you. Add me on FB if you want. (And, yes, this is a real one.)
8. Guys who use pet names right off the bat to greet you in a text message. "Hey Babe…"

171

9. Guys who put up a fake name as their profile name. Who doesn't use their real name?? Automatically suspicious and an immediate swipe left, nope. I came across a name that said GSP. Is that an acronym like FBI? Are you a company? What is that?

10. Guys who are unemployed. Obviously. No explanation needed.

11. I wouldn't recommend guys who are "actors." Check their IMDb. If they are working consistently, I would say that should be fine, but not ones who just have "Extra" on their resume. I know it's a hard knock life, but if they haven't made it yet, they will be putting their career first and not ready to settle down.

12. Guys who have hot chicks in their pictures. Or even worse, when it is obviously an ex-girlfriend and they scratch out her face. Like, seriously dude? There wasn't another picture you could use?

13. Guys with pictures of celebrities in their profile. Like we get it, we all know someone famous. Even the dude who gives me my frappe at McDonald's everyday knows someone.

14. Pictures not showing their teeth, hair, or body. If women have to do it, so do men. We don't need to get catfished. I am not saying if they don't have hair, you shouldn't date them, I am saying they should own their shit since we have to.

15. Pictures with dogs that aren't theirs. Trying to bait women is not cool.

16. Guys who are clearly over 50 and say they are 34. Not joking, my ex's old business partner who I knew popped up on my Hinge account saying he was 45 and he is like 60. You know why they do that? Because girls have age limits. And they want to get those girls who have age limits, because they think they are going to fool them.

17. Another big one is guys with no solo photos, like how the hell are you supposed to figure out which one he is in the picture? You are always hoping it's the hot friend in the photo, and 99.3% of the time it is not the hot friend.

18. When they wear deep Vs or only button the bottom three buttons of a button-up shirt. Like we get it, you like your chest, but why not try to leave it to the imagination and look somewhat like a gentleman?

19. When they wear a Halloween costume. I am not sure I care that much depending on what the costume is, but my friends will say no if they see it. So, I put it in—maybe you know the Halloween costumes they are referring to, or if it is just in general, lol.

20. Rave photos of them tripping balls. Apparently, those are real. I am guessing that is also when they made their profile.

21. Guys who write short messages like "WYD?" or just send the eyes emoji. You deserve more of an effort.

22. Men who are married or in an open relationship and just looking for some side action. Yes, those profiles exist. You can usually tell this when a man has a woman in all of his pictures, but not always. You can also join the women's group in your area called "Are We Dating the Same Guy?" But I would proceed with caution, as some of these women like to think men have red flags when they were just not that into them.

23. Men who wear jean capris. Yep. (Enough said.)

24. Men who say they are self-employed at self-employed. If they can't even say a certain category at self-employed, it's better to swipe left. As well as, self-employed usually means unemployed.

25. Men who wear fur pimp coats and it's not Halloween. Again, yes, I have proof of this.

26. Men who photoshop their body to look skinnier. Men who put filters on their pictures. Like bro, no. I put filters on my photos because I feel like the filter in person.

27. Men trying to be out of a New Kids on the Block music video. The one where they are wearing a no-sleeve zip-up hoodie unzipped to show their abs with a backwards cap.

28. Men who only put up shirtless photos of themselves. Yeah, we get it, you must have worked real hard for that body…I don't want to date and not be able to eat a carb.

29. Men who say they only want something casual. Don't try to bait them into a relationship; they are being honest. If that is all you want as well, have at it. But if you truly want a relationship, no matter how hot they are, you need to swipe left, unfortunately. If you want just sex, have at it, but you will not turn them into a relationship no matter how good in bed you are, remember that. Also, remember they are probably fucking thirteen other girls that are thinking just like you. Stop it. Again, have I done this? Yes. Does it work? No.

30. When a man says he's "open-minded" in his profile, good chance he has ED and is interested in other kinks. That's a swipe left.

31. When his profile says "still figuring it out" as to what he's looking for, he's looking for sex. Swipe left.

32. If a guy only has a WhatsApp number, he is probably from Nigeria and it is a scam.

33. If a dude is laying in his bed with his one arm over his head…it just makes me feel uncomfortable. Next.

34. Guys who leave their bio completely blank. They aren't even making an effort for women to hold a convo. Like "Nice face, I guess." No, ladies, they are looking just to get fucked.

35. Men who have low-quality pictures. Usually meaning they were taken circa 2012, and don't want you to see the real them. Or only two photos that are both extremely far away.

36. My favorite is the dirty mirror selfie…really bro? Clean your mirror.

37. Pics in Vegas with street strippers. Yep…this happens.

38. Someone with no pictures. This is also a thing, and don't know why you would swipe right unless you are super lonely. I also feel that they are probably married.

39. I almost missed fish pics.

40. Standing next to a sports car or any flashy shit.

41. The "Here for a Good Time, Not a Long Time" bio. Translation: He's emotionally unavailable and probably won't text you back after the third drink.

42. Overuse of emojis. Like four tongue emojis, three eggplants, or just fire/fire/fire. If it reads like a 13-year-old's text, he probably talks like one too.

43. "My Kids Come First" in bio. Look, we all respect that—but when the entire bio is about the kids and there's no room for you, it's giving "I want a nanny, not a partner."

44. Men who say "No Drama." That man is the drama. Only toxic dudes think women bring drama. The peaceful ones don't have to say it.

45. "Sapiosexual" in bio. You just learned a new word, congrats. But this usually translates to: "I think I'm smarter than everyone else."

46. "I'm bad at this app." If he's bad at communicating or following through, this is his built-in excuse. Don't fall for it.

47. Profiles that are 90% photos of their kids. Are you dating him or trying to co-parent by next Tuesday?

48. "Must love dogs" but no dog pics. Bro, do you even have a dog? Or did you borrow that line because it sounds wholesome?

49. Guys who say "I don't like talking about myself." Cool, enjoy your monologue while I ask 40 questions to get 4-word answers.

50. Photos with their mom that look like a date. You know the ones. Hugging waist, cheek kiss. That's your mom? Feels like a red flag wrapped in an Oedipus complex.

As Always

If I'm missing some, please contact me: @yourdatingunexpert on Facebook, Instagram, or TikTok and kindly follow. I want to make a cohesive list! I'll be adding these to my website: www.yourdatingunexpert.com so you can check back anytime.

And reminder:

Some dudes just don't know how to take photos. Give them a little cred, they might actually be one of the good ones.

Helpful Dating App Tips:

- If you're unsure about a guy's profile (and over 20% of profiles are now fake or scams), run their photo through Google Reverse Image Search or an app that does that.
- If you're pen-paling a dude, cut it off. He's just keeping you around in case another date falls through. If he hasn't asked you out within a week of chatting, cut it off. In my experience, the good ones ask within the first two days.

Shameless Plug Alert:

If you haven't already downloaded my *Red Flag Bingo*, what are you even doing? Turn your next swiping session into a savage drinking game (or a solo hate-scroll ritual) with the most unhinged profile traits imaginable. It's hilarious, petty, and painfully accurate just like modern dating. Grab it now at https://yourdatingunexpert.com/red-flag-bingo-game.

Messages to Send to Men That Guarantee a Reply

THE FLIRTY BAIT: Sweet with a sting
1. "You seem cute. But I've been wrong before."
2. "I had a dream about you. You were... disappointing. Want to redeem yourself?"
3. "You're either the one or the lesson. Let's find out."

THE FUNNY BAIT: Laughter = response
4. "How tall are you in emotional availability?"
5. "I need someone to open jars and overexplain movies to me. You seem like a candidate."
6. "On a scale from 1 to 'men ain't sh*t,' where do you fall?"

THE WEIRD BAIT: Because confusion = curiosity
7. "Quick question: If you were a chair, how would you emotionally support me?"
8. "Are you the simulation glitch or just here to distract me from my destiny?"
9. "I collect men with questionable hobbies. What's yours?"

THE PSYCHOLOGY BAIT: Reverse the power
10. "You don't strike me as someone who can keep up. Prove me wrong."
11. "I like men who text with confidence. This is your audition."
12. "Most guys flinch at real connection. You game?"

THE SAVAGE BAIT: For when you're feeling spicy
13. "Are you emotionally available or should I block you now and save time?"
14. "I'm only interested in men who know they're the prize, but still act right."
15. "Let me guess…you're 'not like other guys.'"

THE PETTY BAIT: Let's play
16. "I swiped right by accident. Let's see if it was fate or just poor judgment."
17. "I know 3 men like you. One is in therapy. One is in jail. The other's married. You?"
18. "My friends bet you wouldn't respond. Don't prove them right."

THE HIGH-VALUE ENERGY BAIT: You're the prize, act like it
19. "Just a heads up, I don't compete. I attract."
20. "I'm not looking for a pen pal. I'm looking for resonance."
21. "Don't just match my vibe, match my vision."

QUICK FIRE OPENERS
22. "So, what made you swipe?"
23. "Is this going to be a plot twist or a trauma bond?"
24. "I have questions. Do you have bandwidth?"

CLOSERS & POWER FLIPS
25. "I don't need a man. But I could use a good story."
26. "If this is the beginning of a love story, it better be a bestseller."
27. "You text dry, I disappear. Just letting you know the terms."

You are, for sure by now, getting sick of me promoting stuff on Etsy. This book was extremely long and you would have probably gotten bored reading 101 openers, that is why I made another guide. I am going to give you a tip, if you like these, you can plug your style or what you want to say into ChatGPT or an AI you prefer, and it will make prompts for you that are in your own voice. If you don't like your voice, you can get more of these. At the end of this book, I will give you all the games, guides and tools for a deeply discounted rate.

https://yourdatingunexpert.etsy.com/listing/4431488031

Comebacks When They Go Dry

(Because you're not a tumbleweed, and this ain't a ghost town.)

Rule #1: Never beg for attention.
Rule #2: Never act like you noticed the silence first.
Rule #3: Leave him wondering if *you* were the one who disappeared.

The "I'm Unbothered but Sharp" Series
1. "That pause was dramatic. Should I be flattered or concerned?"
2. "Oh good, you're alive. I was about to start a GoFundMe."
3. "Your enthusiasm is overwhelming. Slow down."
4. "You must be exhausted from all this emotional availability."
5. "Didn't mean to interrupt whatever it is you're clearly prioritizing."

The Ice-Cold Power Flip
6. "No worries, I only reply to energy that feels mutual."
7. "My bad, I thought we were having a conversation. Clearly, I was mistaken."
8. "You text like a man with options and no personality."
9. "It's giving breadcrumb. It's giving mid. It's giving… next."
10. "Let me know when your texting plan includes effort."

The Savage Truth Serum
11. "You're not too busy, you're just not interested. It's okay, be real."
12. "Dry texts are usually a sign of one of three things: boredom, a side chick, or emotional constipation. Want to confess which?"
13. "You don't actually like me. You like the attention. Plot twist: it's been revoked."
14. "If I have to carry the convo, I get paid hourly."
15. "Low-effort men get replaced faster than they can type 'lol.'"

The Flip-and-Fade Technique
16. "This was fun. I'll let you get back to whoever's actually getting effort."
17. "I'm gonna dip. Let me know if your vibe ever catches up with your face."

18. "You've officially entered the passive ghost phase. No judgment, I've been there too."

19. "Not feeling the convo anymore, but hope your ego enjoyed the attention."

20. "Thanks for the demo. I'll go with the premium version of connection next time."

The Petty Exit Survey

21. "Quick exit poll: Were you always this boring or did I just bring it out of you?"

22. "What exactly were you hoping to achieve with this... performance?"

23. "Would you say your texting style is: A) Emotionally Avoidant B) Just Lazy C) Trying to get unmatched?"

24. "Before I go, what's the Yelp rating on this conversation? 1-star for effort?"

25. "I need closure. Was it me? Was it you? Or was it your lack of charisma?"

The Last Word That Ends It All

26. "You're cute, but not worth this much confusion."

27. "This isn't ghosting. It's just me letting the conversation die with dignity."

28. "No hard feelings. Just high standards."

29. "You'll think of something clever to say right after I unmatch you."

30. "You're officially archived. Best of luck in your emotionally repressed endeavors."

Swipe-Right Power Lines

(Because you don't chase, you interrupt the algorithm.)

Each line is a trigger. A mirror. A trap. A dare. These aren't about being nice. They're about being unforgettable. Let's break them into sections based on your mood:

I. The Power Entry (Confidence that makes them blink)

1. "Let's skip the pleasantries. What's your emotional availability rating out of 10?"

2. "This app is cursed but you seem slightly less tragic than most."

3. "I don't believe in coincidences. Why are you here?"

II. The Banter Bait (Flirt with a side of challenge)

4. "Tell me something that would make me instantly unmatch you."

5. "You get one chance to make me laugh. Use it wisely."

6. "What's the worst opener a woman's ever sent you? Let me outdo it."

III. The Intellect Hook (For men who think they're deep)

7. "Quick! Describe your soul in three words. No thinking."

8. "Do you believe in fate or free will? This determines everything."

9. "What book changed your mind about something important?"

IV. The Disruptors (Pattern breakers that get a double-take)

10. "This isn't a match. This is a test."

11. "You're not ready for me, but let's pretend for a moment that you are."

12. "Don't try to impress me. Try to be real. Most can't."

V. The Seductive Edge (High-vibe but dangerous)

13. "We'll either kiss or destroy each other. Maybe both."

14. "You don't want nice. You want real. But can you handle it?"

15. "I'm not the safe choice. I'm the one you remember."

VI. The Petty Queens (For days you don't even like men)

16. "Don't be boring. I will disappear mid-message."

17. "Your photos look edited by a man who peaked in 2016."

18. "You're one 'wyd' from getting unmatched."

VII. The Soft Traps (Lowkey, magnetic, deceptively gentle)

19. "What's something you've never told anyone but wish you had?"

20. "What does safety feel like to you?"

21. "Describe the last moment that made you believe in something bigger."

VIII. The Chaos Cards (For when you want to stir sh*t up)

22. "I came here to waste your time and maybe your life. Swipe accordingly."

23. "I will never ask what you do for work. I don't care."

24. "Let's pretend we're already in the breakup phase."

IX. The High-Frequency Power Moves

25. "I attract clarity, not confusion."

26. "I am not auditioning. I am observing."

27. "If your energy isn't intentional, it's invisible to me."

X. The Exit Ramps (If you change your mind mid-message)

28. "Actually, never mind. I saw your bio."

29. "Scratch that. I just realized you're probably emotionally unavailable."

30. "Unmatch in 3... 2... 1…"

If you want 71 more lines, you know what to do:

https://yourdatingunexpert.etsy.com/listing/4431510556

Questions to Ask on a First Date
(Because "What do you do for work?" is not a personality.)

Let's be real. First dates are a weird social experiment wrapped in hopeful chaos. You're sitting across from a stranger, trying to figure out if they're emotionally available or just hot with a good sense of style. The wrong questions can make it feel like a job interview. The *right* ones? They spark something. They pull out the layers, the quirks, the real sh*t people never get asked. That's where connection lives. These aren't your basic "favorite color" type questions. These are designed to crack people open *just enough* to see what's under the surface without making it therapy. Use them to weed out the walking red flags, or better yet, find out if the person across from you actually has a soul. Ask boldly. Laugh freely. And remember: you're not trying to impress anyone, you're collecting data. Now go make that small talk extinct.

First Impression Firestarters
(AKA: Not Your Boring "What's Your Job?" Questions)
These are the warm-up questions that get you out of the "interview zone" and into real energy.

1. What makes you different than most people you know? Forget asking someone to describe themselves that gets you canned answers. This flips it. It tells you what they *notice* about themselves in a crowd. Self-awareness? Confidence? Delusion? You'll know.

2. What's a random fun fact that *never* comes up on a date but should? This one invites play. You want to know if they were once on a game show or have a sixth toe. Let people show you their weird. That's where the good stuff is.

3. What's something you secretly wish you were amazing at? This one reveals dreams not LinkedIn goals, *actual soul cravings*. Do they want to sing in a band? Speak five languages? Cook without setting the kitchen on fire? Now we're talking.

Emotional Depth Checks
These are the questions that gently slide past the mask and ask,
"Hey, is there a real person in there?"
Not trauma dumps just small cracks in the surface to peek at how deep the water goes.

4. What's something that changed you forever even if no one else noticed? This isn't about major life events, it's about inner shifts. You'll see if they reflect, or if they just bounce from moment to moment without ever looking back.

5. What's something you used to believe about love... that you don't anymore? A+ way to assess if they've grown. Do they still think love = fixing people? Do they know the difference between chemistry and compatibility? This one tells you *a lot*.

6. When was the last time you truly felt seen by someone? Watch their eyes when they answer this. You'll know immediately if they're still waiting to be understood or if they've finally found it (even for a moment).

179

Dating Mindset Questions
*Because how someone talks about dating tells you
more than their Hinge profile ever could.*

These questions help you spot emotional availability, baggage, bitterness, or green-flag energy, all without asking, "So why are you single?"

7. What's something dating has taught you about yourself? If they say, "nothing" *run*. If they say, "women are crazy" *sprint*. This question cuts through the fluff and tells you if they've reflected or just rebounded.

8. Do you believe in "the one" or do you think we choose who we love? Philosophical *and* strategic. You'll see whether they're chasing fate or building connection. Also, a peek into how realistic (or delusional) their expectations are.

9. What do you think makes a relationship last and what makes it die? This one separates the surface charmers from the people who *actually think about relationships*. You'll hear their real values fast.

Playful & Adventurous Questions
*For when you want to skip the small talk and jump into the
"what if we ran away together" energy.*

10. If you had a plane ticket to anywhere, no work, no responsibilities, where would you go *right now*? Spontaneity test, location reveal, and emotional compass all in one. This answer says a lot about whether they're a beach bum, a wanderlust soul, or a "Vegas with the boys" walking headache.

11. What's one thing you've always wanted to try, but haven't yet? This one pulls out bucket list energy and shows whether they're adventurous, scared, or stuck in routine. Plus, it might lead to a second date idea (skydiving, anyone?).

12. What's the most spontaneous thing you've ever done and would you do it again? You'll find out if their version of spontaneous is "booked a last-minute trip" or "got blackout and adopted a turtle." Either way? Great story.

Red Flag Radar Questions
*Because "So, why did your last relationship end?"
is way too obvious and way too easy to lie about.*

13. What's something you've *never* been called in a relationship but wish you had? This question cuts *deep*. It'll show you their unmet emotional needs *and* what they know they don't bring to the table yet. If they say "patient," "safe," or "respected" lean in.

14. If your ex was describing you to someone, what do you think they'd say? Self-awareness test. If they say "crazy" or "too much," we might be done here. But if they say "I don't know… probably stubborn but kind?" That's honest. And hot.

15. What's a pattern you've noticed in your past relationships and have you tried to break it? Everyone's got a pattern. Avoidance, over-giving, dating emotionally unavailable people, whatever. This tells you if they've ever looked in the mirror *before* blaming their exes.

Chemistry Builder Questions
For when you want to flirt without losing IQ points.

16. What's something people often misunderstand about you that you secretly wish they saw right away? This one opens the vulnerability door *just* enough. It tells you what they wish they didn't have to explain which is often the most magnetic part of them.

17. What's your "I was totally irresistible in that moment" story? It's a flex, but it's also fun. It shows you how they carry themselves at their best and whether their version of "irresistible" is hot, hilarious, or a walking ick.

18. What's something you've never done on a date... but would love to try? A little suggestive, a little adventurous without being creepy. Plus, if they say "murder mystery dinner" or "slow dancing in a parking lot," you know they've got soul.

The Weird, Witty & Unexpected
For when you're done playing it safe and
want to see if they can keep up with your chaos.

These are the curveballs, the "wait, what?" moments, the stories you'll tell your friends no matter how the date ends.

19. If your inner child ran this date, what would we be doing right now? This one is sneaky sweet. You'll get a glimpse of their playfulness, nostalgia, and maybe a lowkey childhood wound. Are they a fort-building dreamer or a ride-the-shopping-cart rebel?

20. What's your "if they can't handle this, they can't handle me" trait? Confidence check. Also, a *chaos radar*. If they say, "I need a nap every day at 3pm and I cry when I don't get it." Respect.

21. If you had to rate your texting game from 1–10, where do you land and why? Cut through the guessing. This tells you how they communicate AND if they ghost, breadcrumb, or actually reply in full sentences like a grown adult.

22. What conspiracy theory do you *not* believe in... but secretly wish was real? Aliens, Atlantis, lizard people — this question reveals their imagination, playfulness, and *how they handle weird shi*t without short-circuiting.

23. What food would you eat for the rest of your life if nutrition didn't matter? Judgment-free junk food zone. Tells you more than you think like if they've got taste buds or if they've somehow never had real pizza.

Intentional & Soulful

For when the vibe shifts and you're thinking... maybe this isn't just a one-time thing. These are the deep-calm questions. The grounded ones. The ones you save for when you're staring at them mid-date like, "wait... could this actually be something?"

24. What makes you feel most like yourself? This question gets to the core. It shows what brings them home to themselves: nature, music, helping people, disappearing into a book. This is where you find out who they really are when the performance drops.

25. When in your life have you felt the most peace? Everyone talks about "fun" and "sexy," but peace? That's rare. Their answer will show you what environments they thrive in and if they're even capable of stillness.

26. What's a truth you had to learn the hard way but you're grateful for now? This one goes right for the soul. You'll get wisdom, pain, grit and maybe the key to who they've become.

Mic Drop Questions

These are the bold closers, the "I'm not here to waste time" questions, the ones that tell you if it's date two... or delete.

27. What are you *not* willing to settle for anymore in dating or life? No fluff, no games. This gives you their hard lines. The ones they've earned through trial, error, and heartbreak. Watch how fast their face changes when they answer.

28. What's a belief or value you hold now that would've shocked your younger self? This one shows transformation. It reveals where they've done the work or where they still need to.

29. When someone really loves you, how do you know? Words, actions, energy — this reveals their love language *and* their emotional awareness. If they've never thought about it... that's saying something too.

You know how I roll by now. If you want more:
https://yourdatingunexpert.etsy.com/listing/4431521453

101 Places to Find Single Men in the Wild

(Because your future husband is not in your DMs,
he's standing in line somewhere being mid.)

Real-World Tactics: Move Different, Date Smarter

"You can heal your feminine energy all day. But if you keep going to the same three bars, your soulmate is drinking somewhere else."

This is for the woman who's tired of watching everyone else "meet someone" while she keeps running into tech bros, man-babies, and walking midlife crises in cool jackets. It's not you. It's the field. Let's fix it.

1. Date Outside Your Type. Then Again. And Again. If you've been picking "tall, funny, emotionally unavailable" since 2014, it's not working. Date a chef. Date a man who bikes to work. Date a CPA who plays jazz. You're not looking for fireworks. You're looking for something that doesn't need to explode to be real.

Real-World Hack: Expand your radius. Filter for "never married," "wants kids," "over 40," "under 30," or whatever shakes you out of your loop. If you only date 6'2" men with jawlines, you're dating 1.1% of the male population. Congratulations, you've cornered yourself.

2. Go Where the Men Are (Not Where the Girls Go). Most women go to yoga, brunch, and candle-making classes… then wonder why they're single. Men aren't there. You know where they *are*?

- Golf courses
- Entrepreneur meetups
- Dog parks at seven a.m.
- High-end cigar bars (yes, even just for the aesthetic)

Real-World Hack: Once a week, go somewhere you're slightly uncomfortable. Dress like the fantasy version of you that would thrive there. Say nothing. Let them wonder who the hell you are.

3. Always Walk in Alone. You're less approachable when you're with your friends. Period. If you're at a bar, a show, a festival, take a lap solo. Order your drink alone. Look around once. Smile. You just made yourself 500% more accessible without saying a word.

Real-World Hack: Ditch the safety blanket. Men don't want to interrupt your entire friend group. But they *will* ask what you're drinking if you give them a one-second opening.

4. The 15-Second Rule. Make conversation with any man for 15 seconds even if you're not interested. Why? Because it shifts your energy from *closed* to *approachable*. And the universe doesn't care if he's not the one. It just cares that you're open to the frequency of receiving.

Real-World Hack: Use the line: "Wait, I have to ask where'd you get that [drink/watch/shirt]?" No pickup. No pressure. Just engagement.

5. Have a 3-Sentence Story Ready. When he says, "What do you do?" don't launch into your resume. Say something like: "I help women get over men who never deserved them. It's savage. I do R&D for dating." Or "I used to work in tech. Now I mostly work in chaos, caffeine, and cat videos."

Real-World Hack: You need to spark curiosity. Leave room for him to chase *you* with questions.

6. The "Drop One Detail" Trick. Instead of telling your whole life story, drop one interesting line and stop talking.
- "I once had a guy ghost me, then apply for a job at my company six months later."
- "I lived on an island with no Wi-Fi for a year."
- "I accidentally ended up at an orgy once. No further questions."

Say it. Smile. Then sip your drink.

Real-World Hack: Mystery makes you memorable. Don't fill the silence. Let him earn the next layer.

7. Wear a Conversation Starter. A bold ring. A vintage tee. A weird book. A red notebook. Men are simple. They need a hook. Give them one.

Real-World Hack: If you're wearing something a little "extra," stand somewhere still. Let them come to you with, "That's a cool…" It works. Every time.

8. Talk to the Ones You're "Not Sure About." That guy with the okay profile and slightly awkward smile? He could be the best man you've ever met. But you'll never know if you keep chasing aesthetic over essence.

Real-World Hack: If his grammar's good, he has a real job, and he didn't list "banter" as a personality trait? Give him a shot. He's already ahead of 70% of them.

9. Say "Hi" First. But Say It Right. You don't need to be aggressive. You just need to *signal openness.* Try: "You look like trouble in a good way."

"Tell me one thing you're actually proud of."

"I have no opening line, but your energy's great."

Real-World Hack: Don't overthink it. Just start the engine. If he doesn't reply, he's not for you. Next.

THE WILD WILD WEST

This isn't just about location. This is about energy. Go where men feel competent, open, and a little caught off guard. That's when the real ones slip up and show themselves. We're breaking this into categories so you can hunt with intention, depending on your vibe, your time, and your patience level for male behavior.

I. The Gold Mines: Where High-Quality Men Are Actually Paying Attention
1. Upscale coffee shops near business districts
2. Independent bookstores with a finance or entrepreneurship section
3. Hotel bars during conferences

4. Co-working spaces
5. Airport lounges (especially early morning flights)
6. Art gallery openings
7. Cooking classes
8. Wine tastings
9. Charity galas or fundraising events
10. Upscale gym weight rooms (not group classes)

II. The Casual Encounters: Where It Happens When You're Not Trying

11. Your dog park (with or without a dog)
12. Home improvement stores on Saturday morning
13. Farmer's markets
14. Juice bars and smoothie shops
15. Record stores
16. Plant nurseries (a man buying plants = green flag)
17. Running trails or walking paths
18. Beach volleyball courts
19. Your neighborhood bar not a club, a bar
20. The longest line at Trader Joe's (talk while stuck)

III. The Skill Zones: Where They're Focused and Forget to Front

21. Adult rec league sports (kickball, dodgeball, etc.)
22. Rock climbing gyms
23. Community acting or improv classes
24. Martial arts studios
25. Photography meetups
26. Auto shows
27. Public chess parks
28. Live podcast tapings
29. Bar trivia nights
30. Tech expos or startup meetups

IV. The "I Didn't Expect to Meet You Here" Traps

31. Jury duty
32. DMV waiting rooms (the desperation breeds connection)
33. Museum exhibits on a weekday
34. TEDx events
35. Train stations or subway platforms (bonus if you drop your MetroCard)
36. Professional conferences (network *and* flirt)
37. Career fairs (volunteer to help, then scout)
38. Furniture stores (single men pretend they know what they're doing)
39. Ski lodges (by the fireplace, not the slopes)
40. Emergency vet clinics (emotional men = unlocked hearts)

V. The Travel + Adventure Men

41. National parks
42. Solo travel hostels for 30+
43. Language immersion classes
44. Airbnb Experiences
45. Scenic train rides (Amtrak lounge car = gold)
46. Long-haul flights (aisle seat energy only)
47. Group hiking trips or walking tours
48. Boat rentals or kayak clubs
49. Music festivals (look for the ones with jobs)
50. Roadside diners during travel season

VI. The Nerd Herd: Intelligent, Introverted, Potentially Husband Material

51. Sci-fi conventions
52. Board game cafes
53. Computer repair classes
54. Apple store workshops
55. Public library tech help desks
56. Night classes at your local university
57. Vintage comic shops
58. Strategy game meetups
59. VR arcades
60. The one quiet booth in a loud bar

VII. The Fitness + Discipline Men (Watch Out for Narcissists)

61. Boxing gyms
62. Triathlon training clubs
63. Climbing walls
64. Olympic lifting workshops
65. Group runs or 5Ks
66. Tennis courts at public parks
67. Open-water swim events
68. Pickleball tournaments
69. Hot yoga (go late in the day, fewer couples)
70. Men's health expos

VIII. The Money + Mission Men (The ones building things)

71. Real estate investor meetups
72. Wealth-building seminars
73. Stock trading workshops
74. Tech incubator pitch nights
75. City planning or community development panels
76. Startup pitch competitions

77. Financial literacy classes
78. Cryptocurrency networking events
79. Clean tech expos
80. Golf ranges on weekdays

IX. The Creative & Spiritually Awakened Men (Soul + Swagger)

81. Open mic nights
82. Spoken word poetry events
83. Breathwork sessions
84. Sound baths or meditation meetups
85. Book launch parties
86. Screenwriting workshops
87. Music producer meetups
88. Sunday philosophy brunches
89. Non-toxic men's circles
90. A course in miracles study groups

X. The Curveballs: Where You Weren't Expecting It, But BAM! He's There

91. Parking lot of a gym at 6am
92. Local government town halls
93. Public park bootcamp classes
94. Library elevators
95. Costco gas line
96. Knife-sharpening booth at a street fair
97. Dry cleaners on a weekday afternoon
98. Quiet bar on Super Bowl Sunday
99. Tesla charging station lounges
100. Hotel breakfast buffets (solo diners = single)
101. Your friend's boring birthday party. Go anyway, stay 90 minutes, *then decide*

It's not always about *where* you go. It's how open you are while you're there. Head up. Phone down. Eyes engaged. Be magnetic. Be observant. Be the plot twist he brags about later.

Approach Tactics:

How to Get His Attention in the Wild (Without Ever Looking Thirsty)

I. Subtle Ways to Get Noticed (Without Saying a Word)

(Use these when he's nearby and you want him to see you before you speak)

1. Position yourself in his peripheral and laugh like you just heard the funniest thing in your life.
2. Drop something "accidentally" in front of him, but don't look back, he'll bring it to you.

3. Make eye contact. Hold it for one second longer than normal. Then look away slowly.
4. Pull out a book or notebook and look deeply focused, then glance up and stretch. Instant intrigue.
5. Mirror his energy from a distance: stand, sip, or walk the same way. He'll pick up on it, even subconsciously.

II. How to Signal Him to Approach (Without Looking Obvious)

6. Touch your hair or neck while looking around the room slowly. Pause if your eyes land on him.
7. Walk past him and "accidentally" brush shoulders or make gentle contact. Look back just long enough for him to question it.
8. Ask the bartender or barista a question loud enough for him to hear. Something smart or playful.
9. Laugh with your friend while making eye contact with him mid-laugh. Hold his eyes for a split second before returning to your convo.
10. Angle your body toward him when you sit or stand, subtle but psychologically magnetic.

III. Powerful One-Liners to Open Without Losing the Upper Hand

These are quick, casual, and loaded with energy. They make *you* seem bold and unforgettable but still give *him* the space to pursue.

11. "You look like someone I should know."
12. "Are you always this mysterious, or is it just today?"
13. "Quick! Are you charming or just good at pretending?"
14. "I need a male opinion. But only if it's good."
15. "I saw you and had to come over before I made up a whole fake story in my head."
16. "Tell me something about you I wouldn't guess just by looking."
17. "You don't talk much, do you? Is that on purpose or are you waiting for me to say hi first?"
18. "You look like someone who knows where to find good coffee. Am I wrong?"
19. "You look like you're either deep in thought or judging everyone. Which is it?"
20. "Let's skip the small talk. What do you actually want in life?"

IV. Tactics to Draw Him in Without Speaking First

21. Compliment the bartender or server loudly while standing near him. Shows kindness + confidence.
22. Pull out your phone and act like you're texting, but keep glancing his way like he's distracting you.
23. Pretend you're looking for something nearby and ask him for help "Hey, do you know if this place has almond milk?"
24. Ask for a location-based recommendation like: "I'm debating between the IPA and the lager. Got a strong opinion?"

25. Do the "walk away, then come back and ask one question" trick. It looks spontaneous, not premeditated.

V. Closing Energy: How to Leave a Mark If You Walk Away First

26. "You seem interesting. I'll let you come say hi properly next time."
27. "I have to go, but I'm glad I got a glimpse of the mystery."
28. "Nice to meet you. I'm not sure what just happened, but I liked it."
29. "This was fun. Don't let me forget you."
30. "You better be bold enough to continue this next time I see you."

First Date Spots That Are Out of the Ordinary
(Not cute. Not cozy. These are plot-starters. Power moves. Memorable by force.)

These aren't for the situationship you're trying to "see where it goes." These are for the ones you want to either fall for *fast* or eliminate *faster.* Let's structure it by energy and intention so you can pick your battlefield accordingly.

I. Vibes That Say 'I Have Standards and a Story Arc'
1. A speakeasy hidden behind a laundromat
2. A pop-up art installation or immersive exhibit
3. A rooftop jazz night with a dress code

II. Let's Get Cultured, Baby (Without Boring Ourselves to Death)
4. Foreign film with subtitles and post-movie drinks
5. Architecture tour of your city
6. Underground comedy club

III. You Call This a First Date? Exactly. That's the Point.
7. Goat milking or beekeeping experience
8. Archery class in the woods
9. Digging for fossils or gems at a quarry

IV. Fancy Without Feeling Forced
10. Boat-to-table seafood dinner
11. Private yacht sunset ride
12. A perfume-making lab where you create a custom scent

V. Psych Test First Dates (Let's Get Weird Fast)
13. Visit a courtroom and watch a live trial
14. Attend a town hall meeting and whisper commentary

VI. Reckless and Hot (In All the Best Ways)
15. Roller derby match followed by drinks
16. Take a helicopter survival crash course
17. Street food festival where you try everything

VII. Time Travel Dates (We're Not from Here, Apparently)
18. Medieval fair in full costume
19. Roaring 20s party. Fake names required
20. Victorian séance reenactment

VIII. Ultra Intimate Energy with a Twist
21. Bookstore date but you only pick each other books that reveal something you're afraid to say
22. Walk through an unfamiliar neighborhood with no phones and see where you end up
23. Paint a portrait of each other using dollar store supplies

IX. If We Survive This, It's Meant to Be

24. Tandem bike ride on a windy path
25. Indoor skydiving (with high-five photos after)
26. Take a hot yoga class, see who taps out first

X. Low-Budget but Iconically Bold

27. Ask strangers to judge your outfits or make up a love story for you
28. Go to Goodwill and build a "date survival kit" for each other
29. Make the worst possible restaurant reservations and act like it's fine dining

If you want more, there's always more:

https://www.etsy.com/listing/4431544384/101-first-date-ideas-that-arent-boring-o

Tips for Dating Someone New

That new relationship glow? It's everything. The butterflies. The flirty texts. The you-up's that don't feel gross yet. But let's be real, this early stage is *fragile as hell*. One wrong move and you're ghosted faster than you can say, "I thought we had a vibe."

Before you self-sabotage or trauma-dump your way into singledom, here are 20 no-BS tips to keep the spark alive without losing yourself in the process:

1. Romanticize the Damn Moment. Quit spiraling about your future wedding or whether he's texting his ex. Be *here*. Laugh, flirt, enjoy. If you're vibing, vibe. Don't ruin a present moment with a past pattern or future fantasy.

2. Don't Slap on a Label Too Soon. Nothing kills a spark faster than "So...what are we?" two dates in. Let the connection breathe. If it's right, the label will show up when it's ready like Amazon Prime, but for emotional clarity.

3. Try Weird Shit Together. Skip the basic dinner-and-a-movie. Take a salsa class. Visit an escape room. Go axe throwing. Be the chaos they never saw coming, in a good way.

4. Be Just Brave Enough to Be Vulnerable. You don't have to cry about your childhood trauma over appetizers, but don't be all surface either. Let them see the real you: the weird, wonderful, and wounded parts. Real connection lives there.

5. Don't Try to Control the Narrative. If you're already micro-managing their texts or trying to "fix" them, pause. Healthy love doesn't come with a leash. Let people show you who they are instead of assigning them a role in your fantasy.

6. Tell the Truth (Even If It's Awkward). You're not doing anyone favors by pretending you're chill with something you're not. Honest is sexy. And it weeds out the ones who aren't ready for it.

7. Stop Comparing Them to Your Ex. Your new boo isn't your ex. And if they are, therapy. Stop turning your ex into the blueprint or the villain. Create something new with the person in front of you.

8. Keep a Little Mystery. You don't need to drop your life story in the first week. Let the connection unfold. Hold back just enough to make them lean in.

9. Actually, Pay Attention. No one likes feeling like a placeholder. Listen. Ask questions. Remember their favorite coffee order. Be someone who *sees* people. (Read the book *How to Win Friends and Influence People*.)

10. Sprinkle in the Romance. No need to rent a horse-drawn carriage. But a cute voice note? A random compliment? Showing up with their favorite snack? That's romance, baby.

11. Give Them Breathing Room. Neediness isn't endearing, it's exhausting. Miss them? Great. Don't text it 13 times. Let them come to you, too.

12. Texting ≠ Bonding. Put your damn phone down. Text less, talk more. Let chemistry build in person not over an emoji-flooded convo about your favorite pizza toppings.

13. Don't Weaponize Jealousy. Talking about your hot coworker or that DM from your "friend" isn't edgy, it's tacky. Confident people don't need to flex fake options.

14. Mean What You Say. If you're giving a compliment, let it come from the heart. No cookie-cutter pickup lines. Authentic > smooth.

15. Be Kind. Period. Kindness is hot. Period. Say thank you. Show appreciation. Don't make everything about you.

16. Keep It Light, Keep It Fun. Let yourself be playful. Laugh. Tease. Make jokes that don't require a PowerPoint explanation.

17. Ask Real Questions. Surface talk is fine... for elevators. Go deeper. Ask what makes them tick. What scared them as a kid. What they'd do if they weren't afraid.

18. Don't Rush Intimacy. If it's real, it'll build. There's no trophy for who kisses first. Let the moment lead not your anxiety.

19. Unpack Your Baggage... Later. We all have pasts. But if your emotional suitcase is bursting at the seams by date two, unpack that privately first. New connections deserve a clean slate.

20. Keep Living Your Life. Don't ditch your friends, gym routine, goals, or Sunday night rituals just because someone new is giving you attention. A full life makes you magnetic.

Green Flags & Compatibility

Green Flags in Dating

(Proof that healthy, emotionally intelligent, grown-ass men exist and that you're finally ready to meet them there.)

Let's be clear: the good ones are *not rare*. They're just not loud. They're not the chaos in your DMs. They're the calm you keep overlooking because you've normalized tension as chemistry. But these men? They are whole. They are healing. And they are *already doing the work*. You don't need to lower your standards. You need to match their frequency. Here's how to recognize when you've stepped into *safe, grounded, green light love*.

1. They Say What They Mean and Do What They Say. This is the baseline. No decoding. No mixed signals. No wondering. If he says he'll call, he calls. If he says he wants something serious, his actions align. Reliability is his love language.

2. They Create Safety with Their Presence, Not Just Their Words. You feel calm around him. Not because there's no emotion but because he doesn't weaponize yours. Your nervous system relaxes when he walks in, not when he leaves.

3. You Can Tell the Truth and They Don't Flinch. You name a need, a boundary, or a vulnerable truth, and he doesn't punish you for it. He listens, adjusts, and honors it. You don't have to shrink or sugarcoat to be heard.

4. They Respect Boundaries the First Time. You say no, and they don't pout. You need space, and they give it without drama. They don't test your limits, they *protect* them.

5. They Don't Perform. They're Present. He's not love-bombing. He's not acting. He's just *there*. Available. Attuned. You're not addicted to the high because the connection isn't built on adrenaline, it's built on *actual intimacy.*

6. They Handle Conflict Without Collapsing or Exploding. You disagree and he doesn't shut down, gaslight, or blame. He talks it out. He owns his shit. He wants resolution, not domination.

7. They Support Your Dreams Like They're Part of the Plan. He doesn't just tolerate your ambition, he *amplifies* it. He sends you opportunities. He hypes you up. He's not intimidated by your power. He sees it as part of the future he wants to build with you.

8. They Know Who They Are Without Needing to Prove It. There's no posturing. No overcompensating. He's grounded in who he is and he doesn't make you feel small to feel big. He's done the ego work.

9. You Feel More Like Yourself When You're with Him. You're not performing. You're not questioning every text. You're not walking on eggshells. You're laughing more. Breathing easier. You feel like *you*. That's not a coincidence. That's alignment.

10. They Ask Questions That Show They're Actually Listening. He remembers your stories. Asks follow-ups. Brings up things you mentioned once in passing. He pays attention not to impress you, but because he *cares*.

11. He's Got Friends Who Actually Respect Women. The men around him don't talk trash about their wives or roll their eyes at feminism. Green flag men travel in green flag circles.

12. They're Transparent with Their Intentions and Back It Up. You're never confused about where you stand. He tells you what he wants, and it doesn't change when he gets what he wants from you.

13. They're Emotionally Intelligent (and Still Learning). He names his feelings. He doesn't lash out. He knows when to talk and when to listen. And he's still open to learning more about how to love better.

14. He Holds Space Without Trying to Fix You. When you cry, he doesn't panic or offer five solutions. He holds you. He stays. He listens. He's not uncomfortable with your emotions, he welcomes them.

15. He's Consistent Even When Life Gets Hard. Work gets busy, he doesn't disappear. He's stressed, but he still shows up. Green flag men don't use pressure as an excuse to ghost. They communicate through it.

16. He Treats You the Same When You're Not Around. He speaks about you with respect. He protects your name in rooms you're not in. There's no secret second version of him out in the wild. Integrity isn't situational, it's embedded.

17. He Wants to Know the *Real* You. He's not just obsessed with your body, your beauty, your vibe, he's fascinated by your *soul*. He asks where your fire comes from. What scares you. What lights you up. He wants *all* of you.

18. He's Got His Own Life and He's Willing to Make Room for You in It. He's not clingy. He's not codependent. He's stable, independent and still makes intentional space for you, without asking you to shrink to fit.

19. He Apologizes Without Getting Defensive. When he messes up, he says: "You're right. I didn't handle that well." No guilt trip. No explaining it away. Just ownership and action.

20. You Don't Feel Like You're Waiting for the Other Shoe to Drop. This is the final and deepest green flag: peace. You're not anxious all the time. You're not stuck in a cycle of doubt and hypervigilance. You're not trying to make yourself smaller, sexier, more "chill." You're *safe*. And that's what love is supposed to feel like.

GREEN FLAG REFLECTION PROMPTS
(Because sometimes the problem isn't that you can't find good men,
it's that you don't know what to do when you do.)

Read these slowly. Journal honestly. Let this be your mirror.

1. When's the last time I felt *genuinely safe* with someone and what made me feel that way? Describe the moment. Was it how they listened? Showed up? Didn't make you question yourself?

2. Have I ever mistaken emotional chaos for chemistry? What did that cost me? Be specific. Where did you confuse tension with passion? Did it make you ignore someone steady who was showing up for you?

3. What green flags have I seen in the past, but overlooked, ignored, or felt "bored" by? If peace felt unfamiliar, did you sabotage it? Did you walk away from a man who wasn't toxic enough to feel "exciting?"

4. What part of me still equates love with being tested, chased, or earned? Be real: Did you feel more alive when you were proving yourself to someone who didn't even value you?

5. Can I receive affection, attention, and consistency without assuming a catch? Why or why not? If someone treated you well today, would you lean in or brace for the disappointment?

6. Do I trust my body when it relaxes around someone or do I run when it's "too easy?" What would it look like to stay where it feels good instead of defaulting to chaos?

7. What would it take for me to feel worthy of a truly healthy, emotionally available partner, right now? Not after the glow-up. Not after you're "perfect." What would it take to believe you deserve it *today*?

8. Am I drawn to people who want to *know me*, or just *win me*? How can I tell the difference? And more importantly do I still confuse being desired with being loved?

9. What does emotional safety actually look like to me? Not just in theory in practice. How do you know when you're emotionally safe? What does your body do? How does your voice change? What disappears?

10. If a man with all 20 green flags showed up tomorrow, would I be able to *recognize* him, *receive* him, and *keep showing up* for him? And if not… what needs healing in me first?

GREEN FLAG INTEGRATION EXERCISES
*(How to stop craving chaos, and start choosing the kind of love
that won't wreck your soul.)*

1. The "What It Felt Like" Visualization
Purpose: Rewire your body to *want* safety not unpredictability.

How to do it: Close your eyes. Visualize a moment you felt safe, seen, and supported by someone. Doesn't have to be romantic just *secure*. Breathe into the feeling. What did your body do? Your breath? Your shoulders? Now ask: *What if dating could feel like this?* Practice this visualization once a week to make safety your baseline, not your boredom trigger.

2. The "Bored or Safe?" Reframe
Purpose: Catch yourself when your trauma is making decisions.

How to do it: Next time someone *kind*, stable, and respectful texts you and your instinct is "meh" or "he's too nice" pause. Ask yourself:
- Am I bored, or am I just not triggered?
- Am I craving chaos because I think it means passion? Then choose to *lean in* one more time. Respond thoughtfully. Stay curious instead of dismissive.

3. Celebrate the Small Green Flags
Purpose: Reinforce positive behavior instead of chasing drama.

How to do it: After a date (or even a solid conversation), write down *three green flags* you noticed. Examples:
- He followed through with plans
- He asked questions and remembered your answers
- He respected a boundary with zero resistance

This is how you train your brain to seek consistency not adrenaline.

4. Send One Brave Text
Purpose: Break your silence habit and test for emotional safety.

How to do it: Pick someone you're dating (or even just texting) and send one *real* message:
- "I've really enjoyed getting to know you. I'm curious where your head is at."
- "Something you said the other night made me feel really seen, and I appreciated that."
- "I'm looking for something consistent just want to make sure we're on the same page."

Their response will either reinforce the green, or reveal the red. Either way you win.

5. Track Your Nervous System
Purpose: Recalibrate your sense of "normal" in relationships.

How to do it: After any date or deep convo, ask your body:
- Do I feel more grounded or more anxious?
- Was I trying to impress or just being myself?
- Did I feel like I could exhale?

You'll learn very quickly if you're dating from peace or programming.

Dating Compatibility

(Because chemistry is fun, but compatibility is what makes you want to stay in the damn room.)

Let's get something straight: You can be attracted to someone. You can laugh. You can finish each other's sentences and still be *fundamentally incompatible.* Why? Because chemistry is spark. Compatibility is structure. And without structure? The whole thing burns. This chapter is not about how to find someone who "gets" you. It's about how to find someone who can walk with you. Grow with you. Handle you. Hold you. Match you. That's compatibility. And here's what it really takes:

1. You Want the Same Things. Now, Not Hypothetically Someday. Not "I could see myself married someday." Not "Maybe I want kids, maybe I don't." If your timelines and desires don't align now, they probably won't later. Clarity is compatibility. Period.

2. You Communicate the Same Way Under Pressure. It's easy to get along when things are good. But how do you both communicate during stress, misalignment, or misunderstanding? If you shut down and he explodes? *That's not a mismatch, it's a warning.*

3. You're Attracted to Who They Are Not Who You're Hoping They Become. You don't date potential. You date *present-day behavior.* If you're already excusing, fixing, or "waiting until they're in a better place," that's not love that's codependency in makeup.

4. You Laugh Together Like You Share a Secret Language. Not the polite chuckle. Not the forced "haha." I'm talking *gut-deep, soul-level humor* that makes you feel like kids hiding from the teacher. Humor is glue. Don't underestimate it.

5. You Have Compatible Conflict Styles. Can you fight well? Apologize well? Do you both return after rupture with softness and clarity? Because communication without repair is just *talking at a wall.*

6. You Feel Safe in Silence. Can you sit in the same room, doing nothing and still feel connected? If they need constant stimulation to feel close, they're not in tune with your presence. Silence compatibility is intimacy at its core.

7. You Share the Same "Currency of Care." Do you show love in the same ways: touch, words, quality time, acts, gifts? If not, are you *willing to learn each other's languages*? Love languages don't have to match. But they **do** have to be *translated.*

8. You're Both Emotionally Available and Willing to *Stay* Available. Flirting with someone emotionally open is one thing. *Staying* emotionally open when you're triggered, scared, or tired? That's the real test. Compatibility means *emotional stamina.*

9. You're In the Same Season of Life. This isn't about age, it's about *pace.* You can be the same age and living completely different realities. If they're still figuring out who they are, and you're already walking your purpose? You're not aligned. Yet.

10. Your Goals Don't Compete. They Complement. Compatibility means: *your dreams can exist in the same room.* If your vision board makes them insecure, or their lifestyle completely clashes with yours, the relationship will *slowly suffocate you.*

11. Your Boundaries Are Respected Not Negotiated. If they push, twist, or guilt-trip when you express your "no?" That's not miscommunication. That's a **compatibility dealbreaker.**

12. You Share Core Values About the Big Stuff. Love can't hold up long-term if you don't align on the essentials:

- Monogamy
- Family
- Finances
- Faith
- Lifestyle

You don't need to be identical. But you *do* need foundational alignment.

13. You Respect Each Other's Past Without Trying to Rewrite It. They don't need to love every chapter of your history, but they *do* need to honor how it shaped you. If someone tries to minimize, rewrite, or "fix" your past? That's incompatibility in disguise.

14. You're Both Comfortable with Accountability. Compatible people can say: "I was wrong."

"I hurt you."

"I didn't handle that well."

And not fall apart in shame or defense. Accountability is love. *Avoidance is trauma.*

15. You're Drawn to Their *Character* Not Just Their Personality. Charm can fake it. Character can't. You don't just need someone funny, hot, and engaging. You need someone *disciplined, loyal, consistent, and emotionally intelligent.*

16. You Can Navigate Power Dynamics Without Playing Games. Who pays? Who plans? Who texts first? If it's all ego chess, it's not compatibility, it's fear in heels.

17. You're Both Willing to *Grow into* Compatibility Where It Matters. Perfect alignment is rare. But if you're both emotionally mature enough to *lean into discomfort*, learn, adapt, and evolve together? That's golden.

18. You Feel More Like Yourself When You're Around Them Not Less. Compatibility doesn't shrink you to fit the vibe. It *amplifies* who you already are. If you feel smaller, quieter, or like you're performing? It's not compatible, it's just familiar self-abandonment.

19. You Can Talk About the Future Without It Feeling Like Pressure. If just *mentioning* the future makes them sweat, run, or joke it off? Compatibility means *you're both building something*, not just vibing until it dies.

20. You Like Who You Are When You're with Them. The ultimate compatibility check. Do you love the version of you that shows up in their presence? If not, you don't need a better match. You need a *better mirror.*

COMPATIBILITY CHECK-IN:
15 DATE QUESTIONS THAT MATTER

(Because you're done wasting time pretending you don't care about the future.)

1. "What does a healthy relationship look like to you in real life, not just in theory?" You'll know fast if they've actually done the work or just repost Instagram quotes.

2. "How do you usually react when you're hurt or triggered?" Their self-awareness here is everything. If they say "I don't really get triggered," you're not dating a monk, you're dating a red flag with delusions.

3. "What do you need to feel safe and seen in a relationship?" We're not guessing anymore. Let them tell you how they want to be loved and pay attention to whether they ask you the same.

4. "What role do boundaries play in your relationships?" If they flinch at the word, they're not ready for you.

5. "How do you define loyalty beyond physical fidelity?" Because loyalty isn't just not cheating. It's emotional, spiritual, and energetic presence.

6. "What's something you've outgrown that used to define you?" This shows you who they *used to be,* what they've released, and how they process growth.

7. "What does your life look like in five years, realistically?" Not aspirational. Not fantasy. *Realistic.* You want to know if they're building something you'd actually want to be part of.

8. "How do you repair conflict when someone you love is upset with you?" Conflict isn't the red flag. Avoidance is. If they can't answer this clearly, that's your answer.

9. "How do you like to show love and how do you like to receive it?" Early love language decoding saves *so much pain* later. Learn it now.

10. "What's your relationship with money and how do you make financial decisions?" Unsexy? Maybe. Necessary? Absolutely. Compatibility includes shared fiscal values.

11. "What kind of family dynamic did you grow up with and how has it shaped your view of love?" You'll get a *deep* read from this. Watch how they speak about the people who raised them.

12. "What are your emotional non-negotiables in a relationship?" If they haven't thought about it… that's a compatibility answer in itself.

13. "Who do you turn to when life falls apart?" Tells you if they have support systems or expect to make you the sole emotional janitor.

14. "What habits or mindsets are you actively working on right now?" A compatible partner is *in progress*. You're not asking for perfection just movement.

15. "Do you believe relationships should be easy, or require intentional work?" Their answer reveals if they'll bail at the first bump or show up when things get real.

COMPATIBILITY REFLECTION PROMPTS
*(For the woman who refuses to abandon herself
in the name of connection ever again.)*

1. What am I actually looking for in a relationship and have I ever honestly sat with that without rushing to fill the space?

2. What are my top five non-negotiables in a relationship and why are they non-negotiable? (And be ruthless: are they *real*, or are they rooted in fear, ego, or old programming?)

3. When have I felt the most emotionally safe in a relationship and what were the behaviors that created that safety?

4. What patterns have I ignored in the past that ended up costing me deeply? How will I respond differently next time I see them?

5. Do I like the version of myself that shows up when I'm in a relationship? If not, what changes?

6. How do I define compatibility beyond surface traits? What does true energetic alignment *feel* like to me?

7. If I had to write my personal 'Dating Operating Manual,' what would be on the first three pages? (This is your rules of engagement. Your standards. Your code.)

8. What are the ways I self-abandon in dating, and how can I start catching myself before I go too far?

9. How do I want my partner to feel when they're around me and what do I need to feel that way too?

10. Am I looking for a partner or an emotional escape hatch from loneliness, boredom, or pressure? (*Because intention changes everything.*)

Financial Compatibility
*(AKA: Why You Can't Build a Kingdom with Someone
Who Can't Balance a Checkbook)*

Let's get one thing clear: Love is beautiful. Money is necessary. And when those two worlds collide without a strategy, it's a damn mess. You're not shallow for caring about financial compatibility. You're smart. You're protecting the empire you're building. Here's what you need to know if you want a relationship that doesn't end with resentment, secret credit cards, or screaming matches over Amazon Prime purchases.

1. Talk About Money Before You Talk About Moving in Together. If you can't say "what's your credit score?" without breaking into hives, you're not ready for shared bills, shared beds, or shared lives. If he shuts down talking about money, gets defensive, or flips the convo back on you every time finances come up? That's not discomfort. That's immaturity.

2. Your Values About Money Matter Way More Than Your Bank Balances. You don't have to both be rich. You have to both value saving, spending, and growing in a way that matches. *Alignment over amount.*

3. Financial Secrecy Is Emotional Infidelity. Hiding debts, lying about spending, secret gambling habits, it's cheating. Financial lies erode trust just as fast as emotional ones.

4. If You're Building an Empire, You Need a Partner Not a Dependent. If you're hustling, growing, investing, planning, you can't drag a "wing it and hope" energy partner behind you forever. You will outgrow them. Fast.

5. There's a Big Difference Between Temporary Broke and Lifetime Mindset Broke. Everyone hits rough patches. That's life. But if someone's entire vibe is "I'll be broke forever, it's just who I am" run.

6. You Deserve to Be Supported Not Drained. You are not a one-woman scholarship fund. You deserve a partner who pulls their weight, builds with you, and dreams with you not someone who expects you to fund their lifestyle.

7. Your Financial Goals Must Be Respected Not Resented. If he mocks your desire to save, invest, build, that's not love. That's sabotage wearing cologne.

8. Matching Work Ethic Is Just as Important as Matching Ambition. Dreams are cute. Execution is sexier. If he talks big but won't get up early and hustle, the gap between you will grow, and so will your resentment.

9. You Need to See How They Handle Financial Conflict Not Just Financial Comfort. It's easy to vibe when times are good. What happens when a surprise bill hits? A job loss? A market crash? Character shows under pressure, not prosperity.

10. Being "Low Maintenance" Is Not a Badge of Honor. Stop pretending you don't care about money to make yourself more "likable." You're allowed to want a financially stable, financially conscious partner without guilt.

Final Word: Money matters because life matters. Shared goals. Shared visions. Shared values. That's what lasts. Love without financial compatibility isn't freedom, it's a slow death of dreams. Build smart. Date smart. Demand partnership not passengers. Your future self will thank you.

Financial Gut Check:
4 Brutal Questions Before You Build with Anyone

Because no amount of abs, smooth talk, or "potential" will save you from financial chaos if you ignore the signs.

1. Does this man build with me or drain me? (*If you're constantly "helping him out" emotionally, financially, energetically, you're dating a dependent, not a partner.)

2. Can we talk about money openly or does he shut down and get defensive? (*If talking about real-life adult topics makes him squirm like a toddler in timeout, he's not ready for your future.*)

4. If I loaned him money, would I secretly start resenting him? (*Spoiler: YES, YOU WOULD. Never loan a man money. Not because you're cruel but because it kills your libido, your respect, and your power faster than anything else. You are not a bank. You are a goddess.*)

5. Would I still be proud of this partnership if we hit rock bottom together? (*Character isn't proven in prosperity. It's proven when everything's on fire and you're both still standing, back-to-back.*)

Final Word:

If you wouldn't trust him with your money, you damn sure shouldn't trust him with your heart. Build wisely. Love fiercely. Protect your empire like your future depends on it because it does.

Building Emotional Intimacy

(Because love isn't just chemistry, it's emotional courage, and baby, you were made for more than surface connection.)

Let's be real. Most of us weren't taught how to do this part. We were taught how to attract, impress, perform. Not how to *reveal*. Not how to *be held in our truth* without shape-shifting into someone more palatable. But emotional intimacy? That's where real connection lives. It's where relationships stop being fragile. It's where both partners get to exhale and say, *"Finally, I don't have to do this alone."* This chapter isn't about being perfect. It's about being *brave* enough to show up exactly as you are and allowing someone else to do the same.

1. Tell the Truth So You Can Be Seen. Intimacy starts with honesty. Not the polished kind. The kind where you say, "I don't always know how to do this, but I want to try." Say the awkward thing. Say the real thing. Say the thing you've been taught to hide because someone out there is just waiting to feel safe enough to do the same.

2. Let It Be Safe, Not Hard. Emotional intimacy should feel like *relief*, not a performance. You don't have to "earn" your right to be vulnerable. You don't have to prove you're worthy of softness. The right person will meet your open heart with gentleness not manipulation.

3. Start Small but Start Real. You don't have to spill your whole life story on date two. But you *do* have to stop pretending. Try:
- "That meant a lot to me."
- "That made me feel nervous to share, but I wanted to say it." Tiny truths build trust. That's where intimacy begins.

4. Ask Questions That Actually Matter. Surface-level convo won't get you to soul-level connection. Try:
- "What's something you're afraid people might misunderstand about you?"
- "What shaped how you give or receive love?" Depth is uncomfortable only for people who aren't ready for it. Keep going anyway.

5. Don't Flinch When They Go Deep. When they open up, *stay.* You don't need the perfect response. Just say,
- "Thank you for trusting me with that."
- "I'm here, and I'm not going anywhere." Most people don't need to be fixed. They need to be *felt.*

6. Feel It with Them. Don't Just Analyze It. Intimacy isn't a therapy session. It's not about dissecting emotions with a clipboard. It's about being *with* the feeling. If they're hurting, don't go into logic mode. Go into *presence.* Sit beside their truth, and let them feel safe there.

7. Make Space for Emotion Without Judgment. Tears aren't weakness. Fear isn't a flaw. If you want emotional intimacy, you have to normalize emotional expression. Let your date be soft, scared, tender and show that it's okay. That's how we break generational cycles of emotional repression.

8. Be Emotionally Available Yourself. You want someone who's open? Then you have to *be* open too. Stop keeping it cool to look detached. Start naming what you actually feel:
- "I feel connected to you when we talk like this."
- "This conversation is bringing up something I didn't expect, can I be honest?" That's vulnerability. That's power.

9. Build a Safe Place Between You. Your connection should feel like a container. A place where you can both say:
- "I messed that up."
- "I need reassurance."
- "That hit a tender spot, can we talk about it?" Create an environment where softness isn't just allowed, it's *welcomed.*

10. Validate, Validate, Validate. Intimacy deepens every time you say,
- "I hear you."
- "That makes sense."
- "I get why that would feel hard." You don't have to fully understand someone's experience to *honor* it. Validation is the bridge between hearts.

11. Learn Their Language Then Speak It. Emotional intimacy requires fluency in the other person's nervous system. What soothes them? What triggers shutdown? Learn it. Respect it. Don't just speak *your* language of care, learn theirs too.

12. Don't Rush the Connection. Emotional intimacy isn't instant. It builds over time. You water it with consistency, curiosity, and care. The most magnetic love stories aren't built in a weekend. They're built through slow, intentional choosing.

13. Create Shared Moments That Mean Something. Real intimacy isn't just emotional, it's experiential. Cook a meal together. Go for a walk without your phones. Sit in silence and *just exist together.* Intimacy grows in the quiet moments, too.

14. Show Up in the Unsexy Moments. Everyone loves during the highs. But intimacy is built in the lows when one of you is tired, anxious, sick, or overwhelmed. If you can show up without needing to be impressive, *that's love maturing.*

15. Remember That Both Men and Women Need This. Men are not emotionless robots. They are full of fear, love, longing, and hesitation just like us. They are told not to cry, not to need, not to open up. If you want emotional intimacy with a man, show him that he's safe to *feel again.*

16. Let It Be Sacred, Not Strategic. This isn't about being the "cool girl" who never asks too much or the "alpha man" who never reveals weakness. This is about *soul-level honesty.* Let your connection be the one thing in your life that doesn't require performance.

17. Speak Love When It's Hard. When things get tense, use language that connects not attacks. Try:

- "This is important to me. I want us to get through it together."
- "I feel close to you even when we disagree. That matters."

Love doesn't die in conflict. It dies when no one's brave enough to stay soft during it.

18. Own Your Story, Even the Messy Parts. You don't need to pretend you've healed everything. Say, "This is still a tender spot for me, but I'm willing to talk about it." Intimacy isn't about being perfect, it's about being *in process* together.

19. Invite Them In, Don't Demand They Force the Door. Let emotional intimacy be a mutual unfolding. Don't pull it out of someone. Don't try to crack them open. Ask. Invite. Wait. Witness. Let them choose it and let that choice *mean* something.

20. Let Emotional Intimacy Be the Standard, Not the Reward. You don't "earn" closeness after sex, exclusivity, or a three-month trial. You *build* it from day one, by being real. And if someone can't meet you there? Let them go. Don't beg someone to feel you when you've spent your whole life learning how to feel yourself.

EMOTIONAL INTIMACY REFLECTION PROMPTS

(Because it's not just about being open, it's about knowing what you actually want someone to walk into.)

These prompts will help you break your own patterns, soften your own armor, and learn to trust that intimacy doesn't have to feel like tension. Answer them slowly. Truthfully. You don't have to rush this part.

1. What parts of me do I usually hide when I start to like someone? Why do I hide them? This is where the intimacy work begins not in what you say, but what you still feel you *can't*.

2. What does emotional safety *feel* like in my body and when have I felt it before? Close your eyes and remember a moment, any moment, when you felt emotionally held. What changed in your breath, your heart rate, your voice?

3. What makes me feel seen, not just complimented? Heard, not just tolerated? Describe it. Be specific. Because if you can name it, you can start *asking* for it.

4. When someone opens up to me, do I try to fix it, solve it, or sit in it? Why? Be honest. Do you need to be useful to feel valuable? Or can you just *witness* without performance?

5. How do I typically react when someone shares a truth that makes me uncomfortable? Do you shut down? Joke it off? Intellectualize it? Get curious about the defense.

6. What kind of emotional support do I wish someone had offered me when I was younger? Do I give that to others now? Sometimes the intimacy we crave the most is the one we've never seen modeled. That doesn't mean we can't create it.

7. What is one thing I've never said to a romantic partner but have always wanted to? What's the truth you've swallowed in the name of "not ruining the moment?"

8. When I feel emotionally safe, how do I show up differently in love? Do you soften? Laugh more? Speak without overthinking? That version of you, that's the one to protect.

9. What is my default emotional survival pattern withdrawal, over-sharing, people-pleasing, testing, avoidance? When things get too real, what do you do *instead* of leaning in?

REAL-LIFE EMOTIONAL INTIMACY–BUILDING DATE EXERCISES

(For when you're done pretending connection is a mystery, and ready to make it a mutual practice.)

These don't require candles or a deep trauma bond. They just require presence, curiosity, and the willingness to show up with your *actual self.* You don't need to do them all at once. Choose one or two per date and watch what happens when real energy meets real effort.

1. The "Real Questions Only" Walk Date
How to do it: Go for a walk. No phones, no distractions. Each of you gets to ask one question per block. Not light stuff. Think:
- "What shaped your view of love?"
- "What's something most people don't know about you?"

Let the silence land between questions. That's where the intimacy grows.

2. The "Highs, Lows, and Truths" Dinner Game
How to do it: Over dinner or drinks, ask each other:
- What's a recent high point in your life?
- What's a recent low point?
- What's one truth about you most people miss?

This builds emotional rhythm: joy, depth, and self-revelation, all in one conversation.

3. The "Story Swap" Challenge
How to do it: Each person tells one story from childhood, one from heartbreak, and one they've never told anyone on a date. This isn't about trauma, it's about *honesty.* See how they hold your stories. See how they share theirs.

4. The "What's Your Relationship To..." Game
How to do it: Rapid-fire ask each other:
- What's your relationship to money?
- ...to conflict?
- ...to your parents?
- ...to rest?
- ...to success?

You'll learn more in 15 minutes than three weeks of texting.

5. The Eye Contact Test (3-Minute Timer)

How to do it: Sit facing each other. Set a timer for three minutes. No talking. Just eye contact. Notice what rises. Do you feel safe? Do you feel seen? Or do you feel like running? This reveals nervous system truth fast.

6. The "Describe Me" Reflection Game

How to do it: After a meaningful convo, say:

- "Based on this one date, how would you describe me in three words?" Then reflect back your three words for them. This builds *mirroring*: a key component of intimacy and attachment.

7. The "Let Me Understand You" Practice

How to do it: Each person shares one thing that's been on their mind: stress, emotion, joy, anything. The other person doesn't respond. They just say:

- "So, what I'm hearing is..."
- "It sounds like you're feeling..." It's not a discussion. It's a *validation* practice.

8. The "Mini Future Vision" Talk

How to do it: Ask:

- "In a year, what would your life ideally look like?"
- "What does a healthy relationship look like to you?"
- "What kind of love do you think you're ready for now?" Not a proposal just a vibe check on where their heart is at.

9. The "Can I Share Something with You?" Check-In

How to do it: Before dropping vulnerability, ask for permission:

- "Can I share something that feels personal?" This shows *emotional attunement* and creates a moment of mutual consent to go deeper. Respect builds trust.

10. The "Come as You Are" Hangout

How to do it: Low-effort, high-comfort night. No glam. Just comfy clothes, takeout, and the invitation to *just be*. Ask:

- "What helps you feel like you don't have to perform?"
- "What's something you'd love to do with someone you feel safe with?"
  Emotional intimacy thrives in the unfiltered.

BONUS: THE INTIMACY INTEGRITY CHECK (Post-Date Journal Prompt)

After the date, ask yourself:

- Did I feel seen or just admired?
- Did I share or perform?
- Did we go deep or just go through the motions?
- Did this feel like safety or just a distraction?

The answers will tell you everything.

Are We a Thing or Nah?

(Because "go with the flow" is how you end up in a situationship.)

Let's set the record straight: Unspoken expectations breed resentment. Unclear standards invite inconsistency. Assumptions are what keep therapists employed. So, we're not doing that. You're going to define what you expect, demand it unapologetically, and watch the time-wasters vanish like magic.

I. The Expectation Audit: Know What You Actually Want

Before you even think about *what he brings*, check yourself:

- Do you want long-term? Short-term? Situationship with a playlist?
- Are you expecting loyalty while offering ambiguity?
- Do you want a husband but entertain men who "don't believe in labels?"
- Are you emotionally available or just bored?

You can't get what you're not willing to own. If your standards are unclear, his effort will be too.

II. The 10 Core Expectations That Should Be Non-Negotiable

Let's break them down. These aren't "high maintenance." These are baseline.

1. **Consistency**. Not just texts. Energy. Presence. Respect. If he shows up strong, then disappears for three days? He's not busy, he's disorganized or disinterested.
2. **Clear Communication**. You're not a mind reader, and this isn't a code-breaking exercise. You should know where he stands, what he wants, and what he's feeling. If you're guessing, you're losing.
3. **Follow-Through**. Words mean nothing without action. If he says he's going to do something, he does it. If he doesn't, that's not an oops, that's a data point.
4. **Emotional Safety**. You should feel safe to speak your mind, express your needs, and show your weird side without fearing he'll dip, mock, or minimize.
5. **Mutual Effort**. If you're doing all the emotional labor, planning, initiating, and supporting, he's not your partner. He's your project.
6. **Exclusivity (If You Want It)**. Don't assume you're exclusive unless it's explicitly agreed on. Clarity matters. If he avoids this convo, *that* is your answer.
7. **Growth Mindset**. Relationships hit walls. If he can't reflect, adjust, or take accountability? It's over before it starts.
8. **Shared Lifestyle Goals**. Values. Vision. Vibes. Do you both want kids? Freedom? A farm in Montana? A penthouse in New York? If the future looks wildly different, don't try to make it align. It won't.
9. **Respect for Your Boundaries**. If you set a line and he pushes it "as a joke," that's manipulation. Not flirtation.
10. **Affection and Intimacy in Your Language**. Some people give love through touch, others through action. If he can't speak *your* love language, it's going to feel like starvation in a feast.

III. What Unrealistic Expectations Actually Look Like

Let's call ourselves out for a second:

- Wanting him to text you constantly when he's at work
- Expecting him to know what you're feeling without saying anything
- Wanting him to change his personality to match your aesthetic
- Getting mad when he doesn't post you after three dates
- Hoping he'll become "a man of depth" if you just love him hard enough

That's not "high standards." That's delusion. You don't want to be coddled. You want to be met. That means *clear asks, grounded energy, and emotional maturity* from both sides.

IV. How to Express Expectations Without Scaring Him Off

Spoiler: If he's "scared off" by clarity, he wasn't built for you. But if you want to communicate like a high-value, emotionally literate goddess, try these:

- "I'm really enjoying this and want to make sure we're aligned. What are you hoping this turns into?"
- "For me, consistency is attractive. I lose interest quickly when it's hot-and-cold."
- "I'm not expecting perfection, but I do expect presence. I'm too grown for guessing games."
- "If you're not in a place to show up fully, that's okay. Just let me know so I can move accordingly."

Translation: **"I won't chase you, but I will require clarity before I invest."**

How to Handle Mixed Signals Without Losing Your Mind

(Also known as: "Is he into me or is he emotionally stunted?")

One day he's all over you. The next? Radio silence. One minute you're soulmates. The next? "I'm just really busy." Welcome to the dating purgatory of inconsistency, breadcrumbing, and spiritual whiplash. Let's break this all the way down so you never lose sleep, or self-worth, over another mixed-message merchant again.

I. Why Mixed Signals Work on You (Even When You Know Better)

Let's be real. They hit because:

- They activate your brain's dopamine reward loop—unpredictability feels exciting
- You start making excuses for him instead of reading what's in front of you
- You confuse potential with reality
- And part of you thinks *"maybe I can be the exception"*

Spoiler: Mixed signals are always a signal. They just aren't saying what you *want* to hear.

II. What Mixed Signals Actually Mean

Let's translate the chaos:

- "I'm just really busy right now." = You're not a priority. If he wanted to, he would.
- "You're amazing, I'm just not in the right place for something serious." = He wants access to you, not commitment with you.

- "I don't want to hurt you." = He already knows he will.
- He texts you non-stop for three days then vanishes? = You're dopamine, not devotion.
- He says he likes you but avoids plans? = He likes the idea of you. Not the work of showing up.

Real interest is consistent, clear, and grounded. Confusion is your answer.

III. The Four-Phase Response Plan for Mixed Signals

- **PHASE 1: Observe, Don't Perform**. Stop trying to "win him over" when his energy goes sideways. Just watch. Take notes. Stay cool.
- **PHASE 2: Mirror, Don't Chase**. He pulls back? You pull back. Not out of pettiness, out of self-respect. If he doesn't reach out, *you don't either.*
- **PHASE 3: Clarify Once Then Clock Out**. Say what you want *one time*: "I'm looking for something consistent and emotionally available. If that's not you, no hard feelings." Then? Step away. Don't re-explain. Don't convince. Don't wait.
- **PHASE 4: Detach Emotionally Before You Detach Physically**. Pull your energy back before you pull the plug. That's how you avoid spiraling. Unfollow if needed. Mute. Distance. Reset.

IV. How to Stay Sane When You Really Like Him

Here's your toolbox:

- **Anchor in facts, not vibes.** What is he *doing*? Not what is he *saying* or what you *hope* it means.
- **Take your power back through decision, not reaction.** You don't ghost. You exit consciously. With elegance and silence.

V. What to Say When You Call It Out (Without Losing Your Power)

Let's keep it chill, direct, and devastatingly clear:

- "You're inconsistent, and that's a turnoff. I'm not looking for guesswork."
- "If you want something casual, that's fine. I just don't."
- "I don't do almosts. Thanks for the preview though."
- "Your energy's been off. I'm not chasing clarity, it's either there or it's not."
- "No bad blood. I just have a low tolerance for confusion."

VI. Redemption Arc or Delusion? How to Tell If He's Worth One More Shot

He may be worth *a final window* if:

- He acknowledges the mixed signals **without excuses**
- He changes behavior immediately and consistently
- He takes accountability and doesn't try to guilt or flip it

If not? *Silence him. Soft-block him. Journal about it. Then go romanticize your own damn life.*

Final Reminder: Mixed signals are a slow "no" packaged as a maybe. And "maybe" is how they keep you stuck. Clarity is not too much to ask. It's the bare f*cking minimum.

Sarah Melland
How to Know When to Walk Away
(Even If You Really, Really Like Him)
(Because loving someone is not the same as being loved back.)

It doesn't matter how hot the chemistry is. It doesn't matter how good the sex is. It doesn't matter if he makes you laugh, miss him, or cry into your steering wheel. If he doesn't *show up*: consistently, emotionally, honestly, you're not in a relationship. You're in a delusion.

I. The Most Brutal Truth First
You don't walk away when you stop liking him. You walk away when you stop abandoning yourself. You can love someone and still have to leave. You can want someone and still realize they're *not capable* of meeting you. Staying with someone who keeps *almost* showing up will kill your joy. And your confidence. And your standards.

II. Signs It's Time to Walk (Even If You're Not "Ready")
1. **You're always anxious around them.** Not butterflies. Tight chest. Overthinking. Performing.
2. **They keep saying they're "not ready" but still want access to you.** That's not vulnerability. That's control.
3. **You don't know where you stand. Ever.** If clarity hasn't come, it's not coming.
4. **You're always explaining your worth.** Trying to prove you're good enough? Already a loss.
5. **They make you feel too emotional, too needy, too much.** Translation: *They're emotionally unavailable and blaming you for noticing.*
6. **You feel lonelier with them than without them.** You're already alone. You're just sharing the silence.
7. **Every high comes with a crash.** If the connection feels like a rollercoaster, not a rhythm, you're not in love. You're in trauma bonding.
8. **You keep hoping they'll change.** Hoping is not a strategy. And you are not a rehab center.

III. Questions That Cut Through the Noise
Ask yourself:
- Am I chasing who they are, or who I *wish* they'd become?
- Would I want my best friend to date someone who treats her like this?
- Am I growing here or just getting better at surviving?
- If they stayed exactly like this forever, would I be okay with that?
- Does this feel like peace or performance?

If it's performance, it's not love. It's self-betrayal wrapped in romantic tension.

IV. What Makes You Stay (Even When You Shouldn't)
Let's name the lies:
- "But we have such a deep connection…" You can have a deep connection with someone who is deeply wrong for you.

- "But they've been through so much…" You're not their trauma doula. You're a partner, not a fixer.
- "But I've invested so much time…" And how much more are you willing to waste?
- "But when it's good, it's amazing…" It has to be *good when it's hard*. That's the measure.

V. What Walking Away Really Means

It doesn't mean you don't care. It doesn't mean you failed. It doesn't mean you gave up too soon. It means you *finally chose yourself louder than you've been choosing his potential*. It means you loved yourself enough to not wait for someone who never truly showed up. It means you saw the pattern, and instead of spinning your wheels in hope, you ended the cycle. That's not weakness. That's legacy-level strength.

VI. The Aftermath: What to Expect and How to Survive It

- You'll miss him. Even if he was awful.
- You'll romanticize the few good moments. That's withdrawal. Stay grounded.
- You'll question if you were too much. You weren't. You were *too aware*.
- You'll want to reach out. Don't. The silence is sacred.
- You'll feel powerful, then pathetic, then powerful again. Ride it. It passes.
- You'll glow. Eventually. It's inevitable. He'll notice. That's none of your business anymore.

Final Note: The love of your life will not confuse you. He will not make you feel like you're chasing. He will not give you crumbs and call it affection. He will see you, claim you, hold you, and rise with you. Until then? Keep walking. Head high. Spine straight. You're not lost. You're on your way.

Moving from Dating to a Relationship
*(Because it's time to stop collecting connections and
start building something worth keeping.)*

There's a moment in every dating situation where the vibe shifts. The energy deepens. You're texting good morning without thinking. You're no longer wondering who else they're seeing. You're not just dating anymore, you're *orbiting something real*.

But here's the deal: going from casual to committed doesn't happen by accident. It requires clarity, courage, and actual conversations *not vibes, not "seeing where it goes," and definitely not situationships in cute packaging*.

If you're ready to go all in or wondering if your person is, it's time to get real about what moving from dating to a relationship actually looks like.

1. Have the DTR Talk (Yes, Out Loud). No one gets a trophy for "vibing into a relationship." Say the words. Ask the questions.
- "Where do you see this going?"
- "Are we exclusive?"
- "What does commitment look like to you?"

If you're scared to bring it up, you already know the answer.

2. Don't Just Talk Compatibility. Live It. Can you navigate conflict? Travel together without snapping? Handle stress, schedules, family drama? Compatibility isn't just common interests, it's shared *values*, emotional maturity, and lifestyle alignment. Pay attention.

3. Slow Down the Scroll and Lock in Real Time. If you're moving toward commitment, *invest*. That means intentional time together. Go deep. Do nothing together. Build memories. Depth doesn't come from texting 24/7, it comes from *presence*.

4. Meet the People Who Made Them. You don't have to love their mom but seeing them with friends and family is revealing. How do they treat people they're tied to long-term? That's how they'll treat you once the honeymoon fades.

5. Support Each Other's Shit. Goals. Job changes. Anxiety spirals. Parenting stress. The real stuff. If they only show up when it's easy, they're not ready for real. If they hold you steady in your mess, *that's foundation.*

6. Fight. And Then Repair. The first fight isn't a red flag, it's a test. Can you fight fair? Apologize? Sit in discomfort without blame or silence? Healthy relationships don't avoid conflict. They *learn how to return after rupture.*

7. Get Emotionally Naked. This is where it gets real. Talk about fears, insecurities, patterns, triggers. Emotional intimacy is built when you stop pretending you're chill all the time and say, "Here's what scares me but I'm still here."

8. Define What "Relationship" Actually Means to You Both. Monogamous? Long-distance? Living together? Marriage in five years or never? Don't assume you're on the same page, *confirm it.* Misalignment on expectations ruins more relationships than infidelity ever will.

9. Let the Relationship Evolve Without Forcing Milestones. You don't need a proposal by month six. You don't need matching toothbrushes or a shared lease if it's not time. Let the relationship unfold. When it's right, the pace feels calm not pressured.

10. Celebrate Real Milestones, Not Just Instagram Moments. The first time they show up for you when you're sick. The time you disagree and work through it. The day they remember something you said weeks ago. *That's the good stuff.* Celebrate it.

11. Say It. Show It. Repeat. Say you care. Say you're in. Don't make love mysterious. Text "thinking of you." Buy their favorite snack. Commitment isn't one big declaration. It's a hundred small moments where you *choose each other on purpose.*

12. Build Something That's Yours Not Just Something That Looks Good. Pinterest-perfect dates don't mean sh*t if the emotional core is hollow. Don't build a relationship based on aesthetics. Build one based on how you feel when the lights are off and you're just... being.

13. Stay Interdependent, Not Codependent. You don't have to merge your identities to be close. Keep your routines. Your people. Your passions. A healthy relationship is two whole people choosing to walk alongside each other not two halves trying to complete each other.

14. Keep Talking About Boundaries Even When It's Good. Even in love, you get to have space. Say,

- "I need time to decompress after work,"
- "I'm not ready to talk about this right now,"
- or "I love you, but I still need time alone."

That's not distance, it's *respect*.

15. Don't Just Fall in Love, Build It. Falling is easy. Anyone can catch a vibe. But building? That takes communication, courage, and emotional grit. If it's love, *build it like it matters*. Because it does.

CONVERSATION PROMPTS FOR
GOING FROM DATING TO COMMITTED

(For when you're tired of decoding vibes and just want to know what the hell this is.)
Use these casually, confidently, and always from a place of curiosity not insecurity. You're not begging for a label. You're asking for *clarity so you can move accordingly.* Big difference.

1. "I'm really enjoying getting to know you. are we on the same page about where this might be headed?" Soft, open-ended, non-demanding. It starts a dialogue, not a verdict.

2. "I don't want to assume anything. what does dating look like for you right now?" Let him tell you if he's exclusive, casual, or still swiping. And if it's vague? That *is* your answer.

3. "What would commitment look like to you at this point in your life?" This gets you past "do you like me?" and straight to "do you want the same things I do?"

4. "I'm at a place where I'm dating with intention. how do you usually know when you want to make things exclusive?" This puts it on *you* first showing you're clear about your standards while inviting him to share his.

5. "I'm starting to develop deeper feelings for you, and I just want to check in how are you feeling about where we're at?" Vulnerable but calm. You're not forcing anything. You're just checking the emotional temperature.

6. "I've been thinking about the kind of connection I'm looking for and I want to make sure I'm building that with someone who's on the same wavelength. How are you feeling about us?" This shows maturity, self-awareness, and self-respect. It's not a trap, it's a check-in.

7. "Are you still dating other people, or are you leaning toward something more exclusive?" Direct, but not aggressive. Clear > confusing. Every time.

8. "I want to keep showing up with intention, but I need to know if we're moving in the same direction. Can we talk about what this is becoming for each of us?" This is for when it's *been* a minute, and it's time to stop playing pretend.

9. "No pressure at all, I just want to be transparent that I'm looking for something real. If we're not on the same page, that's totally okay, I just don't want to guess." You're giving them an out while still asserting your needs. This is *emotional confidence* in action.

10. "Let's check in. Do you see this as something worth growing into a relationship, or are you still figuring it out?" Use this when it's been consistent and good but unclear. You're giving them space while still asking for truth.

Pro Tip to Avoid the Panic Spiral: Always use a *grounded tone*. Don't start with "we need to talk" energy. Start with "I just wanted to check in with you about something that's been on my mind." Calm energy = better conversation every time.

FLIRTY, FUN, NON-PUSHY TEXTS TO DEFINE WHAT THIS IS

(Because "what are we?" doesn't have to feel like an HR meeting.)

Use these when you're ready to *feel the vibe shift without making it weird*. Drop one in when the energy's good, you've been consistently seeing each other, and you're over dating in the dark.

1. "So are we accidentally in a relationship or am I still allowed to flirt with the bartender?" Lighthearted but low-key genius opens the door with a wink, not a wall.

2. "Not to get all deep in your texts on a random Tuesday, but… are we exclusive or just vibing really hard?" Playful *and* emotionally clear.

3. "If this was a movie, what genre would we be in right now: casual rom-com or slow-burn love story?" Watch his answer carefully. This one's a cute trap.

4. "Serious question: do I need to keep pretending I don't like you this much, or are we past that now?" Bold. Fun. And it gets to the damn point.

5. "Be honest, if your friends asked what I am to you, what would you say? 👀" Let's *not* have you finding out you're "just a girl he hangs out with" six weeks from now.

6. "Okay but *hypothetically*, if someone else asked me out this week, would I say yes or I'm seeing someone?" You're not asking for a title, you're asking for clarity. And that's *power*.

7. "Is this the part where we talk about what we're doing, or are we still riding the 'vibes-only' train?" Casual savage. My personal favorite.

8. "So... do we talk about 'us' or just keep pretending we're both not catching feelings?" Delivered with the right energy? *Unstoppable*.

9. "So I've deleted the apps… should I redownload them or are you gonna make that unnecessary?" Flirty *with a side of savage*. You're putting the ball in his court *without begging for a title*.

10. "If we had to give this thing a name (other than 'vibes'), what would you call it?" You're keeping it casual but calling his bluff on the whole *we're just chillin'* act.

Dating Dealbreakers

Let's be clear: Deal breakers are not "being picky." They're self-respect in action. They're the standards you refuse to lower even when you're lonely, horny, or tired of first dates with men who think "What's up?" is a conversation starter. If you don't know your deal breakers, you're going to keep making excuses for red flags and wonder why you're exhausted and brokenhearted. let's lay it out, loud and clear:

1. Lying and Shady Behavior. If honesty isn't on the table, neither are you. Period. Trust is the bare minimum, not a luxury item.

2. Different Core Values. Love doesn't erase fundamental differences. If you don't align on the big stuff: goals, morals, dreams, it will rot from the inside out.

3. Cheating (or Almost Cheating). If they're hunting for attention elsewhere, *let them hunt.* Alone.

4. Addiction Issues They Won't Face. You can't save someone who refuses to save themselves. Love is not rehab.

5. Zero Compromise Energy. If it's always their way or the highway, give them directions to the nearest off-ramp.

6. Any Form of Abuse: Emotional, Verbal, Physical. No exceptions. No second chances. No "but they're sorry." GTFO.

7. Totally Opposite Relationship Goals If you want marriage and kids and they want casual situationships forever that's not going to magically fix itself. Believe people the first time.

8. Financial Disaster Zone. It's not about being rich. It's about responsibility. If they gamble rent money or hide credit card debt, trust that the chaos will reach you too.

9. Nasty Hygiene or Zero Self-Care. Basic cleanliness is a basic respect. You are not here to date a grown-ass man who smells like microwaved regret.

10. Massive Cultural or Religious Misalignment. Love matters, yes. But so do your deepest roots and beliefs. Honor yours. Don't bulldoze them for romance.

11. Stage Five Clinger Energy. You want a partner, not a human barnacle. Healthy relationships breathe. Needy love suffocates.

12. Wildly Mismatched Sex Drives. If one of you is climbing the walls and the other one is fine with cuddles and prayer circles 24/7 resentment will eat you alive. Chemistry matters.

Final Word: Deal breakers aren't negotiable. They're the fence that protects your future. Every time you let one slide, you're digging your own emotional grave. one little compromise at a time. Know what you want. Know what you refuse. And love yourself enough to walk away the second you see the line being crossed. Your standards are not the problem. Your standards are the solution.

Deal Breaker Reality Gut-Check: Are You Walking Your Talk?

Before you ignore that gnawing feeling in your gut (again), ask yourself these five questions:

1. Am I hoping they'll *change* or loving them as they actually are? (*If you're dating their potential, you're dating a fantasy.*)

2. If my best friend told me this story about her partner, what would I tell her to do? (*Apply the advice you'd scream at your bestie. Loudly.*)

3. Am I scared to leave because I'm in love or because I'm scared to start over? (*Stay because it's right, not because it's familiar.*)

4. What's the deal breaker I keep making excuses for? (*Find it. Name it. Burn the damn excuse book.*)

5. If I saw my future-self five years from now, would she thank me for staying or leaving? (*She already knows. You do too.*)

If these questions made your stomach flip? good. That's not fear. That's your power waking the hell up. You deserve a love that honors you not one you have to survive. Know your deal breakers. And never again apologize for them.

Turn-Ons, Turn-Offs, and the Truth About What Men Are Really After

What Men Are Actually Looking For
(And why it often has nothing to do with you.)

The short version? They want to feel powerful, desired, safe, respected, and like they're winning something rare. The long version? Keep reading. We're going to dissect the male psyche like we're building the Red Flag Rosetta Stone.

I. Let's Be Real First: "Men" Are Not a Monolith

There are *types* and what they're looking for is based on:

- Their **attachment style**
- Their **maturity level**
- Their **ego wounds**
- And where they are in their **emotional evolution**

So, asking *"What do men want?"* is like asking *"What do toddlers want?"* The answer is: **It depends on how healed they are.** So, let's break it down by *categories*.

II. What Emotionally Unavailable Men Want

These men crave intimacy but fear it. So, they chase connection until it feels too real then sabotage it.

They want:

- Chemistry without emotional risk
- A woman who is *deep* but not demanding
- Someone who makes them *feel* something but won't require them to *be* something
- Validation, attention, nurturing but without accountability
- A "safe" container to unravel *without actually being seen too closely*

Translation: They want therapy in a thong. A fantasy woman who doesn't need too much, want too much, or call out their patterns.

III. What Emotionally *Available* Men Want

These are the rare unicorns. And they're not confused. At all.

They want:

- A woman grounded in her own life, with *room* for them not a woman building her world around them
- Emotional connection that feels *safe*, not performative
- Softness that isn't codependent, and strength that isn't guarded
- Fun, peace, laughter, depth, and attraction without performance
- Consistency. Clarity. Partnership. Legacy.

Translation: They want a woman who knows who she is, communicates like an adult, and isn't trying to play games while demanding stability. And yes, they still want to feel desired, powerful, and needed. Not because you're helpless but because you *choose* them.

IV. What Wounded, Performative Men Think They Want

These are the "alpha podcast bros," the "nice guys" with deep entitlement, and the "emotionally mature" men who *read the language but haven't done the work.*

They want:

- The "cool girl" who doesn't nag
- A hyperfeminine peace prize who never challenges their ego
- To be adored like a king without doing the work of one
- Someone "hot but humble," confident but "not too loud," sexy but never *too sexual*

Translation: They want a woman who's been strategically dimmed down to protect their false sense of masculinity. You will exhaust yourself trying to be her. And still be rejected.

V. What Good Men (In Progress) Want

These are men who are healing. Messy but trying. Flawed but *aware.*

They want:

- A space where they can be real without being rejected
- A partner who challenges them without belittling them
- A love that feels earned—not handed to them as a rescue package
- A woman who communicates clearly, calls out their blind spots, and still *believes* in them
- To *feel like a man* not by dominating you, but by *rising alongside you*

They don't want a babysitter. They want a mirror. **And a teammate.**

VI. The Wild Truth: Sometimes It's Not About You at All

A man may not choose you because:

- He's not ready to see himself clearly
- You trigger his deepest insecurities by simply existing in your power
- He's still addicted to the thrill of chaos
- You're *too emotionally safe* for a man who hasn't built internal safety yet

You're not too much. You're too accurate. You're not intimidating. You're emotionally clarifying. And some men simply aren't ready for that.

Final Word: So, what do men actually want? The real ones? They want a woman who is fully herself. Who isn't performing femininity for male approval. Who can love without losing herself. Who invites not demands growth. Who is soft because she's strong, not because she's scared. Who is a mirror, not a mask. And until one of them proves they're ready for you? Don't waste your softness on someone still performing masculinity for sport.

What Turns Men On During Dating
(And no, it's not just cleavage though that never hurts.)

Attraction doesn't start in the bedroom. It starts in the moment he can't predict you, control you, or stop thinking about you. Let's break down the real turn-ons: the ones that get in their head, under their skin, and leave them *slightly ruined* for anyone after you.

I. Confidence That Isn't Performative
The biggest turn-on? You knowing you're the prize. Without asking him to confirm it. Confidence turns men on when it's:
- Grounded, not loud
- Calm, not overcompensating
- Present, not self-obsessed
- You being comfortable with silence, eye contact, and not rushing to fill the space

When you don't need his attention, you command it. When you don't need his validation, you become magnetic. That's erotic.

II. Being Challenged (Gently, But Decisively)
You want to know what short-circuits the male brain in the best way? A woman who's not afraid to say:
- "I don't agree, but I get why you think that."
- "That joke didn't land, try again."
- "I don't tolerate that kind of talk."
- "I like you. But I like me more."

Respectful challenge = mental stimulation = primal fire. Men are used to being either praised or avoided. But when you *stand grounded in your truth* and still flirt? That's game over.

III. Sensory Confidence
Men are visual, yes. But they're also sensory creatures. Turn-ons they *won't admit*:
- The scent of your skin lingering after a hug
- The way you lean in when you talk, *then* pull back
- The curve of your wrist, neck, collarbone *not just what's exposed*
- The sound of your voice when you say their name with a smirk

You don't need to be naked. You need to be *intentional.*

IV. Playfulness with Depth
Men light up when you're:
- A little unpredictable
- A little chaotic in the right way
- Down to play, but not to be played with
- Emotionally aware but still quick to laugh

Let him be serious. Let him lead. Let him show off. Then one-line him into oblivion with a joke he didn't see coming. That contrast? It turns them on more than a dress ever could.

V. Unavailability to Bullsh*t

The ultimate turn-on? A woman who *could* be into him… but won't settle.

- You don't need to explain your standards. He *feels* them.
- You can laugh at his charm but you're not seduced by it.
- You can disappear the moment he shows inconsistency, and he knows it.

This isn't coldness. It's self-respect laced with sensuality. The moment a man realizes you're not like the others, because you don't need the game to feel powerful, you'll turn him on *and* level him up.

Final Word: Yes, men are visual. But the right men? They're aroused by something far deeper.

- Your energy when you walk in
- Your standards when you speak
- Your silence when they expect a reaction
- Your ability to want them *without ever needing them*

That's the turn-on. That's the difference between a girl he liked and a woman he can't forget.

What Turns Men Off During Dating
(Also known as: "Why He Said You Were Amazing
Then Disappeared into the Matrix")

He was into you. He flirted. He initiated. He made plans. He called you sexy. And then... *poof.* Or worse, he started acting "busy." The truth? You didn't do anything "wrong." But you *might* have triggered one of the subconscious male icks that shut their brains (and d*cks) off faster than airplane mode on a toxic text. Let's break down the real turn-offs. the ones they rarely say out loud, but absolutely respond to.

I. Overeagerness (AKA Energetic Thirst)

Nothing flattens a man's attraction faster than a woman who's too available too fast. Turn-offs in this zone:

- Replying too quickly every time
- Over-texting when he's slow to respond
- Planning your wedding after one night of banter
- Getting offended when he doesn't mirror your excitement
- Making him your emotional outlet by date two

Men want to feel desired not devoured. They want to win, not feel like they were drafted by default.

II. Overexplaining Yourself (AKA Talking Yourself Out of the Throne)

You know what's hotter than justifying every thought or emotion? Saying what you mean and letting it sit. Turn-offs here:

- "Sorry if that sounded weird..."
- "I just want to explain what I meant earlier…"
- "I know I can come off intense but—"
- "I'm usually not like this, I just…"

Stop auditioning. You're not here for a role in *his comfort zone*. You're the whole damn plot twist.

III. Complaining About Other Men

This is a subtle sabotage move. It's giving "I'm still in my villain origin story" energy. Turn-offs:

- "Ugh, men never know what they want."
- "You're not like other guys… I think."
- "My ex was such a narcissist, he—"
- "Guys on dating apps are all trash."

IV. Energy That Feels Controlling

This doesn't mean you're bossy. It means you're trying to manage the date, the vibe, the outcome: everything. Turn-offs here:

- "So, what are we?" on date two
- "You probably won't like me once you get to know me…"
- Passive-aggressive digs disguised as flirtation
- Telling him how to respond, feel, or behave constantly

If he feels like he's being micro-managed? He'll tap out. Fast. Men don't want to be babysat. they want to *choose* to show up. If you pre-script it, it's over.

V. Hyper-Masculine Energy Disguised as "I Don't Need a Man"

We get it. You're independent. You pay your own bills. You open your own doors. You installed your own TV. But if your energy says "I dare you to try to add value to my life, peasant" he won't rise to the challenge. He'll back away *gracefully and terrified*. Turn-offs:

- Refusing to receive
- Mocking chivalry
- Constantly reminding him how replaceable men are
- Acting like vulnerability = weakness

You can be strong without treating softness like it's contagious. Men aren't scared of your power. They're turned off when you use it as armor.

VI. Body Language + Vibe Killers

1. **You don't smile at all**. Not "smile more," not "be pleasant" but if your resting face is contempt and your vibe is ice queen performance art, *there's no invitation for connection.*
2. **You sit like you want to leave**. Arms crossed, body angled away, purse clutched in escape mode. He'll notice. And emotionally check out before the check comes.
3. **You act like you're too good for the place**. If the entire night is you making snarky remarks about the venue, the wine, or the food, he's already deciding who to ask next time instead.

VII. Sexual Energy Gone Weird

1. **You make everything a test**. Pretend you're not interested to "see if he chases?" Cool. He's gone.
2. **You use sex as bait**. Flirting is great. But men *know* when you're using sexual energy to hook them, while internally calculating how long to make them wait.
3. **You lead with judgment, not desire**. Constantly sizing him up, micromanaging his order, criticizing his clothes. He's not turned on. He's mentally filing a restraining order.

Bonus Round: Micro-Icks They'll Never Tell You Turned Them Off

1. You order like you're high-maintenance on purpose
2. You say "I'm not like other girls" (instant L)
3. You wear perfume that reminds him of his aunt
4. You ask if he still talks to his ex during the appetizer
5. You tell him, "I usually don't go for guys like you"

Final Word: You don't need to change who you are. But you do need to ask: **Am I leading with power or protection? Clarity or control? Attraction or anxiety?** Because what turns men off the fastest isn't how you look or what you wear. It's the *energy you bring into the room*, the one that either invites connection… or sends them back to Hinge.

Red Flags, Decoded

(Categorized. Clarified. And ready to save your sanity before you waste six months on a walking trauma response.)

Not every red flag means "run immediately." But if you're stacking these like poker chips, you're not building a relationship, you're gambling with your peace. Red flags are patterns, not one-offs. Trust the *pattern*.

EMOTIONAL RED FLAGS

When their inner world is a black hole and they expect you to fix it without blinking.

1. Lack of Accountability. If they *never* take ownership for their screwups, it's always their ex, their boss, their parents, Mercury retrograde, you're dating a victim, not a partner. "I'm sorry you feel that way" ≠ an apology.

2. Uncontrolled Jealousy. They're suspicious of everyone: your barista, your dog walker, your coworker from accounting. They think loyalty = surveillance. No. That's paranoia dressed as love.

3. Emotional Dumping Without Reciprocity. You know their entire trauma timeline but they know nothing about yours. They use you like a therapist, but flinch when you bring up your own feelings? *Emotional imbalance* is not intimacy.

4. Inconsistent Affection. They love bomb you one week and emotionally ghost the next. This is not romance, it's nervous system abuse.

BEHAVIORAL RED FLAGS

This is the stuff they show you early, if you're paying attention.

5. Disrespect (to you or anyone else). Watch how they treat the waiter. Their mom. A stranger. You are not special, you're just *next*. Mocking your or belittling you, even if he is joking. That's a nope.

6. Dishonesty (Even Over Small Sh*t). If they lie about things that don't even matter, imagine what they'll do when it *does*. Half-truths are still lies. "I didn't mention it" is not transparency.

7. Poor Communication. They dodge real conversations, change the subject when things get emotional, or hit you with "idk" every time you try to talk deeper. That's not mystery. That's emotional immaturity.

8. Breadcrumbing. They text just enough to keep you hooked but never move anything forward. This is not "busy." This is *strategic laziness* from someone who wants your energy without commitment.

CONTROL + POWER DYNAMICS
When you feel more like a project than a partner.

9. Controlling Behavior. If they're trying to tell you how to dress, who to hang out with, or where to be, you're not dating. You're being managed.

10. Guilt-Tripping or Emotional Manipulation. They flip every situation to make you feel like *you're* the problem. You end up apologizing when *they're* the one who crossed a line. This is a playbook, not a personality.

11. Invasive Curiosity. They need access to your phone, your passwords, your location... and call it "being open." Nope. That's not closeness. That's surveillance.

12. Rushing Intimacy. "I've never felt this way about anyone." "I think you're my soulmate." In week one. You're not in love, you're being *lovebombed.*

BOUNDARY-CRUSHING BEHAVIOR
If someone can't handle your "no," they're not ready for your "yes."

13. Pushing Physical or Emotional Limits. Whether it's touching you too soon or asking invasive personal questions you've said you're not ready for. *No* is not a debate.

14. Testing Your Limits for Reactions. They joke about cheating, play hot-and-cold, or intentionally trigger jealousy "just to see how much you care." That's manipulation, not flirtation.

15. Guilt After Setting Boundaries. You say, "I don't feel comfortable with that" they get moody, distant, or call you "sensitive." This is a control tactic. You're not difficult, they're just used to people folding.

LIFESTYLE RED FLAGS
Compatibility ≠ chemistry. You can vibe with someone
who is completely wrong for your life.

16. No Goals, No Growth. They're coasting through life on autopilot. No ambition, no self-awareness, no plans. That's not "go with the flow." That's dead weight.

17. Unresolved Ex Drama. If their ex is still their emotional support line or their main villain, you're entering a war that has nothing to do with you.

18. Mismatched Values. If you're into depth, growth, and loyalty, and they're into partying, sarcasm, and avoiding all responsibility, you're not "opposites." You're *incompatible.*

19. Inconsistent Effort. You don't need a grand gesture. You need follow-through. If they only step up when they're about to lose you, that's not love. That's desperation dressed in flowers.

20. They "Don't Believe in Labels." Translation: They want all the benefits of a relationship with none of the responsibility. *Don't argue with this, believe them.*

BONUS RED FLAG: YOUR NERVOUS SYSTEM HATES THEM

You're anxious. You're second-guessing everything. You're in a constant loop of decoding texts, seeking validation, and explaining your own reactions. Baby girl, your *body* knows.

RED FLAG REFLECTION WORKSHEET

(Because your intuition has been screaming, and it's time to listen.)

Use this worksheet anytime you start feeling unsure about someone you're dating or when your gut knows something is off, but your brain keeps trying to justify it.

INSTRUCTIONS: Go line by line. Be brutally honest. This is not about judging yourself, it's about protecting your peace before another emotional entanglement eats your time, energy, and self-worth.

SECTION 1: PATTERN IDENTIFICATION

1. What are the red flags I've noticed so far?
(List them in your own words. Get specific. Vibes don't count. Write behaviors.)

_____

_____

_____

2. How many of these have I seen more than once?
Circle one:
- Once
- Twice
- Repeatedly
- It's basically their personality

3. Have I ever made excuses for this behavior?
Circle all that apply:
- "They're just stressed"
- "They had a tough childhood"
- "They're not used to someone like me"
- "I don't want to seem too sensitive"
- "Maybe I'm overthinking it"

4. What has my body felt like around them lately?
Check all that apply:
- Tight chest
- Uneasy stomach
- Trouble sleeping
- Anxious before/after seeing them
- Constant need to seek reassurance
- Feeling like I can't fully relax

227

SECTION 2: BOUNDARIES + BEHAVIOR

5. Have they crossed any of my stated boundaries?

If yes, how did I respond?

_____

_____

6. Do I feel safe to speak my mind with them? Why or why not?

_____

_____

7. Have I minimized anything to keep the peace or avoid being "too much?"

Describe a recent moment where you swallowed a truth to stay likable.

_____

_____

_____

SECTION 3: ENERGY ACCOUNTING

8. Since dating them, have I felt more…

Circle one for each:

- Clear or Confused?
- Secure or Anxious?
- Seen or Misunderstood?
- Grounded or Off-balance?
- Valued or Tolerated?

9. What parts of myself have I started hiding, shrinking, or silencing?

Be honest. Who are you _not_ being in this connection?

_____

_____

SECTION 4: REALITY CHECK

10. If a close friend told me they were experiencing what I am, what would I tell them to do?

_____

_____

11. Am I waiting for a version of this person that doesn't actually exist? What do I keep hoping they'll become?

_____

_____

12. What would leaving (or pulling back) give me space to feel again?

_____

_____

FINAL PROMPT:

What's the truth I've been avoiding and what's the smallest action I can take today to honor it?

Shameless Plug (because I don't play):

If you want the *ultimate decoder ring* for men's trash behavior, I built you the ***Red Flag Translator***, a savage companion guide that breaks down every excuse, line, and gaslight with zero mercy. This book gives you the survival strategy, but the Translator? That's the dictionary. Grab it and never wonder "what did he mean by that?" again.

https://yourdatingunexpert.com/red-flag-translator

Types of Men to Avoid

You don't need to learn another lesson the hard way. Here's your cheat sheet.

Each type includes:

- 🪧 The Flag
- 💣 Why He's Dangerous
- 💭 What You'll Think It Is
- 🔍 What It Actually Is
- 🤞 What to Do

1. The Love Bomber

🪧 Floods you with praise, gifts, and connection fast.

💣 He's manufacturing intimacy without building it.

💭 You'll think: "Finally, a man who knows what he wants."

🔍 It's emotional cocaine.

🤞 Run when intensity replaces consistency.

2. The Wounded Narcissist

🪧 Talks about his trauma constantly, but has no accountability.

💣 Uses pain to excuse cruelty.

💭 You'll think: "He's just been through a lot."

🔍 He's weaponizing his wounds.

🤞 Compassion ≠ a free pass for damage.

3. The Girl-Hater

🪧 Low-key hates women but masks it as "preference."

💣 Calls women "females," complains about makeup, weight, independence.

💭 You'll think: "He's just honest."

🔍 He's indoctrinated and bitter.

🤞 Misogyny isn't a personality, it's a disqualifier.

4. The Almost Boyfriend

🪧 Acts like your man but avoids the label.

💣 Has all the benefits of a relationship, none of the responsibility.

💭 You'll think: "We're basically dating already."

🔍 If he wanted to claim you, he would.

🤞 If it's unclear, it's a no.

5. The Rage Bottle

🔺 Seems calm, but explodes randomly.

💣 Has no emotional regulation.

💭 You'll think: "He's just under a lot of stress."

🔍 His silence isn't peace, it's pressure.

✌️ Emotional safety isn't optional.

6. The Sexual Opportunist

🔺 Pushes boundaries early, frames it as "passion."

💣 Only present when things are physical.

💭 You'll think: "He just really desires me."

🔍 He just wants access.

✌️ If he disappears after sex, he was never there.

7. The Secret Keeper

🔺 Vague about his life, friends, past, and phone.

💣 Withholding is how he keeps power.

💭 You'll think: "He's just private."

🔍 He's hiding something or someone.

✌️ Love thrives in transparency.

8. The Praise Hunter

🔺 Needs constant validation, or he spirals.

💣 Will become jealous, controlling, or withdrawn if not center stage.

💭 You'll think: "He just needs reassurance."

🔍 He's feeding on your energy.

✌️ Affirmation shouldn't feel like babysitting.

9. The Ghoster Who Returns

🔺 Disappears when it gets deep, reappears when you detach.

💣 You're not a partner, you're a backup plan.

💭 You'll think: "Maybe the timing just wasn't right."

🔍 No, he just needed an ego boost.

✌️ Close the door. For good.

10. The Clout Chaser

🔺 Only shows up when you're thriving.

💣 Wants your light, not your soul.

💭 You'll think: "He's proud of me."

🔍 He's addicted to proximity, not partnership.

✌️ If he claps more than he connects, he's not your guy.

11. The "Empath" Who's Actually Just Codependent

🔺 Claims to feel deeply, but takes zero space for himself.

💣 Smothers you, panics if you set boundaries.

💭 You'll think: "He's just really loving."

🔍 He doesn't know where you end and he begins.

✌️ Love without autonomy is control.

12. The Jealous Jailer

🔺 Tries to isolate you under the guise of love.

💣 Polices your clothes, friends, or social media.

💭 You'll think: "He just wants to protect me."

🔍 Control isn't care, it's a trap.

✌️ Run before he erases you.

13. The Daddy Reenactment

🔺 You're dating him to fix something your dad broke.

💣 The dynamic feels eerily familiar… and unsafe.

💭 You'll think: "This time, I'll be chosen."

🔍 This time, you'll be retraumatized.

✌️ Don't confuse recognition with compatibility.

14. The Career Cult Leader

🔺 Obsessed with hustle, growth, and "winning."

💣 No space for your needs unless they fit his calendar.

💭 You'll think: "He's just really ambitious."

🔍 He's emotionally unavailable and calls it purpose.

✌️ If love feels like a productivity metric, log off.

15. The Emotionally Void Stoic

🔺 Never expresses feelings. Doesn't comfort, doesn't share.

💣 You're in a relationship with silence.

💭 You'll think: "He shows love in different ways."

🔍 Maybe. But you're lonely.

✌️ Emotional intimacy is non-negotiable.

16. The Socially Acceptable Sexist

🔔 Says he's "old-fashioned" or "traditional."

💣 Wants obedience, not partnership.

🧠 You'll think: "He's just confident in gender roles."

🔍 He's masking power dynamics as romance.

✋ You're not his 1950s fantasy.

17. The Situationship Specialist

🔔 Perpetually in limbo. Doesn't define it, ever.

💣 Wastes years of your life while keeping options open.

🧠 You'll think: "It's complicated."

🔍 It's not. He just won't choose you.

✋ Confusion is a no.

There are 50 arch-personality types I have decoded and you can read them all here, if you are interested.

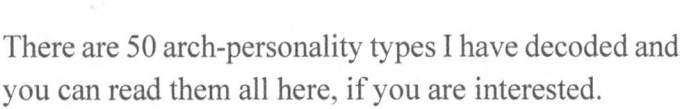

https://yourdatingunexpert.com/men-decoded-the-unholy-field-guide

THE THREE PATTERNS THAT COST WOMEN YEARS
Recognizing Emotional Manipulation Patterns

Emotional manipulation is not always obvious. It is not always loud. It is, more often, the erosion of your sanity through a series of almosts. Almost an apology. Almost a commitment. Almost love. This chapter breaks down the 10 most insidious emotional manipulation patterns used in modern dating. These are not surface-level red flags. These are the psychological weapons men use to confuse, control, destabilize, and drain you while making it feel like your idea.

PATTERN 1. Gaslighting

"Maybe I am too sensitive…" No. You were being trained to distrust yourself.

✦ **What It Is (Clinical Depth):** Gaslighting is a deliberate psychological tactic where a person manipulates you into doubting your memory, your perception, and your sanity. It is systematic reality distortion designed to gain control. In psychology, it's classified under emotional abuse and often coexists with narcissistic or borderline personality traits. Over time, it fractures your ability to self-reference, causing anxiety, dissociation, self-blame, and sometimes a complete emotional shutdown.

✦ **What It Sounds Like:**
- "That's not what I said."
- "You're imagining things."
- "You're way too emotional."

- "You always twist things."
- "You're remembering it wrong."
- "You're crazy, just like your mother."

These aren't just dismissals. They are intentional erasures of your emotional truth. Their goal? Make *them* the authority on what's real, and make you dependent on their version of events.

✦ **The Psychological Weaponry:** Gaslighting uses three manipulative levers:
1. **Denial of truth:** Even when you have proof, they deny it. This creates cognitive dissonance.
2. **Projection:** They accuse you of what *they're* doing to confuse and destabilize.
3. **Isolation:** They erode your trust in others and in yourself, so you start confiding *only in them.*

✦ **Why It Feels Like *Your* Fault:** Because gaslighting is often subtle and progressive. It starts small: a correction here, a dismissal there. But over time, you begin to:
- Question your memory
- Apologize for things you didn't do
- Rationalize their coldness

This is not weakness. This is a trauma response to invisible harm.

✦ **What It Looks Like in Dating Today:** Modern gaslighting has evolved. It doesn't always scream. It's often **wrapped in therapy speak** or masked as concern:
- "I just think you're projecting your past onto me."
- "You're acting like you have trauma to heal. Why don't you go journal about this instead of blaming me?"
- "I never said I wanted a relationship. You assumed that."

This is weaponized calm. It's emotional abuse dressed in mindfulness. Don't confuse vocabulary for integrity.

✦ **The Way Out (Healing Begins Here):**
1. **Document everything.** Write it down. Keep a journal. Save the texts.
2. **Talk to someone safe.** You need an outside witness to reality.
3. **Speak your truth without needing approval.** Even if they deny it, name it for yourself.
4. **Detach from the narrative.** You don't need to prove abuse to the abuser.
5. **Rebuild your self-trust.** You didn't misremember. You were manipulated.

Reframe this truth: Gaslighting didn't make you crazy. It made you survive confusion so well that now you're fluent in subtle harm. That's not weakness. That's proof of your strength. And now, you'll never be fooled again.

Emotional Extraction: Reclaiming Sanity After Gaslighting

<u>Deprogramming Practices</u>

These are practical, grounding tools to help you start unhooking from the internalized voice of the gaslighter and restore your self-trust.

1. Reality Reconnection Journal. Every time you feel confused, log the facts. Break the cycle of internal chaos by documenting *your* version of what happened without needing permission or agreement.

Prompt:

- What did I see or hear?
- How did I feel?
- What did I make it mean?
- Is this how I'd respond if I fully trusted myself?

Over time, this becomes your proof. Your archive of truth. Your soul's receipts.

2. The Mirror Talk Ritual. Once a day, look in the mirror and say:

- "I am not crazy. I am remembering what he wanted me to forget."
- "My intuition is not broken. It was silenced."
- "I don't need anyone to believe me. I believe me."

3. Body Signals Check-In. Gaslighting disconnects you from your body. It keeps you in your head, spinning for clarity that never comes. Start asking:

- Where do I feel that unease?
- Is my chest tight?
- Does my gut clench around this person?

Your body remembers. Let her speak. Let her guide.

4. The One Safe Witness. Gaslighting thrives in isolation. Choose one emotionally safe person to start naming what happened to. Not to be believed just to be heard. Say: "I don't need you to fix it. I just need someone to witness what I went through so I can stop pretending it wasn't real."

Closing Truth: You Were Never Crazy. You were intuitive. You were observant. You were *dangerous* to someone who needed you confused. Gaslighting wasn't just emotional abuse. It was an attempt to erase you. You survived it. Now we rewrite the voice in your head.

PATTERN 2. The Hot-and-Cold Manipulator

"But when it's good, it's so good…" That's how they keep you hooked.
Chaos isn't chemistry. It's control.

What It Is (Psychological Breakdown): Hot-and-cold manipulation is a psychological tactic based on intermittent reinforcement: a pattern where affection, attention, or validation is given sporadically and unpredictably to create emotional dependency. It works not because it feels safe, but because it creates a high. A *chemical addiction to hope and confusion*. You start mistaking the dopamine hit of "finally getting closeness again" for love. You think the high means connection. But what you're actually experiencing is survival-based bonding.

What It Sounds Like
- "Sorry I've been distant... I've just had a lot going on."
- "I'm all in just scared sometimes, that's all."
- "You know how much I care... I just get overwhelmed."
- "You mean a lot to me, I'm just not good with feelings."
- "I always come back, don't I?"

Translation: *I give just enough to keep you hopeful and disappear just enough to keep you chasing.*

Psychological Function
1. **Addiction via Intermittent Reward**. Your nervous system becomes chemically trained to crave their return after emotional withdrawal. The unpredictability makes you chase the next "good moment" like a slot machine.
2. **Control Without Commitment**. They maintain power because you're never sure where you stand. The inconsistency keeps you emotionally off-balance and unable to detach.
3. **Shame Loop Activation**. When they go cold, you assume *you* did something wrong. You start shape-shifting to win back the warmth.

This is not connection. It's a trauma reenactment.

How It Shows Up in Dating
- He lovebombs, disappears, then comes back like nothing happened
- He gives intense attention, then ignores messages for days
- He's hyper-affectionate when you pull away, but cold when you're vulnerable

You're not crazy for holding on. You were trained to.

Why It Hurts: Because it mimics passion. It feels like fire. But what you're actually experiencing is nervous system dysregulation disguised as desire.
- You start making excuses for his inconsistency
- You chase highs instead of stability
- You forget what it's like to feel loved without anxiety
- You believe "this must be love" because the lows are so low, the highs feel transcendent

The Most Dangerous Variant: The Wounded Showman. He shows up intense, emotional, magnetic. But once you get close, he disappears only to reappear *just when you start to detach.* He paints himself as misunderstood, too damaged to love fully, but too sincere to be called a player. You feel chosen. Then discarded. Then chosen again. He doesn't commit. He casts you in the story he wants to believe about himself until the role exhausts you.

Healing & Nervous System Repair After Hot-and-Cold Manipulation
Love should never require withdrawal symptoms.

1. Pattern Exposure Exercise: Print the Receipts. Your brain romanticizes patterns when they're scattered so it's time to bring the cycle into focus.
Write it out like a timeline:
- Day 1: Intense connection
- Day 3: Ignored message
- Day 5: Random call out of nowhere
- Day 7: Warm again
- Day 9: Emotional shutdown after I opened up
- Day 10: Flirty and back like nothing happened

Then ask: "If this timeline was a script, what genre is it? Is this love? Or is this an emotional hostage film where I'm the main character and don't know how the scene ends?"

2. The Nervous System Break Pattern. Your body has been trained to expect loss after connection, and silence after joy. That's the trauma loop. Let's rewire it:
Daily practice:
- Put one hand on your heart, one on your belly
- Close your eyes
- Breathe in for 4, hold for 4, exhale for 6
- Say: "I am allowed to feel safe when it's good. I do not have to brace for the drop. I do not chase the high. I return to myself."

Repeat this every time you feel that aching pull to check your phone, re-read old texts, or replay the last good moment.

3. Ritual of Final Reconnection: Say Goodbye to the "Good Version." This is where most women stay stuck. You're not chasing *him*. You're chasing the version of him you met first.
Write a letter to that version. Begin with: "I loved you. You weren't real. You were the role he played long enough to win my heart, but not long enough to keep it. I know now that love doesn't vanish like that. Love doesn't make me beg for clarity. I release you. I no longer grieve an illusion." You can burn it. Or read it aloud until the ache breaks.

4. Name the Craving for What It Is. Every time you feel the urge to text him, to chase that next high, name it. Don't shame it. Say: "This is not love. This is a withdrawal symptom. I am not missing him. I am missing relief from the pain he caused. I won't bargain with my soul for 15 minutes of connection." This stops the cycle of blaming yourself for *wanting* the pain to end and lets you name the real wound underneath: you were trained to confuse inconsistency with intimacy.

Final Reframe: The connection wasn't real. The chemicals were. But love is not an adrenaline spike. Love is safe. steady. slow-burning. You'll remember: you don't chase someone who drops you after kissing your soul. You choose the kind of love that never asks you to earn your next hit.

PATTERN 3. The Fixer Fantasy

"If I just love him right, maybe he'll become everything I see in him."
No, he won't. He's not your soul mate. He's your slow death.

What It Is (Psychological Breakdown): The Fixer Fantasy is the emotional trap where you fall in love not with the man in front of you, but with his potential. You become invested in who he could be if only he healed, evolved, committed, or woke up. He never claimed to be that man. You just *saw* the possibility and got hooked on the transformation. This is not compassion. This is projection disguised as loyalty.

What It Sounds Like
- "He's been through a lot. He just needs someone to believe in him."
- "I know he loves me… he just doesn't know how to show it yet."
- "He's growing. He's working on himself."
- "If he could just get out of his own way…"
- "We've had so many breakthroughs. He's not like this with anyone else."

Translation: *I've become emotionally attached to a man who isn't real, but I've seen glimpses, so I stay.*

Psychological Function
1. **Hope as a Drug**. Your brain becomes chemically tethered to the *idea* of who he might become. You confuse effort with progress. You mistake pain for proof of meaning.
2. **Emotional Overfunctioning**. You take on the role of therapist, motivator, project manager. You believe your love can "bring him back to life." In reality, **you are slowly dying in the process.**
3. **Codependent Conditioning**. You were likely trained to see your worth through what you *give*. So, you give until your self-worth depends on whether or not *he improves*.

But he won't. Because **you became the solution, so he never had to face the problem.**

How It Shows Up in Dating
- You feel "needed" more than loved
- You confuse chaos with depth
- You feel guilt about leaving him "in the middle of his healing"

You're not growing together. You're trying to *drag* him into becoming someone you can finally rest with.

Why It Hurts: Because every time you see a glimpse of the man he *could* be, your nervous system rewards it like a win. But it's not a win, it's a trap. He'll change just enough to keep you hopeful, then collapse back into the comfort of your overfunctioning. And when it ends? You don't just grieve the relationship. You grieve the future you built in your mind that he never even signed up for.

The Most Dangerous Variant: The Emotionally Unemployed Visionary. He has big dreams. Big plans. Big feelings. But no follow-through. No consistency. No evidence. He says all the right things. Reads the right books. Uses the buzzwords. But when it comes time to build? To repair? To commit? He shuts down. And you call it trauma, not **emotional laziness.** This is not your soul mate. This is your *unfinished draft* of a man.

Healing & Release After the Fixer Fantasy

You were not wrong to see potential. You were just never meant to mother it.

1. Grieve the Illusion, Not the Man. What you lost wasn't *him*, it was the future you wrote in your head. The version of him who:

- Got therapy
- Held your hand during conflict
- Showed up for the life you dreamed out loud
- Became the man you knew he could be

But that version never existed. So, you're not healing from heartbreak. You're healing from projection withdrawal. Write this out: "I was in love with a possibility not a partner. I was faithful to an idea not a reality. And now I grieve the fiction so I can reclaim my future."

2. Rewrite the Role You Played. You weren't stupid. You were *wired to nurture*. But now it's time to call it what it was. Make two columns:

- Left: What you did to "help" him
- Right: What it cost you

Examples:

- "I coached him through emotional shutdowns" → "I became emotionally starved"
- "I stayed patient through inconsistencies" → "I normalized instability"

Then say: "I forgive myself for thinking love was a rescue mission. I am not a rehab center. I am a revolution. I do not serve men who want to be worshiped for their potential."

3. Break the "Maybe He'll Be Better for Her" Spell. This one is poison. But let's burn it now.

Repeat: "If he becomes better for someone else, it's because I did the work he *refused* to do. That's not my failure. That's *his*. And if he ever becomes the man I saw in him, it will not undo what I endured." Let her have the man he *may* become. You're done living in the half-life of who he *never was*.

4. Declare the End of Emotional Apprenticeships. Say it. Write it. Tattoo it on your damn soul: "I no longer date men for their potential. I no longer mother grown adults. I no longer confuse loyalty with martyrdom. I do not invest in unfinished men hoping they become safe."

"From this moment forward, I only walk beside those already walking. I am not your ladder. I am the mountain."

Final Reframe. You didn't fail. You graduated. Love doesn't fix people. It doesn't heal them. It doesn't raise them from the emotional dead. That's their job. And your job now? To love from overflow, not obligation. To choose partners, not projects. To become everything you were building for someone else *for yourself.*

Trash Lines Men Say

These are not red flags. These are straight-up exits.

Each one includes the quote, the roast, and (optional) a suggested clapback or translation. You can format this as a rapid-fire section, a TikTok-ready series, or include commentary after each.

1. "You'd be perfect if you just lost a little weight."

▷ Translation: *I want a Build-A-Bitch, not a human.*

🔥 Clapback: "You'd be tolerable if you never spoke again."

2. "I usually date models, but you've got something…"

▷ Translation: *You're a downgrade I'm trying to spin as a compliment.*

🔥 Clapback: "And you've got something too! The audacity."

3. "You're not my type, but I'd still f*ck you."

▷ Translation: *I don't like you, but I like access.*

🔥 Clapback: "Congrats on being the human version of mold. Unwanted, but everywhere."

4. "You're too pretty to be single, what's wrong with you?"

▷ Translation: *I assume women only exist for men's approval and possession.*

🔥 Clapback: "Being single isn't a flaw, thinking like you is."

5. "Can I raw dog you or is this like… a whole thing?"

▷ Translation: *I treat health and consent like optional side quests.*

🔥 Clapback: "Your pullout game and decision-making both seem questionable. Hard pass."

6. "My ex was crazy."

▷ Translation: *I was the problem, but I'm too emotionally immature to admit it.*

🔥 Clapback: "Cool, she probably said the same about you."

7. "You're not like other girls."

▷ Translation: *I think insulting other women will flatter you.*

🔥 Clapback: "No, I'm worse. And more self-aware."

8. "I can't give you what you want right now."

▷ Translation: *I absolutely could, I just won't.*

🔥 Clapback: "Then don't waste my sparkle, king."

9. "You're lucky I'm even into you."

▷ Translation: *I weaponize low self-esteem as foreplay.*

🔥 Clapback: "You're lucky I haven't called pest control."

10. "I like to be honest. Most girls can't handle that."

▶ Translation: *I'm not honest. I'm mean and blame you for reacting.*

🔥 Clapback: "You mistake cruelty for character. Therapy's that way."

11. "I don't want anything serious… unless it's with the right person."

▶ Translation: *I'm pre-rejecting you in case I want to come back later.*

🔥 Clapback: "That person isn't me. Or anyone with taste."

12. "Wanna come over and chill?" (*first text ever*)

▶ Translation: *I am the human version of unsalted rice.*

🔥 Clapback: "Sure, I'll bring Monopoly and a taser."

13. "You're way out of my league… but I'll still hit it."

▶ Translation: *I know I don't deserve you. I'm hoping you don't realize that yet.*

🔥 Clapback: "Not even in your dreams, honey."

14. "You're too emotional."

▶ Translation: *I don't understand feelings and I'm blaming you for having them.*

🔥 Clapback: "And you're too emotionally constipated to matter."

15. "You're high maintenance."

▶ Translation: *You have standards and I'm not meeting them.*

🔥 Clapback: "And you're under-resourced. So, we're even."

16. "I just don't want to hurt you."

▶ Translation: *I already am.*

🔥 Clapback: "Then leave before the damage requires scar tissue."

17. "You're lucky I'm not a cheater."

▶ Translation: *I think not being a literal villain makes me a hero.*

🔥 Clapback: "You're lucky I'm not a felon."

18. "You knew what this was."

▶ Translation: *I said something vague once and now I'm using it to justify treating you like trash.*

🔥 Clapback: "Yeah, it was a mistake."

19. "Let's just see where this goes."

▶ Translation: *I know exactly where this is going: nowhere.*

🔥 Clapback: "It's going to the block list, that's where."

20. "I'm not on social media."

▶ Translation: *I'm hiding something or someone.*

🔥 Clapback: "Cool. Neither is the FBI when they're undercover."

21. "My last ex still hits me up."

▶ Translation: *I love unsolicited validation and passive chaos.*

🔥 Clapback: "Good. Now you can reply from the same device you're blocked on."

22. "I'm just being honest." *(after saying something cruel)*

▶ Translation: *I use 'truth' as an excuse to be emotionally abusive.*

🔥 Clapback: "And I'm just being honest, you're basic."

23. "You're overthinking."

▶ Translation: *You noticed something real, and now I'm trying to make you doubt it.*

🔥 Clapback: "No, you're under-behaving."

24. "I don't want to ruin what we have."

▶ Translation: *I like having sex and attention without consequences.*

🔥 Clapback: "Babe, it's already ruined. We just haven't declared it dead yet."

25. "You're too independent."

▶ Translation: *I'm insecure and need someone who feels like a project.*

🔥 Clapback: "Then go build a robot."

26. "Why are you being so sensitive?"

▶ Translation: *I don't want to be held accountable, so I'm attacking your reaction.*

🔥 Clapback: "Why are you being so disposable?"

27. "Don't catch feelings."

▶ Translation: *I want the benefits of intimacy with none of the accountability.*

🔥 Clapback: "Don't worry. I only catch flights and red flags."

28. "You don't need makeup."

▶ Translation: *I'm going to neg you while pretending it's support.*

🔥 Clapback: "And you don't need opinions, but here we are."

29. "I'm just not ready for someone like you."

▶ Translation: *I know I'll be exposed if I stay.*

🔥 Clapback: "Finally, something we agree on."

30. "You're lucky I didn't ghost you."

⚑ Translation: *My standards for basic human decency are subterranean.*

🔥 Clapback: "Ghosting would've been a mercy, actually."

31. "Don't worry, you're not like the girls I usually hook up with."

⚑ Translation: *Insult + neg + passive confession of being trash.*

🔥 Clapback: "Shame. I was hoping to be one of the girls who left you first."

32. "You're just hard to love."

⚑ Translation: *I'm incapable of loving someone complex and it's easier to blame you.*

🔥 Clapback: "And you're easy to forget."

33. "I'm just vibing right now."

⚑ Translation: *I'm emotionally unavailable but sound cool when I say it like this.*

🔥 Clapback: "Then go vibe with someone else's time."

34. "You're lucky I'm loyal."

⚑ Translation: *I haven't cheated yet, but I want credit for not being a sociopath.*

🔥 Clapback: "That's the bare minimum, not a brag."

35. "I thought you were different."

⚑ Translation: *I'm punishing you for having boundaries like every other woman I've drained.*

🔥 Clapback: "I am. I left."

Want more dissections of the trash lines men say?
Catch my savage *Men Decoded* series on YouTube, where I rip apart the most cliché, manipulative, and ridiculous one-liners in real time. It's raw, hilarious, and will make you side-eye half the bios you see tonight.
https://youtube.com/playlist?list=PLstOVerax_jQW2H2PMWMy1Ey_8k_C-5bS&si=_VJb2TWp3l8UEdHl

What Emotionally Healthy Men Actually Say

A Love Letter to What's Still Possible

This isn't fantasy. This is what it sounds like when a man has done the work. He speaks to your nervous system, not your triggers. He doesn't confuse vulnerability with weakness, he lives in truth, grounded in self-awareness. Let this be your reminder: you are not asking for too much. You've just been speaking to men who offer too little.

1. "I want to understand you not just agree with you."

💬 *He knows connection doesn't require total sameness just presence.*
This man listens to hear you, not to fix you.

2. "Let's talk about it. I'm not going anywhere."

💬 *He doesn't flee when things get hard.*
He stays. Even when it's messy. Especially when it matters.

3. "You're allowed to feel what you're feeling."

💬 *He doesn't regulate you. He holds space.*
No defensiveness. No minimizing. Just calm, safe containment.

4. "What do you need from me right now?"

💬 *He doesn't assume. He asks. And then listens.*
He's not guessing how to love you. He's inviting you to show him.

5. "I was wrong, and I want to make it right."

💬 *He takes accountability without theatrics or ego.*
Apologies don't scare him, they soften him.

6. "You don't have to shrink to be loved by me."

💬 *He wants the whole you, not the edited version.*
Your bigness, boldness, brilliance welcomed, not tolerated.

7. "I'm attracted to how you think."

💬 *He's not intimidated by your mind. He's turned on by it.*
Smart women don't scare him, they inspire him.

8. "I've worked hard to break the patterns that used to run me."

💬 *He knows healing isn't a trend, it's a responsibility.*
He doesn't use his trauma as a personality. He transformed it into self-awareness.

9. "Tell me more. I want to understand your world."

💬 *Curiosity, not criticism. Depth, not defensiveness.*
He wants your story not just your body.

10. "I feel safest when we're honest with each other."

💬 *Emotional safety is his foundation, not your job to build.*

He doesn't weaponize honesty, he shares it gently.

11. "I don't need to be needed. I want to be chosen."

💬 *He's not looking for a woman to complete him just one to walk beside him.*

Partnership, not pedestal.

12. "I love how you take up space."

💬 *Your power excites him not threatens him.*

He doesn't need to dim your light to feel bright.

13. "I care about how you experienced that, even if I didn't mean to hurt you."

💬 *He understands that intent and impact are not the same.*

He doesn't defend. He listens. He makes it safe to feel.

14. "I want to know how you love and how you feel loved."

💬 *Love isn't a guessing game, it's a language he's fluent in.*

He's not afraid to ask. He's excited to learn.

15. "I've got you. You don't have to do this alone."

💬 *He doesn't flinch when you're in pain.*

He meets you there not with pity, but with partnership.

16. "Your independence turns me on."

💬 *He doesn't want to rescue you; he wants to rise with you.*

Your strength isn't a threat. It's foreplay.

17. "I'm proud of you not for what you do, but for who you are."

💬 *Your worth isn't tied to your productivity in his eyes.*

He celebrates your essence, not just your achievements.

18. "Let's slow down and figure this out together."

💬 *He's not rushing to end the conversation; he's invested in resolution.*

This man doesn't run from hard moments. He leans in.

19. "I trust you and I trust myself with you."

💬 *He's not just grounded in you. He's grounded in himself.*

He doesn't seek control, he brings clarity.

20. "What matters to you, matters to me."

💬 *Your priorities become shared space not separate lanes.*

He joins your world, not just visits it when it's convenient.

21. "I want us to be better, not bitter."

💬 *He sees conflict as a bridge not a battleground.*

Healing with him doesn't mean losing your dignity.

22. "I want to be the kind of man who makes you feel safer, not smaller."

💬 *He watches how his words land not just how they sound to him.*

He values your softness as much as your fire.

23. "I can hold your story without needing to rewrite it."

💬 *He doesn't interrupt your healing with his ego.*

He honors your journey, scars and all.

24. "You don't have to earn love here."

💬 *There is no hustle. No pleasing. Just being.*

And being is enough.

25. "Even if we don't end up together, I'll never regret knowing you."

💬 *He holds love with open hands, not clenched fists.*

His love isn't possession, it's presence.

26. "I want to grow with you not compete, control, or correct you."

💬 *He's not trying to lead you, fix you, or outrun you. He's walking with you.*

27. "It's okay to need me. I won't use it against you."

💬 *He doesn't see your vulnerability as leverage. He sees it as intimacy.*

28. "I want to know what you're afraid to say."

💬 *He invites your truth, even when it's messy. Especially when it's messy.*

29. "If you ever feel like I'm not showing up fully, I want you to tell me."

💬 *He's not afraid of feedback. He craves growth, not ego preservation.*

30. "I want to support your dreams not just benefit from your peace."

💬 *He's not here to be healed. He's here to build something with you.*

31. "You've changed me in the best ways."

💬 *He lets love shape him. He sees you as a catalyst, not a convenience.*

32. "Being loved by you makes me a better man and I don't take that lightly."

💬 *He values the relationship because it calls him higher. And he rises to meet it.*

Healthy love doesn't feel like a high. It feels like finally landing somewhere you never thought existed. A man who is emotionally mature won't need to convince you. His words will match his presence. And his presence will feel like peace.

Why He Ghosted

Let's call it like it is: Ghosting is the modern man's cowardly go-to exit strategy. It's lazy. It's weak. It's passive-aggressive silence wrapped in a blanket of emotional immaturity. One minute you're vibing, flirting, sharing a drink and a story, maybe even locking lips and then *poof*, he faded like a fantasy he was never capable of living up to. So, what the hell happened? Let's break this down, *UnExpert style*. No fluff. No coping quotes. Just the real damn reasons why men ghost and what it actually means when it happens to *you*.

1. They Don't Care Enough to Try. This is the headline. The gut punch. The one we *never* want to admit. This is the top of the list because it's almost always the truth. If he ghosted, he didn't care enough to keep trying. That's it. If you meant something real, he wouldn't vanish. If you were *her*, he wouldn't risk losing you. You didn't scare him off. You didn't text too much. You didn't show up too strong. He just didn't care *enough*. And that sucks, but it's also your freedom slip.

That doesn't make you unworthy, it just means *he was never the one*. If a man wants you, you'll know. If he doesn't, you'll be confused. And baby, if you're confused... he's already gone.

2. He Got What He Wanted. Let's be honest: a lot of men are out here trying to *borrow intimacy without returning it*. Whether it was emotional validation, attention, a little ego boost, or a casual hookup once he got his fix, he ghosted like an addict in relapse. Some men use dating apps like vending machines. They take what they want and leave the wrapper behind.

3. He's Talking to 12 Other Women. Dating apps turned men into slot machine gamblers. Men swipe like it's their job. He's not looking for love. He's swiping for dopamine and talking to multiple women at once. He's ghosting you mid-convo while texting "wyd" to someone else. Don't internalize that. That's not rejection, it's *addiction* on his end. This doesn't mean you weren't amazing, it just means he was playing a numbers game. Don't compete in a race you never agreed to run.

4. Avoidance is Easier Than Accountability. Most men weren't taught how to communicate or face discomfort. So instead of saying, *"Hey, I'm not feeling this,"* they panicked and choose silence. Why? Because he was never taught how to communicate with women he's not trying to sleep with. If he can't manage a simple text, he's not managing anything meaningful. It's not classy. It's not noble. But it *is* lazy and typical.

5. He's Emotionally Unavailable (and Doesn't Even Know It). A lot of men *think* they're ready for a relationship... until a real woman walks in. Then suddenly he's "just figuring things out" or "not in the right headspace" or "too busy." You've heard all the excuses. Translation: *he's emotionally constipated and your presence made him realize he can't handle depth*. No babe, he's just *not ready for you*. And that is ok, you will find someone that is. Don't let this bring you down. Keep going you ferocious feline.

6. The Fantasy Died After the First Date. Harsh but true. Sometimes, a man is into the *idea* of you. The way you looked in photos. The version of you he imagined in his head. Then he meets the actual you, fully formed, honest, opinionated and instead of adjusting his expectations like a grown man, he bailed. Ghosting is his immature response to disappointment. Not your problem.

7. He's a Conflict Avoider (aka a Nice Guy). Nice guys ghost too. They *especially* ghost. Because heaven forbid, they hurt your feelings directly. He'll vanish and hope you "get the hint" instead of being honest. These are the same dudes who say "you deserve better" in their Hinge bios. *Cringe.*

8. He's Going Back to His Ex. This one burns. You were the rebound trial run. He won't tell you that. But if he ghosted out of nowhere after a great time, it's not about *you* at all, it's about the *unfinished mess* he crawled out of. And just like that, he disappears back into the emotional dumpster fire he never healed from.

9. He's a Narcissist Who Needed an Ego Hit. Ghosting is a favorite weapon of emotionally manipulative men. Narcissists love the chase. They love knowing you like them. They love the high of making you feel special, then pulling away. But the second they feel like they've "won," they bounce. These men don't ghost you because of who *you* are. They ghost because of who *they* aren't. If it feels like a pattern, trust that it is. Block, delete, cleanse.

10. You Triggered His Insecurity. Sometimes, you walk in too confident. Too radiant. Too "I'm not here to be picked, I am the damn prize." And that energy intimidates the shit out of men still playing small and haven't done the work. Instead of rising to the challenge, they retreat into invisibility and ghost just to feel in control again. His fragility is not your burden.

Bonus: **He Wanted a Yes Girl, Not a Real One**. Did you set a boundary? Show self-respect? Say something that challenged him? Congratulations you triggered the flight response in a man used to getting away with mediocrity.

What Does It Mean If He Ghosted After a First Date? First date ghosting stings differently. It feels personal. You got ready. You showed up. You shared stories, jokes, maybe even a kiss. And then *nothing*. Let's rip the Band-Aid.

If he ghosted after one date, he didn't feel a spark or he didn't want to pursue it. And instead of saying that like a human adult, he vanished like the spineless jellyfish he is. It doesn't mean you weren't good enough. It doesn't mean you did something wrong. It doesn't mean you have to second-guess every word you said or every bite of that shared charcuterie board.

It just means he wasn't your person, and that's a blessing in disguise. You want someone who sees you and can't wait to text you the next day not someone who disappears like a scared raccoon.

For Good Measure: **He Couldn't Handle a Woman Who Knew Herself**. You weren't needy. You weren't fake. You didn't perform. You were just... you. And that scared him. Not because there's something wrong with you, but because you weren't playing the pick-me game he's used to winning.

How to Not Take Ghosting Personally (Even When It Feels Like Rejection)

It's hard. Especially when you liked him. Especially when you felt hope. Let's go deeper than "it's not you, it's him," because your brain *already knows* that, your nervous system just hasn't caught up. Here's how to hold your power and stop internalizing it:

- **Stop replaying the date like a crime scene.** Don't try to reverse-engineer the date. If you liked him, your brain will scramble for evidence that you messed up. It'll go through what you wore, what you said, how you laughed—like you're the murder suspect and the vibe was the crime scene. Stop. There's just him, being done. You didn't miss a clue. You didn't say the wrong thing. You didn't "ruin it." He just wasn't your person.
- **Accept that rejection can feel personal even when it's not.** Your body reacts to ghosting like a loss, because it is. It's the death of a future you were starting to fantasize about. You have to grieve that. But grieving isn't the same as *blaming yourself*. Cry, yes. Spiral? No. When your brain starts asking "Was it me?", answer back: "No. It was him. And I'm not arguing with silence." Don't let silence lower your self-worth. His ghosting isn't a mirror. It's a reveal. He showed you he can't communicate. Let that be enough.
- **Remember: Attraction is not validation.** Just because *you* wanted *him* doesn't mean his lack of interest means *you're unworthy*. You saw potential. He didn't. That doesn't erase your value, it just reveals his taste. You liked the *possibility*. You liked the *idea*. And that's okay. But don't confuse a fantasy with a loss of actual love. You didn't lose love. You dodged a lie.
- **Let silence be your answer.** Ghosting is a message. It's not the one you wanted but it *is* clear. Let silence end the conversation so you can start a better one with someone else or, honestly, with yourself.
- **Mute. Block. Cleanse.** Energetically or literally. Clear the texts. Mute the story views. You don't need his ghost hovering in your inbox.

How to Escape the "Why Didn't He Want Me?" Spiral

Because sometimes even knowing all the above doesn't help. You still feel rejected. Here's how to break the loop:

1. Breathe, then interrupt the thought. Your brain is building a false narrative. Stop mid-thought and say, "This isn't truth. This is anxiety looking for control."

2. Write down what you *actually* want. Not "I wanted him to like me." What do you *really* want? Safety? Connection? Passion? Write it out. If he couldn't give you that, then this wasn't a loss. It was a detour.

3. Cleanse the energy. Delete the thread. Mute the story views. Burn the notes app fantasy wedding plan. *Clear the static.* You're not begging for crumbs when you remember you're the bakery.

4. Create a "B*tch, He's Not It" playlist. Yes, seriously. You need sound medicine. Turn on a song that makes you feel *dangerous in the best way*. (Need help? I've got a savage list. If you read my books, you know there is always a playlist and you are welcome! It includes: "Fuck You" by Silent Child, because that is my jam right now; "Goodbye" by Kristinia DeBarge, an underrated post-ghosting bop; and "I'm Too Sexy" by Right Said Fred, because sometimes you need campy delusion, plus many more jams.)

https://open.spotify.com/playlist/3Qe8VY22iUp6fa3WOHF7Cl?si=Yz7nj213TaqHYMm3TFLuWg

20 Iconic Lines to Say to a Guy Who Ghosted (For YOU, Not Him)

Let me be clear: *you don't owe him anything*. And if I were you, I wouldn't say a damn thing. Act like it doesn't effing bother you. You don't have time for that loser. But if you *must* say something for *your* peace, not his response (because, God knows, he ain't replying. Here are some lines to set yourself free:

1. "If you lost interest, you could've just said that. Ghosting isn't confusing, it's pathetic."
2. "I hope your communication skills one day match your flirting energy."
3. "Disappearing isn't masculine. It's just emotional cowardice."
4. "If silence is all you've got, I'll take that as closure."
5. "Thanks for the clarity, your absence spoke volumes."
6. "Damn. I was two days away from making you my emergency contact. JK. Go soar."
7. "I was about to fake-laugh at all your jokes for a solid month. You missed a golden era. Blessings."
8. "Wild. I already picked our couple's Halloween costume. It involved wigs. You'll never know."
9. "No worries. I already named a plant after you. It's thriving without sunlight too."
10. "I was dangerously close to introducing you to my group chat. That was almost your big break. Stay humble."
11. "Ghosted? Respect. I, too, have fled from emotionally healthy situations."
12. "All good. You gave beige sweater energy anyway. Rooting for your evolution."
13. "Honestly? You were cute. But so are cookies. And I gave them up for skin clarity. Take care, legend."
14. "Damn, I was just about to ask for your Netflix password and your birth time. Ha! Give me cred, that was funny."
15. "Damn. I even shaved above the knee for you."

16. "I was really looking forward to trauma-bonding and ignoring all your red flags for at least three months."

17. "Honestly, thank you. I was dangerously close to catching feelings *and* an STD."

18. "All good. I've been ghosted by hotter men with worse grammar."

19. "Was really looking forward to finding your baby photos online and pretending it wasn't weird. Alas."

20. "You ghosted before I could accidentally fall for your *almost* charisma. Close one for both of us."

Savage Reframes for Getting Ghosted (That'll Make You Laugh, Not Cry)

Because if he ghosted you, you probably avoided bad sex, a gaslighting situationship, and him asking to split the bill at Chili's.

1. Getting ghosted is just God's way of saying: babe, that d*ck had no stroke.

2. He didn't disappear. He got spiritually evicted.

3. He ghosted you? Good. That man had 'performative missionary' energy anyway.

4. You didn't get ghosted. You got upgraded back to your peace, your playlist, and your power.

5. Girl, the only thing he would've blown was the vibe.

6. He vanished before you had to see his apartment. That's a blessing, not a heartbreak.

7. You didn't lose a man. You lost a walking podcast opinion with two pillows and no ambition.

8. You got ghosted? That's your ego detox. He was a distraction dressed as a potential.

9. Ghosting is just the universe saving you from answering 'what are we?' six times over lukewarm Pad Thai.

10. Feel proud. You were too much woman for a man who still follows Instagram models like it's a job.

Final Word from Your Dating UnExpert: Ghosting doesn't mean you weren't good enough. It means he wasn't ready. Or real. Or honest enough to just say the truth. Stop romanticizing inconsistency. Stop giving energy to silence. Stop turning "he disappeared" into "what did I do wrong?" Because when someone leaves without a word, they're not rejecting you. They're disqualifying themselves. And you, my love, are still *so wildly worthy*, no matter who didn't text back.

Are We Dating the Same Guy?

As much as I am all for women helping women, this group, if you join it, needs to be taken with a grain of salt. Proceed with caution. Don't get me wrong, I think this group is needed for situations like: if the guy is married, if he has domestic violence charges, if he's raped a woman, has STDs, fake accounts, or anything else that *actually* matters. This group should not be used to rant, judge, or belittle men who just didn't want you.

I was berated by a man on my social media account @yourdatingunexpert. He called it a *female supremacy group* and couldn't believe I was in that group as a dating expert. One, I'm not a dating expert. I clearly state that I do the dumb shit in dating *so you don't have to* which, in reverse, makes me an expert in what not to do.

I let him say his piece. He asked how I would feel if there was a men's group of similar caliber, doxxing women and spreading lies. In this group, you're not allowed to post a last name, but there are photos. I told him, "You must have been a victim and not-nice things were said about you."

He went on another rant about how he was going to screenshot our conversation and *blast me everywhere.* I told him, "Do it."

I will tell it like it is in this book and exactly how I feel about *Are We Dating the Same Guy*. I also told him: "Now I see why these women say terrible things about you. Just from this brief encounter, you absolutely have anger issues and women should be scared to date you." Then I blocked this dude who I've never met, and who didn't even follow me. Women have a right to know about men like him and he proved his own point.

Here's the real breakdown (from about three months inside):
- Married or in long-term relationships: **15%**
- Domestic violence: **10%**
- Fake accounts: **10%**
- STD checks: **5%**
- Advice (not relevant to any man): **10%**
- Memes or funny shit (also not relevant to any man): **15%**
- Vouching for a good guy (there's also a group for that): **5%**
- Meetups (just looking for girlfriends to hang out with): **5%**
- Girls ranting about red flags: **25%**

The numbers could be lower or higher. I'm not getting too technical. But the percentage of women ranting about red flags is probably *a lot* higher depending on the group. So again, proceed with caution.

Girls in this group you should *not* embody:
The Bitchy "There Are No Good Men" Girl
These women should not be dating. Point blank. Periodt! These women haven't healed. These women will not find men, because they are constantly finding something wrong with every

single one. As a woman who has used dating apps in multiple cities and has found great guys in *all* of them, you're either picking trash or you're just a negative human being that needs healing. I have found great men in both Los Angeles *and* Cape Coral, Florida. Big or small, there are great men in every city. So, stop being this bitchy, woe-is-me victim of terrible men. It's not them. It's you. Figure your shit out.

The Private Investigator Girl

Now, I love me some cyber-stalking and investigative reporting, but these girls take it to a whole new level. They have apps that can look up phone numbers. They pay for TruthFinder or whatever the hell it is to search every man's history. They go above and beyond the call of duty to make sure the guy they're dating has never even gotten a speeding ticket.

Don't be this scared human being. It's not good for your mental health. Most dudes are fine. They don't have records. They're not married. They're not catfishing you. They're just regular guys looking for something real. You look absolutely crazy. And no dude wants that. There *are* checks you should do:

- Get their last name before going on a date.
- Google them real quick.
- Check court records *if you want* whatever makes you feel safe.

But if a guy already makes you feel unsafe *before* you've even gone out with him? Don't go out with him. That's the beauty of online dating: *next*.

The Tattle Tale Girl

This girl is no friend to women. This girl is fucking *desperate* for a man's attention. This girl is gross with a pick-me persona. She is the epitome of shit on your shoe. She's not a woman you want in your life ever. I don't care if you're best friends with the guy being posted. You never, ever, fucking ever screenshot something and send it to him.

In some situations, this could put the woman who posted it in *actual danger*. You don't know how the man will react even if you *think* you do. And if you think this little "heads up" will earn you brownie points with the guy you're talking to? It won't. He'll view you as a narc, you sadistic freak. Get the fuck out of the group, you sorry-ass excuse for a woman. You shouldn't even have the grace to call yourself a woman.

Yes, I don't like when women completely bash a guy who probably didn't deserve it. That's why I'm writing this. So that other women *don't* judge a guy based on one girl's mouth or thirty girls who are mad because he wasn't interested. But that still doesn't entitle you to tell a man he was posted in the group.

The Word of the Month Girl

These are the girls I want every woman to watch out for. They are *everywhere* in this group. These girls love their buzzwords. Narcissist. Gaslighter. Toxic. Lovebomber. Most of them have zero idea what these words actually mean.

They throw around clinical terms like confetti and turn every ick into a trauma diagnosis. Most of the time? The guy was just emotionally unavailable or not interested. That doesn't make him a narcissist. Let me say it again: Every single person has narcissistic tendencies. It's called being human. So, stop diagnosing people based on one red flag that wasn't even red.

The Oversharer Girl

Ohhhh this girl goes IN. Ten paragraphs. Screenshots. Play-by-plays. Crying emojis. Birth charts. You name it. She dated him for two weeks and now we've got a full dissertation with references. It's not informative, it's emotionally messy. It's not brave, it's *oversharing in a public forum full of strangers*. Girl, take a breath. Screenshot it to your best friend. Not 48,000 women who don't know you and are too bored to care.

The Judgmental Girl

This girl hates everything. His hat? Gross. His job? Lame. His dog? Too small. His text response time? Disrespectful. His favorite show? Problematic. She swipes through dating apps like she's the Queen of England with a red pen. She's not looking for a boyfriend, she's casting a *movie*. And newsflash? Most of these women aren't any more emotionally stable than the guys they're roasting. You don't like him? Move on. But stop trashing real people just for a laugh in the comments.

The "Let's Bait My Boyfriend" Girl

I can't believe I even have to say this… But if you are creating fake profiles or recruiting other girls to DM your boyfriend to "test his loyalty," you've already lost. You don't trust him. You don't trust yourself. And you've officially entered unhinged territory. That's not protection. That's a self-fulfilling prophecy. Let the man go and stop humiliating yourself.

Whew. That's the tea. Do I think the group has value? Absolutely. Do I think a *lot* of women in there are posting from a place of pain and not truth? Also, yes. So be wise. Watch how people speak. And don't become the very woman you wouldn't trust either.

These aren't bad women. These are women acting from unhealed fear, insecurity, and group validation. And becoming one of them will cost you more than it protects you.

You're the Red Flag: How to Know If You're the Problem (and How to Fix It)

Hard pill: sometimes, it's not them. Sometimes, it's you.

This chapter isn't here to shame you, it's here to free you. Because if you're brave enough to own your red flags, you're brave enough to stop repeating the same dating disasters. Let's make something clear: you can be a good person and still be toxic in love. You can be smart and still self-sabotage. You can be healing and still be the hurricane. This is your mirror. Grit your teeth and look.

1. You Think the Chaos Means Chemistry. You're bored when it's stable. You chase drama and call it passion. Deep down, calm feels unsafe.
Fix It: Learn to regulate your nervous system. Peace isn't the absence of love. It's the presence of emotional maturity.

2. You Fall in Love with Potential. You date men like fixer-uppers. You're addicted to being the one who "saves" him.
Fix It: You're not his therapist. Date someone *present*, not just *promising*.

3. You Weaponize Your Healing. You think your trauma makes you deep. You demand grace but don't give any. You use "I'm working on myself" to excuse bad behavior.
Fix It: Healing is not a shield. It's not a brand. It's a responsibility.

4. You Expect a Psychic, Not a Partner. You get mad when he doesn't know what you need. You never ask for it, but punish him for not intuiting it.
Fix It: Say it. Out loud. With clarity. Emotional maturity includes directness.

5. You Think Jealousy = Love. You snoop. You test. You make him earn trust he hasn't even broken yet.
Fix It: Heal the wound where you expect betrayal before it happens. He's not your ex.

6. You Confuse Validation with Intimacy. You need compliments to breathe. You panic if he doesn't chase. You confuse anxiety for attraction.
Fix It: Learn to self-source your worth. A partner should enhance you, not complete you.

7. You Date to Prove Something. To your ex. To your friends. To the timeline in your head. He's not a man. He's a trophy for your ego.
Fix It: Want love because it *feels right* not because it looks right.

8. You Criticize More Than You Connect. Nothing is ever enough. You nitpick. You "just want him to do better."
Fix It: Men don't grow under pressure, they withdraw. Trade control for curiosity.

9. You Want Him to Read Your Mind. You say "it's fine" when it's not. You want him to chase after your silence.
Fix It: Clarity is kindness. Confusion is cruelty.

10. You Perform Instead of Being Real. You change your vibe to be what you *think* he wants. You lose yourself trying to win him.
Fix It: Authenticity is the hottest thing you can wear. If you have to shape-shift to keep him, he's not your person.

11. You Need the Upper Hand. You play games. Hold back affection. Wait three hours to text.
Fix It: Real power is not manipulation, it's emotional courage. Drop the act.

12. You Call Every Guy a Narcissist. But really, you just don't handle rejection well. Not every man who doesn't want you is broken.
Fix It: Not everyone is meant to choose you. And that's okay. You still win when you walk away with your peace.

13. You Disappear When It Gets Real. You say you want love, but ghost anyone who actually shows up.
Fix It: Love can't land when you're still hiding. Be brave enough to receive.

14. You Cling to Red Flags Out of Loneliness. You stay too long. You convince yourself you can make it work. You'd rather be wrong than be alone.
Fix It: Solitude is where standards are born. Make peace your baseline, not chaos.

15. You Say "Men Are Trash." But you keep choosing trash, ignoring gold, and then blaming men for the pattern.
Fix It: Your picker isn't broken. Your self-trust is. Rebuild it. You know better now.

16. You Confuse High Standards with Impossible Expectations. No one's good enough unless they're psychic, rich, healed, hot, funny, and read your mind.
Fix It: There's a difference between having standards and building a prison.

17. You Trauma-Dump Instead of Build Trust. You overshare on date one and call it "vulnerability."
Fix It: Let trust earn its way into the room. You don't need to bleed to be seen.

18. You Think Emotional Intensity = Compatibility. If it's not obsessive, you think it's not real.
Fix It: Real love won't hijack your nervous system. It will soothe it.

19. You Keep Score. Who texted first. Who paid last. Who wins.
Fix It: Dating isn't a competition unless you're trying to lose connection.

20. You Romanticize Struggle. You think love is something to "fight for" instead of something that flows.
Fix It: Healthy love doesn't need to be rescued. It just needs to be chosen.

Final Truth: It doesn't make you weak to admit you've been the villain in someone else's story. It makes you stronger than 99% of the dating pool. Because now? You're not just looking for love. You're becoming the version of you that can *sustain* it.

Why Nice Guys Finish Last

(And Why They Shouldn't, You Idiot)

If "he's just too nice" comes out of your mouth, congrats! You just bench-warmed a perfectly good man while chasing a human smoke alarm. Let's be clear: we are *not* talking about the fake "nice guy" who holds doors and expects sex like it's a reward sticker. We're talking about the real ones: emotionally safe, kind, grounded, open-hearted men who actually want connection. And what do women do? We friend-zone them. We ghost them. We label them as "meh" while salivating over a guy who texts "wyd" at two a.m. like it's a love language.

THIS IS EVOLUTIONARY. BUT YOU'RE NOT A CAVEMAN.

Back in the Paleolithic era, survival wasn't cute, it was brutal. A woman needed to know:
- Could this man protect me?
- Could he fight off threats?
- Could he keep me and my offspring alive?

So, the nervous system evolved to *scan for strength*. Physical dominance. Tactical awareness. Command. Even today, thousands of years later, those primal attraction cues still run in the background especially under stress.

The problem? In modern dating, toxicity mimics strength and safety gets misread as weakness. That's why emotionally unstable men who dominate space, speak over you, and vanish when things get real often *feel more magnetic* than the guy who listens, asks, and holds space. But it's not magnetism, it's your trauma trying to feel at home.

TEN PSYCHOLOGICAL REASONS WOMEN IGNORE GENUINE NICE GUYS

1. They don't activate the threat response. If your attraction blueprint is built on high-stakes emotional instability, then calm men don't register as "exciting." Translation: Your nervous system isn't calibrated for healthy love. It's calibrated for emotional survival.

2. Kindness without edge feels one-dimensional. Some nice guys *are* boring. Why? Because they've learned to please, not to lead. Their niceness is rooted in fear, not confidence. That's not kindness. That's approval-seeking. And women can smell it.

3. They don't challenge emotional patterning. Nice guys don't trigger our self-worth issues. They don't make us chase. So, if our entire identity is wrapped in earning love, we feel lost. Safe love requires you to sit still with your value, not audition for it.

4. They don't match the aesthetic of power. Culturally, we associate power with detachment, aloofness, and status. The guy who's emotionally available doesn't *look* powerful, even though he probably is. We equate tension with value, not presence.

5. The dopamine system prefers unpredictability. Biochemically, the brain loves a reward loop especially one that's inconsistent. The man who ghosts, then lovebombs, then disappears again? That's literal neurochemical chaos. The nice guy is consistent. That means no hit. No high. No crash. And for a dysregulated woman? No interest.

257

6. They don't create urgency. A woman with unresolved attachment wounds often equates emotional urgency with emotional importance. The nice guy's calm, steady presence doesn't light a fire and that feels like a lack of chemistry. Stability doesn't feel urgent, but it's the only thing that lasts.

7. Women aren't taught to trust pleasure. When a relationship feels too easy, we assume it's fake. That's because many women learned love through labor, pain, or unpredictability. The nervous system rejects what it didn't earn even if it's exactly what it needs.

8. They don't mirror her self-doubt. Women subconsciously pick men who reflect how they feel about themselves. If she's full of doubt and insecurity, a man who mirrors that chaos will feel "right." A grounded man doesn't match her vibration so she doesn't trust him. The nice guy feels foreign. The toxic guy feels familiar.

9. They're not performers. Nice guys show up as they are. No chase. No games. No status theater. And because most of modern dating is performative, women mistake authenticity for lack of effort. If there's no show, some assume there's no depth. But that's a trauma response not discernment.

10. He reminds her what she's not ready for. A nice, healthy man often exposes the parts of a woman she hasn't healed, the intimacy she craves but hasn't yet become. That's terrifying. It's easier to reject him than to rise into the version of herself that could actually receive him.

THIS IS A *YOU* PROBLEM

If you keep choosing men who hurt you, avoid you, or confuse you and call the safe ones boring, it's not because they're too nice. It's because your inner compass is cracked and you don't recognize peace when it shows up. You're not broken. You're wired for survival, not intimacy. You've built your attraction map around emotional danger. That's not your fault, but it *is* your job to unlearn it.

THE NICE GUY, EVOLVED

Let's redefine him:
- He's grounded, not passive
- He's kind, but not spineless
- He has emotional availability with backbone
- He knows who he is and doesn't need to dominate you to prove it

He is emotionally safe, psychologically mature, and still a protector, but in 2025, that looks like:
- Knowing how to sit with your tears
- Handling hard conversations without ego
- Being a partner, not a savior
- Having purpose that isn't rooted in control

He doesn't need to be the loudest one in the room. He *is* the room. And when your body is healed enough to receive him? He will feel like the deepest breath you've ever taken.

FINAL TRUTH: Nice guys don't finish last. *They finish healthy.* It's not that they aren't strong enough. It's that we aren't calm enough to receive them. So next time a safe, available, kind man shows up and your body says, *"He's too nice…"* ask it this instead: "Or am I just too used to chaos to recognize peace?"

PART IV

THE WILD CARDS
SPECIAL CIRCUMSTANCES &
REAL-WORLD COMPLEXITY

Special Situations

Dating After Divorce
(Because you didn't walk through that wreckage just to fumble the rebuild.)

Divorce doesn't just change your relationship status. It rearranges your soul. Whether it ended in fire or in silence, divorce leaves you standing in the ashes of the life you thought you were building and now, you're supposed to "get back out there" like you didn't just survive an emotional earthquake?

Let's be honest: *dating after divorce isn't cute.* It's vulnerable. It's complicated. It's you trying to let someone in again after watching love fall apart in real time. But here's the thing: You're not broken, you're *rebuilt.* You're not too much, you're finally *too wise* to play small. And you're not behind, you're just *done pretending that bare-minimum love is enough.* So, here's how you date post-divorce not from fear, not from loneliness, but from *power.*

1. Let It Hurt First. Like, Really Hurt. You cannot skip this. Sit with the grief. Let it hollow you. Mourn the dreams that didn't happen. Then get up and promise yourself this: *next time, I will not abandon myself to keep something alive that was already dead.*

2. You Are Not Your Divorce Story. Yes, it shaped you. Yes, it changed you. But you are not just "divorced." You're a whole woman with her own rhythm, her own lessons, and her own damn timeline. Don't shrink your identity to a chapter you already closed.

3. You Don't Owe Anyone the Details of Your Divorce. You're allowed to say, "It ended, and I've grown a lot since then." You don't need to overshare or relive the trauma to prove your honesty. Share your story when it feels sacred not when it feels performative.

4. Your Children Are Not a Side Note. They're a Sacred Filter. If you're a parent, your kids are not a burden. They are not baggage. They are *your legacy.* And anyone who sees them as an inconvenience is not your person. Period.

5. Rebuild Your Identity Without the Marriage Narrative. Who are you outside the role of wife, caretaker, fixer, or martyr? What do *you* like? Want? Crave? Get reacquainted with the woman you silenced to keep the peace.

6. Don't Compare Every Date to Your Ex. Good or Bad. Your ex was a chapter. Not the blueprint. Don't waste time trying to find the opposite of them—or the replica. Every new person deserves a clear slate… until they prove otherwise.

7. Your Life Is Not on Pause Until You "Find Someone" Again. You are not waiting to be chosen. You're *choosing yourself* over and over until someone rises to meet you. Live. Build. Heal. Thrive. And let love be the *bonus not the rescue.*

8. Love Will Look Different Now and That's a Good Thing. It won't be fire and obsession. It'll be slow. Calm. Present. Safe. You'll mistake it for boring at first until you realize this is what stability feels like.

9. You Get to Love Again Without Shame, Without Fear, Without Apology. Divorce didn't ruin you. It *refined* you. You don't need to justify why you're still open to love. You're not "trying again" you're *choosing better*. And this time? It's gonna be different. Because *you're different.*

CONVERSATION PROMPTS FOR DATING AFTER DIVORCE

(Because this time, it's not about being chosen, it's about choosing consciously.)
These aren't interrogation tactics. These are soul-level check-ins. You've already lost yourself in someone once. Now you ask better questions, *early*, to make sure you never do it again.

1. "I've learned a lot about myself since my last relationship. What's something your past taught you that changed the way you love?" You're not hiding your history. You're owning your growth. This reveals if they've actually evolved or just repeated.

2. "What does commitment look like to you now?" Ask it straight. Divorce teaches you that everyone defines "serious" differently. You're not here to guess.

3. "How do you handle conflict when it shows up in a relationship?" You've been through the silence, the screaming, the stonewalling. Now you need to know if they *regulate or react.*

4. "What does emotional safety feel like for you and how do you offer it to someone else?" This is how you find out if they have actual emotional intelligence or if they just say nice things and hope for the best.

5. "What kind of life are you building right now, and what role would a partner play in it?" You're not looking to be someone's plan B. This filters out the driftwood from the men with *direction.*

6. "How do you feel about dating someone who's been through a divorce?" This one reveals everything. Watch their tone. If they flinch, joke, or get weird, you just got your answer.

7. "If we both decided to be exclusive, what kind of relationship would we be trying to create?" Skip the title. Ask about *vision.* Commitment is nothing without shared direction.

8. "Have you ever stayed too long in a relationship? What finally made you leave?" This tells you if they know how to *walk away from dysfunction* or if they only leave when it's burning down.

9. "When things get hard, how do you show up in a relationship?" You want someone who doesn't run from emotional weather. Their answer will show you if they lean in or shut down.

10. "What are your personal non-negotiables in relationships now?" You're not asking to perform. You're checking for *clarity.* Because if they don't know… they're not ready for you.

DATING AFTER DIVORCE: RED FLAGS & GREEN FLAGS
(Because you don't need another heartbreak to finally trust your gut.)

GREEN FLAGS
If you see these, lean in.

1. He respects your healing and doesn't rush your readiness. He's patient, not pushy. He doesn't get weird when you set boundaries or need space to process your pace.

2. He's clear and intentional about what he wants. No guessing games. No "let's see where this goes." He knows what kind of connection he's available for and tells you upfront.

3. He holds space without trying to fix you. He listens, stays present, and doesn't make your past about him. He's not intimidated by your truth, he honors it.

4. He's done his own inner work. You're not his therapist. He's self-aware, accountable, and has receipts for the lessons he claims to have learned.

5. He responds to conflict with regulation, not rage or retreat. No disappearing. No exploding. He shows up, communicates, and doesn't punish you for being human

6. He sees your kids (if you have them) as part of the package, not an obstacle. You don't have to shrink your motherhood. He respects it. Period.

7. He checks in not to control, but to connect. He sends the "How's your day?" texts not because he's insecure or suspicious, but because he genuinely *wants* to know how your heart is doing. He's tuned in, not intrusive.

8. He doesn't punish you for being guarded, he earns his place slowly, consistently, and without ego. He doesn't flinch when you hesitate. He doesn't guilt you for needing time. He stays. Gently. Without pushing. Because he's not here for access, he's here for *real connection.*

RED FLAGS
If you see these, walk. No explaining, no fixing, no "maybe if I just…"

1. He says he's over his ex, but can't stop talking about her. Either he's still angry or still attached. Both are your exit cue.

2. He downplays your divorce or makes jokes about "baggage." That's not humor. That's judgment. He doesn't get to minimize your pain to make himself feel clever.

3. He moves *fast* emotionally or physically. Love bombing after divorce is real. If he's planning vacations after three dates or calling you "wifey" on week one, it's not romance, it's control in disguise.

4. He disappears when conversations get real. Emotionally unavailable men love surface intimacy. The minute you go deep? *Gone.* Don't chase.

5. He compares you to his ex, especially as a "compliment." "I'm so glad you're not crazy like her." Translation: *He's the problem, and he will say the same about you next.*

6. He doesn't ask about your healing. He just wants access to the healed version of you. If he can't sit with the full picture, he doesn't deserve the love you rebuilt from ruins.

7. He gets defensive when you bring up boundaries. Pushback is not passion. Respect is the bare minimum. If he makes you feel bad for protecting yourself? *Bye.*

8. He treats your softness like a weakness. If he jokes about you being "too sensitive," avoids emotional conversations, or shuts down your vulnerability with deflection or control. He's not strong, he's scared. And you're not here to babysit someone else's unprocessed wounds. Your softness is sacred. Not negotiable.

Bonus: He makes your intuition feel like an inconvenience. If he's constantly making you question your gut, downplaying your concerns, or flipping the script to make you feel dramatic? That's not miscommunication, it's manipulation. *You didn't survive a divorce to gaslight yourself into round two.*

He expects intimacy before building emotional safety. Whether it's physical, emotional, or logistical, if he's rushing access to the most vulnerable parts of you before earning trust, he's not interested in *you.* He's interested in what you can *give* him. Real love takes time. And if he won't earn it? He doesn't get it.

Dating with Children

(Because love doesn't stop when you become a parent,
but your standards sure as hell better rise.)

Dating when kids are involved is a whole different game. You're not just protecting your heart, you're protecting theirs. That means you move slower, think smarter, and never let romance override your responsibility. Whether you're a single parent or dating someone with kids, this chapter is about doing love *maturely, intentionally,* and without the fantasy-fueled chaos that breaks more than just hearts.

1. Don't Introduce Just Anyone. Your kids don't need to meet your "maybe." Wait until you've built a foundation, had hard conversations, and know this person is a real contender. You're not hiding your kids. You're *protecting their peace.*

2. Talk to Your Kids Like They Matter Because They Do. You don't need to give them a play-by-play, but don't leave them in the dark either. Let them feel included in a way that's age-appropriate and emotionally safe. Kids can sense when something's changing. Give them security, not confusion.

3. Make Your Kids the Priority, Not a Plot Twist. This isn't a "surprise, I have kids" situation. Be upfront from the start. If someone's not okay with your children being a core part of your life, they're not your person. Period.

4. Plan Dates That Make Sense for Your Reality. Kid-free nights? Amazing. But sometimes life means park playdates, early dinners, or meeting during extracurriculars. Don't apologize for your life. Invite someone who *wants in on it.*

5. Let the Relationship Unfold Slowly and Naturally. Blending families is not a sprint, it's a slow build with a lot of feelings involved. Give your kids (and your partner) the grace of time. Let the bonds form *organically.*

6. Respect the Co-Parent Dynamic (Even If It's Messy). This is not the time for ego. If there's an ex in the picture, stay grounded. Respect the boundaries. Don't speak negatively about them around the kids. Be the *peace*, not the drama.

7. Protect Your Time Like the Gold It Is. You're juggling a lot. Make space for your kids *and* your needs. That means saying no when you're too tired, and yes to help when it's offered. Don't let dating become another full-time job.

8. Be Ready to Walk Away If Your Kids Aren't Safe or Respected. If your partner minimizes, dismisses, or competes with your children, *leave.* Fast. You're not looking for a savior, you're looking for a stable, emotionally mature presence who sees your family as a whole.

9. Be Honest About Your Bandwidth. You can't give what you don't have. Be upfront about your energy, time, and priorities. If someone expects 24/7 availability, let them know you've got humans to raise. That's not an excuse, it's a *standard.*

10. Don't Use Your Kids to Justify Staying in a Dead-End Situation. "Stability" doesn't mean settling. Your kids deserve to see you *loved well*. Staying in a relationship out of fear or guilt teaches them to do the same. Show them what *healthy* looks like.

11. Give Their Kids the Same Grace You'd Want for Yours. If your partner has children, remember: those kids didn't ask for this either. Don't force a bond, don't expect instant closeness. Show up, be consistent, and earn their trust *slowly*.

12. Talk About the Future Early Blended Family Edition. Don't avoid the hard questions:
- Will we live together?
- What role will we play in each other's kids' lives?
- Are we aligned on parenting values?
  This isn't about rushing, it's about clarity.

13. Be the Safe Space When Emotions Get Messy. Your child might act out, feel jealous, or resist the new dynamic. That's okay. You're the adult. Be the emotional anchor. Validate their feelings even when they're hard to hear.

14. Trust That You Still Deserve Epic, Beautiful, Soul-Filling Love. Having kids doesn't make you less desirable, it makes you *wiser. Fiercer.* More *emotionally fluent.* The right partner will see your parenting journey as a strength not a burden. Never, ever settle for less than someone who sees *all* of you and still says, "I'm in."

CONVERSATION PROMPTS WHEN DATING SOMEONE WITH KIDS
(Because "he's a good dad" is the bare minimum and you're trying to avoid becoming his next unpaid nanny-slash-therapist.)

These aren't interrogation questions. They're intentional, casual check-ins that help you spot whether this man is grounded, available, and capable of *emotional responsibility* or just using his kids as an excuse for chaos and inconsistency.

1. "What's your custody schedule like?" This shows you're curious and respectful of his time but it also helps you clock whether he's consistent, involved, or one of those "every other weekend when it's convenient" dads.

2. "How do you balance dating and parenting?" Translation: Are you actively making space for something new, or am I just filling dead time between soccer games and your emotional avoidance?

3. "How do you and your ex co-parent?" Pay attention here. If he blames her, calls her crazy, or starts ranting, *run.* If he's respectful and mature about it, that's a green flag.

4. "What kind of relationship are you hoping I have with your kids… eventually?" Not now, but *eventually.* You want to know if he's looking for someone to co-parent on date five, or if he's giving things time to evolve naturally.

5. **"What do your kids already know about your dating life?"** This shows you how transparent he is with them and how seriously he takes protecting their emotional space.

6. **"How do you typically handle disagreements with your co-parent?"** You're looking for emotional regulation here. If he says, "I just avoid her" or "we scream and get over it," that's not high-vibe behavior. You want *communication and boundaries*, not drama.

7. **"What's one thing you've learned about yourself through being a parent?"** A man who's done any kind of emotional growth through fatherhood is gold. If he can't name *anything*, he may be stuck in survival mode or emotional immaturity.

8. **"What kind of support do you need as a parent when you're dating someone?"** His answer will show you whether he wants a partner… or a replacement mother figure.

9. **"How do you discipline your kids when they act out?"** You don't need to agree on everything, but this will help you learn his values: Is he gentle? Strict? Checked-out? You're not parenting *with* him yet, but if that's the future, you want to know now.

10. **"What does a great relationship look like to you when there are kids in the mix?"** You're looking for vision here. Does he have a healthy picture of what love, parenting, and partnership can look like together or is he winging it with trauma and vibes?

CONVERSATION PROMPTS FOR SINGLE PARENTS DATING SOMEONE WITHOUT KIDS

(Because if he's going to be around your child,
you need to know he's not emotionally 12 himself.)

These questions are all about protecting your peace, clocking their maturity, and checking their readiness not just for love, but for the layered, sacred reality of dating someone who already has children. You're not just dating for fun, you're dating for alignment, peace, and long-term emotional safety.

1. **"Have you ever dated someone with kids before?"** Their answer gives you context. If they say "once and never again" *clock that.* If they say "not yet, but I'm open and curious," that's a much different energy.

2. **"How do you feel about being part of a relationship where I already have children?"** You want clarity here, not sugarcoated vibes. Are they truly open to the reality or just excited about the idea?

3. **"What's your comfort level with not being the center of my universe 24/7?"** Blunt? Maybe. Necessary? Absolutely. You need someone who understands your priorities without catching feelings when they're not always first.

4. **"What does being a partner to a parent mean to you?"** This tells you whether they see themselves as a bystander, a support system, or something else entirely. You want to know how they view their *role*, now and long-term.

5. "Would you ever want to have kids of your own?" You need to know if your paths align or if you're headed in totally different directions. Clarity now saves heartbreak later.

6. "How would you handle it if my child didn't immediately take to you?" If they say "I'd win them over," that's ego. If they say "I'd respect their space and take my time," *that's the energy you want.*

7. "What kind of family dynamic did you grow up with?" This opens up important backstory: how they view parenting, discipline, emotional safety, and what "normal" looked like to them growing up.

8. "What would your support look like when I'm overwhelmed or burned out from parenting?" You're not asking them to fix your life. You're asking them to *show up emotionally.*

9. "What does your ideal weekend look like?" Sneaky good question. If they say "parties, last-minute travel, staying out all night," they may not be ready for family energy. If they say "connection, calm, quality time" you're getting closer to alignment.

10. "What do you admire most about people who are parents?" Watch how they answer. If they talk about sacrifice, strength, patience, you're dealing with someone who *sees you.* If they joke or change the subject, you've got your answer too.

Age Gap Dating

(Because at 40, I can date the father, the son,
or just adopt the whole damn family business.)

Age gap dating isn't weird anymore. It's standard operating procedure. You're grown. They're grown. You're not looking for a second childhood or a third divorce, you're looking for connection, chemistry, and someone whose emotional maturity matches their jawline. Dating older? Dating younger? It's all fair game *as long as you're leading with your power, not your insecurity.* Here's the real breakdown:

1. Own the Gap Without Making It the Relationship's Whole Personality. You're not his "hot older woman." He's not your "cute young project." Ditch the stereotypes. Build the connection.

2. Don't Ignore Life Stage Differences Just Because the Chemistry Is Fire. Yes, the banter is great. Yes, the bedroom is a revival. But does he want kids and you're one Google search away from early retirement? Talk about the real sh*t early.

3. If You Feel Like His Mom, You're Already in the Wrong Role. You're not raising him. You're not reminding him to book his dentist appointment. You're dating not parenting.

4. Shared Values Matter More Than Shared Birth Years. Forget matching playlists. Are you aligned on ambition, loyalty, life dreams? Because TikTok trends fade. *Character doesn't.*

5. Be Ready for Side-Eye from Strangers, Friends, and Family. People will project. Laugh it off. Your relationship isn't up for committee approval.

6. Energy Over Age. He could be 25 with the emotional maturity of a golden retriever or 55 and still rocking trauma from 1992. You're not dating numbers, you're dating *energy.*

7. Don't Romanticize Immaturity Just Because It's Wrapped in a Hot Body. He's fun, spontaneous, lives in the moment and also can't hold a job, book a reservation, or manage his emotions? Yeah, pass.

8. Financial Conversations Aren't Gold-Digging. They're Grown-Ass Discussions. You're not looking for a wallet. You're looking for a man who can stand next to you, not climb on your back financially.

9. Protect Your Future While Enjoying Your Present. Love the now. Protect your assets. You're not naïve, you're seasoned. Romance is beautiful. *Prenups are too.*

10. If He Tries to "Teach" You Life Lessons You Didn't Ask For, Run. There's a difference between wisdom and condescension. If it feels like he's dating you for an audience, not a partner? Exit, stage left.

11. Never Dim Your Power to Seem "Relatable." You don't need to downplay your success, your scars, your age, or your standards to make a man feel less insecure. Let them rise or let them watch you walk.

12. Long-Term Reality Check: Can This Last? Real talk:

- What happens when you're 50 and he's 32?
- Or when he's 68 and you're still ready to climb mountains? Dream the dream, but also *plan the plan.*

13. Remember: You're Not a "Cougar" or a "Trophy" You're a Whole Damn Force. Drop the labels. You're not a cliché. You're a woman who knows her worth and refuses to box it into someone else's comfort zone.

14. If It Feels Good, It's Nobody's Damn Business. If you're happy, respected, loved, and aligned, guess what? Their opinions, side-eyes, and outdated narratives don't pay your bills or fuel your joy. *Love out loud. Love without apology.*

AGE GAP DATING: RED FLAGS & GREEN FLAGS
(Because you're not about to fall for a hot mess in a younger package or a well-dressed narcissist with retirement benefits.)

GREEN FLAGS
If he shows these signs? You might actually be onto something real.

1. He respects your stage of life even if it's different than his. No weird energy about your career, your age, your kids, or your freedom. He doesn't flinch. He *admires*.

2. He's emotionally regulated regardless of age. Whether he's 27 or 57, he can name his feelings, own his sh*t, and talk through tension without ghosting, gaslighting, or going silent.

3. He supports your goals without competition or control. Your glow-up doesn't threaten him, it *inspires* him. Whether he's retired or still building, he knows how to clap for you.

4. He doesn't infantilize you (if you're younger) or play daddy (if he's older). You're equals. Full stop. No weird power plays. No patronizing tone. Just real respect.

5. He's not hiding you. If he's proud to show up with you at work, around friends, online, greenest of flags. Secrecy is not sexy.

RED FLAGS
Run. Fast. These are the classics with a twist.

1. He fetishizes your age instead of seeing *you*.
"You're so mature for your age."
"You're the hottest older woman I've ever dated."
If he's leading with your number, he's not here for your *depth*.

2. He uses the age gap to control the pace or power of the relationship. Watch for things like:

- Love bombing
- Fast-forwarding commitment
- Acting like he knows best "because he's older"
  That's not wisdom. That's manipulation with a birthday.

269

3. He makes your life experience a punchline.

"Back in your day..."

"Wait, you've never heard of this?"

If he turns your lived experience into a bit, *he's not secure enough to date a woman with range.*

4. His friends don't know you or act weird when they do. If he's not integrating you into his world, or if you feel like the side piece at the retirement party or the music festival, *you're not the priority.*

Cultural and Religious Considerations

(Because love can cross oceans,
but only if you're willing to listen, learn, and lead with respect.)

Dating someone from a different cultural or religious background can be one of the most beautiful, expansive experiences of your life, but only if you stop trying to mold them into your worldview. This chapter isn't about being politically correct or walking on eggshells. It's about *real connection through real curiosity.*

If you're not willing to honor someone's identity, roots, and spiritual rhythm, you're not ready for anything serious. But if you are? You're stepping into a love that can *stretch and soften you in all the best ways.* Here's how to do it with grace:

1. Start With Respect, Not Assumptions. No one owes you an explanation for their culture or religion, but if they choose to share it with you, listen like it's sacred. Because it is. Your way isn't "normal" it's just familiar. And theirs is just as valid.

2. Ask Real Questions and Stay Open to the Answers. If something confuses you, ask. If something feels unfamiliar, *get curious not critical.* Don't pretend to know what you don't. Say:
- "Can I ask more about that?"
- "How do you celebrate that holiday?"
- "What's something about your culture people usually get wrong?"

Let them be your teacher and don't make it a debate.

3. Understand the Weight of Family and Community. Some cultures are highly communal. Some families are deeply involved. This isn't "controlling" it's how loyalty and legacy are passed down. If your partner's family has a voice in their decisions, honor that. You don't have to agree but you *do* have to respect it.

4. Learn Their Rituals and Rhythms. Prayer. Fasting. Sacred holidays. Dietary laws. Modesty. Rituals of grief or joy. These aren't random traditions. They're tied to identity. Even if you don't share their practice, *honor their devotion.*

Show up by saying:
- "Is there anything you'd like me to be mindful of?"
- "How can I support you during this time?"

You don't need to convert. You need to *care.*

5. Celebrate What Matters to Them. Learn their holidays. Try their food. Ask about the stories behind their customs. You don't have to get it perfect. You just have to show that you *want* to get it. Participating in what they love builds trust that you're not just dating them, you're learning their world.

6. Consent Still Comes First, Always. Different cultures and religions have different dating norms around physical touch, commitment, even who they're "allowed" to date. Don't push. Don't assume. Don't take it personally if they need to move slower. Honor their pace without pressure.

7. Address Conflict with Empathy, Not Ego. If there's a misunderstanding rooted in cultural or religious difference, *don't double down.* Ask:

- "How does this land for you, based on your experience?"
- "What does this look like from your perspective?" Approach it like a bridge not a battlefield.

8. Talk About the Long-Term Realities. If this gets serious, ask the hard questions:

- How do we raise kids?
- Are there expectations from your family or community?
- What traditions do we want to blend and what might we keep separate?

Avoiding these convos doesn't protect love. It *undermines* it.

9. Do Your Own Research. It's Not Their Job to Educate You. Google is free. Read about their faith. Watch documentaries about their culture. Ask thoughtful questions *after* you've shown the effort. When someone sees you're willing to learn on your own, it shows respect without expectation.

10. Find Your Shared Values and Build from There. At the end of the day, it's not about matching backgrounds, it's about matching *character.* Do you both value family? Integrity? Growth? Faith? Do you want the same things, even if you come from different starting points? Shared values don't erase differences. They *anchor* your connection through them.

Bottom line: Dating across culture or religion isn't a novelty, it's a responsibility. But it can also be one of the most soul-expanding journeys you'll ever take. Love is not about "sameness" it's about *sacred difference honored through mutual respect.* If you can stay curious, patient, and humble, you just might build something deeper than anything you've known before.

COMPATIBILITY CONVERSATION STARTERS

(For couples from different cultures, religions, or upbringings who want to go deeper without assumptions, pressure, or weird vibes.)

Use these organically on walks, during dinner, in texts. The key is curiosity, not critique. You're not looking for perfect alignment. You're looking for *clarity, respect, and potential harmony.*

1. "What were relationships like in your household growing up?" This opens up conversation around gender roles, emotional expression, marriage, love and what they're modeling or rejecting.

2. "What does your culture or religion say about dating and how do you feel about that now?" This helps them separate what they were taught from what they believe. It shows you're interested in their personal truth, not just their background.

3. "Are there any holidays or traditions that really matter to you?" Not just the ones they celebrate, but the ones that *move* them. This helps you prepare to show up meaningfully when it counts.

4. "How important is faith or spirituality in your daily life?" Whether they're deeply observant or more fluid, this reveals how faith (or lack of it) shapes their worldview and future plans.

5. "What's something about your culture or religion people often misunderstand?" This builds trust fast. You're offering them space to be seen *accurately*, not just through a Western or outsider lens.

6. "How do you imagine raising kids if your partner has different beliefs or traditions?" Even if you're not thinking about kids now, this question opens the door to long-term vision and non-negotiables.

7. "Are there any customs or boundaries in your dating life I should be aware of or respect?" This question is pure gold. It's proactive, humble, and deeply respectful. It lets them name their pace, preferences, and sacred lines.

8. "What kind of partner support feels most meaningful to you in your culture or faith?" This opens a conversation about gender expectations, emotional roles, and how *you* can support *them* on their terms.

9. "What parts of your culture or religion are most connected to who you are today?" This invites them to name what's important without feeling like they have to explain everything.

10. "What values do you hope your future relationship is built on, no matter who you're with?" This one brings it all home. Past belief systems aside, this asks: who are *you* now, and what kind of love are you here to create?

Communication & Conflict

Effective Communication Skills
(Or: How to Say What You Mean Without Triggering a Breakup or a Lawsuit)

Communication is more than words. It's vibe. It's energy. It's the difference between "let's go out again" and "please lose my number." Master these, and you're no longer a walking misfire, you're a magnetic, emotionally intelligent force of nature. Here's your *no-BS* guide to *dating like a communicator, not a cautionary tale.*

If you can't say it, don't date.
You can't build connection without communication. Period. You're not just learning how to talk, you're learning how to *be understood*. If you want a real relationship and not just another situationship that ends in "I don't know what we were," here's what you need to know:

A survival manual for the modern dating battlefield. No fluff. Just facts.
If you're not communicating clearly, you're not dating, you're just confusing each other with vibes and assumptions. These aren't "soft skills" these are non-negotiables if you want to build *anything* real.

1. Active Listening. If you can't actually hear them, you can't connect. That means you stop scanning the room, rehearsing your next line, or comparing them to your ex in your head.
How to use it: When they're speaking, make it your job to *get it*. Not just the words but the emotion underneath. Ask follow-ups like: "Wait, what was that like for you?" or "Can I ask what you meant by that?"

   Give *verbal feedback* while they talk: "That makes sense." "I get that." "Wow, really?" This shows you're tuned in not just waiting to talk about yourself.

2. Open and Honest Expression. Saying "I don't know" when you *do* know? Withholding because you're afraid of being "too much?" That's how you sabotage something before it starts.
How to use it: Practice saying the real thing, even if it's awkward. "I'm having a good time and want to see you again." Or "I'm not feeling a romantic spark, but I've loved getting to know you." If you're confused, say "I'm feeling a little unsure where we stand, can we talk about it?" Say the thing. Don't overthink it into oblivion. Clarity is a love language.

3. Nonverbal Communication. Words are 10% of what people pick up. The rest? Your body, tone, pace, posture, eye contact, energy. You could say all the right things and still come across closed off.
How to use it: Watch your physical presence. Are you leaning in or pulled back? Are your arms crossed? Is your tone warm or robotic? If you're interested, show it. Sit forward, make eye contact, smile when they say something funny even if it's awkward-funny. Energy is communication.

4. Empathy. Empathy means you stop reacting from your lens and start responding from theirs. Most people don't want to be fixed. They want to be felt.

How to use it: When they share something emotional, pause. Don't one-up them or pivot to your own story. Try saying:

- "That sounds really heavy. Thank you for sharing it."
- "I can't fully relate, but I hear you. And I get why that'd affect you." And if you don't get it, ask: "Help me understand what that felt like for you."

5. Asking Thoughtful Questions. Dating without curiosity is just small talk with cocktails. Real connection comes from asking better questions not the recycled "so what do you do?"

How to use it: Ask questions like

- "What's something people misunderstand about you?"
- "What's shaped your view of relationships?"
- "When do you feel most like yourself?"

Use follow-up questions too. Don't just move on. Stay in the answer. Get to the *why*, not just the *what*.

6. Clarification. Miscommunication kills more potential than cheating ever will. If something they said confused you, don't pretend you understood, ask.

How to use it: Say things like

- "Can I clarify what you meant when you said you're not looking for anything serious?"
- "When you say you're 'bad at texting,' should I expect days of silence or are we talking 12 hours?"

It's not confrontation, it's collaboration. Make no assumptions. Clarify everything.

7. Giving Constructive Feedback. You're allowed to say when something didn't land for you as long as you're not throwing grenades while you do it.

How to use it:

- "Hey, when you made that joke about my job, I laughed it off, but honestly, it stung a little."
- "I noticed you kind of shut down when I brought up exclusivity. Can we talk about what came up for you?"

  Give feedback without accusation. Use "I felt…" not "You did…"

8. Naming and Respecting Boundaries. Boundaries are not "walls" or "tests" they are guidelines for what keeps you feeling safe, valued, and connected.

How to use it:

- Say: "I like to take things slow physically."
- Or: "I'm not ready to talk about past relationships yet."
- Or: "I need a heads up before last-minute plans." Then *hold the line*. If they can't respect your boundary, that's your answer.

9. Responding to Their Boundaries with Maturity. The second someone says "no" and you flinch, guilt-trip, or argue, you've revealed your emotional age.

How to use it: When someone gives a boundary, say

- "Thanks for telling me."
- "I appreciate you being direct." If it disappoints you? That's okay. Still doesn't mean you get to push it. Respect is hot. Pressure is not.

10. Conflict Resolution. Conflict isn't a sign it's wrong. It's a sign you've reached the part where truth gets tested. But how you handle it determines everything.

How to use it: When a disagreement comes up

- *Pause before reacting.* Ask: "Can we talk this through instead of letting it build?"
- Own your part. Say: "I see where I could've done that better."
- Stay on topic. Don't stack every old complaint onto one moment.
- Listen without getting defensive. No eye rolls. No walking away mid-sentence. Stay. Work it out.

11. Stating Intentions Early. Letting someone build an emotional connection without telling them what you're *actually* looking for? That's not chill, it's manipulative.

How to use it: Whether you want commitment, casual, or "seeing where it goes," *say it upfront.* Try

- "I'm not in a rush, but I'm looking for something meaningful."
- "I'm in a casual season right now, but I believe in being honest and respectful." This saves everyone time and prevents silent heartbreaks.

12. Matching Energy Without Playing Games. If they're engaging, show up. If they're pulling away, don't chase or guilt, just recalibrate. Communication is a mirror.

How to use it: Notice the rhythm of texts, tone of conversation, level of effort. If you're always initiating and they're half-hearted, *address it.* Say:

- "I really enjoy talking to you, but I'm starting to feel a bit one-sided. Are you still interested?"

  Don't play hard to get. Play *honest to be respected.*

13. Recognizing Emotional Availability. If someone dodges hard conversations, disappears when things get real, or laughs everything off, that's not lighthearted. That's avoidance.

How to use it: Ask questions that gently test for depth:

- "How do you usually handle conflict in relationships?"
- "What does vulnerability mean to you?" If they freeze or joke it off, that's your intel. Don't try to teach someone to swim while you're drowning.

14. Naming the Vibe Shift. If the energy's changed, say it. Most people feel it but pretend not to notice, hoping it'll self-correct. Spoiler: it won't.

How to use it:

- "Hey, I've noticed things feel a little different lately. Am I imagining that, or are we both feeling it?"

  This opens the door for a real convo instead of a slow fade built on silence and confusion.

276

15. Using Silence Intentionally, Not Punishingly. Taking space is healthy. Going silent to teach them a lesson? That's emotional manipulation dressed in a trauma response.

How to use it: "I need a little time to process, and I want to respond clearly. Can we talk later tonight or tomorrow?" This way, you're not ghosting, they know where you stand. And when you *do* come back, be clear. Don't punish them for not mind-reading while you disappeared.

16. Checking in Instead of Assuming. If something seems off, don't spiral in your head. Don't assume you did something wrong. Just *check in.*

How to use it:

- "Hey, just checking in. Are we good?"
- "I'm feeling a little off energy, and I wanted to talk about it instead of assuming." This is how adults stay connected instead of unraveling in their heads and blaming it on "vibes."

17. Giving Space Without Withdrawing. You don't need to over-talk to show you care. Sometimes people just need room to breathe. Space isn't rejection. It's rest.

How to use it:

- "I can tell you've got a lot going on. I'm here if/when you want to talk. No pressure."
- "Let me know if you need some space. I'll respect that and be here when you're ready." Space is communication *if* you name it. Ghosting isn't.

18. Emotional Regulation During Conflict. Getting triggered isn't the problem, projecting it onto someone else *is.*

How to use it: Pause before you respond. Ask yourself, "Am I reacting to *them*, or to something old inside me?" Own it. Try:

- "That hit a nerve. I need a second to respond instead of react." This shows *emotional intelligence*, not weakness.

19. Consistency Over Time. Anyone can communicate well for a week. The skill is doing it *after the high wears off,* the butterflies fade, and real-life hits.

How to use it: Don't just say what you feel. Keep showing it. Don't let communication die once you've "got" them. That's how people end up feeling emotionally abandoned in relationships. Keep checking in. Keep listening. Keep asking, "How's your heart this week?"

20. Making the Other Person Feel Safe to Be Honest. You want honesty? You have to *make room for it.* If they feel judged, punished, or dismissed every time they're real, you've made the truth unsafe.

How to use it: When they open up, *thank them.* When they disagree with you, *listen without defensiveness.* When they're scared, *don't fix it, hold space.* Try:

- "I really appreciate you telling me that."
- "You're safe to be honest with me. I'd rather hear the truth than be comforted by a lie." Trust is built in the moments you could get reactive, but choose to stay open.

21. Communicating Through Awkwardness. Because most people ghost not out of malice, but discomfort.

What's missing: How to *stay* in awkward, emotionally murky conversations without panicking or emotionally ejecting.

How to use it:
- "This is a little hard for me to say, but I want to be honest anyway."
- "I'm not sure how to explain this well, but I'd like to try." Normalize awkward moments. If you can name it without dramatizing it, you create emotional safety.

22. Repair After Miscommunication. Communication isn't just about getting it *right*, it's about *repairing* when you get it wrong.

What's missing: How to revisit a conversation that didn't go well instead of ghosting, withdrawing, or pretending it never happened.

How to use it:
- "I've been thinking about what I said the other night and I don't love how I handled it."
- "Can we revisit our convo from earlier? I don't feel like I expressed myself clearly." *Most people never hear this. When you do it, you stand out.*

23. Understanding Their Style vs. Yours. Because not everyone communicates the same and mismatched styles create unnecessary friction.

What's missing: How to identify and navigate differences in expression (direct vs. indirect, emotional vs. logical, fast vs. slow processors).

How to use it:
- "When something's bothering you, do you usually need to talk it out right away or sit with it for a bit?"
- "What's the best way to check in with you when we hit tension?" Adapt your style *without abandoning your truth.*

24. Expressing Appreciation Consistently. Appreciation is communication and if it's missing, things die even when everything else looks "fine."

What's missing: How to communicate *positive emotions* regularly not just problems or logistics.

How to use it:
- "I felt really safe the way you handled that conversation."
- "I love how thoughtful you are. It means more than you know." Affection, praise, and gratitude don't wait until it's missing to express it.

25. Regulating When You're Overstimulated. Some people shut down *not* because they don't care, but because their system is overwhelmed.

What's missing: Teaching your partner (and learning yourself) how to recognize signs of emotional flooding and pause instead of pushing through.

How to use it:
- "I'm starting to feel overwhelmed. Can we take a beat and come back to this in 30 minutes?"
- "I want to keep talking, but I need a second to ground myself first." This is especially critical for anxious or avoidant daters.

PRACTICE CHECKLIST:
HOW TO ACTUALLY COMMUNICATE LIKE A PRO
(NOT A PANICKED TEENAGER)

This isn't theory. These are actionable, in-the-field exercises and mindset shifts to *rewire how you show up* in conversations, dates, and emotional situations.

DAILY HABITS TO BUILD COMMUNICATION MUSCLE

1. Reflect before reacting.

→ Every time you get triggered, pause. Ask: *"What's the story I'm telling myself right now? Is it true?"*

Journal the real emotion underneath before sending a single text.

2. Practice naming your feelings without needing resolution.

→ "I'm feeling anxious right now, but I don't need you to fix it. I just wanted to share where I'm at."

Try that with a friend or date. Watch how your nervous system responds when you're just *seen.*

3. Clarify instead of assuming—once a day.

→ Pick one interaction daily (text or real-life) where you want to assume something… and *don't.* Instead, ask:

- "Hey, just to clarify, what did you mean by that?"
- "Can I ask where your head's at?"

ON-DATE PRACTICE EXERCISES

4. Mirror + Validate their response at least once.

→ Try saying:

- "It sounds like that really impacted you."
- "That makes sense why you'd feel that way."
  Then shut up. Let them sit in being understood. That moment alone builds *more intimacy than compliments ever could.*

5. Ask one meaningful question that isn't about surface stuff.

→ Examples:

- "What do you wish more people understood about you?"
- "What's something you're currently learning about relationships?"
  Then follow up with curiosity. Don't pivot away too fast.

6. Name something you appreciate clearly.

→ End the date with:

- "I really liked how you talked about your sister. That was sweet."
- "You're really thoughtful. That stood out."
  Gratitude builds connection, and most people don't hear it enough.

BREAK THESE HABITS IF YOU WANT TO BE TAKEN SERIOUSLY

7. No more vague texting.

→ Stop saying "maybe," "idk," or dropping half-truths to keep things light.

Say: "I'd love to hang out again. What does your week look like?" Or say: "Hey, I think we're on different pages, but I've really enjoyed talking to you."

8. Don't ghost ever again.

→ Instead, copy/paste this if you're trying to end it respectfully: "Hey [Name], I've appreciated getting to know you, but I don't feel a romantic connection. Just wanted to be honest and not leave you guessing. Wishing you the best." You don't owe everyone your heart, but you do owe them closure.

9. Stop performing.

→ Show up as *you*. If you're anxious, name it. If you're awkward, laugh about it. Pretending to be chill only guarantees you'll attract people who aren't safe for your real self.

WEEKLY SELF-CHECK QUESTIONS

Ask these once a week, or after a date:

- Am I listening more than I'm performing?
- Have I said what I actually feel, or what I think will keep them interested?
- Have I been clear about my needs, wants, or boundaries?
- Have I been honest? *not just in facts, but in tone and intention?*
- Did I respect *their* communication style too, or only focus on mine?

BONUS INTEGRATION: THE MIRROR DRILL

(Use once a week to rewire old patterns)

Stand in front of a mirror and say:

- "It's safe for me to speak my truth."
- "I don't have to shrink to be loved."
- "I release the need to be chosen. I choose clarity."
  Then, write down one situation this week where you'll *practice* being clearer, braver, or more direct.

Effective Conflict Management
(AKA: How to Fight Without Burning the Relationship to the Ground)

Love isn't tested in the good moments. It's revealed in the tension. If you don't know how to fight, you don't know how to love. Let's get something straight: conflict doesn't ruin relationships. Poor communication does. Passive-aggression does. Stonewalling does. Screaming, shutting down, scorekeeping that's what erodes love until it's just resentment in lingerie. If you want a healthy relationship, you don't need to avoid conflict. You need to master it.

THE PSYCHOLOGY OF A FIGHT
When conflict happens, your nervous system enters survival mode:
- **Fight** (attack)
- **Flight** (avoid)
- **Freeze** (shut down)
- **Fawn** (people-please)

Most couples never learn how to regulate this. Every disagreement becomes a war, a withdrawal, or a desperate performance. Until you can name your pattern, you're just reenacting your childhood in adult relationships.

THE GOLDEN RULES OF HEALTHY CONFLICT
1. Assume They're Not the Enemy. If you start the conversation trying to *win*, you've already lost. The goal isn't victory, it's connection.

2. Speak From Your Body, Not Your Blame. "I feel hurt when you cancel plans" hits differently than "You never show up." If your tone feels like a courtroom, expect defense not resolution.

3. Never Fight to Prove a Point. Fight to Understand a Pattern. If this keeps happening, what's underneath it? Trigger? Insecurity? Unmet need? That's the real conversation.

4. Regulate Before You Communicate. Take a walk. Breathe. Cry it out. Write it down. Then speak. Your nervous system should not be leading the conversation.

5. Stick to One Topic at a Time. Don't turn every conflict into a greatest hits album of every past mistake. That's not resolution. That's emotional ambush.

6. Call a Timeout if Needed. "I love you. I'm too heated to talk right now. I need 30 minutes." That's maturity. Not avoidance.

7. Use Repair Statements
- "What I said wasn't fair. Let me try again."
- "I want to understand you better. Can we slow down?"
- "That landed wrong. Let me clarify."

Repair isn't weakness. It's leadership.

COMMUNICATION SKILLS THAT ACTUALLY WORK

- **Reflective Listening**: "What I'm hearing is that you felt dismissed when I didn't respond. Is that right?"
- **Clarifying Questions**: "Can you help me understand what that felt like for you?"
- **Ownership Language**: "That was on me. I didn't realize how that came across."
- **Non-Negotiable Respect**: You can be angry but never cruel.

CONFLICT RED FLAGS

- Mocking, belittling, or name-calling
- Weaponizing silence
- Emotional dumping with no accountability
- Needing to "win" every fight
- Threatening to leave during every disagreement

These aren't just communication issues. They're relational landmines.

REFRAME: CONFLICT IS INTIMACY TRAINING

Every argument is a mirror. It shows:

- How you handle discomfort
- How you treat someone when you're hurting
- What your nervous system does when triggered
- How willing you are to stay in the room when things get real

Love isn't built on compatibility. It's built on *repair.*

FINAL TRUTH

If you can't argue with someone, you can't grow with them. Conflict isn't a breakdown. It's a portal. If you walk through it with awareness, clarity, and respect, what's on the other side is deeper trust. Not every disagreement is a dealbreaker. But how you *handle it* might be. So, fight but fight well. Fight for each other, not against. Fight to understand, not to dominate. And above all? Never lose sight of the love underneath the tension.

Expressing Needs & Boundaries

Here's the harsh truth nobody taught us growing up: If you don't express your needs and boundaries, someone will walk all over them and they won't even know they're doing it. And guess what? That's on you. Not because you deserved it, but because you never *stated the rules of engagement.*

What Needs and Boundaries *Actually* Are (and Aren't):

◆ **A need** is what makes you feel safe, seen, and valued.

◆ **A boundary** is where you end and someone else begins.

◆ **A need is not a demand.**

◆ **A boundary is not a threat.**

You're not begging for basic decency. You're *clarifying the standards* for being in your life.

Why Most People Screw This Up:

- They think setting boundaries will scare people away. (*Good. Let it scare the wrong ones off.*)
- They think expressing needs makes them "needy." (*Wrong. Healthy needs filter out the emotionally bankrupt.*)
- They think being chill and flexible will make someone stay. (*Spoiler: It won't. It just makes you easier to take advantage of.*)

How to Actually Express Needs and Boundaries (Like a Goddamn Queen):

1. Get Clear with Yourself First. If you can't articulate what you need, no one else can guess it. Before you open your mouth, check in:

- What makes me feel respected?
- What drains me?
- What behaviors are deal-breakers?

Self-awareness before self-expression. Always.

2. Say It Early Not After You're Hurt. You don't wait until after someone has stomped all over you to awkwardly mumble, "Um, actually, I kind of didn't like that..." You set the tone from the beginning. Clear is kind. Early is protective.

3. Use "I" Statements, Not Blame Grenades. Example:

◆ Weak: *"You're so disrespectful. You never call me back."*

◆ Powerful: *"I need consistency in communication to feel valued in a connection."*

You're not attacking. You're informing. What they do with that information tells you *everything* you need to know.

4. Stay Calm When You Say It. Your boundaries lose power when you deliver them through panic, rage, or tears. State them the way you would your Starbucks order:

- Calm.
- Clear.
- No apologies.

If they freak out? **Congratulations. You just dodged a bullet wearing cologne.**

5. Enforce It Without Drama. Setting a boundary means you're ready to walk if it's crossed. No tantrums. No lectures. No "one more chances." Cross my line, lose my presence. Simple. Final.

Final Word: If you expressing a need scares someone away, if you stating a boundary makes someone defensive, if you protecting your peace makes someone uncomfortable: Good. You just exposed what would have destroyed you later. You're not asking for too much. You're asking the wrong person if it feels like too much.

Speak your truth early. Speak your truth often.
And don't be scared when the wrong ones disappear.
That's not rejection, that's divine editing.

Savage Boundary Scripts
(Steal these, tweak these, own these but never stay silent again.)

For Expressing a Need:

◆ **"I need ___ to feel respected and secure when I'm building a connection."**
Examples:

- *I need consistent communication to feel respected and secure.*
- *I need honesty about intentions to feel respected and secure.*
- *I need follow-through, not just words, to feel respected and secure.*

For Setting a Boundary:

◆ **"If ___ happens, I will ___ because protecting my peace is not negotiable."**
Examples:

- *If you disappear without communication, I will lose interest because protecting my peace is not negotiable.*
- *If you make jokes at my expense, I will leave because protecting my peace is not negotiable.*
- *If you can't respect my time, I will move on because protecting my peace is not negotiable.*

For Reinforcing a Boundary Without Drama:

◆ **"That doesn't work for me."**
◆ **"I respect myself too much to stay in situations like this."**
◆ **"I'm not available for this kind of energy."**
◆ **"I wish you the best, but I'm exiting this conversation."**
(Short. Calm. Deadly effective.)

For a Non-Negotiable Goodbye:

◆ **"I don't do warnings. I do standards."**

◆ **"You're not a bad person. You're just not my person."**

◆ **"I'm not angry. I'm clear."**

Closing Reminder: "Boundaries don't push away the right people. They expose the wrong ones faster."

Boundary Declaration Card
(Fill this out. Save it. Live by it.)

◆ **My Core Non-Negotiables Are:**
(Example: honesty, consistency, emotional maturity)

➔ _____

➔ _____

➔ _____

◆ **If someone crosses these lines, I will:**
(Example: walk away without explaining, protect my peace without guilt)

➔ _____

➔ _____

◆ **My Reminder to Myself:**
(Choose one or write your own)

- "I am not here to beg for basics."
- "My standards are my protection, not my punishment."
- "The right person will honor my boundaries effortlessly."
- _____

Final Command:

"I am the guardian of my peace. I do not bend for chaos disguised as connection."

Scripts for Boundary-Setting
(AKA: How to Shut It Down Without Shrinking Yourself)

You're not a bitch for having boundaries. You're just no longer available for bullshit. Most women aren't "too emotional," they're just under-boundaried and overexposed. Boundaries aren't walls. They're doors with locks. They say: this is how I let love in. This is how I keep disrespect out.

Below are full-spectrum boundary scripts for almost every scenario from the subtle manipulator to the sweet guy who's just not your person. These aren't passive-aggressive. These aren't overly apologetic. These are rooted, clear, and emotionally clean.

WHEN HE'S BEING VAGUE OR INCONSISTENT
- "Hey, I'm not into confusion. If you want to see me, make a real plan. If not, I'm good keeping it moving."
- "I'm not the girl you text at midnight when you're bored. If you're interested, show up like it."
- "If I'm not a priority, I'm not available. Simple as that."

WHEN HE CROSSES A LINE PHYSICALLY OR EMOTIONALLY
- "That didn't sit right with me. I need you to know that I don't accept [insert behavior]. Respect is non-negotiable."
- "I don't tolerate being spoken to like that even when someone's upset. Let's try again when it's calm."
- "I'm not here to teach someone how to treat me. If you don't already know, I'm not the one."

WHEN HE LOVEBOMBS THEN DISAPPEARS
- "You come in hot, then disappear. That's not sexy, it's chaotic. I'm out."
- "If your attention is a rollercoaster, I'd rather walk."
- "You're not confusing. You're just inconsistent. And that's not something I entertain anymore."

WHEN HE WANTS SOMETHING CASUAL AND YOU DON'T
- "Totally valid that you're not looking for something serious and just as valid that I'm not wasting my energy on someone who isn't."
- "I'm not judging you for not wanting more. But I *am* choosing not to invest in something that leads nowhere."
- "I don't do situationships. Wish you the best."

WHEN HE GASLIGHTS YOU OR DEFLECTS
- "I know what I felt. I don't need to debate my reality."
- "You don't get to decide what hurt me. That's not your call."
- "Deflecting accountability isn't a personality trait. It's a red flag."

WHEN HE KEEPS PUSHING AFTER YOU SAY NO

- "I already gave my answer. Repeating yourself isn't going to change it."
- "You pushing my boundary just made the answer a permanent no."
- "Consent isn't a debate. It's a door that closes the second you ignore it."

WHEN HE GETS DEFENSIVE AFTER FEEDBACK

- "You don't have to agree, but if you care about me, you'll at least try to understand."
- "I'm not attacking you. I'm asking to be heard. If that's too much, then so am I."
- "If feedback makes you shut down, this won't work. Growth requires discomfort."

WHEN HE TRIES TO COME BACK AFTER MESSING UP

- "I don't hate you. I'm just not offering a second round of what broke me the first time."
- "Forgiveness doesn't mean re-entry. I've moved on."
- "I respect your growth. But I've outgrown the version of me that would say yes again."

WHEN HE JUST WON'T RESPECT YOUR TIME

- "I don't chase people to get what I deserve. I align with those who show up."
- "If this is how you handle communication, I'm not your person."
- "It's not a scheduling issue. It's a priority issue. And I'm not interested in begging to matter."

CLOSING LINE

Every time you set a boundary, you tell the universe: "I'm not available for breadcrumbs. I'm available for the real thing." Use your words. Use your spine. Use your silence when needed. You're not cold. You're clear. And clarity is the new seduction.

WHY YOU KEEP FALLING FOR POTENTIAL (AND HOW TO STOP)

You saw his brokenness and called it mystery. You saw his chaos and called it chemistry. You saw his potential and called it a future. And now you're exhausted.
Let's get real. You didn't fall in love with him. You fell in love with what he *could be* if he healed, evolved, stopped ghosting, went to therapy, got his act together, or finally realized how amazing you are. This is your wake-up call. Not to shame you. But to break the cycle of building your life around half-finished men.

WHY WE FALL FOR POTENTIAL (THE PSYCHOLOGY)

1. You equate love with labor. If your love language is "fixing him," you're not in a relationship, you're in a rescue mission. When your worth is tied to being "the one who saves him," you'll never stop choosing men who need saving.

2. You mistake inconsistency for depth. He opens up once, then disappears. He trauma dumps, then ghosts. And you confuse those fleeting vulnerable moments for emotional intimacy. A spark is not a foundation. And chaos is not character.

3. You were never taught to receive. If you grew up earning love, performing for it, or chasing emotionally unavailable parents, a man who makes you work for every crumb feels familiar. Healthy love will feel foreign until you unlearn the need to prove you're worthy.

4. Fantasy is safer than reality. You can't get hurt by the man in your imagination. But you *will* get shattered trying to date someone who only exists there. He's not a project. He's a person. And if he's not showing up, he's not ready and that's not your job to fix.

SIGNS YOU'RE IN LOVE WITH POTENTIAL, NOT A PERSON
- You spend more time *hoping* he'll change than actually enjoying who he is
- You defend his behavior to your friends because *"they just don't see the good in him like you do"*
- You're waiting for the version of him that only shows up in rare bursts
- You're emotionally invested in who he could become not who's in front of you now

WHAT IT COSTS YOU
- Wasted time and emotional bandwidth
- Self-doubt and confusion
- A distorted sense of what healthy love even looks like
- The slow erosion of your self-worth from constantly over-giving and under-receiving

HOW TO STOP FALLING FOR POTENTIAL

1. Date what's in front of you. Not the highlight reel. Not the backstory. Not the promises. Ask: *If nothing ever changed, would I still want this?*

2. Honor consistency over charisma. That emotionally solid guy might not make your stomach drop but your nervous system won't be in a panic either. That's not boring. That's *safe*.

3. Build a self-worth that doesn't need to earn love. You don't have to be impressive, useful, or hyper-tolerant to be loved. You get to be loved *as you are*.

4. Stop thinking your love is medicine. Healing is a solo job. You can inspire it, but you cannot *do* it for him. Stop auditioning to be his emotional nurse.

TEXT SCRIPTS TO SHIFT THE POWER
(AKA: How to Flip the Energy Without Losing Your Dignity or Your Edge)
You don't need to yell, chase, ghost, or play games. You just need language that holds power. the kind that shifts energy without shaking hands. This isn't about manipulation. It's about mastery. Most women were never taught how to regulate the dynamic when it starts to spiral how to interrupt the pattern and *reclaim the frame* without rage, silence, or begging. These scripts are for that moment when the vibe shifts, the game starts, or you feel the ground slipping under your feet. You don't spiral. You don't perform. You don't plead. **You redirect. You rise. You reset the energy in one move.**

WHEN THE POTENTIAL HASN'T POTENCHED

- "You have so much potential. But I've realized I'm in love with who I want you to be not who you're choosing to be. That's on me. I'm stepping back."
- "You're a good man just not the right man for me to keep pouring into while I dry out."
- "I deserve a relationship that doesn't need to be rescued. I'm done holding space for a version of you that hasn't arrived."
- "You keep showing me glimpses of someone I could love. But I'm not building my life around glimpses anymore."
- "Your growth is your responsibility. Not my reward. I'm walking away with love but I *am* walking away."

Psychology: This shuts down future-faking and stops you from auditioning for a role that doesn't exist. It's self-trust over hope, reality over potential.

WHEN HE GOES COLD OR DISTANT

- "Hey, feels like the energy shifted. If you need space, that's cool. Just don't string me along."
- "I'm picking up on the shift. If this isn't working for you, you're allowed to walk and I'm allowed to let you."
- "No hard feelings. Just not staying where I'm unsure I'm wanted."

Psychology: This disarms avoidance and puts you in self-trust instead of panic. It shows emotional maturity and removes their power to ghost you first.

WHEN YOU FEEL THE NEED TO CHASE OR CLING

Instead of sending that needy paragraph:

- "Hey, I just realized I've been over-explaining myself to someone who hasn't earned that access. Stepping back."
- "I deserve reciprocity, not confusion. Gonna re-center."
- "When it feels like I have to perform for connection, I know it's time to come home to myself."

Psychology: Interrupts anxious attachment patterns. Shifts you back into self-leadership without rage or collapse.

WHEN YOU NEED TO SET A CHILL BUT CLEAR BOUNDARY

- "I like where this is going, but I move with intention. If that's not aligned, no hard feelings."
- "I value direct communication. If that's not your style, we probably won't vibe."
- "I'm not here to be an option. Take your time just don't waste mine."

Psychology: Creates subtle pressure without emotional demand. Men with integrity rise to it. The rest weed themselves out.

WHEN HE'S LOVE-BOMBING BUT YOU FEEL OFF

- "Appreciate the compliments but consistency means more than intensity. Let's see where this goes."
- "This feels fast. I'm not in a rush. If it's real, it'll hold."
- "I've learned not to confuse intensity with intimacy. Slow is sexy."

Psychology: Disarms false urgency. Centers you in discernment. Keeps you out of fantasy bonding.

WHEN YOU WANT TO TAKE A STEP BACK WITHOUT CREATING DRAMA

- "Hey. I've been reflecting and I want to pause. Not to punish. Just to realign."
- "I need a little distance to hear my own voice again. If it's real, space won't break it."
- "I want to want this. Right now, I'm not sure. So, I'm going to take a breather."

Psychology: Interrupts emotional entanglement. Shifts the frame. Restores your own clarity.

WHEN YOU'RE DONE, BUT STILL EMPOWERED

- "I don't have anything unkind to say. Just no desire to keep doing this."
- "There's no villain here. Just a version of me that refuses to keep chasing patterns that don't feel safe."
- "I appreciate the time, but my peace is non-negotiable. Be well."

Psychology: Ends the pattern without dramatics. Leaves no room for re-entry. Positions you as sovereign.

BONUS TRUTH BOMBS FOR POWER SHIFTS

(Use these sparingly. They land like thunder.)

- "The version of me that would have tolerated this no longer exists."
- "I don't chase what's mine. I align with it."
- "If you wanted to, you would. And if you don't, I will."
- "I'm not mad. I'm just not interested anymore."
- "You taught me something. And I'm grateful. Now I'm gone."

FINAL TRUTH:

Power isn't in the volume of your voice. It's in the precision of your words. You don't need to scream to shift the energy. You just need clarity, conviction, and the courage to walk when the energy stays below your standard. The shift doesn't happen when he changes. It happens when you do.

PART V
THE GOSPEL OF
DATING TRUTHS

Before the first date
"You are not getting ready for a man.
You are preparing the world for a woman like you."

You're staring at your closet. Overthinking the text. Wondering if this is going to be worth it or just another chapter in the anthology of almosts. Let me tell you something. The world doesn't need you to be perfect tonight. It needs you to show up real. Because you, exactly as you are right now: too much, too guarded, too hopeful is already worthy of being chosen, even if tonight isn't the night it happens.

Put on the outfit that makes you feel most *like her* that future you who laughs during sex, eats pasta with her fingers, and kisses someone who actually gets it. Not because he's sitting across from you. But because she's always been inside you, waiting to be embodied.

And maybe tonight it will click. Maybe the eye contact will linger. Maybe something will move. But maybe it won't. Maybe he'll talk too much. Or too little. Maybe he'll remind you of your ex in the worst way. And maybe, at the end of the night, you'll come home, kick off your shoes, and feel that familiar ache of *"Not this one."*

But here's the truth: You showed up. You tried again. You risked softness in a world that rewards silence. And that? That's divine resilience. Dating is not for the faint of heart. It's for the woman who can look rejection in the eye and still believe in intimacy. So, go. Smile. Order your favorite drink. Say what you mean. Laugh too loud if it feels good. You're not auditioning. You're witnessing. You're not trying to get picked. You're deciding who's allowed to walk beside a woman like you.

And even if this night ends in silence, in confusion, in a story you'll only tell once. You will rise. You will shine. You will come home to yourself again. Because *you* are the constant. And nothing not awkward silences, not mediocre men, not mismatched chemistry can dim a woman who remembers her own worth. Now go make them feel lucky just to sit across from you.

1. **You're not getting ready for him. You're stepping into the mirror to meet yourself.** This night isn't about him. It's about the woman staring back at you becoming more of herself every time she dares to show up, even when it's inconvenient, uncertain, or lonely.

2. **You've already survived worse than an awkward dinner. So tonight? Is light work.** You've cried on bathroom floors, stared at phones that never lit up, and felt heartbreak like a burn. One man's small talk isn't going to shake a woman who's rebuilt herself from silence.

3. **Let it be fun. Not perfect. Not strategic. Just fun. That's where the magic hides.** You're not applying for a job. You're tasting connection. Real magic doesn't come from playing it right, it comes from playing at all.

4. **The butterflies mean you still believe. That makes you dangerous in the best way.** Butterflies don't mean fear. They mean potential. You haven't gone cold. You still believe in something worth showing up for and that makes you powerful as hell.

5. **You're not here to impress. You're here to observe. Let him audition for once.** Flip the script. This isn't "I hope he likes me." This is "Does he even belong here?" Observation is power. Detachment is divine.

6. **Put on that outfit that makes you feel like the final boss in a love story. Then walk like the plot just started.** You're not dressing for compliments. You're dressing for alignment. Be the version of you that makes every entrance a scene.

7. **You don't need to tone it down. You need someone who's hungry for your full volume.** You've dimmed for jobs, for friends, for almosts. But not tonight. The right one won't be scared of your intensity. They'll feel at home in it.

8. **Let the night unfold without gripping. Detachment is seductive. Curiosity is power.** Don't try to control the outcome. Let the energy speak. Real chemistry doesn't need a plan, it needs space.

9. **You don't have to be "chill" to be worthy. You can be fire and still be soft.** You're allowed to care. You're allowed to feel. The idea that you need to seem "cool" to be lovable? Burn it.

10. **This isn't about forever. It's about one moment of honest connection. Let that be enough.** Stop measuring every conversation by its potential wedding date. Sometimes healing starts with one good laugh and ends with clarity.

11. **Even if he's not "it," tonight still counts. Every date is one step closer to remembering exactly what you want.** The more you try, the more you refine. And one day, you'll realize every "no" was sharpening your "hell yes."

12. **You're not asking for too much. You've just outgrown places where too little was normal.** Desire isn't demanding. It's directional. Let your preferences be the gatekeepers to better rooms.

13. **You are not nervous, you are electric. He should be the one adjusting his frequency to handle your energy.** That flutter in your chest? That's your field expanding. Don't mistake excitement for weakness.

14. **Stop Googling if he's your type. You are the type. He's just lucky to witness.** You're not here to fit his mold. You're here to break his pattern. Let your presence disrupt.

15. **Your only job tonight is to feel like yourself. That's where chemistry actually lives.** You don't need to perform. You just need to show up rooted. That's when real attraction activates.

16. **Don't shrink. Don't edit. Don't dim. If he can't hold your fullness, he's not the container.** The truth is this: the more "you" you are, the faster the wrong ones fall away.

17. **It's not about who texts first. It's about who shows up real. Keep it honest.** Chasing and games are over. Show up with presence. The ones meant for you will meet it.

18. **If it's not him, it's not wasted. You still got dressed like a legend and made someone's night.** Even your "no's" leave an impression. You're unforgettable whether they get a second chance or not.

19. **You are not here to be chosen. You are here to be mirrored, matched, met.** Forget the audition. Love doesn't come from begging. It comes from being witnessed in wholeness.

20. **You've already won. You stayed open. That's the rarest, boldest, most sacred thing you can do.** Vulnerability isn't weakness, it's divinity. Showing up with hope in a world like this? That's power.

After Ghosting

1. **You weren't ghosted. You were redirected.** This isn't abandonment, it's divine filtration. What feels like rejection is just the universe removing the ones who couldn't hold you.

2. **You didn't lose him. You lost the illusion.** What hurts isn't the person, it's the story. And now that story is over. Burn the plot. Begin again.

3. **If he could disappear that easily, he was never here in the first place.** His absence isn't a mystery. It's a message. Let the silence speak louder than any apology could.

4. **Ghosting is closure delivered in coward's packaging.** You don't need his words to move on. His disappearance *was* the answer.

5. **Your worth isn't measured by someone's ability to communicate.** You're not hard to love. You're hard to play. And that's why he vanished.

6. **You didn't do too much. He just had too little.** Your presence demanded presence. He couldn't deliver it. That's not your burden.

7. **If he disappeared, it's because he couldn't stand in the truth of you.** Real connection demands vulnerability. Some men flee at the first sign of depth.

8. **You're not overreacting. You're under-appreciated.** That ache you feel? It's your nervous system detoxing from inconsistency. Don't apologize for having emotions.

9. **The urge to chase is your trauma speaking. Let it sit. Let it pass.** Ghosting can trigger old wounds. But healing means you no longer beg silence for answers.

10. **He did you a favor. He revealed himself quickly.** Be grateful it didn't drag on. Some men take years to show their emotional cowardice. He took days.

11. **You are not a loose end. You are the entire book.** Just because he didn't read you fully doesn't mean the story stops there.

12. **His silence doesn't diminish your light. It just shows where he's still in the dark.** Some people ghost because they can't even face *themselves*, let alone you.

13. **You don't need revenge. You need re-centering.** His karma is the loss of you. Yours is the glow-up that follows.

14. **Not everything unfinished was meant to continue.** Some things don't need a next chapter. Some things end mid-sentence and still give you the ending you needed.

15. **You don't need to send that last message. He already got the memo.** And if he didn't? Let him wonder. Let the silence haunt *him* for once.

16. **Stop stalking the void. Refreshing won't resurrect clarity.** Close the app. Mute the thread. Step out of purgatory. That's how the healing starts.

17. **You're not crazy. You just sensed something he wasn't brave enough to admit.** Intuition is not delusion. Your body always knew. He just didn't confirm it, because he couldn't handle what you saw.

18. **Ghosting isn't about you being unworthy. It's about him being unequipped.** Emotional intimacy takes courage. Some people just aren't built for depth.

19. **The right one won't disappear when it gets real.** He'll lean in. He'll get curious. He'll stay even when it's messy. Wait for *that*.

20. **You rise, even here. Especially here.** This is your ashes-to-phoenix moment. Not because he left. but because you stayed with yourself.

When you're spiraling

For when you're crying over a man who hasn't texted in two days, stalking his Venmo, rereading texts like sacred scripture, and wondering if you imagined the whole damn connection.

1. **You're not crazy. You're just emotionally invested in someone who isn't invested back.** And that imbalance? It messes with your nervous system. You're not unstable. You're misaligned.

2. **Stop checking the messages. They won't read any differently this time.** He didn't say more than he meant. He said less than you deserved. That's the part to remember.

3. **The spiral is your brain trying to solve something your soul already knows.** You keep reanalyzing because you *don't want the answer to be silence*. But it is. And it's enough.

4. **You can't logic your way out of disappointment. You have to feel your way through it.** Let it ache. Let it sting. Then let it pass. Trying to figure him out won't save you. But claiming your peace will.

5. **Your intuition isn't overthinking. It's just louder than your denial now.** You've known for days that something's off. This spiral? It's just your heart catching up.

6. **You don't need another sign. You need to stop gaslighting yourself.** Every time you excuse his behavior, you betray your own knowing. And you already know enough.

7. **The more you try to fix it, the further you fall.** Stop sending lifeboats to someone who jumped ship without a word. You're not his rescue squad.

8. **You are not hard to love. You are hard to lie to.** Men ghost women who make them feel seen. Your truth scared him, not your intensity.

9. **The obsession isn't about him, it's about what he activated.** This isn't even about *him*. It's about your need to prove you're worth staying for. And babe, you already are.

10. **He didn't change. You just finally saw him clearly.** The pedestal cracked and the fantasy fell. That's not loss. That's liberation.

11. **Take your phone. Put it in another room. Go outside. You'll survive the hour.** One walk, one breath, one real-world moment that's how you cut the psychic cord.

12. **You don't have to be over it. You just have to stop feeding it.** Pain doesn't go away when you ignore it, but it grows when you rehearse it.

13. **You are not begging him. You are begging the feeling to go away.** And it will. Not because he replies. But because *you* decided to let go.

14. **There's no closure at the end of a breadcrumb trail.** You don't need to reach the end to know it leads nowhere.

15. **He's not thinking about you right now. But you are. That's enough pain for two.** So, release him. And return to the only mind you can control: your own.

16. **Every time you rewatch that story, you stay trapped in the fiction.** It's not a romantic mystery. It's a failed audition. The curtain closed. Walk off stage.

17. **Your spiral doesn't make you weak. It makes you real.** You're feeling because you're alive. But don't confuse intensity with truth. Pain is loud but it's not always right.

18. **Get out of the fantasy. Get into your body.** Move. Breathe. Touch your skin. Eat something warm. This is how you come home.

19. **He didn't ghost you. He revealed his ceiling.** You wanted depth. He brought you silence. Now you know.

20. **This spiral is a portal. Not a prison.** If you stop resisting it and feel it fully, it will break open into clarity. That's how the healing starts.

After a Bad First Date

For when your mascara outperformed the man. When the vibes were off.
When the check arrived and so did the regret.

1. **Just because you got dressed doesn't mean it had to be worth it.** You don't owe the universe a return on your lipstick. You tried. That's the win.

2. **You weren't too picky. He was just too plain.** Don't let them gaslight your standards. Boredom is a red flag too.

3. **You didn't waste your time. You confirmed your taste.** Clarity is never a waste. Sometimes the best outcome is the exit.

4. **It wasn't chemistry. It was caffeine and noise.** Don't mistake surface-level charm for connection. Some men are just rehearsed.

5. **You're not jaded. You're just tired of pretending you're having fun.** Exhaustion isn't bitterness, it's wisdom in disguise.

6. **Your intuition checked out in the first five minutes. The rest was social obligation.** You knew. Your body always knows. Trust it next time.

7. **Just because you matched doesn't mean you're meant.** Algorithm ≠ alignment. Swipe fatigue is real. Rest.

8. **Don't confuse disappointment with failure.** The night didn't go wrong. It just wasn't right. There's a difference.

9. **You're not too much. You were just in a room too small.** When the conversation has no oxygen, that's not your fault, it's their capacity.

10. **The ick was the gift. Now you can delete in peace.** Honor the discomfort. It's your body trying to lead you home.

11. **You didn't need a love story tonight. You needed a reminder of what not to entertain.** Sometimes the contrast is the teacher. Let it teach you.

12. **You're not being negative. You're just finally being honest.** Toxic positivity has no place in the dating trenches. Call it what it was.

13. **You don't owe him a second chance just because he was "nice."** Bare minimum behavior doesn't earn bonus rounds.

14. **Let tonight be a comma, not a conclusion.** Don't spiral into the story that "there's no one left." One bad date isn't proof. It's a page.

15. **You were still the best part of that evening.** He'll remember your presence long after you forget his name.

16. **If you left feeling smaller, it wasn't attraction, it was an energetic mismatch.** Real connection expands you. Shrinking is your cue to leave.

17. **You didn't mess up. You just didn't click.** Not every date is a reflection of your flaws. Some are just… not it.

18. **Take off the heels. Order food. Laugh about it. Then let it go.** Decompression is sacred. So is pizza.

19. **You're not dramatic. You're just unwilling to waste time pretending.** Disappointment is valid. So is high discernment.

20. **The best dates aren't the ones that go perfect. They're the ones you don't have to recover from.** And when that date arrives? You'll know. Because you won't feel the need to fix it.

When He Texts "u up?" (And Other Ghostly Bullsh*t)
For the messages that resurrect nothing but your standards.

1. **"u up?" isn't a question. It's an insult.** Translation: *Are you available for low effort, zero commitment, and probably bad sex?* The answer is no. Forever no.

2. **If he can text you at midnight, he can text you at noon.** Late-night access with daytime silence? That's not romance. That's rationed validation.

3. **Responding to crumbs guarantees you never get the feast.** He'll keep sending garbage as long as you keep opening the bag.

4. **"Wyd?" is not a check-in. It's a vibe check and he's failing.** You deserve substance. Not a six-letter breadcrumb that could've gone to five other women.

5. **If he didn't ask about your day, your dreams, or your damn name, he's not interested in your soul. Just your silence.** And we don't give sacred energy to men who haven't earned a conversation.

6. **You are not a vending machine for validation.** He doesn't get to push a button and receive your attention. This is not a drive-thru.

7. **Don't answer. Screenshot it. Send it to the group chat. Then go take a bath.** You don't owe closure. You owe yourself a laugh and a glow-up.

8. **Every time you reply, you vote against your own self-worth.** Silence is a ballot. Cast it wisely.

9. **You are not the warm body he defaults to when his ego gets cold.** You're the fire. You don't light yourself for moths.

10. **Delete the thread. Mute the number. Reclaim your nervous system.** Because one day, he'll text "u up?" again… and you'll genuinely forget who he was.

When you forget who TF you are

For the days when your crown feels heavy, your hope feels thin, and you start wondering if maybe it really *is* you. This is the voice that pulls you out of the mud, dusts you off, and reminds you: you've been that girl all along.

1. **You didn't lose him. You lost your center. Get it back.** This isn't about the guy. This is about the moment you started bending to fit inside something smaller than you were built for.

2. **You are not hard to love. You just stopped loving yourself first.** Self-abandonment always makes the world feel colder. Come back to your own arms.

3. **You've survived every heartbreak, every almost, every silence. And you're still here.** Still powerful. Still intuitive. Still worthy. You don't need a win to prove your resilience.

4. **You've made yourself smaller to be chosen. It didn't work. Time to go big again.** Shrinkage only attracts men who fear your fullness. Re-expand. Let them disqualify themselves.

5. **Your loneliness doesn't mean you're broken. It means your standards are working.** You're in the gap between who you were and who you're becoming. Honor the quiet.

6. **You forgot your magic. That's all. It's still here. Still glowing. Just waiting.** Pick it up. Put it on. No one took it. You just set it down.

7. **Stop mistaking low effort for compatibility.** You've been convincing yourself that breadcrumbs are a meal. They're not. You deserve more than "bare minimum and vibes."

8. **If he couldn't see you, it doesn't mean you weren't shining.** It means his vision was never strong enough for your light.

9. **Every spiral is sacred. It shows you where you're still healing.** You're not regressing. You're returning to your truth, layer by messy layer.

10. **The woman you're becoming would never tolerate what you used to beg for.** And that's why it hurts, it's the shedding before the shift.

11. **Your power didn't leave you. It just got buried under doubt.** Let the fire come back. Even if it starts as a spark.

12. **You don't need to get over him. You need to get back to *you*.** He's not the destination. He was just a detour with a lesson.

13. **You are the plot twist.** Every chapter he didn't show up in? You were writing a better ending without him.

14. **You weren't too intense. You were too *awake* for someone still sleeping.** Let them snooze. You've got worlds to build.

15. **There is a version of you who never doubts herself. Ask her what to do.** She knows. She always has. Sit quietly. Listen.

16. **Comparison is the thief of intuition.** Stop scrolling for answers in other people's love stories. Your story isn't late, it's legendary.

17. **You don't need a break from dating. You need a reunion with your worth.** The apps aren't the problem. Your exhaustion is the symptom. Fill your own cup again.

18. **You've already been through hell. This is just a detour through doubt.** Keep walking. Keep breathing. The fire didn't kill you. It refined you.

19. **You're not meant to be liked by everyone. You're meant to be *unforgettable* to the right one.** Rejection isn't loss. It's redirection toward resonance.

20. **You're still her. Bruised maybe. Tired, sure. But her. The whole f*cking force.** And when you remember? The world moves differently. It always has.

101 Dating Success Stories

Real Stories. Real Hope. Read This When You're About to Give Up.

Before you scroll through these, let me say this: These are real stories. Pulled from the depths of Reddit threads, internet forums, comment sections, and anonymous blogs. Names have been changed. Details have been masked. But the moments? The magic? The *against-all-odds* wins? Every bit of it is true.

This chapter isn't here to sell you a fantasy. It's here to remind you that love: *real, healing, surprising, sometimes inconvenient love* is still happening. Right now. To women just like you. Women who were ghosted, overlooked, lied to, disappointed, and damn near gave up. And then… it happened. So, if you're spiraling, exhausted, or ready to swear off dating forever, read one of these. And remember: *it only takes one yes to erase a hundred nos.* Let's begin.

1. She Deleted the App… Then Redownloaded It One Last Time. Her thumb hovered. She almost didn't swipe that night. But on her last scroll, there he was. Same hometown. Same weird favorite book. They met for coffee the next day. Married 18 months later.

2. They Matched Over a Joke About Pineapple on Pizza. She thought his prompt was dumb. He thought her reply was brilliant. One joke turned into six hours of messages. Now they share a Spotify account, a lease, and a king-size bed.

3. She Went Alone to a Friend's Birthday Party. She almost didn't go. She stood in the corner for the first 15 minutes. Then a guy dropped his drink near her, apologized, and started a conversation. They've been inseparable since.

4. He Ghosted Her. Then Came Back with an Apology and Therapy Receipts. She blocked him after the second disappearance. Six months later, he sent a message owning everything. Therapy, growth, consistency. She gave him one last shot. Now they're engaged.

5. She Met Him at the DMV. Yes, the DMV. She was annoyed, in sweats, zero makeup. He complimented her keychain. They joked about the lines. They got coffee that same afternoon. They've been together ever since.

6. She Shot Her Shot in a Comment Section. He posted a funny reel. She commented something savage. He replied. Then DMed. Two months later, he flew to her city. They've been doing long-distance *and* therapy, together ever since.

7. They Bonded Over a Shared Uber. New Year's Eve. Surge pricing chaos. She jumped in with strangers to split the ride. One of them ended up being him. A shared ride turned into a shared life.

8. She Got Set Up by Her Ex's Sister. It was messy. It was weird. But her ex's sister *loved* her too much to let her settle. The new guy? Absolute king energy. Total opposite of her ex. They're now a blended family.

9. She Found Him in Her DMs Months After Ignoring Him. He'd messaged before. She never replied. Then one night, she cleaned out her inbox, saw his message, and replied out of curiosity. Their first date lasted nine hours.

10. He Almost Canceled. So Did She. But They Both Showed Up Anyway. It was raining. She had cramps. He was exhausted. But they showed up out of respect. No sparks at first. Then she made a sarcastic joke. He laughed so hard he spilled his wine. They never stopped talking.

11. She Was the Plus-One to a Wedding She Almost Skipped. Her friend begged her to come. She didn't know anyone. She showed up in a dress she hated, sat at the "leftover" table and ended up seated next to the groom's cousin. They slow-danced once. He asked for her number. They're now planning their own wedding.

12. They Were Neighbors for a Year and Never Spoke. She saw him in the elevator, in the mailroom, always with earbuds in. Then one day, the power went out in the building. They met in the hallway. Talked for two hours in candlelight. Now they live together on a different floor.

13. He Liked Her Story. She Liked His Dog. Instagram. He replied to her story about anxiety. She replied to his story about his pit bull. A few days later, they met for lunch. He brought the dog. That was two years ago. They now co-parent the pit bull.

14. She Thought He Was Too Nice. Then She Saw Him Handle a Crisis. She almost ghosted him after two dates. Too available. Too boring. Then she witnessed him help a stranger who collapsed in public: calm, present, compassionate. Her attraction lit up like fire. They've been together ever since.

15. They Met Because Her Friend Lost Her Purse. It was chaos at the bar. Her friend was sobbing. He stepped in to help. Found the purse in the back booth. Stayed to make sure they got home safe. Exchanged numbers. The rest is perfectly chaotic history.

16. They Matched. Then Didn't Talk for Six Weeks. He forgot to reply. She forgot she even matched with him. Then one day, he sent a message: "I know I'm late. But I had to say something." She responded. Turns out, he was late but worth the wait.

17. She Slid into His DMs Over a Recipe Post. He posted a lasagna. She joked that it looked illegal. He replied with "Wanna be my taste tester?" They had their first date in his kitchen. She never left.

18. They Bonded Over Shared Disdain for Small Talk. Their first date was awkward. He said, "Can we just skip this part?" She laughed and said yes. They ended up talking about death, childhood wounds, and their biggest fears. And then they fell in love.

19. He Got Her Coffee Order Wrong. It Became Their Thing. He ordered a caramel macchiato. She hated caramel. But she was too awkward to say anything. So, she drank it. Now every year on their anniversary, he gets her the "wrong" drink. It's become their joke.

20. She Was Crying in Her Car. He Tapped on the Window. She was going through it: bad date, bad week, everything. She was crying in a Target parking lot. He knocked on the window.

Asked if she was okay. Didn't hit on her. Just held space. That turned into coffee. Coffee turned into something sacred.

21. They Met Through a Dog That Ran Away. His dog escaped his yard. She found it in her driveway. Returned it. He was embarrassed and flustered. She found it charming. A week later, they went on their first walk with the dog, of course.

22. She Wrote an Open Letter to Her Future Partner. He Found It. She posted it on Medium. A few weeks later, she got an email: "I don't know if I'm him, but this cracked something open in me." She replied. They're now in a long-distance relationship that neither saw coming.

23. She Asked Him Out as a Dare. Her friends told her to shoot her shot with the cute bartender. She did. He laughed, said no one ever asks *him* out. They dated casually. Then seriously. He still calls her "The Dare."

24. They Matched at the Worst Possible Time. She was about to move. He was recovering from a breakup. But they kept talking. Talking became visits. Visits became love. She stayed. So did he.

25. He Showed Up to Help During a Hurricane. She was volunteering at a relief shelter. He was passing out supplies. Their eyes met over granola bars and bottled water. Sometimes, love shows up where survival lives.

26. She Said "No Thanks" Three Times Before Saying Yes. He was persistent but respectful. She declined his invitation three times. Then one day, something in her shifted. She said yes. They've been together five years. Sometimes, *the timing just needs to catch up.*

27. They Reconnected Over an Old Facebook Memory. She tagged him in an embarrassing prom photo. He commented, "Best worst night ever." They caught up. That night turned into a date. The date turned into reconnection. The reconnection turned into forever.

28. They Met in an Airport Security Line. Shoes off. Laptop out. He made a joke about TSA pat-downs. She laughed. They ended up seated two rows apart. He asked for her number before landing. They now fly together everywhere.

29. She Took Herself on a Solo Date and Got Interrupted. She was at a wine bar, reading a book, minding her business. He walked up and said, "I know this is weird, but can I buy you another glass?" She said yes. Then he sat down. Then he stayed.

30. They Matched on Hinge. Then Found Out Their Moms Were Best Friends in College. She brought him home for dinner. Her mom gasped. His mom screamed. Apparently, they were roommates back in the day. The moms were the flower girls at the wedding.

31. They Fell in Love Over a Shared Lyft Ride. It was a glitch. Both ordered separate Lyfts: same name, same pickup point. The driver shrugged, said "get in." They laughed the whole ride. Now they share a last name.

32. She Asked for the Manager... and Ended Up Dating Him. Her food was wrong. She was annoyed. The manager came out, fixed the issue, and made her laugh so hard she forgot why she was mad. He wrote his number on the receipt.

33. They Met in a Divorce Support Group. It was raw. It was real. Neither was looking. But something about their honesty cracked them open. Healing together turned into building something new.

34. She Sent the Wrong Text to the Right Stranger. It was supposed to go to her friend. Instead, she accidentally texted her old landlord. He replied with "wrong number... but hey, how are you?" She laughed. Now they're together.

35. He Was Her Real Estate Agent. She didn't find the perfect apartment but she did find him. They bonded over bad landlords and worse coffee. Now they live together in a place they picked as a couple.

36. She Was Crying in the Bathroom at a Concert. He noticed her eyes were red when she came out. Asked if she was okay. She said, "Not even close." He said, "Wanna dance it out anyway?" That night changed everything.

37. They Reconnected Over a Spotify Wrapped Post. She posted her top five artists. He commented "I can't believe you still listen to that." It had been seven years. Their playlist has looked the same ever since.

38. She Broke Up with Him. He Came Back Two Years Later—Healed. The breakup hurt. But she stood her ground. Two years later, he messaged her: "You were right. I wasn't ready. I am now." She believed him. This time, it worked.

39. He Was Her Lyft Driver. She was crying after a bad date. He asked if she was okay. She said, "Can you just drive around for a while?" They ended up parked, talking for two hours. He asked her out the next week.

40. They Met at Jury Duty. She was bored. He offered her gum. They joked about the case the entire lunch break. Neither got selected for the trial, but they ended up selecting each other.

41. They Met in the Comments on a TikTok. She made a savage comment. He replied with something even funnier. They took it to DMs. That turned into a three a.m. FaceTime. The rest? Algorithm magic.

42. She Said "No More Musicians" and Then Met Him at Open Mic Night. He sang a song he wrote about his ex. She rolled her eyes... then approached him anyway. They've been writing new verses together ever since.

43. They Were Assigned the Same Partner in a CPR Class. "Sorry in advance if I panic," he said. "Same," she laughed. They ended up practicing mouth-to-mouth, then got coffee after. First save was each other.

44. She Helped Him Find His Lost Dog. She posted in a community group. He messaged her crying. She brought the dog home. He brought flowers. They fell in love over gratitude and wet paws.

45. They Met While Arguing Over Who Was Next in Line. Both were stressed. It was late. They snapped at each other in line at CVS. Then laughed. Then flirted. Sometimes a spark starts with fire.

46. He Laughed at Her Hinge Prompt and Sent a Voice Note. She wrote "I'm only here for emotional intelligence and playlists." He replied: "Challenge accepted." His playlist worked. So did he.

47. She Got Stood Up but Stayed for a Drink. The guy never showed. But the bartender did. Talked her through it. Made her laugh. Wrote his number on the receipt. Two years later, he proposed right there at the bar.

48. They Were Assigned Seats Next to Each Other at a Charity Gala. She almost bailed. He didn't want to go alone. They both said yes to someone else's invite and ended up meeting the person they didn't know they were waiting for.

49. She Replied to His Instagram Story on a Whim. He posted a photo of his dog in a sweater. She messaged: "Unforgivable fashion crime." He laughed, responded with a photo of himself in the same sweater. They've been matching ever since.

50. They Matched During a Citywide Power Outage. No one could go out. So, they FaceTimed. Then again. Then again. When the power came back on, they met in person and already felt like they'd known each other for years.

51. She Missed Her Train. He Missed His Flight. They Met at the Coffee Shop in Between. They were both annoyed. Both killing time. He asked if he could share her outlet. She said, "Only if you make me laugh." He did. They've been connected ever since.

52. They Matched on Three Different Apps Before Talking. Same faces. Same bios. Never messaged. Then one day she saw him again and said, "Okay, universe. I get it." She messaged first. They've been together three years.

53. She Liked His Shoes. He Liked Her Laugh. It was a mutual friend's game night. They barely spoke just enough to notice each other. A week later, he asked the host for her number. Their second date lasted 10 hours.

54. They Met at a Friend's Funeral. Grief made them raw. Honest. Human. They talked about regret, memory, and love. From that shared softness, something sacred grew.

55. They Matched, But Neither Was Sure Why. She didn't think he was her type. He thought she was out of his league. Their first date was awkward. Their second? Effortless. Sometimes connection doesn't start with sparks—it starts with truth.

56. She Gave Him Directions. He Gave Her a Reason to Stay in That City. He asked for a street. She gave him a walking tour. They talked the entire time. When he left town, he kept calling. When he came back, it was for her.

57. They Met at a Bookstore Over the Same Novel. She reached for it. So did he. They joked. They talked about the plot. He bought her a copy. She still keeps it on her nightstand next to his glasses.

58. He Was the DJ. She Was the Girl Who Requested a Song That Changed His Night. She asked for a deep cut. He smiled like she'd passed a secret test. After his set, he found her in the crowd. They've been in sync ever since.

59. They Were Both Recovering from Heartbreak and Didn't Expect Anything. She was guarded. He was grieving. But they met at a support event and talked about love like it was a language both forgot. Now they're fluent.

60. She Thought She Was Being Catfished. He Thought She Was a Bot. They both almost unmatched. Then one of them finally said, "You real?" The other laughed. Now they joke that the algorithm almost fumbled their fate.

61. They Kept Bumping Into Each Other for Weeks. Same coffee shop. Same dog park. Same Sunday market. Finally, she said, "Okay, this is getting weird. Should we just talk?" They did. Now they share groceries.

62. He Walked Her to Her Car After a Networking Event. It wasn't flirty. Just kind. She thanked him and drove home. But something about the conversation stuck. She emailed him the next day. Now they share a last name.

63. They Fell in Love While Co-Parenting Their Dogs. They lived in the same apartment building. Their dogs became best friends. So did they. They now take all four of them on road trips.

64. She Moved to a New City and Made a Joke in a Group Chat. He replied. One message became 37. They met at a coffee shop the next day. She says that was the moment the city felt like home.

65. They Got Paired for a Trivia Night by Accident. She didn't know anyone. Neither did he. The host threw them together. They lost horribly. Then got drinks. They've been winning at love ever since.

66. She Sent Him a Voice Note by Mistake. It was meant for her best friend. "I don't even think I like him that much." He replied, "Rude. But fair." It broke the tension. They laughed. Then dated. Now married.

67. They Met Volunteering at a Voter Registration Booth. She liked his sarcasm. He liked her clipboard command energy. They registered 87 voters that day. And fell in love over the long game.

68. They Matched Because They Had the Same Therapist (Unknowingly). They realized it on the second date. Same counselor. Different days. "So, we're already doing the work," he joked. They both laughed. The therapist got invited to the wedding.

69. They Saw Each Other at the Gym for Six Months Before Speaking. She noticed his smile. He noticed her playlists. He finally said, "You run like you're being chased by a plot twist." That line started their whole story.

70. She Gave Up on Dating, Then Met Him at Her Niece's Soccer Game. He was the uncle of another kid. They bonded over folding chairs and bad referees. A week later, he invited her to brunch. It's been blissfully domestic ever since.

71. He Sent a Calendar Invite for Their First Date. She thought it was a joke. "Dinner with the girl who deserves better." He wasn't joking. He showed up early. Now he shows up for everything.

72. They Fell in Love Over Game Night Trash Talk. Uno got intense. She called him out for cheating. He was mortified. Then intrigued. Then obsessed. Now they play as a team and still fight dirty.

73. They Reconnected at a Mutual Friend's Baby Shower. They dated briefly in their twenties. Now in their thirties, they were both single and evolved. They locked eyes. The past fell away. The real thing started.

74. He Sent a Thank You Note After a First Date That Didn't Lead to More. She declined a second date. He replied: "Thanks anyway. That conversation gave me clarity I didn't know I needed." Six months later, they reconnected. Now they're building clarity together.

75. She Said No to the App Until Her Therapist Challenged Her. "Try for 30 days," she said. Day 26, she matched with him. Day 28, they met. Day 90, they moved in together. Her therapist now claims partial credit.

76. They Were Both Wearing the Same Band Shirt. She noticed his. He noticed hers. They pointed. They laughed. "Show me your favorite track," he said. That song now plays at every anniversary.

77. She Brought Her Dog to Their First Date. He Brought Treats. He didn't flinch when the dog barked. He asked its name like it was a person. Her dog loved him first. She fell shortly after.

78. She Caught Him Staring at Her in a Laundromat. She rolled her eyes. He waved. She smirked. He walked over and said, "You look like you're doing laundry *angrily*." They've been teasing each other ever since.

79. He Found Her Old YouTube Channel. She hadn't updated it in years. He commented anyway. "This made me feel less alone." She replied. One video led to forever.

80. They Met During a Fire Drill at Their Office Building. Neither worked in the same department. But standing outside for 30 minutes changed everything. They call it "the emergency that saved us."

81. She Matched with His Best Friend First Platonically. There was no spark. But the best friend said, "You have to meet someone." She did. And this time, the spark set everything on fire.

82. They Both Reached for the Last Pumpkin at Trader Joe's. She said, "Rock paper scissors?" He said, "You can have it if I get your number." They both got what they wanted.

83. They Met While Sitting Next to Each Other at Jury Selection. They didn't get picked. But they picked each other. Now they call their love "a federal offense."

84. She Didn't Like Him at First. Then He Brought Her Soup When She Got Sick. The slow burn is real. Kindness over charisma. Presence over performance. They're still going strong now with better recipes.

85. They Reconnected Through a Shared Fitness App Challenge. They had a mutual friend. Joined a steps competition. Started DMing. Turned competition into connection. They now run side by side.

86. He Asked if He Could Sit at Her Table in a Crowded Café. She was annoyed. Then intrigued. He read the same book she was holding. She made space. Now they share every table.

87. They Met in a Zoom Breakout Room During a Virtual Conference. Awkward silence. He broke it with a dad joke. She laughed in spite of herself. They met in person three weeks later. The chemistry held up.

88. They Matched Because They Both Quoted the Office in Their Bios. She wrote "I feel God in this Chili's tonight." He replied with "Bears. Beets. Soulmates?" That was it.

89. They Got into a Debate on Reddit. Totally anonymous. It got heated. Then curious. Then flirty. Then private messages. Now they moderate a relationship subreddit together.

90. They Reconnected at Their 10-Year High School Reunion. Neither remembered the other clearly. But something clicked. That awkward small talk turned into a three-hour walk around the city. It hasn't stopped.

91. They Met When He Returned Her Lost Wallet. She left it in a cab. He found it. Drove to return it. Refused a reward. Asked if he could buy her coffee instead. She said yes.

92. She Made the First Move Terrified. She almost deleted the message. "I like your smile." He replied: "I like that you said something first." Sometimes, courage pays in full.

93. He Helped Her Carry Groceries. Then Helped Her Heal. They lived in the same building. One day she was struggling. He noticed. That act of service became a pattern. So did love.

94. She Was His Waitress. He Left His Number on the Check. She almost rolled her eyes. But something told her to text. He tipped well. Loved better. She tells that story with a smile now.

95. They Met at a Spiritual Retreat in the Middle of Nowhere. No phones. No makeup. No distractions. Just presence. Two strangers met in silence. By the last day, they couldn't stop talking.

96. She Was Supposed to Go with Someone Else. Her date canceled. She went anyway. Sat next to a guy who said, "First date?" She said, "Was supposed to be." He said, "Can I fill in?" He did.

97. They Found Each Other During a Social Media Cleanse. She deleted everything. He was off-grid for a year. They met in person, through a friend, no algorithm involved. Sometimes the best matches aren't coded.

98. They Met at a Silent Disco and Didn't Speak for an Hour. Just eye contact. Dancing. Smiling. When they finally took the headphones off, she said, "So you *can* move." He said, "So can you." Magic followed.

99. He Was the Friend She Never Considered Until She Did. They were close. No lines ever crossed. Then one night she looked at him differently. He'd been waiting all along.

100. They Got Stuck in an Elevator Together. Ten minutes. No phone signal. No distractions. Just two people in a box with nothing to do but talk. The doors opened. Their story began.

101. She Gave Up on Love. Then It Found Her Anyway. No apps. No dates. Just a quiet coffee shop. A book. A stranger who said, "That's my favorite too." And a voice inside her that whispered, *"Don't give up now. Not yet."*

THE LAST UNEXPERT ADVICE

You Did It, Bitch.

You made it through the delusions. The dick droughts. The ghosting. The spirals. The silence. The hope that tried to kill you and the fire that brought you back. You didn't just finish this book. You passed the fucking course. You are now a savage unicorn part velvet, part dagger. You are as fierce as fire, and as soft as silk.

You can kiss like a daydream and walk away like a storm. You can love with your whole chest but never again at your own expense. You have *standards with teeth*. Boundaries that don't shake. You flirt with fate. You ghost the ghosts. You don't beg for crumbs you bless your own table. You are not "too much."

You are the exact frequency the right one's been waiting to find. And when they do? You won't be surprised. You'll be ready. Now go. Live. Swipe. Sashay. Delete. Reinstall. Love. Leave. Laugh. Rise. Repeat. The wild is waiting for you.
Unleash her.

All the Dating Survival Tools

Inside *The Dating Survival Bible*, you'll find a full arsenal of interactive games and tools designed to turn insight into action. These are not cute journal prompts or filler exercises. They are pattern-breaking, clarity-inducing frameworks that help you spot red flags faster, stop overthinking, and make confident decisions without spiraling. Each game is built to be used in real time, whether you're dating, texting, stuck in a situationship, or trying to exit one with your sanity intact.

Normally, these tools are sold individually for over $50. For readers of this book, everything is unlocked for **just $9.99** because clarity should not be a luxury item. Scan the **QR Code** to access the entire vault instantly. PROMO CODE: **SURVIVALGODDESS.** No upsells. No nonsense. Just the tools you need to stop guessing and start trusting yourself.

https://www.etsy.com/listing/4433179467/the-dating-survival-toolkit-19-dating

- Know Your Flirt
- Text Like Your Flirt Style
- First Date Power Moves
- The Ultimate Body Language & Trash Men Decoder
- The Model Soulmate Blueprint
- The Exit Strategy
- The Self-Love Installation
- The Dating Anxiety Reset
- He's Probably Dead
- What's Your Attachment Flavor
- 101 Dating Affirmations that Actually Work
- Love Is Already On Its Way
- Bad B Rejection Recovery Journal
- 101 Dating App Prompt Answers That Actually Get Replies
- 101 Messages to Send Men on Dating Apps That Guarantee a Reply
- 101 Swipe-Right Power Lines
- 101 Questions to Ask a First Date
- 101 First Date Spots That Are Out of the Ordinary
- 101 Dating Ideas

Other Glow-Up Books By Sarah Melland

The Breakup Band Aid

In Sarah Melland's debut self-help satire, she rips off a 12-step program and caters it to a breakup, all while sharing her personal catastrophic stories of how she tried to get her ex back multiple times and failed miserably. This "How Not To" book gives you everything you supposedly need in a breakup book. Plus, helpful insights as to how not to have a nervous breakdown or a restraining order. It will make you laugh out loud, cry uncontrollable tears, get in shape, travel around the world, and make you glow like the shining confident person you were always meant to be.

Practicing Love

Practicing Love takes the reader beyond the "veil of consciousness" to a place of self-reflection and inner peace, beyond the conscious thoughts that create chaos in our lives. The book leads readers through their own personal journeys, emphasizing how finding love within ourselves is essential for transforming how we view our external world. It is about self-discovery and the importance of manifesting the vibration of love in our lives. Everything within and around us is energy. Understanding how we direct this energy, both positively and negatively, with our thoughts and feelings is the key to making dramatic changes in our lives. It is time for humanity to raise its collective consciousness through unconditional love and service to others.

The AI Empire Builder Blueprint

The AI Empire Builder Blueprint is the ultimate guide/workbook for women who feel stuck, overwhelmed, invisible, or exhausted by starting over again and again, yet still sense a spark inside them that refuses to die. This book is for the woman who knows she's meant for more. For the woman who needs a side-hustle that can grow slowly while she heals. For the creative woman whose ideas spiral too fast to organize. For the woman who's tired of feeling miserable, depressed, unheard, unseen, and unsure what her purpose even *is* anymore.

All books available at https://yourdatingunexpert.com/buy-therapy

About the Author

Sarah Melland is not here to teach you how to "manifest a man" or communicate your needs into the void. She is here to tell you the truth. The kind that saves you years, dignity, and at least one emotionally unnecessary situationship.

She is the creator of **Your Dating UnExpert**, a blunt, funny, psychologically sharp platform dedicated to decoding modern dating behavior, exposing red flags, and helping women stop romanticizing confusion. Her work blends pattern recognition, lived experience, behavioral insight, and humor sharp enough to cut through denial.

Sarah earned her degree in Mass Communications from Arizona State University, graduating Summa Cum Laude, where she developed a deep understanding of media, messaging, psychology, and how narratives shape behavior. She has since written numerous books focused on empowering women, reclaiming personal agency, and building brands from passion rather than performance. Her work centers on turning lived experience into clarity, language, and systems that actually help people move forward.

She writes the way your smartest friend talks after one glass of wine. Honest. Observant. Slightly savage. Deeply validating. She has spent years studying dating dynamics not from theory alone, but from the front lines. The ghosters. The slow-faders. The men who "aren't ready" but somehow keep circling back. The women who keep wondering if they're asking for too much when they're barely asking for effort.

The Dating Survival Bible was born out of frustration with advice that tells women to soften, wait, or try harder. This book is a refusal to keep playing that game. It is a field guide for emotional clarity in a culture built on mixed signals. No fluff. No pretending bad behavior is a love language. Just clarity, language, power shifts, and permission to trust what you already feel.

When she's not writing, Sarah builds digital tools, guides, and frameworks that help women turn insight into action and passion into sustainable brands. Her work has become a lifeline for women who are tired of questioning their instincts and ready to stop performing for connection.

She believes dating should not feel like a psychological endurance test.
She believes clarity is kindness.
And she believes if you're confused, that's already your answer.

Welcome to survival mode.

Facebook: www.facebook.com/yourdatingunexpert
Instagram: @yourdatingunexpert
TikTok: @yourdatingunexpert
YouTube: www.youtube.com/@ohmymelons